ADVENTURES OF A BRITISH SIGNALS DESPATCH RIDER

Adventures of a Royal Signals Despatch Rider

E. S. NICHOLSON

UPFRONT PUBLISHING
LEICESTERSHIRE

Adventures of a Royal Signals Despatch Rider
Copyright © E. S. Nicholson 2003

ISBN 1-84426-213-8

First published 2003 by
UPFRONT PUBLISHING LTD
Leicestershire

Printed by Lightning Source

Many thanks to Elizabeth and David
Without your help this book could never have been made

CONTENTS

Chapter 1

MY FIRST HOME

When I was born, our home was in the crescent down George Street in Cottingham. It was 18 December 1915, soon after the Great War was declared. My dad was away from home in the army, so my mother went to my dad's relatives in Hull for my birth. Before the war, my dad worked as a chair maker and also a cabinetmaker. His brothers also worked at the same furniture manufacturers and their father was the foreman. Dad was in the Territorials, so therefore he was called up as soon as the war began. He was in the East Yorkshire regiment and he made rapid progress and was soon promoted to Drill Sergeant.

He went to Sandhurst, Officers Training College at the same time as the Prince of Wales and they passed out at the same time and were both the same age, 21-years-old. He went to France and was acting Captain and was fighting at Mons when he received a wound that left his left hand useless.

My mother was a machinist and in those days there was very little in the way of transport. So she had to walk from Cottingham to Hull, and back, after a hard day's work. My mother was brought up at Cottingham. Her name was Ethel May Grant before she married. I was the second child. My brother was called Stanley William.

When the war ended, my dad set up a business making furniture. He managed to get an ideal building for his work. It was near the village square. It was like a barn with a granary upstairs.

In those days there was hardly any machinery and one of my dad's sayings was, 'You should never make anything by hand if a machine can do it.'

He bought some machines and he made some. They were placed upstairs. Downstairs was a store for wood. Belts and pulleys and shafts were used for driving the machines. He was handicapped with the left hand being useless. The hospitals had tried to persuade him to have it amputated. But he refused, and in doing so, got less money, as the War Pension would have been greater for having lost an arm. This resulted in us being poor, as the family grew. We had an addition to the family: Leslie Arthur was born. Stan and I went to Cottingham School. Stan liked school, but I thought it was a waste of time and so I only went when I couldn't get away from Stan and Mother. My dad had the right idea and said, 'I could learn more in his workshop than at school.' So when I wasn't in school, I was at the workshop.

I soon learnt to recognise the sound of the kid catchers' big boots on the wooden stairs and would get under my bench. The kid catcher would ask if I was there and my dad would say, 'Do you think I would have him here when he should be at school?' and give the poor chap a good telling-off for his stupidity. The business was going well and I remember about a cinema being built not far away from our 'works'. My dad got the contract for supplying the chairs. This was a good help and kept him busy for quite some time because he did all the work himself.

In those days, the cost of going into the cinema was two jam jars. That made jam jars very valuable and sometimes very scarce.

Sometimes lingering in the queue, would be one or two little kids minus the glass money. I watched them carefully to make sure no one scrambled into my pockets, as I would have been in trouble as well as them.

He didn't neglect the home either and it was a home to be proud of with the most beautiful furniture. There was a doctor living in Cottingham who was an admirer of fine furniture and like our home, his home was also a home to be proud of. A leg on one chair had become damaged. The doctor spent a long time searching for someone to repair the chair leg, but as that wood was rare in this country, he had no success until he told my dad about it. The chair was repaired with wood exactly like the rest of the chair and due to Dad's skill, it was an invisible mend. The doctor was delighted, but also puzzled and never knew from where the wood had come. But I knew my crafty dad had removed some of the upholstery and from there he had taken a piece of wood to repair the leg.

I liked Cottingham and like all good families, we used to walk about and our favourite walk was along Grange Road and towards Skidby Mill. I remember my grandparents well (Mr and Mrs Grant). I thought Granddad was a Russian because he had a white pointed beard under his chin. Grandma was an invalid and Granddad used to push her out in a wicker bath chair. On Sundays I went to the Methodist Chapel with Granddad.

My eldest brother was Stan. He was one and a half years older than me. Les was one and a half years younger than me. He got the nickname Pug.

When I was born, my dad's parents wanted me to be christened Ernest Sydney, but my other grandparents wanted Jack. So I was christened as my dad's parents wished. But I got called Jack. So they were all happy.

As we got older we were allowed to go out on our own. We used to get a penny as pocket money and we'd go to the railway station to watch the trains. We would get chocolate out of a machine, but Les thought he was old enough to smoke, so he put his penny in a different machine, which gave him a cigarette. He would take it home to smoke and get a good hiding. We also went to chalk pits at Skidby to play.

Dad's hand was giving him a lot of trouble and his health deteriorated. Going to hospital became regular and the business began going downhill and eventually closed down. This was a bad thing for Stan and I because we were very interested in woodwork.

At this time, one of my dad's brothers, Uncle Arthur had become manager at the furniture factory and in later years, one of his sons became manager. We were at a disadvantage because our dad had fought for his country and had become an invalid.

Although my dad liked cars and motorbikes, he also liked riding a pushbike. After being brought up in a street in Hull, he enjoyed the peace of the countryside. Stanley also enjoyed the outings. It would be much better than sitting in a pram and being called a lovely baby girl.

During the time when my mother was taking me out in my pram, my dad, thinking he should help with childminding, was making a sidecar for Stanley, which he fitted, to his pushbike. A lot of sidecars that went onto pushbikes were made in the years to follow, but I think the one my dad made was the first one in Britain.

Chapter 2

MOVING TO WITHERNSEA

Withernsea is the most southerly of the Yorkshire coast resorts in East Riding of Yorkshire. We went to live in a council house, which was one of a row of houses called Owthorne Cottages on North Road. Dad made a good start by having the council at court for swindling. Included in the rent was an amount of money that the tenants should not have been paying. Dad beat the council and they had to give the money back.

We liked our new home and didn't miss Cottingham. There was the fresh air blowing off the sea, and the sands. There were donkeys and ice cream. At weekends we had visitors leaving via the railway and new visitors coming in. We were there with barrows and old prams to transport heavy cases for them and we became rich when the weather was fine and could make as much as five shillings. But this had to tide us over the times when the weather was bad. They then carried the cases themselves, rushing to get away as fast as they could go.

We had nice neighbours and I remember the people next door best. They were Mr and Mrs Hewitt and they had three children the same ages as we were. There were fields, at that time, to play in, and we used to play cricket mostly. Mr Hewitt played golf and it wasn't long before Dad had a set of golf clubs and they went to the golf course together.

We spent a lot of time on the promenade. The Dreweries (a family well known for their fishing) had fish shops in the town, and we would watch for their fishing boat, tossing and rolling, and wait for it coming in. It would be towed to the top of the slipway, stop and be surrounded by people wanting to buy fish.

We watched the Pierots and Punch and Judy shows. My dad's uncle had a fish stall and we would talk to him while he dressed crabs. There was a bandstand and we used to sit and listen to the music. We left Withernsea and moved about for two years, and then came back to Withernsea. This time we went to south end, into a bungalow near the petrol station.

I would be about nine and a half years old and my education made very little progress while we flitted from one place to another.

I liked the school and I was looking forward to going back amongst children I knew. The large playing field and football pitches were the most important to me. I made good progress and was chosen captain of our class. I went into the under-fourteen football team and played at centre forward. We reached the final, but were unlucky with the weather on the day of the match. The snow was coming down quickly. Someone told me that the match was cancelled so I went to the cinema.

Before I had reached a seat, my name and a message came over. 'Will E Nicholson go to the school as soon as possible with his football gear.' I reached the school as quickly as I could, which was not very quick with the awful conditions. It wasn't fit for football, but then the people in charge were not playing.

The ground was awful and the ball seemed to weigh a ton. It was impossible to play any good football. About five minutes from the end, no one had scored so I made my last desperate attempt to get the ball in the net. I dropped back a bit and the centre half received the ball and passed it to me. Dribbling was out of the question so I kept the ball between my shins and forced it passed the defenders and into the net.

After this game I was picked for the senior football team. We had two or three rugby games, but that was all. I played hockey on roller skates, but didn't play enough to get good at it.

I learnt to be a boxer to defend myself from bullies. My first lessons came suddenly one evening. I had to walk from school, which was quite a long way, and when I was about half a mile away from home, a big lad came up to me and wanted a fight. We got stuck in and I had no chance and he bashed me up. After I had finished my tea, my dad said to me, 'Tomorrow when you see that lad, you are going to bash him up.' I thought, *could I use a magic wand in one evening?* Within half an hour of my finishing my tea, my dad was teaching me the art of boxing. I got quicker with my hands and feet and before the end of the lesson, I could deliver a left swing and a right uppercut like a flash.

As I was walking home the following afternoon, I was looking forward to seeing 'Jimmy Bully', but he was not there. But my wish came two or three days later. I went into action and dropped him with a left uppercut. I never had any more trouble with bullies.

Stan played football and played well, but cricket was his favourite game. He was a good bowler and he delivered well-pitched bowls, which suited me as I played wicket keeper and was usually the top scorer. In one match, Stan took all ten wickets for a low score.

Dad wasn't so interested in hitting a little ball and walking to it just to have another swipe at it. The bungalow didn't suit him so he was looking for something better.

My dad bought two knitting machines. The needles of one machine went in a circle; this one was for knitting socks and stockings. The other machine had the needles in a straight line for knitting jumpers and scarves and lots of other flat woollen items.

He wasted no time in teaching us how to use both machines, so instead of buying us lads socks and jumpers, we got balls of wool and knitted them ourselves. In those days there weren't any nylon tights, but dad did a good trade with his silk stockings. He seemed to like making them, but I bet his eyes gleamed when he was measuring ladies' legs, and I reckon he liked that part of the job best. The knitting machines seemed to just fade away and the last time I saw them, the rust had almost devoured them.

My dad liked music, especially when a good piano player was playing. He bought a piano and soon learnt how to play it. He was a good singer and I liked to hear him playing the piano and singing.

I liked to hear a mouth organ and so I bought one and tried to play it. I remember Dad telling someone that I could have bought a piano with the money I had spent on mouth organs and I still couldn't play one. My playing sounded all right to me, but perhaps that was because I didn't understand music.

When my dad came back from Uncle Sydney's funeral, he brought Uncle Sydney's herringbone coat and two of his bowler hats. The coat would not fit Mother either. I must have been harder up for clothes than anyone else so it was decided that I would be the lucky lad. Uncle Sydney was a full-grown man. I was a seven-year-old lad so the coat did need slight alterations.

Dad was good at making things with wood so making slight alterations to a coat didn't trouble him and he was soon chopping large pieces off with the big scissors. It's a pity he didn't have a tailor's small dummy, because I must have put it on a hundred times and each time it fitted across the shoulders. By the time he had finished it the shoulders still fitted, but nothing else did. It must have been a slack fit because I wore it for years.

When a good tailor who knows his job well is altering a well-cut coat, he does not touch the pockets as it spoils the style. Therefore my pockets reached to below my knees. My dad had picked out the best of the bowler hats for himself and gave the other one to Pug, my brother. One thing, which Pug hated, was getting washed. By wearing his bowler hat there was no need for washing his ears and the back of his neck, which made life easier and pleasurable.

Chapter 3

EASINGTON, MY FAVOURITE VILLAGE

Dad, whom I will refer to as Ernie from now onwards, found a new home for us and we must give him credit for his good effort and 100 marks out of a possible 100. The place was Easington, and we found it to be very interesting. It is a coastal village about seven miles north of Spurn Point. The people were very friendly, hard-working and happy. I was eleven-years-old at that time.

When you reached Easington from Patrington, there was a T-road. The left road went to Dimlington, Out Newton and to Withernsea. The right road went to the centre of the village. This part was called balk end. Two detached cottages faced Patrington Road. One of these became our home. The other one belonged to Mr Carrick and his wife. They had a daughter living with them, but sadly their young son died in the street during a wedding.

We had to go to a water pump outside the school for our drinking water. From our cottage we had to turn right, pass the Carricks', and pass our one-acre field and we were there.

Easington School was just a small country school; our teacher was also the headmaster. His wife taught at the infants' school and another lady taught the juniors. Naturally Stan and I didn't waste time getting together and we had a fairly good football team. A jumble sale was soon organised and football gear was bought with the takings. Likewise with cricket, and I can still remember the faces as we opened our first cricket bag and took out the new shiny bats and the rest of the gear. At that time, aviation was getting a lot of publicity and Amy Johnson, a Hull girl, was becoming a very famous flyer. We felt really important when she came to our dances, which we held in school. Easington Gala and Sports Day was the highlight of the year. I won the under fourteen 100 yards race and I came third in the under twenty-one 200 yards race. The cash prize came in very handy.

Our place must have been a small farm at one time, but it was still big enough to keep us busy. There were two gardens behind the cottages. One belonged to our neighbours, the Carricks and the other one was ours. A path divided them, and ours led to the barn. Behind the barn was the fold yard with the brick buildings flanking the opposite side. The gate at the left-hand end of the fold yard led to our paddock, which was just one acre. Beyond the paddock the school stood, with the schoolhouse facing us and to the right of the paddock was one acre of garden. While we were at school, old Ernie would mark out plots of land about fifteen feet square and no matter what other plans we had for the evening, these pieces of garden had to be dug and raked before anything else could be done. Coming from our home and turning left led to the centre of Easington. Next to our cottage was a row of seven cottages. Two of our school friends lived in one of them. They were Freda and Ron Medforth. They had a brother who was in the Royal Navy. Their father used to grow his own tobacco. The broad leaves could be seen climbing on his garden fence. In a yard at the other side of the road belonging to Mr Cousins, were two traction engines. One of the traction engines was driving a threshing machine. The blacksmith's shop faced us as we approached the left-hand corner. Just round the corner were two cottages and behind them was the church farm. On the other side of the farm buildings and not visible from that side of the road, was the large thatch-roofed tithed barn, which was built in the fourteenth century. By the size of the barn, I would think the vicars of days gone by were better off than the vicars of today.

A wall encircled the church. Both the church and the wall were built of round cobbles from the seashore. Conveniently situated for the benefit of hymn singer's throats, at the left-hand side, was the Marquis of Granby, and between this pub and the Coastguard houses there was Charlie Medforth's shoemaker's shop. I don't think there were boots in and around Easington that hadn't been made in this little black wooden shop. The road to Kilnsea ran straight on and passed the village square. The famous old wooden seat stood on the right, against the church wall, and faced the square. This is where the old and the young congregated during the evenings to listen to the daily news to do with the happenings on the farm or on the shore or when out fishing in the small boats. The old farm workers could tell interesting stories about the farms and farm folk and sometimes this conversation would be of great interest to us young lads. I used to like to go to the seat when I had time during the evening. There was a gate in the wall, which led to the church by a footpath through the churchyard, for people walking from the village square.

Most of the old fishermen had spent some time in either the Royal Navy or the merchant navy and could thrill us as they spun their yarns about those days. The old men of the land could tell us about fields, which they had worked in, that now lay beneath the waves. Due to this rapid washing away of clay cliffs, areas of uneven patches of clay would be visible at high tide and during very rough seas these could move about. This was very dangerous for launching a lifeboat. The lifeboat house was at the side of the road about one hundred yards from the cliff. The lifeboat was launched by eight horses, which had to be brought from the farms as quickly as possible. We often heard them running past during the night from the mill farm and as soon as they were yoked to the boat, they would run down the slipway across the beach and into the water until the boat was floating. Then the horses would be unhitched and they'd come back onto the beach. I can remember one terrible stormy night when the horses got among the treacherous clay and some of them stumbled and rolled into the rough sea. By a miracle there were no casualties. The Spurn lifeboat reached the distressed vessel and saved the entire crew. But they were not the first there every time. Also, we had the Easington Rocket Brigade and the Holmpton Rocket Crew who rescued sailors from ships that had come too near the coast to shelter and had ran aground, by breeches buoy (a method of rescue involving an object resembling breeches slung over a rope).

One road followed the church wall then turned left in front of the tithed barn. This was the back road and led to Humberside. One road carried straight on towards the sea, but the Kilnsea road branched right just after the coastguard tower. Kilnsea was about two miles from there. Just before it reached Kilnsea, the road crossed a sea wall, showing evidence of the changing coastline over the years in that part of Holderness. Spurn peninsula was at one time further to the East. It was washed away and then later reformed by eroded sand and gravel being swept down the coast and meeting the strong tide of the Humber.

Easington people were the best people I have ever known, and amongst them were heroes, brave and tough. We had the lifeboat crews who went in dangerous, rough weather when waves were as high as houses. Also the coast is well known for high tides, currents and mud flats.

There was always something for us to do at Easington. On Saturdays we played football or cricket. We went on our bikes to other villages to play. We always had a good team. My brother Stan was our best bowler. I was the stumper and top batsman. As well as enjoying the games, we were all friendly and it was good to talk to the lads who belonged to the other villages. Rides on our pushbikes were also a happy time when the weather was good to us.

Sunday was a religious day; I went to the Wesleyan chapel. The Webster family, who had the shop near the square, were Wesleyans. Peter Webster was at school with us.

The Medforth family were churchgoers. Reverend Holt was the parson. Because of the different religions, Ron Medforth and I had to go our different ways when we reached the church and then I would wait for him outside the chapel.

One day Ron asked why I didn't go to church. We talked about this for a while and decided that I would go to church to see if I liked it and Ron would try the chapel. When I went into the church, they all stared at me and I felt like coming out. But before I found a seat, Mrs Holt came, looking very stern. Her voice bellowed these few unchristian words. 'You are not church, you are chapel, we don't want the likes of you in here.' I couldn't get out quick enough and decided Ron could have his church.

The chapel was on Seaside Road and so we usually went to the seashore and walked along the cliff tops. But sometimes we went along the Kilnsea Road. After a mile, we turned right, as that road went to Humberside. On the left was a farm belonging to Mr Lawson. John and Olive were schoolmates. I was attracted to their rabbits because they were so loveable.

I wanted a rabbit and Ron wanted me to have one because he didn't have a rabbit, so we began to talk about getting one. We needed some wood to make a hutch, and wood comes from out of the sea. We rode our bikes to Humberside and we saw something bobbing about in the river. It was quite a long way out, but the tide was bringing it towards the shore. We sat down to wait as we had plenty of time. But it soon came drifting towards us and we could see that it was a large bundle of wood.

It came ashore where we were sitting. It was tongued and grooved, just what we wanted. It was heavy as it was soaked in sea water, but we had it at home as soon as possible, every single board as it was too good to leave behind.

We had to wait for it to dry out and then we made the hutch. We went to see Mr Blashill. His farm was on the left at the right hand corner, on the way to Humberside. Clubley's farm was on the right hand side. This was where Denise and Gordon lived. They had some pigs in the fold yard. We used to get on their backs and they would run round the fold yard and rub up against a wall to get us off their backs. I reckon we would have had sore backsides if Mr Clubley had seen us.

Mr Blashill let us have some hay and straw, two turnips and some rolled oats. We were very excited when we went to collect our rabbit. It was a chinchilla about six-weeks-old.

This set Ernie off wanting rabbits, but he didn't say so. One day he came home with two well-bred Angoras (rabbits). Because of their long coats he made hutches in the barn. They were more like cages with a wire-mesh bottom and trays to catch the droppings. Breeding rabbits isn't difficult so we soon had lots of baby rabbits. Ernie was the boss so he didn't feed them himself, that job was left to me.

Ernie bought some Kaki Campbell ducks. He was really feeling like a farmer. Then he met Mr Johnson, known as Piggy Johnson. He had a Berkshire Gilt with five young ones. Ernie bought the Gilt and the piglets. Now Ernie was a farmer, we had rabbits in the barn and across the fold yard we had the ducks and the pigs. There were also three or four bullocks belonging to Mr Quinton living with us.

We loved the Berkshire Gilt, because she was so friendly. She used to lie on her back to have her belly stroked and tickled. She followed us about and if we were busy, she would stand and look at us. She was more like a dog.

When we went to school she would be looking for a gap in the hedge. When she found one she would force her way through and the next minute she would be in the playground looking for us. The headmaster would look through a classroom window. I liked this bit as I would have to take her home and I never rushed to get back to the classroom.

When the young pigs were three-months-old, the selling price was high. Ernie sent them to market and got the benefit of the good market. This encouraged him to think about pig breeding.

The lady pig had another litter, but by the time they were about six-weeks-old, the sale price had dropped to rock bottom. This upset Ernie and so he took the piglets away from the mother and sold them for five shillings each. He then gave the mother a large amount of food to fatten her up so that he could sell her. This gave her milk fever and our loving pig died.

We dug a large grave and buried her and placed a large vase of flowers on the grave. We also made a wooden cross. I think it was the saddest day we ever had at Easington. It proved that Ernie wasn't a farmer.

Ette and Ernie were going to Hull for the day. They must have thought that Pug and I would perhaps get up to mischief so they gave us a job to do. It wasn't a very nice job either. The fold yard and the loose boxes required mucking out, so that is what we had to do.

From the fold yard to where Ernie wanted the manure in the garden, was a long way, and we only had one barrow and that was only half the required transport for efficient output.

Barbara, my sister, was eighteen-months-old and so she had finished with her pram. It was a lovely pram with large chrome wheels, bars and was well sprung. It was scandalous to have such a lovely piece of transport doing nothing. So our transport was doubled at no extra cost.

We worked very hard and finished the job expecting to be rewarded with a large piece of silver. But when our ungrateful parents arrived home they were only interested in the muck-covered pram. We didn't know that Audrey was waiting to be born and would expect a nice shining pram. For all our good work we received nothing but a good telling-off.

In the old days before there were boxing booths and stadiums, bare-fisted boxers did their boxing in a field and the spectators formed a ring. I suppose such an event would have taken place at Easington in years gone by. But you would not expect it to happen when I was at Easington, but it did.

I was under the impression that everyone liked me, but I was wrong. There was a girl called Olive who was a bit sweet on me. But she had a brother who was a lot older. He had been in the Army and I reckon he would have been at least eighteen-years-old. He didn't like me, but I have no idea why. He told the men on the seat he was going to bash me up and arranged the time for the fight.

I went to the seat and waited for him and the old guys were getting excited about it. When he came to the seat, they all got up on their feet and began to walk to a field near Humber Lane with Buckley and I walking side by side in front of them. They were all chatting and guessing who would be the winner, but neither Buckley nor I spoke a word.

We strode into the field and the two gladiators removed caps and jackets and someone took these to look after them. We stood ready and someone shouted to us to start the fight.

I did not go for him, I let him chase after me and I used my feet to side step him as Ernie had taught me. To fight him all the time would have exhausted me. So I just kept jabbing and dodging. He would rush at me with his head low so I waited for an opportunity to land a hard left to his ribs and a right to his jaw. My chance came and it rocked him and from then on I kept on punching him. Then I gave him a good left to his solar plexus and a smashing right to the temple and he went down for the count.

Someone took him home and I went to the seat feeling proud of myself. They had all enjoyed it very much. I was boasting about not getting hurt. My right wrist was still clenched so I tried to open it, but my fingers refused to budge.

One man said, 'That's no wonder, the way you hit his head. Hit an Irishman and you might as well hit a gate post.' It was all right for the spectators; they had enjoyed their evening. But my friend Olive was so upset over her brother, she wouldn't have anything else to do with me.

They didn't have far to go when they took Buckley home. He lived down a back lane, which started at the square. The Fleetwood family also lived down this lane. They were very decent and friendly; they had a son called Burt, and a daughter Peggy. Both were at school with me. Peggy delivered milk for Mr Carter whose farm was opposite Webster's shop. Peggy was my sweetheart. My socks were just worn out; in fact a pair of woollen sleeves on my legs remained. So before I got socks, I had to earn some money. I was in luck because old Eggy, the schoolmaster, wanted two-penny worth of rhubarb. We had loads of it and my price was two pence for thirty sticks.

Before school I had to feed the rabbits. There were about sixty, counting the babies. I had to collect a full sack of rabbit meat from the roadside to give to them. After feeding the rabbits I went for breakfast.

The time was going too quickly for me and I ran down the garden. I picked thirty nice young red sticks and rushed off to school. They had all gone in and were sat down, but I was about five minutes late. Eggy just stared at me as if there was something wrong. I had not had time to get a wash or brush my uncut mob of hair. My hands were stained from the rabbit greens and the rhubarb. I had my usual, and only grey jumper on, which was almost worn out and had never had a wash. My shorts were smart apart from wanting a wash in boiling water and stain remover.

'You're late,' he said. 'Why are you late?' he asked.

I thought it was very obvious, but I thought I had better give him an answer. I glanced round the class and saw the blooming kids enjoying things. 'Because I had to get your rhubarb.'

I was standing there with the thirty sticks of rhubarb under my left arm and it was getting heavy. Then he came out with a typical teachers' remark, which was, 'If you had been picking rhubarb for someone else, I would have to cane you, so I must cane you for picking it for me.' So he got his cane and began tapping my right arm with it. I did not understand so he said, 'Hold your hand out.'

So I held my left hand out; anyway, I had held it long enough. I looked down at the thirty sticks of the stuff and thought it was a lot for two pence; I ought to have charged him sixpence. A very angry voice said, 'Pick it up.'

'No, it's yours now so you pick it up,' I said.

The kids were enjoying the pantomime, but by the look on the red face that glared at me I do not think Eggy could see the funny side of it all. You could say that the sound that came from his trembling mouth was a gentle plea for help. 'Pick it up, Lawson,' shouted his nibs. John Lawson did not move. 'You pick it up, Medforth,' came the next hope. But Ron Medforth remained seated. Next it was Dennis Clubley and then Jim Biglin, but the sticks of pie stuff remained on the deck.

Angry and with a look of defeat, he bent his long slim body over and began to pick it up.

As I was leaving school he gave me two pence. He smiled at me and thanked me; we were friends again. He was a good teacher and I liked him for that. I think I was his favourite because I was a sportsman. Our cricket and football teams won a lot of games against neighbouring village schools. I had reached the Yorkshire sports, which was good for such a small school. I got ready for the 100 yards race. I felt I was in the best condition and looked forward to being first.

The names were called and the runners lined up and were set off. But I was devastated my name hadn't been called. My dad was with me and he played up hell. I had been left off the programme. The race should have been run again, but the officials said, 'No'. Eventually they said that I could, but on my own. I ran, but my time was a lot more than my usual time.

While we were at Easington our best outings were the walks to Spurn because there was a wonderful romance about it. There were no roads from where the public road ended and the only means of transport to Spurn was the train. This consisted of the engine, named Kenyon, which pulled a carriage, which had lost all its doors and windows, and a long flat-floored truck. We often had a day at Spurn. If Kenyon were leaving Kilnsea, we would enjoy a ride; otherwise we would walk, striding from one sleeper to the next. This would stimulate our appetites for the food that was given to us by the good people of Spurn. It was a very remote place for the few soldiers, the lifeboat men and lifeboat crew. But that was not the reason why we were made so welcome. It was more than that; those people were a marvellous type, and brave, for where could you find a more dangerous job than manning the lifeboat. The currents in the mouth of the Humber were extremely dangerous, as is the South Yorkshire coast in stormy weather. This lifeboat crew was in fact the only professional crew in Britain. The Bull Lightship is about 1 mile south of the Spurn Lightship.

During low tide, the large trawlers and cargo would be two or three miles out, waiting for high tide before sailing into the Humber. The lighthouse is 120ft high. It was built in 1895 and is the third Spurn Lighthouse. The other two, whose bases remain, were built in 1852 and 1776. Looking across the Humber and almost due east from Spurn, is that delightful Lincolnshire resort of Cleethorpes, and a little further along the river is the port of Grimsby, and then Immingham. Turn north and enjoy a lovely view of the south tip of Holderness. Almost immediately, the eyes go on Patrington because of the superb tower and 180ft spire of its fourteenth century church. But one must remember to have a closer look at this beautiful church, which deserves its title, 'Queen of Holderness'. Hedon is in the distance, twice as far away from Patrington and in almost a straight line. Hedon can be picked out from miles around by the splendid tower of St Augustine's church. This church has been given the title, 'The King of Holderness'. Hedon is one of the oldest boroughs in England whose first charter goes back to 1170. In the town hall is a very old civic mace, beautifully decorated and showing a crown and the Royal Arms of England and France.

Withernsea, with its promenade and amusements, shows up well. The lighthouse is unique because it was built away from the sea and stands behind the town. It is a fine lighthouse. If one can picture it, one can see the sailing ships of the thirteenth century. Sailing into the ports of two towns, out there between the two lightships, a scene of many years past will be produced by the mind's eye. Because out there, below the waves lie two towns. One of these towns was Ravenser at the end of the land jutting out from the mainland. It was a very wealthy and prosperous town even more important, as far as its port was concerned, than Hull. Then a new strip of land appeared early in the thirteenth century and on it was developed a town called Ravenserodd. By the year 1235, Ravenserodd had a port, and in a few years, quays were built. Ravenser became important and wealthy, but the sea that was responsible for the land in the first place, began to destroy it. As parts of the town were being washed away, the rich merchants began to leave, taking their businesses and wealth to Hull and Grimsby. By the end of the year 1400 nothing remained of these two towns. In the garden of Hollyrood House in Baxtergate Hedon, is a 20ft high cross, known as the Kilnsea cross. It was washed up at Kilnsea in 1818 and it is believed to have been erected on Ravenser in the year 1200. Hedon had two havens and a mile of two quays, but it was two miles from Paull, which stands at the side of the river. Likewise there is Patrington Haven, which is about two and a half miles from the riverbank. Sunk island is the reclaimed land which amounts to 6,000 acres of rich agricultural land which is the outcome of centuries of reclamation of silt and mud from the river. I liked Easington and the wonderful people, but the time had come when I thought I should get a job. My mother suggested that I should go to Uncle Bill's farm. He was my mother's brother. The idea of going to Bill

Grant's farm seemed brilliant, as I was a lover of animals especially horses.

Therefore, at the age of thirteen and a half years, I left home and walked to my Uncle Bill's farm, about eighteen miles away. I cannot remember much about that journey, but I remember quite plainly turning round and seeing my mother standing at our front door waving to me. I waved back and walked on, with nothing but the clothes I was wearing and one shilling and eight pence in my pocket.

Chapter 4

GETTING SETTLED DOWN ON THE FARM

It was a very long walk for a young lad and I must have been hungry and very tired when I reached North Park Farm. There was a large porch, which had some shelves containing some pot plants and under the shelves on the floor were Wellington boots, hobnailed boots and ladies' shoes. Milking smocks hung from nails on one wall. I walked through into the kitchen, it seemed massive and likewise the table that stood down the middle of the kitchen.

Uncle Bill and Aunt Eve had two sons, George and Laury, and two daughters Kath and Olive. George was married to Dolly. They had a baby called Kenneth. The farmhouse was big. George had part of the house at the back that was equivalent to a largish house. Therefore they had plenty of room in their part of the house.

It was a dairy farm of 350 acres. To milk the seventy cows Uncle Bill, Aunt Eve, George, Kath and Olive all turned out morning and evening. George was the herdsman and Laury was foreman and horseman. There was a young man who was the wagoner. Also, there were several labourers. The wagoner and I slept in a back bedroom in George's part. There were lots of trees across the back of the farmhouse and part-way along the side. When the wind was strong, those trees swayed and howled and made all sorts of ghostly noises that made me very frightened. The toilet was at the bottom of the garden near the trees. The door would often be blown open adding to the noises, the hinges would be creaking and the door slamming. The food was good; for breakfast we had bread and meat with plenty of fat on it and a big slice of pie. Dinner was potatoes and vegetables and meat with plenty of fat, and a big slice of pie. For tea again we had bread, and meat with plenty of fat on it, and a big slice of pie. For supper you got nowt. Sometimes we got a pudding at dinner times, either a milk pudding or steamed. Anyway we got plenty to eat.

I soon settled down because I loved animals and living on the farm was great. When I went to infants' school I could never find the school and I would always be at my dad's workshop. On the days when my map reading was at its best, I would finish up at school. My excuse for being missing a few days was, 'I had to go to my farm in Australia.' The teacher never argued, so I thought she believed I had a farm in Australia. Therefore, I was not afraid of going to school just for a day now and again. There was a lot of work to do on this farm and now and again I thought of home and my friends, going to chapel and having a walk on the seaside. But most of all, I missed my brothers and sisters.

I worked with George mostly. I brought the cows in from the grass field, and they strolled to their places in the cow houses. George would have put the food out for them and brought the buckets from the dairy. By this time the gang would have come in clad in their milking smocks and ready for pulling the cows' teats. I soon learnt to do this and got my fair share of seven cows to milk twice each day. Olive was the youngest; she was seventeen-years-old. We soon became very good friends and I helped her with the poultry. Sometimes on a Saturday, or Sunday afternoon, Aunt Eve would let me scrub the kitchen floor. She was a very sweet lady.

I liked Dolly; she was a lovely person and very kind to me. She was not a country girl. Her home was on Hedon Road in Hull. She had a sister who was also very nice, and two brothers. These two lads played rugby and I think that is how George got to know Dolly, but I don't know. Kath was a lovely blonde girl who was courting a butcher's son, so I did not get to know her very much.

I liked Laury. Everyone liked Laury. He was big and strong and very good-looking. He could entertain you, as he knew a lot of songs and rhymes like: 'The dogs they had a meeting, they came from near and far.'

I did not work with Laury as he was with the horses, which was a shame because I loved horses. But I worked with horses later. For the present I had the cows, pigs and sheep to tend to, so I never ran out of work.

Of course I had to go to school, but I had a week off and then on the next Monday it would be my first day at a fresh school. This did not bother me because changing schools was like a bad habit. My dad was never a lover of landlords so we never stayed in one place long before the landlord and father were falling out. Once, we were moving and all ready to go and some of us were on the removal van, and some went with Father on the Royal Enfield 1000cc V Twin. But I had to go on my bike. Daddy shouted a few instructions, but I still did not have any idea where we were going. They all cleared off and I went to get my bike. It had a puncture, but luckily I had a puncture outfit. I was about eight-years-old. I was never reported as a missing person, so evidently I had reached my destination.

We lived at Hornsea for a while. The bungalow was near the mere. When the tide came in our garden got well watered. But when it was an extra high tide, Mother got all the room floors washed. Mother was never made to be so clean. We were soon on the move again and Daddy had long since decided it was easier to flit than pay rent.

We moved to a village called Seaton, about five miles away from Hornsea. There was no school there so really we shouldn't have had to go to one. We didn't have a school kids' union so we could not do anything about it.

We had to go to Sigglesthorne School. It was a very long walk for us young kids and we had to get up very early. By the time it was dinnertime, we were very hungry and tired. This agony did not last long as one day it came to a very abrupt halt.

We walked to school as usual and settled down to our learning. Then the classroom door opened and there was Father shouting for his children. We trooped outside and there on the road, waiting patiently for us, was a removal van with table and chair legs stuck out through the back end. Whatever was it; just a blooming furniture van on its way to our next abode.

Chapter 5

BURSTWICK SCHOOL

I was looking forward to going to school to be with kids of my own age. But first I had my morning's work to do. The cows were waiting at the field gate heavy with milk. They were Friesians, well known for giving high yields. Jersey cows gave rich creamy milk so Uncle Bill had six of them to improve the Friesians' milk. I milked my seven cows and went for my breakfast. After breakfast I fed the pigs and then went to get ready for school. I had a long walk to school and arrived at 10 o'clock. The headmaster was also our teacher. He was fairly tall, clean-shaven, good-looking and wearing a well-cut grey suit. He spoke well and was very polite. I thought I was lucky to have a teacher like that. 'Don't worry about being late and go to that desk over there,' he said. I glanced at the kids and thought, *They are glad to see me, and very amused at the way I was dressed.* I had no trouble with the lessons. Although I had been to different schools, my education was in advance of Burstwick School. I had not learnt much at the country schools, but I had been to Newland Avenue and Sidmore Street Schools in Hull and also Withernsea School and they were all very good schools.

Eventually it was 4 o'clock and I did not waste much time getting out of school and running to the farm. It would soon be milking time and I had to feed the pigs and then get the cows in. By the time I had got to the big dining table, I was very hungry, and tired. I did not think I would find time or have the chance to play football. But I was in for a very happy surprise as we had a game of football at school. I was a good footballer, so I was well liked by the lads and lasses.

The teacher and I became very good friends. Like me, he had a great love for rabbits. I had some lovely ones when I was at home at Easington. They were Angoras and Chinchillas. Teacher had mostly black and tan rabbits. His buck and doe had won prizes at big shows. He had a young rabbit from the buck and the doe. It was really beautiful and would have been good enough for the big shows. Except for its teeth. Rabbit's teeth keep on growing, but the top and bottom rub together, which keep them their normal size. This young rabbit's teeth did not rub together. Teacher gave it to me and I was proud to own it, but filing its teeth was a regular job and a tedious one, as you had to be gentle and careful.

Everything was going all right at school and on the farm. Sometimes after tea I was with Olive. We always had some jobs to do like finishing collecting eggs and we always had to lock up the hen houses. The days were getting longer and you always had a few old hens reluctant to call it a day and would refuse to go to bed. This was quite annoying when you had been up since half past five.

About three months before I went to the farm, a mare was having a foal. There were complications and the mare died. The foal was all right and of course looking after it became another job for Olive. His name was Tishy and he was always with us. Uncle Bill did not like him and he felt that it was a waste of good hay and corn and he would never be any good. I could imagine him as a grown horse and someone taking him to pull a plough. I reckon he would just turn his head and dive under the traces and gallop home.

The weather was getting hotter and the farmers were busy with hay. Some of the lads were going swimming in a drain and I thought it was dangerous, but I cannot remember anyone coming to any harm. At that time a lad was riding home from school on his bike and a car hit him and killed him. We were all very sad at school. He was in my class and lived at a farm on Preston Road. I had been looking forward to going to their farm to visit him. His family and the Grants were very good friends and lived at the next but one farm from ours. He was a nice lad and was sadly missed. I got on very well with my classmates and so I soon had some good friends. But one lad wasn't so friendly. He was the blacksmith's son. He was a big lad and his arms looked strong as if he had swung a hammer quite a lot. He was a real bully, so I didn't have any time for him. One day he told me he was going to bash me after school. I was disappointed about it because I got on with everyone else. He held his fists ever so high to protect his face. I gave him a tap to his solar plexus. His hands dropped and he got a left swing and a right uppercut, and he'd had enough. The next day he had great pleasure in telling me his big brother was coming to school at 4 o'clock. I told him it was a pity he was not bringing his dad for a right uppercut. His brother did not last long, but his sister came the following day. They say attack is the best form of defence, but how can you attack a girl. It was the hardest fight I had ever had, but I am glad to say she didn't get hurt.

The afternoon's milk went to a Mr Lawson who lived on Hedon Road near Marfleet. He had a round and delivered the milk the next day. George used to take the milk in the Trojan. I liked being with Olive during the evenings, but I preferred to go with George. I liked Mr Lawson very much. He was a sportsman like George and their conversations were good to listen to. Young Lawson, his son, was an amateur boxer and quite good. We used to do some sparring and his dad would be saying, 'Hit him Jack, hit him harder.' I preferred not to do as I was told.

Sometimes I got a ride out to Hull on Saturday evenings. George rode for Hull Speedway, but he never took me to the track. I would be dropped off as soon as we reached Hull and

Dolly and young Ken would go another two or three miles to Dolly's mother's. I would walk about and make my own way to Dolly's mother's house. We would stay there until George came to take us home.

I used to be well dressed in my second hand clothes – the jacket, which was three sizes too big and my heavy upturned hobnailed boots, went well with my oversized jodhpurs. As I walked about the town lads stared at me, I do not know why. They seemed to know I was a country lad. I reckon it was because of my fresh complexion.

To have to walk about Hull and be stared at and have some cheek from spotty faced youths was not my idea of having fun. Most of all, I did not want to work on farms all my life. Therefore, I naturally got interested in that bull on the army recruiting posters. *That's the life for me; I'll be a general in three to four years.* I made up my mind to go to the recruiting place as soon as I was fourteen-years-old. At last I had something to look forward to.

Chapter 6

SHOW DOGS AND SPEEDWAY.BIKES

Uncle Bill had some smooth-haired fox terriers. He was showing two of them on Saturday. At least that is what he thought. He had me holding them on a table while he prepared them for the judges, pulling a few hairs out from here and sticking them in somewhere else and that sort of thing. Uncle Bill looked forward to dog shows and was very happy as he worked on the dogs, never swearing even once. However, Saturday was not a good day. There were some evil spirits about on the farm. To begin with, one of the vehicles fell poorly and couldn't be put to rights without some delay. This was disastrous because that only left old faithful, a Trojan van. Disastrous because George also had a hobby. He was a Speedway Rider and so he had to go to Hull speedway track at the same time as Uncle Bill wanted to go to the dog show.

George and his mechanic, George Twiddle, devised a plan of action. It was a scheme where I played an important part; a part, you would think was very unfair if you were any sort of sportsman.

Without fail, Uncle Bill would spend at least twenty minutes in the lavatory, and these two wizards of the speedway had taken advantage of this regular habit. The lavatory was a double-seated affair, situated down the garden behind the house where Dolly and George lived. Double seated lavs were a regular feature on the farms in those days. One was not expected to waste time waiting for someone to finish, but to join him or her, and enjoy a conversation. Personally, I can think of better places to enjoy a conversation. But nevertheless, this is where Uncle Bill would be sitting before going out for the afternoon, or as in this case, before not going out in the afternoon.

The time arrived for me to take up my position in the garden behind a thick bush. From this position I could see the path, which led to the lav, and also the two Georges could see me. I heard the garden gate open and sure enough it was Uncle Bill. He looked so pleased with himself, a sure indication that he was confident about bringing home a silver cup.

He went in and gently closed the door behind him. The couple of bad lads received my signal, and they wasted no time in loading the bike, which was followed by spares, tools and riding gear. Having done this, the pair of them got into the cab and the engine was started and almost before the second cylinder had time to fire, there was a frightening noise from Uncle Bill and such dreadful words for my young ears to be receiving. The door was flung open with such force that it rocked madly to and fro on the hinges. He was accelerating now and struggling to pull up underpants and breeches as he went. He sped left at the garden gate from where he could see 'old faithful'. The old Trojan chugged away, taking its time to reach the road, with Uncle Bill in pursuit, waving and shouting and trying to hold up his breeches, which were getting out of control. Then suddenly it happened. He tripped over something and his feet went airborne, and his nose prepared for a landing, resulting in such a belly flop. But he didn't hurt himself because he went 'splash' in a lovely soft mixture of mud and cow muck. It must have been his lucky day, but somehow he didn't seem to be enjoying it. The chugging Trojan chugged its way to the speedway, and was unloaded and the bike made ready. George had done well on the previous Saturday, so naturally he was keen and looking forward to the repeat performance. But did he deserve to be treated with such kindness. I am sure he didn't and he wasn't. He made a good start and was doing very well. But while on full throttle, he suddenly changed to become an acrobat cum ballet dancer or something. I said, 'I don't think this is a wise move.' Well, as George didn't come round until Tuesday afternoon, it proved I wasn't as thick as I looked. George's absence caused a lot of inconvenience and Uncle Bill was very cross, saying nasty things, like the bike should be in hell. I told him I didn't think that would do the tyres much good. But he was in no mood for my nonsense so I kept quiet. We went to see George Twiddle, George Grant's mechanic on the Sunday morning after the latter came round to see how the bike was getting on. George Grant and I had already done a good two-and-a-half-hour's work, washed the cow muck from behind our ears and devoured our breakfast. But when we arrived at Twiddle's house, he had only just emerged from his bed. Watching him sitting there, bleary-eyed and leisurely making a plate of bacon and eggs disappear, made me quite envious. However, as we sat and listened to what he had to say and drinking the tea his mother had made us, I came to the conclusion his bit of luxury had been well earned. The Twiddle hammer had been put to good use, working until late into the night until all the bent bits had been put right. In fact the bike was ready for being transported back to the farm. As soon as we got the bike back to the farm, it was taken for testing. It was a field where the drain ran along the bottom end.

The engine was well tuned and our mechanic was only too pleased to show off its speed as he headed down the field towards the bottom end. The place was almost reached where the throttle would be momentarily snapped shut and the bike flicked over, executing a well-controlled power slide right round the bottom end of the field. Well, that is what would have happened if a cartwheel hadn't made that deep rut. The bike has to have both wheels on the ground before it can perform its magic and before Twiddle had managed to persuade it to change direction, he was running out of the field. Therefore, no one could blame Twiddle for parting company with the bike and finding his own way down. But even so, and being devoid of all tail fins on his boots, he had the necessary skill to place himself in a convenient position to enable his legs to be seen sticking out above the reeds. George was used to pulling cows out when they had got stuck in the mud. Therefore, with his knowledge and having got Twiddle safely on firm land, George could see at a glance that he needed no medical attention apart from a good swilling down with a hosepipe. So he pronounced him fit enough to run to the farm for a rope to haul out the bike. All this looked funny to me, but not to George and the other George. *Very strange chaps*, I thought. But Uncle Bill's reaction gave evidence of the wisdom of that saying, 'He who laughs last, laughs best.'

By the time the afternoon's milking had been done our mechanic had washed down and dried the bike and had noted what components required attention. Dolly had arranged to spend some time in the evening with a friend who lived at a nearby farm. Therefore, as soon as tea was finished, she went out. She had and still has a charming personality and was well liked amongst the farm folk. But she was very fond of her friends who lived in Hull and would always prepare well for their visits to make sure they enjoyed being with her and George. She had visitors coming the next day, so she had been very busy. The furniture had been rearranged for the benefit of their comfort. The afternoon had been spent making cakes and sausage rolls.

Advantage had been made of Dolly's absence, and the bike was wheeled into the comfort of the living room after furniture had been pushed aside to make room for the workers. 'Have a sausage roll,' said George taking a couple for himself. They were really delicious after the rough and ready farm baking, and there was such a large pile of them we thought, not having any idea that visitors were coming. We worked on the bike, taking care with the assembly, without noticing the time or the dwindling pile of sausage rolls. The bike was almost finished and we would just have time to get it out of the way and tidy up before Dolly returned. But life is not as easy as that. The door opened and in came Dolly. She stood and stared for a second or two as if she couldn't believe it. 'What the devil's going on in here?' she said. Her eyes almost popping out of their sockets. I could see that she was a little vexed. George was kneeling by the side of the bike, throttle slide held in his left hand. He looked at her, gormless-like, with his jaw dropped and mouth, wide open and half a fag sticking to his bottom lip. One did not need a degree to see he was a cowman. His battered hat on the back of his head gave away his trade, with the flattened cloth above his right side of his forehead stuck up with sweat and black and white hairs from the sides of cows during milking. His braces were removed from his shoulders and his breeches, which were tucked inside his black leather leggings, needed no support from them. Twiddle looked like an innocent child standing there behind the bike in his blue overalls, wiping his hands on a dirty piece of rag. Dolly's eyes were getting used to the light now after the darkness outside and began to focus on the disarranged room. 'What a damned mess! Oh, what a mess! Get that damned thing out of here. Come on, get it out before I put a hammer through the blinking thing, and where's my rug and where's my...?' She stopped as she saw the table, minus the best part of an afternoon's baking. 'Well you greedy pigs,' she said. I looked at the clock and decided it was my bedtime. I wished them good night. I knew I would have to wish very hard. The peace and quiet of the evening had been shattered. It wasn't long before I heard Twiddle going on his way. I bet he was glad to get outside the door.

Uncle Bill had a very hearty laugh. When he was in a good mood, he wore a tweed cap, good quality shirts and a nice tie.

His sports-type jacket was well cut and very smart. He always wore smart breeches and highly polished knee-length boots.

But Uncle Bill wasn't always in a good mood. One day I saw him curse and swear at an old workman for ages while the poor man trembled in his boots. I remember one morning when we turned out to do the milking. It was a lovely fine day and everyone was happy. But sometime later, Uncle suddenly changed from a happy soul to a raving lunatic.

As I walked across the yard, I saw Tishy in the paddock enjoying his breakfast of grass. He looked up and stared at me and then galloped to the gate, which was shut and fastened by the sneck.

We had finished milking and were going to the house for breakfast. The churns were lined up and ready to be put into the milk float. The lids of the churns were set at an angle to leave a space for the air to cool the milk. When we came out the house, all the lids were scattered around on the ground and Tishy had his head as far as it would go in a milk churn. He had drunk a gallon or more from each churn. When Tishy lifted his head from the churn, he looked very happy and contented and I thought, *he likes milk better than grass.* I don't think Uncle's thoughts were like mine and Tishy was lucky to escape being so many tins of corned beef.

Chapter 7

A SHEEPDOG, HORSES AND A DEAD FOX

One extra duty I had was looking after the sheep. In the field were two young horses: one of the horses was a light riding horse as used for fox hunting, and the other one was a young racehorse. They were both two-years-old, so I looked after those as well as the sheep. Uncle Bill did not have a lot of sheep, but he took in sheep belonging to two other farmers. Therefore I had a lot of sheep in a very big field. Seeing that I wasn't a trained shepherd with trained dogs, I had a very difficult task.

One day, Uncle Bill brought home a sheepdog. He had given £5 for it. It was black and white and a lovely looking dog. I took it with me not knowing what would happen. The dog was very keen and soon rounded up the sheep and took them to the far corner of the field. I didn't want them there, as it was a long walk for me. I took the dog the next day and again it took them to the far corner.

The dog wasn't helping me and I thought it was useless. Actually it was I who was useless and the dog would have been wondering why the shepherd was not giving it any signals to let it know what to do. I didn't take it anymore and so the dog stayed in the yard.

Kath was courting a butcher's son called Cedrick. Can you imagine a pretty young girl wanting to court a bloke called

Cedrick? He had a motorbike that sounded like a biscuit tin of pebbles shaken vigorously. The dog, when it wasn't tied up, always chased Cedrick and snapped at his feet and legs. He wore a sheepskin motorbike coat, with a sheepskin collar. Any sensible sheepdog would take him for a mechanised ram running away at that time. I had a visitor, my brother Les (Pug). The dog was tied up near the back door. After we had dined, Aunt Eve gave Pug a plate of scrapings like extra greasy fat meat and told him to give it to the dog. As Pug was scraping this rubbish onto the dog's dish, he took a bite of Pug's bum. The dog had taken a glance at the greasy plate and could only blame Pug for the cruelty.

Pug's bum required some medical attention so he had to drop his pants and Aunt Eve applied iodine to the bitten bits.

When Cedrick was told about the dog preferring Pug's bum, he went all sympathetic over Pug and not the dog. These were his very words: 'If that dog bites me I will shoot it.' The back door was shut and the dog got no warning of Cedrick's intentions. The dog did bite Cedrick and he tied it to the gatepost, went into the house and came out with Uncle Bill's gun and shot the poor dog. I thought it was a rotten thing to do and I was very upset. After all, Uncle Bill had bought the dog for me. I liked it and if I had been taught to give the dog commands, we would have got on very well.

One day, the young racehorse was missing. One thing, which worried me, was the horses used to chase each other round the field and I was afraid that they would slip into the drain. I ran back to the yard and shouted to George who ran to the house to get help. I carried on with my work with the sheep and when I got back I was told the worst; the horse had slipped over the drain bank and broken its neck.

One day, George was walking along the side of the drain when he saw something that looked like a dog, halfway down the bank. It was a dead fox that had been shot, so George took the fox home. That evening we had to go to his mother-in-law's house and I went with him. Dolly's sister was also at the house. George proudly took the fox into the house to show them how lovely a fox is with its lovely coat and big bushy tail. But he also wanted to tell them how the fox became dead.

It was a good story with all the details. He had cunningly stalked this cunning animal and with a crack marksman's skill, he had shot it. But later George made the mistake of telling someone else the story, someone who should not have been told.

About a week later, he visited Dolly's relatives again. But this time the swank had turned to pity, and the story was quite different. He told us he was in trouble with the master of the hounds who was going to have him at court for shooting a fox as 'the foxes belonged to the hunt.' George looked sad and hoping for some pity he said, 'But I didn't kill it.' His listeners only laughed and there was no pity for George. I do not know what happened next, but I don't think he went to court.

Chapter 8

THE HORSES AND WAGONS

We do not see horses and wagons nowadays unless it is at a show. I do not know when the horse wagon was designed, but I know it must have been by a genius because it never changed. The people who built them must have been very skilled. The body I think is perfect with the curved shelf at each side of the well-constructed body, and wooden wheels.

Blacksmiths made the axles, which gave the wheels the correct angle of tilt to enable the wagon to run in a straight line and easy to manoeuvre into a corner and out again without too much strain on the horses' collars from the pole.

The hoops for the wheels had to be perfect and a good fit, after they had been heated to a high temperature and lowered onto the wheel. The blacksmith also made the turntable for the front steering and the caps and hooks for the swingletrees and also the traces and chains. The skill of the painters and sign writers completed the wagon and added to its charm and good looks.

Fixed onto the turntable is the pole. Two horses are needed to pull the wagon, one at each side of the pole. The pole has two chains fixed at the front. One chain hooks onto the harness of one horse and the other chain to the other horse. Therefore, one horse will steer one way and the other horse will steer the wagon in an opposite turn.

All the pulling weight is on the horses' shoulders. Therefore, the collars must be well made and a perfect fit, otherwise the horses' shoulders will soon become sore. The pull on the traces must be even and to achieve this you have swingletrees. A swingletree has the same action as the beam on top of scales.

On the front frame of a wagon you have two hooks, one on each side of the pole. A centre ring on the swingletree goes on the hook and the traces are hooked onto the ends of the swingletree.

Horses and wagons took corn to the millers and on these days the horsemen would be up extra early to make sure the horses were well groomed with harness and brass looking its best.

The horses knew that they were going on a trip out and would be snorting and raring to go. But they always seemed happy to be home. They would be pleased to be unyoked from the wagons and walk slowly to the pond for a well-earned drink. There was no hurry, they were back and had done their day's work.

So by the time they had walked to the stable and into their stalls, the men would have put hay in the cribs and corn and chaff into their troughs. It is very important that their troughs are kept clean with no traces of the last meal, as horses are very particular about their food. The horsemen would then go for their food. When they returned to the stable they would give the horses another feed, and about half an hour later, their final feed.

Chapter 9

HARVESTING

Harvesting then as today, is the most important time of the year because without the harvesting, we would not get any wages. Apart from that, the difference between harvesting then and harvesting now is almost unbelievable. It began when the reapers were invented. They took the place of scythes and workmen went to the farms to destroy the reapers because they were putting lots of people out of work. Binders took the place of reapers a long time before I went to Grant's farm. Nevertheless, the binders had some faults.

It was harvest time and as well as looking forward to a long holiday from school, I was looking forward to helping with the harvest. Perhaps I did not realise that harvest meant working from very early morning until the darkness of night. I could not have imagined that sweat would be pouring down my face and neck and my mouth would be very dry, and I would be starving hungry before the middle of the morning. I was only thirteen-years-old, but who would worry about that.

The binder was dragged out of the shed and had a good brush down; someone emptied a large can of oil onto all moving parts. Someone took out the knife, which cuts the corn and cleaned it well and lubricated it, also the knife housing where it slides backwards and forwards driven by a linkage from one the wheels. The knife would be sharpened and put into place and linked with the connecting rod. The spare knife would be taken from its box, examined and sharpened if necessary.

A ball of binder band would be placed on its spindle and threaded through the needles. The knotter would be tested to see if it tied the band all right. When the maintenance jobs were done, the horses were yoked and the binder taken to the field. By this time the men at the field would have finished their job.

These men would have gone round the field scything, a full sweep of the scythe. As they went along, they would have raked up the corn, pulling it to their legs. A handful of the corn would be twisted to make a band to tie up to make a sheaf.

The open-out of the field is completed and the binder is pulled into the field and begins cutting the corn. The men who have opened-out the field would start stooking the sheaves. Stooking must be done right otherwise they will not stand up to the rain. To start stooking, you decide where to put your first row, as all the rows should be the same distance apart and facing north and south. The first pair of sheaves should be in the middle of the stook after the other four pairs of sheaves have been put in place. When a field has been well stooked and the sun is shining on it, it looks quite good.

It was a lovely sunny day and George and I went to help with the stooking. At times like this it was good to be on the farm and everyone was in a happy mood. We talked and sang a few well-known songs and the field was soon stooked and that was a good job well done. Laurie would be doing the stacking later, so he was busy doing the base for the first stack. This had to be the correct size, as also the stack height had to be right. In other words, the stack would contain the amount of corn we could get through exactly in one day on thrashing day.

The first field to be stooked will be ready for loading and taken to the stackyard if the weather has kept dry and the sun and warm winds have ripened the corn. Sometimes large clouds would appear and the rain poured down. This would be the end of harvest until the sun came back. Muck plugging came after harvest. This was a hard and dirty job that lasted a long time. Therefore, on wet days during the summer, muck plugging became a regular job. So the horses were yoked to the wagon and into the fold yard we went, armed with muck forks. The people who made muck forks were under the impression that all farm workers were big and strong. I was little and fairly strong and by the end of the day, my back had lost all its elasticity and I would be walking like an old man. The manure was solid with the cattle pressing it down for four months, which made bringing up a forkful of the stuff very hard work. When you slung it high onto a wagon it felt like a hundredweight on the fork.

The sun began to shine and there was a warm breeze. I was glad we would soon be able to continue with the harvest. I was not glad for long.

The stooks were dry at the outside, but were wet through on the inside. We had to go and pull the stooks over and remake them with the wet on the outside. After a few minutes you were as wet as the sheaves and you stayed wet for the rest of the day.

The weather stayed dry and some of the corn was ready to bring in. 'Waggoner' was the head lad. He was tall and well built and he had seen a few harvests and made a lot of loads of corn. He and his horses were impatient to go and get the first load. They set off at a gallop. They were shire horses and their large hooves thudded on the ground as they went past where I was watching. They appeared to be glad to get away from the muck plugging, and to be dashing off to the cornfield. I thought it was a magnificent sight, two lovely horses galloping by with their wagon and the wheels saying, 'Knap, knap,' as they should do when they are good wheels and hubs.

After a little while 'Third lad', went by. (There is a foreman, then the 'Waggoner' and then Third lad). He wanted to be in the field as 'Waggoner' finished loading. Next another pair of horses and wagon went by. He wanted to be in the field as soon as 'Third lad', had finished. As he went by me, 'Waggoner' went by with his load. There is some skill in making a good load, but it is practice that makes perfect. When you have laid the sheaves neatly in the bottom of the wagon, you place sheaves along the shelves with the bottom of the sheaves looking outwards. Also, you lay sheaves across the back and the front with their bottoms looking outwards.

Next you put a row of sheaves onto the sheaves you have just laid across the front of the wagon, but the opposite way round with the tips of the corn up to the bands of the front sheaves. Do the same at the back of the wagon then put about six sheaves in the middle. That is one course done, so do exactly the same again to make two courses. When completed, the load should look like the back half of two ducks stuck together. The makers of the wagons have been good to us by making the shelves a little higher at the outer edge with lovely curves from front to back.

When the two courses have been completed, start at the front again and put the sheaves across as before and bind them with a row of sheaves with the corn up to the bands. Go to the back and do the same and another row of sheaves to fill the middle. Start at the back this time and do exactly the same as before. When the sheaves are placed to fill the middle, they will be the opposite way round to the others. This will bind the front and the back equally.

You need to finish your load with a single row of sheaves. Therefore, after the two courses just mentioned are completed, the rest of the courses are reduced by one sheaf at the back and the front, until there is just one sheaf as just mentioned. Making a load is very easy when you just have one man forking to you. But if there are two forkers, you have to work quickly if you want your load to reach the stack yard over bumps and cartwheel gullies.

Unloading is easy at first, but you must not dawdle, as it is bad for you if a load is waiting while you are finishing yours. As the stack becomes higher, the dust and bits of straw and chaff stick to your sweating face, neck, arms and hands. If the corn is barley you also get the spikes sticking to you and through your socks until they look like a couple of porcupines. You had to put up with this from first light until it got dark. An onlooker would see the romance in a pair of well-groomed horses pulling a wagon. But for the workers at that time, it was slavery and poverty. Making a corn stack was different to making a load on a wagon. The middle of the stack had to be higher than the outer edges so that the sheaves were sloping downwards to prevent the rain running into the stack.

The stacker had to be skilled at the job and a very hard worker, as it was tiring work. It was usual to have three men on the stack. One man was at the edge of the stack and he took the sheaves from the wagon loader. He passed them into the middle of the stack and this man passed them to the stacker. If it were a good team, the one passing to the man in the middle would make sure that the sheaves were correctly placed. Likewise, the man who was passing to the stacker would make sure that the stacker had only to pull the sheaf a couple of inches for it to be where he wanted it. Stackers did not like people trying to put the sheaves in the correct place, as this was their job. Also, they hated it when a sheaf went too far and hung over the edge an inch or two because then they would have to lift the sheaf to bring it back. But when you think about it, they had to keep up with the wagon men. They had to put every sheaf in its correct place and by the time the stack was complete, the stacker would have stood on and handled every sheaf in the stack.

When all the corn had been brought in and all the stacks made, the stacker would set about making them look good. They were proud of their stacks. There would be lots of long bits of straw poking out from the bottom of the outer sheaves. He would go and get his sickle from its hiding place. It has a long handle and the knife is very sharp. With this, he lashed off the long bits and the stacks looked a lot better.

The next job is thatching. The Thatcher, Luke, and his helper, a young lad called Graham, began to collect up what was necessary for thatching. There were kneepads, wooden pegs, a ball of binder twine, and some good long winter wheat straw. They would rake all the short loose pieces of straw off the top of the stack. Then they would prepare the straw by getting a handful and shaking it and pulling it through the hand to get rid of short pieces of straw, and level the ends. They would wet it to make it lay better. When they had an armful ready, Luke took it onto the stack and shook it out to cover about 18 inches wide and about 3 inches thick. Graham had to work hard to keep Luke supplied with straw if he didn't want to get shouted at. Luke would go all the way round the stack laying the straw and knocking in the pegs. He tied the binder twine to the pegs to hold down the straw. When he laid the next course it covered two thirds of the course and so on, until they were to the ridge. The ridge was straddled by an extra thickness to make sure no rain could get through. Luke went all the way round the stack on his ladder and using shears to trim the bottom course of the thatching. This completed one stack, but there were others to thatch.

It was the end of harvesting for that year and there was lots of stubble to plough. To walk slowly behind a plough with two lovely and obedient horses was the best experience in the world. When we were in the middle of a great big field, even I could sing my head off in spite of having a flat croaky voice, lacking knowledge in music and not knowing all the words.

The muck plugging got into full swing and everyone was looking happy and some were even singing. I thought there must be something good about spreading manure all over the field. I'm sure I would rather have been going round the Isle of Man on a fast Matchless. But to see the old men on their pushbikes made me think that maybe they would rather be on the muck carts than on a fast Matchless. Strange how people differ. At last the last load came out of the fold yard. Muck plugging was followed by other exciting pastimes like cleaning out ditches and cutting hedges.

Laurie had made a good job of the corn stacks. They were neatly trimmed and the thatching was excellent. But one stack remained without trimming up. That was because the threshing men were coming to pull it to bits.

I watched the steam engine coming through the stack yard gate. It was something worth stopping to look at. I marvelled at the power of that steam engine, its beauty and quietness. There was a kind of romance about the hissing steam and the low thud, thud, and seeing the moving parts, so well balanced and so clean.

The threshing engine was pulled to the stack to stop in the exact place. No shunting, no sliding. The threshing men were experts and highly skilled. The threshing machine wheels were jacked-up and chocks placed under them. There were spirit levels built into the sides and ends of the threshing machine because it was essential to have it dead level. The steam engine drove the threshing machine by a long belt, making accurate setting up essential. Therefore, the engine driver drove the engine to the thresher, placing it in the exact position with the belt pulley on the steam engine in a perfect straight line to the pulley on the threshing machine. There were three men on the stack and two men on the threshing machine. One cut the bands on the stooks and fed it into the machine. An elevator placed at the end of the threshing machine fed the straw to the men making the straw sack.

Carrying corn was a good job if you were strong enough to carry sixteen stone sacks of wheat all day. It was against the law for lads under seventeen to carry corn. Sometimes it is loaded onto the wagons to go straight to the millers or taken to the granary. 'Waggoner', and 'Third Lad', would always carry the corn. But what about the chaff that came out with all the muck and dust from the big hole in the bottom of the threshing machine. This was the most horrible job of all, and this would have to be done by the youngest lad who would most likely be fourteen-years-old. The lad had a dustsheet and he had a rake for raking the chaff onto his sheet. Then he took hold of the four corners, pulled them together, twisted them and slung the load onto his back. It was so big that from the back you could only just see his boots. He had a long way to take it to suit the farmer. He had always to go through the fold yard. The fold yard would be full of cattle, and pigs and so all the doors had to be opened and shut after him. Very often when he tried to open the fold yard door, there would be an old cow's arse pushed against it. The chaff would be piling up all the time and the poor lad would have to run back to the machine with his face covered in sweat and the dust and muck from out of the chaff. How much extra money in wages would it have cost the farmer to have two young lads moving the chaff? One shilling I would guess. But it wasn't only in farming that young lads were treated badly in those days.

Chapter 10

FOURTEEN-YEARS-OLD

At last I reached the ripe old age of fourteen and I would soon be a soldier boy, at least that is what I thought. I liked everyone at the farm especially Dolly; she was like a mother to me. I liked farm work and I liked animals, but I also liked to play football and cricket. But most importantly, I wanted to ride in the tourist trophy races on the Isle of Man. When I became a soldier boy, I would be a despatch rider and perhaps I would go racing and the army would sponsor me.

One afternoon, George was taking Dolly and Aunt Eve to Hull to do some shopping. I asked if I could go with them and George said 'Yes'. They dropped me off at Hull and told me to meet them at six o'clock. I went as quickly as I could to the recruiting office. On arriving, my heart just slumped into my boots, as I was so upset to see the doors closed. I stood looking at the door as if it would suddenly open and let me in. I was surprised to see a short stocky man coming towards me. He looked to be about 45-years-old and not well dressed, but not scruffy. 'What are you doing here?' he asked.

'Well I came to join the army,' I answered.

'Then you are very lucky that they are closed, so you had better get off home and don't let me see you round here anymore,' he said, and I thought to myself, *no wonder the army are down on manpower with him around.* I waited for him to tell me more and he did not take any inviting, as he most certainly didn't have any love for the army. He gave me the benefit of his experiences in far distant lands with such good effect, that I didn't go back there until I was almost twenty, when I joined the Royal Corps of Signals on the 29 November 1935.

Now that I was working full time on the farm I received a wage. It was two shillings per week. I spent it mostly on clothes, but the title of the best-dressed youth eluded me. I shall never forget how one particular week's wage went. A double tooth had been giving me pain all week, so when I received my wages, I went to the dentist. I asked him what the charge was for extracting a tooth. His reply was 'Two shillings and sixpence.' I told him I was sorry, but I only had two shillings. He said that he was also sorry, and that I would have to return when I had enough money. That meant having toothache for another week. It turned out that this dentist was no gambling man, and so I turned to go. Then he said, 'I'll tell you what you can do, sonny. If I don't use cocaine, then the cost of extracting the tooth will only be two shillings.'

I didn't want another week of pain so I agreed to let him take it out this way. It was a double tooth and he had a struggle to get it out. He would press it down to loosen it and then give it a jerk. This action was repeated three or four times before it was eventually extracted. Chinese torture couldn't have been any worse. The pain was terrible and it lasted all week so I was no better off than if he had waited another week when I could pay the extra sixpence. So that is how I had my tooth out. There were some lovely people about those days. But that was only one tooth; I had much worse coming to me.

My birthday was on the 18 December. It was a working day, but I did get a treat when I went to see George and Dolly in the evening. There was a present for me, a pair of socks and Dolly had made a birthday cake.

Laurie and the other horsemen came in and we had some music and Laurie told some of his tales like:

The doggies had a meeting
They came from near and far
Some came by motorcycle
Some came by motorcar.
Each doggie passed the entrance
Each doggie signed the book
Then each unstrapped his arse hole
And hung it on the hook.
One dog was not invited
It sorely raised his ire
He ran into the meeting hall
And loudly shouted fire.
It threw them in confusion
And without a second look
Each grabbed another's arse hole
From off another hook.

But that's the reason why sir
When walking down the street
And that's the reason why sir
When doggies chanced to meet
And that's the reason why sir
On land and sea and foam
He will sniff another's arse hole
To see if it's his own.

I wished everyone a good night and thanked them for a good birthday. I went to my bedroom and was soon in my bed. I was very tired, but the wind blowing through the trees making their ghostly sounds kept me awake for a while. Then I slept soundly until the clock struck the very early getting-up time.

A few days later, when Kath and Uncle Bill returned home from their morning milk round in Hull, Kath came into the house carrying a huge fat turkey. This was the first sign that Christmas was here.

The day before Christmas Day, Aunt Eve, Dolly, and Olive were very busy in the kitchen and there was a lovely smell of baking. There was also work going on outside. We were working hard to make less work for Christmas Day.

There was an extra cartload of turnips brought from the field, which we put through the turnip chopper for Christmas Day feeding, and likewise the cow cake that went through the rows of teeth in the cake crusher. Chaff is a main part of the feed for the horses, sheep, and cattle. This is a first class oat straw chopped up small and fed with rolled oats, so we needed quite a big pile of it to see us through Christmas.

Hay was cut in cubes from the haystack. There were two shapes of knives and I could never make up my mind, which was the best. One knife was an inverted triangle. The handle of the knife was made of wood and was shaped like the letter T with the bottom bolted to the knife.

The other knife was shaped like a kidney bean with the handle coming at a right angle. One thing I remember best about them is that it didn't matter how cold you were before cutting hay, you would be sweating before you had finished.

Straw was pitched from the stack onto a flat cart and taken into the fold yard for bedding down cattle. After this was done, more straw was brought into the fold yard for bedding down the cowshed, stable, pigsties and small calves.

When we had done what we could for Christmas Day, there was still plenty to do for that day. The horses would have to be turned out of the stable into the fold yard. They would go for a long drink and a roll over in the fold yard straw. When the horsemen had completed their work in the stable, that is cleaning the floor, putting fresh bedding in the stalls and hay in the rack and feed in the troughs, they would call the horses. They would go to their own stall and wait for the men to tie them to the trough by their halter.

Then there was the grooming to do and another feed to give them and shaking up of the bedding and sweeping of the stable floor. When the horses had eaten their feed, they had turnips to crunch.

Then late afternoon, the horsemen had to start again with the watering, feeding, and bedding down. We had the same to do with the cows plus milking them and feeding the pigs and the calves. The sheep were all right and there weren't any missing.

We were all out of our beds at the usual time and on with the work. Uncle Bill and Kath set off with the milk for Hull. They were just a little earlier than usual, which was good as they usually arrived back at around 12 o'clock and the sooner they got back, the more time they would have to get ready for their Christmas dinner.

The rest of us were washed and changed into our best clothes by about 10 o'clock. What a wonderful feeling it was to be dressed up and waiting for dinner.

The ladies worked very hard and when we went into the large kitchen and sat at that very large table, we felt like millionaires. The spread on the table was unbelievable and to be able to just sit on your chair and have the lovely dinner placed in front of you, was like a dream.

We had plenty of time to relax after dinner before starting work again. The work gave us an appetite for the Christmas tea, which was also first rate and a credit to the ladies.

In the evening, we entertained ourselves with songs and stories about the people we knew and the funny things, which happened on the farms.

A week went by and the New Year was 1929 and I was fourteen-years-old. As I had left school, I was more involved with the general work on the farm. There were hedges to cut and dykes to clean out. Picking up the hedge cuttings and loading it on a cart and taking it to burn, wasn't the best of jobs and everyone involved in it was very glad when it was finished.

I was very busy with the sheep as it was lambing time. You have to spend a lot of time near the sheep as you could save the life of a ewe and the lamb just by being there when the ewe is having a difficult time. Normally the head comes first; with its front legs one at each side of the lamb's head.

If you only see one leg and the other trailing behind, just by being there to help, could save the lamb from dying. Then came the time for castrating and cutting off the lamb's tail. That was when I felt sorry for them. What looks better than seeing a lamb shake its tail?

You have to be on the lookout for foot rot and be able to treat it. Then there are ticks, which bore into the sheep's skin and flesh. At that time of the year when ticks are bad, you have to take the sheep to a sheep wash to kill the ticks.

The horsemen are busy ploughing and they want the land dry for cultivating and preparing for sowing. The previous year, there was a field that was fallow. It was ploughed four or five times and the fold yard manure spread all over it. That field would be sown mostly with wheat, but part of it would be sown with turnip seed for the current year's crop.

Drainpipes about 5 inches thick in diameter drained the fields. The ground was ridged giving a slope at each side of the ridge for water to run down to where the drainpipes were laid under the surface about 2ft down.

To maintain a good slope from the ridge to the drainpipes was done by ploughing. The foreman or the 'Waggoner' would start at one side of the field. He would have three poles. He would put the first pole in the ground at the end of the first ridge. Then he would walk to halfway along the ridge and push the second pole into the ground making sure it was right on top of the ridge. He then stood the third pole up where it would be in a straight line with his first two poles.

He began to plough, throwing the soil onto the top of the ridge. His return run would also throw the soil on top of the ridge. Therefore, he would have a furrow at each side and he would keep ploughing until he reached where the drainpipes were underground. He ploughed the next piece the same, finishing off at the drainpipes. So his plough was always turning the ground over towards the ridge and keeping a good slope. The rainwater seeped through the ground into the pots that drained the water into a ditch.

Chapter 11

MOVING TO PAULL

Uncle Bill had bought a farm at Paull called Rose Farm. This was about six miles away so we had a job on. We had a large herd of cows and lots of sheep and pigs. But I was glad when it was finished and we could settle down again.

I liked everything about Rose Farm and Paull suited me. It was a short walk across one of our fields to St Andrew's Church that was on the main road from Thorngumbald. A short walk from the church and you were in Paull. There is a promenade and a lighthouse. At the other end of the village is a boat-making yard. From the promenade you can see Hull docks and as far away as Beverley, on a clear day. Across the river you can see Cleethorpes, Grimsby, and Immingham, and I could breathe the lovely fresh air from the sea. This was more like home to me and I was feeling very happy. But nevertheless, I didn't want to work on farms all my life and farm wages would not get what I wanted. I was interested in cars and motorcycles and I wanted to do well on racetracks with cars or bikes. I was interested in engineering of many types.

I tried to work out my next move, but I couldn't think of a way out. The future is not ours to see. So therefore I had no idea that soon my work on Uncle Bill's farm would end as suddenly as it had started.

Our Friesian bull looked all right to me, but Uncle Bill thought it was time it was pensioned off, so he purchased a very well bred young Friesian. I had the job of looking after this young bull and we soon became used to each other. Nevertheless, I didn't think he could be trusted, so I was very careful not to let him get me in a corner. One day when I was getting the cows into the cowshed from the fold yard, the young bull was snorting and sending straw and manure flying with its horns and front legs. 'Is tha thrang?' a (busy) voice called.

I looked up and saw that it was Mr Hardwick, leaning on the fold yard gate. I liked Mr Hardwick; he was a pleasant man. He always had a smile on his round red face and his friendly blue eyes twinkled as he spoke. His heavy-looking corduroy jacket was open as always. I used to think it must have been a waste of time putting buttons on farmers' jackets. He was wearing a thin black tie, which was tucked into his mustard-coloured waistcoat. His breeches were made of the same material as his jacket. Corduroy was the favourite material amongst the farm workers. It was expensive, but hard-wearing and I often wished I could afford it. Looking at Mr Hardwick you could see that the leggings had been knocking about for a long time. Over the leather was a thick skin made up of cow muck collected over the years and this was reinforced by splashes of milk that had gone sour.

'Is tha' thrang lad?' he called again. He could see I was, but he had asked a question and he wanted an answer.

'Yes we are always busy, there's plenty to do here,' I said.

'Tha's getting a fine young bull there lad, but bah gum, you must watch 'im or eel 'av tha,' he warned. 'Tha needs ta 'andle that un, avan yer gotten a whip,' he said.

'No, I only wish I had,' I replied.

'Bill's late 'ome today,' he said.

'Yes, they are late, but I don't think they will be long,' I replied. 'Did you want to see him?' I asked. It paid to ask daft questions; it made one more sociable or something.

'Weal, I just wanted to ask 'im if 'ed sell ma that thea young dog. Ah reckon it warr a well bred little dog and mebby Bill ud let ma ave im cheap if tha's nowt for im ta do.'

I was trying to think of an answer when Uncle Bill arrived. 'Now then, Hardwick, what are you after? No you can't have that bull if that is what you're thinking,' said Uncle Bill.

'Ah wa' just telling lad, e owt ta ave a whip to calm im wi. Al send 'im yan in mornin',' said Mr Hardwick, as they walked away to carry on the conversation in the middle of the road, which was typical of farmers. They were still there an hour later. By that time they would have forgotten about the dog and the bull and would be talking about general farming activities. I'm glad to say the whip had not been forgotten and I received it the next day. When I cracked that whip, Billy the bull was more frightened of me than I of him.

Chapter 12

HAYMAKING

I think haymaking time was the best of all the other farming jobs and it is the best time of the year. The horses are turned out into the field to sleep and the cows are out in the grass field except at milking time. This cuts out a lot of work and more time to be busy with hay.

Usually a pair of horses is sufficient to pull a reaper. If the going is hard work, you can have a third horse at the front of the other two horses. The reapers were the same as binders that were used for cutting corn, but without the sails and the means to make stooks.

One horse pulled the hay rake because it was of light construction. It consisted of the horse shafts, a little framework and two wheels, a seat for the driver and a long lever for releasing the hay from a number of curved rakes, which picked up the hay and carried it until the man on the rake pulled the lever, and the hay fell out. The finished job would be rows of hay across the field.

The hay was left for a couple of days to dry. Then we went with our hayforks and turned it over three or four times. When it was ready for gathering, it was put into heaps. Then a pair of horses would come trotting into the field with the wagon, the horseman and two forkers.

When this wagon was loaded, another wagon was there and so on until all the hay had been stacked. I had worked hard at Uncle Bill's for a year, so I asked if I could go home for a few days. I wasn't very pleased when Aunt Eve said, 'You can go home on Saturday when you have finished your work.' I was annoyed because I thought she should let me go when I had done my day's work on the Friday.

I can't say how much I was looking forward to being at home with my family. There's no place like home where you can talk, take time eating your meals and relax in an atmosphere, which you can only get at home. I was also looking forward to being amongst motorbikes and having a race with Pug. I hoped it would not be long before I was having a race with George Grant and his friend Dot Adams. He was called Dot because his racing bike was a DOT (Devoid Of Trouble).

I was very tired when it came to Friday night and so I had a good sleep before getting up extra early on the Saturday morning so that I could get the cows in, feed them and get everything ready for when the others came to do the milking. The sooner the milking was finished, the sooner I could get the pigs fed and be off on my pushbike, heading for home.

I went to get my whip from the cow house where I kept it, but it wasn't there. I couldn't find it anywhere and had to go without it. By the time I reached the field, most of the cows were already coming to the gate. When I called them they all began to come except one old cow, which was doing a bit of courting with the bull at the far end of the field. I kept on calling, but it seemed they had better things to do and refused to take any notice of me.

Unfortunately they had to come in because the cow had to be milked. So I had to go and fetch them. When I was within a few yards of them the cow looked at me, put its nose down to the ground and charged. I could only shout and lash out with my feet as I had nothing to defend myself with and then the bull joined in. As the bull came for me, the cow ran off. At that time the bull seemed a bit afraid of me and I managed to chase it off. As I backed towards the hedge it came for me again. I dodged it and managed to chase it off again and then backed again towards the hedge. By this time the bull was in a rage, snorting and sending grass sods flying. It came for me again, and once again I was able to dodge it and back a few more paces towards the hedge. I decided that next time I would make a dash for the hedge. I turned and was looking for a gap in the hedge where I would be able to dive through. I saw a gap, but as I turned the mad bull charged towards me and I hadn't a chance to do anything. It knocked me over and I hit the deck with a thud. I was dazed, but I managed to stagger to my feet. I grabbed the ring in its nose and lashed out with my heavy boots, kicking it under its chin. It bellowed and pulled back and I lost my grip on the ring. I went down again and its massive head was over me. I fought like a tiger and tried to get up. Its horn hit me in my mouth. The roof of my mouth was damaged, my lips badly split and teeth scattered. I fell to the ground, face downward, exhausted and with blood pouring from my mouth. I thought I had lost my last fight. I murmured, 'Goodbye everyone.' I waited for the bull to kneel on me to finish me off. I waited and it seemed like ages. Everything was so still and quiet and I thought the bull must have left me. But I dared not move. I heard a voice very faintly as if it was coming from a long way off. 'Get up and run. Hurry, get up and run,' the voice was saying. My Uncle Bill had arrived just in time to save my life. He had fought the bull off with a hayfork and as I looked up, the bull was chasing him. He was striding out like a champion and with a leap that would have done justice at the Olympics, he cleared the hedge. Deciding this was no time for getting enthusiastic about the athletics, I made the effort to get to my feet. Then I passed out and cannot tell you anymore about it, because when I came round I was in that big kitchen and someone was giving me medical attention. I expect they had sent for the vet.

I did go home that day, but cannot remember how I got there. But although it may seem strange, I do remember that I didn't have my two shillings for my week's wage. Aunt Eve may have given it to me, or she may have put it in my pocket, or she may have forgotten it in the confusion. I never returned to ask her, but what I do know for certain is that the last week with Uncle Bill was a dead loss.

Some years later an old farmer said to me, 'I reckon ya Uncle must be the richest farmer in Owlderness.' I thought to myself, *In that case ar reckon ar owt to gan und ask him for ma two bob.*

Chapter 13

GOING TO KILNSEA

It was strange being at home in a house, which was new to me. There was the Bluebell pub and next to it was Bluebell cottage. We had the cottage. There was a plaque on the side of the pub, which recorded that it was built in 1847 and was 500 yards from the sea. When we were there it was only half that distance. There was a heavy gun battery situated between the pub and the shore.

To the front of the pub and the cottage, only half a mile away, is the River Humber. The road goes to the Spurn Peninsula about half a mile away.

The school-going children of Kilnsea had to attend Easington School and because of the distance, which I reckon would be about three miles, the Kilnsea school bus was available for them. This was a four-wheeled flat cart with a canvas top making it look like a covered wagon from the Wild West. A dark brown horse pulled the cart, which was driven by the owner, Mr Tenyson. Mr Tenyson's farm was at Kilnsea. He had a large moustache. Mrs Tenyson was a very nice person. She had long, curly ginger hair. Likewise, I recall one of the daughters who had the loveliest red curly hair.

Because the children went to Easington School, we already knew them before we went to live at Kilnsea. There was Crags Clubley's children, who lived opposite the church and were our friends at school. Mary was just a little older than Stan, Fred was my age, and Esther was Pug's age. Stan had gone to a high school after leaving Easington and was in lodgings in Hull. Mary and Fred were working and so I felt a bit lonely during schooldays.

Although Pug was younger than Stan and I, he was the first to have his own motorbike. When he was six-years-old he was more interested in motorbikes than any toys and would always be with Ernie when he was working on cars and motorbikes.

Ernie had a Rudge Malti that was made in 1913 and in very good condition. He gave it to Pug when he was seven-years-old. Pug loved his Rudge and he kept it in good condition with lots of loving care. He was a very good rider and good at maintaining the Rudge. Therefore, he had his Rudge motorcycle that we rode about on when he came home from school.

I didn't have time to settle in before I was on the move again. The nearest dental surgery was at Withernsea, about ten miles from home. It was therefore arranged for me to go to my Grandma's (old Ernie's mother). She had a shop in a street off Beverley Road. There was a dental surgery very near, and as I would have to go several times for treatment, this would be the most convenient way.

We set off on our journey in style, with me sitting in the single-seater sidecar. It had a small oval windscreen and a curved boot nicely streamlined from the top of the seat backrest, and there was no top. I suppose if you wanted to be kind you could call it a single-seater sports type. We were soon onto the straight length of road and old Ernie whipped the throttle lever as far back as it would go. I looked at him with some amusement as he sat, crouched forward, his face set and stern below his cap, which was pulled down to his eyebrows for fear of it becoming airborne due to the strong high wind, which was created by the tremendous speed. I tried to see the speedometer, but I couldn't; we must have been almost reaching thirty-five miles per hour. The beautifully balanced engine of the Bradbury was really buzzing now, well perhaps not buzzing, but doing at least six hundred revs per minute, with Ernie hanging on to full throttle.

Eventually we were there and almost frightened to death by the clanging of the great bell above the shop door. Almost immediately, my grandma appeared in the doorway from the living room, so delighted she was to see us. Or was it because she expected some customers with lovely cash to spend? Ernie did not hang about for long. He had a few words with the dog, which was fastened in the backyard with a long length of clothesline. It was a nice dog, looked like a greyhound, but it was not a greyhound, and its long toenails were an indication that it didn't look like that on account of over-exercising. I came to the conclusion that if overfeeding was bad for dogs, this one must be very healthy. Ernie suggested the dog should go to Kilnsea as the fresh air and exercise would be good for it. Having said this he cleared off, perhaps back home or most likely to see an old flame.

The living room was overcrowded as living rooms always were in those days. The furniture was of the highest quality and so it should be as the Nicholsons were in the furniture trade. In the centre of the room was a beautiful polished table over which was a heavy green tablecloth with edges of hanging baubles. A large grandfather clock was stood between the kitchen door and room window. I had a look through the window at the garden. It was a nice size considering that it was down a street off Beverley Road. At the straight side of the path down the centre, which led to the greenhouse, were shrubs and plants giving a lovely display of colour.

There was always bread rising in large earthenware bowls in front of the spotless highly polished coal range. My aunt used to rise very early every morning except Sundays, to bake bread, pies and cakes to sell in the shop. On Sundays she went to church, and taught the children at Sunday school. There were two parrots, a grey one, which was always talking, and a green one, which didn't talk at all.

There was also my other aunt. She had ginger hair and I have heard it said that ladies with ginger hair are sexy. It was not for me to say whether she was or not. Therefore, I will give a description and you can draw your own conclusion. She was the sick one; the one who kept the family doctor in luxury. Her hair was straggly and held in a bun on the back of her narrow head. By her complexion you may think she had sailed the seven seas. But she hadn't, she suffered from yellow jaundice. Below the long black dress you could just see her black laced-up type calf boots. On her matchstick legs, were splayed-out duck feet.

When my granddad came in from work, the parrot would say, 'Bob's come home, put the kettle on.' Bob wasn't much trouble to anyone. As soon as the meal was finished he would go to the greenhouse and stay there until the old woman had gone to bed. As soon as she was out of the way, he would go to the pub at the corner of the street and stay there until closing time.

I had been going to the dentist for about six months and the dentist had completed his work on my mouth, so I was ready for going home. Pug would come for me on the Saturday.

The dentist was a very good one. There had been a lot of work to do, but he was very considerate and patient not doing too much in one visit. Eight front teeth had been broken off at my gums. It was necessary to do some lancing to remove the roots, which were shattered and most of my remaining teeth required straightening.

I went once each week for the first month. Then I went alternate weeks for two months. This was giving my gums chance to heal and for him to keep a check on his work. I was using TCP mouthwash three times a day. This helped the healing and kept my gums healthy.

When my gums had healed, they were still tender and needed time to shrink and harden. So after another month he took impressions and made a top and bottom plate for eight missing teeth. The dentist's work took about five months. But the TCP treatment went on for years, and also the pain, which was caused by the cold. The women had to go out on the Saturday afternoon and when Pug came, I had to tell him that we must not leave until they returned. How to amuse ourselves in a dismal room was a problem, until we realised that although the grey parrot could talk, there had been something missing in its education. It didn't seem to know any swear words. This we thought was terrible and without a moment's hesitation, we gave ourselves the task of completing its education. We spent about two hours repeating all the swear words we knew over and over again. But that overgrown sparrow never said a word. We were so disgusted we called it all the nasty things we could think of, but still no word from Polly. Eventually the ladies returned from their gallivanting and began to get tea ready. This was usually giblets, which were brought onto the table in the large jar as they had been bought in the market. I think the jar of giblets would cost about two pence and as they lasted for two or three meals, they were able to eat them without feeling miserable about it. But they always had a good spread on the table. But before the giblets were downed, someone would gather up the pies and they would be taken into the shop. I had already told Pug about this, therefore before the giblets had been eaten and the pies done the disappearing trick, I noticed Pug had his eyes on a nice big pie. He winked at me, then cut the pie in half. The old dears never had the misfortune to see such shocking behaviour in all their lives.

I had to ride the pillion of the Bradbury because the dog occupied the sidecar, during the journey to Kilnsea. The piece of clothesline was still attached to the collar so we decided to tie it to the sidecar, as we didn't want to have him doing the disappearing act. But how best to do this was not an easy problem. If he only had it short he would not be able to jump out, or would he? That was the problem. After careful consideration we let him have plenty of rope, then if he jumped out he could start running and we would stop and put him back into the sidecar. But our precious hound had no intention of leaving the comfort of that seat. After that miserable backyard, this was the best day of his life. He couldn't have looked more pleased if he had just become best dog in the show at Crufts. I wondered what was going on in his mind as he took in the sights of Hull. With Hedon behind us, we were on the winding country roads, and I forgot about our passenger. When I did glance at the sidecar it was empty. At the end of the taut line and not being able to make up its mind whether to run or skate, was our precious hound. I shouted to Pug, 'The dog has jumped out of the sidecar.'

The reply was as can be expected, 'Yer wot, don't know what yer say.'

He noticed an absence of doggy and slammed on the brake. I knew we had slammed on the brake because I could hear the scrape, scrape, from the hard blocks of fibre as they rubbed on metal. No one had ever been slung over the handlebars with these brakes. We came to a halt eventually, much to the dog's relief. The need to save up for claw clippers was no longer a necessity. In fact, had he skated much further he would have been a new type of Daschund. I thought he was in need of the kiss of life, but Pug didn't seem very keen about that. We put him back in the sidecar and there he remained to the end of the journey. He enjoyed being at the seaside; his favourite pastime was chasing seagulls on the sands. He was with us for a long time, but I cannot remember what happened to him. I hope he never returned to that backyard.

About a week after I had come home from my grandma's, Ernie called to see them, but found his relatives to be very cross indeed. On his return home he looked at Pug and me and began to laugh. He had been told that his two beastly boys deserved a jolly good beating and he had been ordered to administer the punishment by Grandma, without fail. The incident with the pie was bad enough, but on the Sunday the vicar had been brought home for tea. Just when he was busy sucking the delicious meat from a sparrow's neck, a spluttering and muttering overcame him, which almost caused him to choke. This was brought on by the grey parrot coming out with the biggest beakful of the choicest swear words imaginable.

Chapter 14

LIVING AT KILNSEA

I had some good luck just before we left Kilnsea. I was just strolling about in Kilnsea and stopped by at a house with its garage doors wide open. I noticed a motorbike inside the garage. I suppose I had a cheek because I went into the garage to have a look at it.

A man came into the garage and he had a surprise when he saw a very interested lad checking over his motorbike. We had a chat about motorbikes and when he realised that I knew quite a lot about them and I was so interested, he asked me if I would like to buy it. That did not make me happy because I didn't have the money to buy a motorbike. Nevertheless I asked him how much he wanted for it. The engine wasn't there so it should be cheap.

He said, 'Five shillings. It's worth a lot more than that, but you seem to be a good lad and I know you would like to have it.'

'Could I give you a shilling a week?' I asked. 'Yes, that will be all right if you don't forget,' was his reply!

It was a Wooler motorcycle. Woolers were noted for their advanced design and one special feature was the suspension, which was unique in those days of ridged frames. Sliding blocks, which were held by coil springs, sprang both the front and the rear wheels. Each have a short spring at the bottom and a longer spring above the sliding block. They had a long petrol tank, with a domed extension, which extended beyond the forks and steering head. The forward part of the tank was for the engine oil. Because of the long round yellow tanks, the bikes were nicknamed, 'Flying Bananas'. I was upset over the absence of the engine because this like the rest of the bike was of unusual design. There was a Singer engine on the floor of the garage. It was a 250cc side valve and a very neat little engine. It was nothing like the Wooler engine, but this was no time for getting choosy over trifles so I asked him if I could have it and he said, 'Yes, you need an engine.' After a little studying, hack-sawing and drilling, the bike was ready for a run. It went very well and my only regret is that I have not still got it as it is the only Singer motorcycle engine I have ever seen. Pug's Rudge was too fast for my bike, but this may not have been the case with the Wooler engine. But two bikes were better than one and we enjoyed ourselves.

The layout of Kilnsea hadn't been constructed for the benefit of Pug and me, having only one decent corner. After this corner was the long straight road to Easington. Chasing Pug along these would not have done the little engine any good.

The school broke up, the covered wagon put away and Neddy turned out to grass. Also, Stan came home and he looked worse than Granddad Nick's dog we had brought from Hull and would have benefited by being turned out to grass with the horse. It would appear that Grandma's was not the only house where giblets were the main diet. But after a week of Ett's cooking (my mother's cooking) his ribs had stopped showing through his overcoat.

Along the coast, northwards past Withernsea is a small agricultural village called Tunstall, and halfway down the seaside road from the village of Tunstall, there are two coastguard houses. But these were no longer required for coastguards, and we received word that one of these was becoming vacant. This was excellent news, which steered

Ernie into action. As our hero went down that road I saw him as a despatch rider with urgent operation messages, and a big German on his BMW, in hot pursuit. As time went by, excitement gripped us at the prospects. We even looked forward to Ernie coming home, something we had never looked forward to before, or since. But our sweet daddy did not disappoint us – the mission had been successful. I could have kissed him, if I had not just had my tea.

Chapter 15

GOING TO TUNSTALL

We didn't like the house at Kilnsea. There was nowhere to keep our bikes and the roads were unsuitable for motorbike racing practice. We did not waste any time either. In fact, before the Bradbury engine had time to cool down, Stan was at the controls with Pug on the pillion and me in the sidecar, heading in the direction of our next home. It was not long before we were pulling up in front of the coastguard houses. We did just glance at the house. It looked all right to us, but it was not important, as it was only to live in. But we were very pleased with the big shed in the garden. Of course in that area the only consideration, which limited the size of a shed was the available space. As all the wood came off the seashore, the only difference in cost was the amount of nails one purchased. We had a look at the seashore. The tide was out and there was a beautiful stretch of hard sand. The cliffs were not very high and disappeared into sand dunes and sea grass about one quarter of a mile at Sand-le-Mere giving access onto the sand for bikes. As we set off for home, we were so happy we burst into song and sang all the way home. They were good for young motorcyclists, and for old ones too. Many an old boy has gone to look in his garage on the morning after a night out to see if his motorbike was there and on seeing it there, wondered how he had managed to get home.

The Royal Enfield remained as last used for moving to Kilnsea, with the strong boards fitted to the sidecar chassis. Therefore, as soon as the house became vacant, Pug and I began to move the bits of motorbikes and cars from the shed at Kilnsea to the one at Tunstall. The Royal Enfield with its 1,000cc V twin JAP engine was very useful for taking these heavy loads, and was also very fast on the return journey when empty.

The young motorcyclists of today may wonder about the cost of running all these bikes. Well, it wasn't such a problem because although the Bradbury may have had a road licence, I'm sure that none of the others had one. Petrol was just under one shilling per gallon and those engines did not gobble it like today's bikes do. Fourteen years of age was the limit for riding a motorbike. Pug was only just thirteen, so he could not have a licence. Stan and I were old enough, but not rich enough to get a licence. So it turned out rather cheap. A policeman round those villages was a very rare sight indeed, and he would only have a pedal cycle and even our bikes were faster than a police bike.

Tunstall hadn't a school and neither did it have a Mr Tenyson, so the children had to walk the three miles to Roos School. I managed to get a job at Mr Laycock's farm in Roos. It was a six-and-a-half days per week job and I had a wage of £1 a week, which was very good as some married men with families were only getting £1 10s per week. I had to hand over seventeen shillings and sixpence per week for my keep at home, so I did not get very rich. I must have eaten a lot. I wonder what made me such a greedy pig.

For the present, motorbikes had priority as we would start racing the following year and there was a lot of practising to do. It was decided that Pug's Rudge would do to start off with, but I was in need of a suitable bike. Ernie was extremely enthusiastic and helpful. He surprised us by dismantling his Humber, which he had owned for fifteen years, which must have been heart-rending. He hacked away at the old fashioned frame and when the frame was ready, we built up the bike, using mostly NUT parts. (NUT stands for Newcastle-upon-Tyne). In those days when most petrol tanks fitted between the two top tubes of the frame, NUTs had a lovely shaped saddle tank. The bike turned out lovely to look at and marvellous to ride.

Riding on the hard sands was very good for practice, and we became very good at broadsiding, throttle control and race tactics. We also learnt the art of falling off when the bike had reached a point when it was not possible to rectify a fault. To reach the sands we had to go along the seaside to the cliff and turn right on the cliff top and along a footpath, until we came to the end of the cliffs. We would get the full advantage of the journey by making it a race. If Ernie was available he would start us off, sometimes it would be a clutch start and sometimes it would be a push start. Ernie was very critical and pointed out any mistakes, which we made. 'Wheelies' were certainly not allowed, nor was the slightest tendency to wobble as we went through the gears. He would say, 'What's the use of making perfect bikes if you put them all out of balance when you change gears?'

One day we set off to go to the sands. I got the best start, but Pug was only just behind. As I began to brake and go down my gears, Pug passed me on my left. I thought he was out to overtake me so that he could get onto the narrow footpath, which ran along the cliff top, in front of me. We were not supposed to pass each other there because it was too dangerous. I put extra pressure on my brakes to give him room to corner then I realised that something was wrong and that Pug would not be cornering. His throttle slide had jammed in the fully open position. Being a born rider, he did the correct thing and kept his bike going in a straight line without touching his brakes, and went over the edge of the cliff. This did not do my concentration any good and by the time I had got things sorted out and was able to look over my shoulder, Pug had already made contact with the sand. My only regret is that we did not think of measuring the jump because some years later when I was in the Signals' Display Team, they would say what was considered to be the world record. It would be just over 70ft; I wish I could shake them by telling them how far Pug had jumped.

A policeman, who lived just outside Tunstall village on Hilston Road, had retired. There was a field near where he lived and so with his mind on the need to have something to do, he bought it. But half the field was sufficient for his needs. Ernie negotiated for the other half and obtained it on a five-year lease. Now Ernie was taking a big gamble because his idea was to build a bungalow and then when the lease ended, he would buy the land. Of course this legal stuff did not concern us lads. All it meant to us was we were going to have a grass track. We had become fed up with the sands. For one thing the tide did not suit us, as very often the tide would be right out during working hours, and lapping on the cliffs during the evening when we wanted to practice. Another thing was that salt water and sand is bad for bikes. But good things do not come easy, and there was an awful lot of work to do before we could indulge in burning petrol again. As soon as Ernie had completed the marking out, we began digging out for the foundations. It was getting near the end of the year and Ernie began to pray for some rough weather. I cannot say where he did his praying because he did not go to church. But what matters is that we got plenty of rough weather during that winter. Of course, Ernie did not like the winter any more than anyone else did; therefore I must give an explanation for this strange request. Most of the cargo boats were bringing in wood, which is a very valuable material when one is building a bungalow. When the sea is rough and the strong winds are blowing, the boats will shelter near land. It very often happens that a cargo boat with its heavy load runs aground, and to refloat it, part of the cargo is dumped overboard. Well two miles north from this field were the high cliffs at Dimlington, which I expect would give some shelter because this is where they ran aground. About a mile from the field there was a bend in the coastline, which forms a small bay. The bend brought the cliffs very near to the Tunstall-Hilston road. This was Ernie's wood supply, and we were the slaves.

A boat ran ashore, which was carrying large planks of wood; Ernie was delighted as it was just what he wanted for the floor battens. It was very hard work dragging the soaking wet planks up the cliff and across to the road where the Royal Enfield waited to be loaded up. Most of the wood was washed up near the bay, but not all of it and we had to carry it as much as two miles. As we trudged over the soft sand weighed down with Ernie's gift from the gods, our bones felt like seizing up into a solid mass.

Having got well supplied with planks, he was muttering to the gods again, 'I want some more joists,' he said. Sure enough he got his wish and another boat with pit props ran aground. I am not sure about his building methods, as I was going to my regular job and only helped him with the wood from the shore. But I believe he had placed the planks (which I think would be joists) at a good distance apart. Next he squared off the pit props and fitted these across them. The construction of the outside walls consisted of concrete panels (which he made of course) fitted into wooden frames. There was an inside and outside panel, which was separated by a 1½ inch air space. People had to pay a small charge for the wood from the beach. A cargo boat was forced to dispose of valuable cargo as a means of getting refloated. A customs officer would visit houses in the district and calculate a price, which the people had to pay him for their wood, which they had collected. Of course, he only saw what Ernie showed him and knew nothing about that, which was out of sight at the far end of the field. Pug was very useful when we were getting wood up the cliffs because he was very strong for his size and demonstrated this with an almost unbelievable feat. He and Alan had gone to the cliff tops to see if there was any wood washing up. They saw something bobbing about in the water and waited to see what it was. It was a body of a drowned man. Pug got it on his back and carried it to the top of the cliffs. I reckon this would be twice as difficult as carrying a live man.

We built a shed in the field, the wood for the frame coming off the beach, but it was covered with matchboard, which I paid for. I was not being generous, the shed would be used as a tuning shop for the bikes, but first it became a joiner's shop in which Ernie made all the doors and windows for the bungalow. Ernie was very highly skilled at woodwork and within a short time there was a pile of doors and windows to be fixed in place, and the bungalow went up very quickly.

While Ernie was getting on with the bungalow, we were left alone to get on with the bikes at the coastguard house. We gave the bikes a good clean to get rid of the sand and then removed the engines and gave them a good clean before stripping them. Our tuning consisted mostly of a good examination of components and a few hours of polishing valve ports and flywheels and grinding in valves. We had a good look at the cams, but resisted the temptation to improve on the cam profiles and that I reckon was a wise move. Also, we were relieved to find no play on the big end bearings, as splitting flywheels and reassembling was a job that we didn't tackle at that stage, apart from assisting Ernie. However, we did succeed, either with skill or luck, to get the compression ratio to suit the fifty-fifty mixture of Tetraethyl and Benzene, and also to get the timing and carburation spot on. When we set up the carbs, we tried main jets until we found the one, which gave maximum speed, and used the next size upwards. I believe this improved the performance when racing on grass and scrambles. With those old carbs we used to get a slight splutter when broadsiding. This was improved by slightly weighting the float. We got a lot of fun out of those bikes and a lot of satisfaction out of tuning them up, because we just messed about, sometimes making performance better and sometimes worse, but learning all the time.

One day, Ernie had a brilliant idea for accelerating out of corners. This consisted of an ignition cut-out operated from a button on the handlebars. Instead of closing the throttle, the ignition was cut and the gas would build-up in the cylinder. Then as the sparks were switched on again, the bike would go like a rocket. Well we thought something might go like a rocket, but we were not sure what it would be. So we told Ernie to try it on his Bradbury first. Well we had a lot to learn and we couldn't expect to think up good ideas without crazy ones as well.

The day of our first grass track racing dawned. The Citroen had been fitted with a rack at the rear and one on the roof. Pug's bike went on the back and mine on the top. After all the careful tuning, we made the mistake of placing my bike on its side, which proved we had a lot to learn. We didn't have oil seals in the gearbox, only an oil slinger for keeping the gearbox oil away from the dry clutch, which had become a slipping wet clutch by the time we had reached the grass track. Almost all the gearbox oil had found its way past the output bearing and completely soaked the clutch.

As I worked on the clutch, I could see that even to have trouble had its compensations, by way of offers of help from the riders, which made me feel I was already a racing motorcyclist. But there was nothing spectacular about my performance during that first outing, just a third place in one of the heats. But I soon began to realise that chasing each other round the track was only part of the pleasure that comes from motorcycle racing. I think it is that extraordinary atmosphere in the paddock, which makes one proud to be part of it. Motorcyclists are and always will be wonderful companions. So much so that if some competitor is in need of a component, which is in your spares box, then he must have it and be given help with the fitting of it, to get him onto the starting line on time. The possibility that he may only give you a rear view of his bike in the race has nothing to do with it at all, for this is true sportsmanship. This is motorcycle racing, which gets into the blood, and then once it is there, it stays there. So if you should have chance to come across two ancient old geezers racing round hospital grounds in their wheelchairs and if they are leaning over the sides on corners, you can bet your life that you are looking at a couple of motorcyclists of days gone by.

Pug's performance was about the same as mine during that first day. We had forgotten all about the racing tactics, which Ernie had taught us, having plenty on, just riding round. The fine art of racing came later because the only real practice was from racing.

I cannot remember when we moved from the coastguard house to the bungalow, but due to an incident with a fire, I know for certain that it wasn't until after a few race meetings. Therefore, let me give you the gen leading up to this little fire. We had been to a grass track event, but I cannot remember when, but I can remember by this time we had become used to racing in a crowd and able to take advantage of what Ernie had taught us about getting a flying start and riding together. It was one of those race days when everything went well. When we received our prize money we thought it would be a good idea if we went to Hull and got rigged out with new clothes. Now this was something that we knew nothing about as you already know. Therefore, it is not surprising that the shop we favoured with our custom was one, which everyone knew (except Pug and I) sold best quality rubbish at favourable prices. I'll bet the shop assistants couldn't eat their tea for laughing. As soon as we got back home we changed into our new togs. It's a pity we did not have our photos taken. I reckon we could have got booked up anywhere as a comic pair. What I remember best is the hats, as these were trilbys that were extra high with large brims. We got on our motorbikes for a ride, perhaps just to show off our togs to villagers. We would have looked better on horses with that gear. We had travelled about halfway along the seaside road when Pug's bike caught fire. The only thing we had for smothering out the flames were these big hats and they were ruined.

We moved to the new home and called it, 'Belle Vue'. We marked out the track, a bend on each of the two straights, making it less monotonous than just plain oval. We preferred it to the beach; in fact, we never rode on sands again. But I almost did at Filey the following year. The reason I did not ride at Filey is a little complicated because a girl was involved. I had started courting, and as she was such a nice girl, I cannot understand why she fell for me. Unless it was because I was so handsome, or was it because of my unusual perfume, a mixture of petrol, oil and farmyard manure. Her home was in Knaresborough and she had come to work in a house in Burton Pidsea. Therefore, she may have been lonely, a situation which unfortunately, was not improved by being my girlfriend, due to the bikes being in need of some attention whenever I had a date. Having me not turning up after waiting for about an hour made her cross. But apart from this small lack of understanding, she was really a nice girl. If someone tells you that absence makes the heart grow stronger, tell him or her to get lost. Because to say that my love for her was any less, would have been a very feeble description indeed. Perhaps what was needed was the expert advice from a woman's magazine. But not having the wisdom for such a wise move, I sat down and wrote her a letter containing much passionate nonsense, and a bit about me deciding not to race at Filey as I would rather have a day out with her.

I rushed off with my masterpiece as I did not want to miss the post, and as I passed the busy roadmen standing talking at the side of the road by the church, I gave them a friendly wave because their foreman and Ernie were friends. By the time I had reached the postbox, being an unreliable idiot, I had lost the letter. I searched on the verge, but there was no letter to be found. The roadmen looked very cheerful when I passed them again. It's so nice to see men happy at work, except when a love letter with a load of sloppy nonsense has gone missing. The road foreman sitting astride his Ariel motorbike was outside Belle Vue talking to old Ernie. A sheet of writing paper was over the glass on the headlamp where everyone could see it. These two old geezers also looked very pleased with themselves. This wasn't my day, but one must never give up. I wrote another letter and made sure I posted it, but I had missed the post and would be lucky to get a reply before Saturday morning. I dashed into the workshop hoping to read that she still loved me, but did she? Diagonally across the paper were just two words: Not interested.

I went to Filey, but it was too late to take my bike, but I wasn't bothered about that as I wasn't keen on having it covered with sand. At Filey I watched some people riding about on the sands and then I went for a stroll. What a boring day, I would have got more excitement out of taking my two aunts and the grey parrot out for the day. I don't think I ever saw that girl again.

The grass tracking had ended for that year and one Sunday, Pug and I were playing about on our bikes, doing a bit of trick riding and anything to amuse us. The paperboy arrived and stayed for a while as he often did, to watch us on our bikes. Our place was the last of his round, so he did right to relax for a while. He brought the papers from Withernsea in a barrow, with the handle of the barrow fixed onto the frame of his cycle just below the seat. Just for a bit of fun, we asked if we could fix the barrow onto the back of Pug's bike so that I could have a ride in it. But the idea was to have him in the barrow so that we could scare him just a little. He was very keen about it so it was fixed behind the motorbike and I sat in and enjoyed a very steady ride. Then he got in and Pug went fast until the barrow was swinging right out as Pug went round the corners. But we had such a disappointment, that beastly boy enjoyed every bit of it. I wish I could remember his name, as he may have become an expert sidecar passenger for all I know.

Grass track racing was all right, but what we really wanted to do was road racing, but a good bike was too expensive for us to be able to buy. But we were lucky in having two good friends in Sid Miles, who had Water Tower Garage at Halsham and his brother Harold, who had a small motorbike business in Hull. They were the nicest chaps you could wish to know and they had already given us some help with the bikes. Sid died at an early age leaving his wife, a girl, and a boy. The boy was not very old at the time, but he managed to keep the garage going and it is still a good business. Harold's small business did well and he still has a small showroom just off Anlaby Road.

Harold had taken in a very fast Calthorp, Black Prince model, and a tuned AJS engine. But it was not a camshaft AJS engine, just the pushrod 350cc. I only wish it had been the Cammy engine. Pug had the Calthorp and I have forgotten what the price was. But as I had the AJS I do remember that its price was £2 10s, and it had only done forty-five miles. My bike was not suitable for making into a road-racing machine because it was too low. In fact it had become too low for the grass. It was made for the leg trailing style and by this time (1932), the present day style was becoming popular.

Going out to work was against Ernie's religion as far as he himself was concerned. But as soon as Pug left school, there was pressure on him to get fixed up with work. Having very little to choose from, the job he got was on a farm on Sunk Island. This was worse than terrible for someone like Pug because a lad must be born and bred into farming. It was a job where a lad was hired out for a year. He lived in and roughed it with the rest of the hired lads. His pay I reckon would have been about £7 or £8 for the year's work. The farm lads didn't spend a lot of money. They would go to Hull once a year to get hired out, where the farmers all met, which I think was in the vicinity of the cattle market. During winter evenings they would stay in the stables, sitting on the corn bins, looking at the horses' backsides. Then at about 9 o'clock they would give the horses another feed, shake the horses' beds up, bringing the straw to the rear to keep the horses clean. The cribs would be filled with hay and then the lads would retire to their beds.

When I went to see Pug on the first day at work, I did not expect to see a happy face. He was almost in tears. It was dark and there was no one in the yard so I told Pug to go up to his bedroom and collect his belongings while I went to the stackyard to find a ladder. We didn't bother closing the bedroom window or returning the ladder back to the stackyard; we hadn't time for that. We were soon on the motorbike zooming down the road, never to return.

When Alan left school, Ernie had a job ready for him. It was on Withernsea Council, sweeping streets. He had a barrow and a brush, and he had a shovel for picking up the horse muck. He had no ambitions as regards getting a gold watch for long service. He hated the job and also hated Ernie for getting it for him. In fact he still hasn't forgiven him for it. But the job did not last long. During his first week, an ancient councillor had to be driven somewhere and there was no chauffeur available. Alan could drive; in fact, he was quite a good driver although he was only fourteen years of age. So Alan had to drive old Grumpy to this place where he had to go. The following day he had to be driven again, and once more Alan was given the job. I don't know if the old gout was playing up or not, but old Grumpy made the mistake of criticising Alan's driving. They were in the middle of town and his nibs could not drive, so Alan drove into the middle of the road and left him. That was the end of that job. Alan's next job was in a garage and that was better suited to Alan's talents.

Many years later, during the war and in the middle of a big chunk of desert, a young officer was talking to his men and telling them about his dad who had been the Mayor of Holderness. 'One day he was visiting Withernsea and a young lad was given the job of driving my dad back to Bridlington. He asked the driver to go across the road to pick up another councillor. The cheeky young beggar asked my dad why he couldn't walk across the road. When they reached the corner where you turn to Hornsea, my dad said, "We will turn right here if the driver doesn't mind". But this lad stopped the car in the middle of the road just round the corner.'

Alan said to the young officer, 'That cheeky driver was I.' The officer didn't believe Alan, as anybody could have said it. But after the officer had asked Alan a few questions about his dad he realised that in fact Alan was the lad who had no respect for the Mayor of Holderness.

Pug moved on to another farm after escaping from Sunk Island, but that was not so bad as it was on a farm in Tunstall. His first job was in a turnip field with a mule and cart. He was managing fine considering driving a mule wasn't a bit like driving a car or a motorbike. In fact everything went well until he came back to the farm at 12 o'clock. It wasn't a tidy farm by any means. The gate hadn't been fastened and it was swinging to and fro on its hinges. Pug stopped the mule and dismounted from the cart. But before he could get hold of the gate to fix it open, 'Muley' had put himself into gear and tried to get the cart through a half-open gate, which resulted in converting the gate into firewood. Pug shouted, 'Please stop 'Muley',' or whatever it is one says to make a mule halt. But the mule had gone deaf and also hungry and could think of nothing else but a trough of oats. A ladder on the ground was the next to become firewood as one of the wheels went along the spells, breaking everything. It would appear there was nothing abnormal about these happenings for this farm because the farmer was evidently satisfied with Pug's performance and kept him on. Likewise, it would appear he had passed his driving test and continued to drive the mule and cart for many months to follow. But he never really managed to master the mules' braking system that remained unreliable to say the least.

Ernie, being a proud parent, was very interested in our work, and while he sat up in bed knocking back eggs and bacon and cups of tea and reading the morning papers, he would ask my mother if his dear children had gone to work. What he actually said was, 'Hasn't them lazy beggars gone to work yet?' He was also interested in our wages and by the time he took his cut for our board, they had almost diminished. But any money that we received for overtime and jobs on the farm machinery in our spare time went towards building up our garage business. Therefore, at the time when we received the Calthorp and the AJS engine, we had enough space to build a good racing bike. The NUT (Newcastle-upon-Tyne) petrol tank, which was nicely painted and had the name 'ESN Special', painted on its panels was naturally fitted to the new bike.

We had an excellent track for testing the bikes and also ourselves. It was five miles per lap and all maintained free of charge by the council. At least it was free to us. We started off from Belle Vue along the narrow rural road. We had to brake hard and go down the gears for a very sharp left-hander near Dimlington. Then to the T-junction onto the Roos road. This was a much better road than Kilnsea and has some fast bends. Reaching the outer part of Roos, we turned and went down the almost dead straight road to Tunstall, which is 1 mile. We kept the bikes flat out for the length of the road, shutting off as we reached the dip just before the left corner that took us onto the Main Street. The straight-through exhaust pipes really crackled as we went along Main Street with its houses right near the side of the road, and past the church to complete a lap. We were thrilled by the way the bikes handled and the exhilarating speed. It was exciting and often frightening. We were grateful for the roads that I have just described, as we were never troubled by traffic. Nowadays it would be very dangerous for two young lads to race round those same roads, as they would be very lucky to do half the circuit without having a vehicle pull out in front of them.

The people of Tunstall were very good and seemed to put up with the noise simply because they were interested in our racing. The old church, which was built of cobbles from the beach, as were other village churches in Holderness coastal areas, is very near to the road side. When we went by during a service, some of the old folk thought the church would fall in on them. As soon as we heard about this we stopped practising on Sundays. Sometimes the Withernsea police received a complaint and they had to come out to investigate. But Ernie always had plenty of time to wave us in before the police came. I believe it was the police themselves who sent word to Ernie to say that they had to come out to us. I am not sure about that, but the police were very good to motorcyclists at that time. I entered for West Park road races and began to prepare my bike for my first road race meeting in (1931) at the age of sixteen, but Ernie would have nothing to do with it, as he said the track was too dangerous because it was lined with trees. I agree with him now, but at the time I just thought he was a silly old fool. When people are young and full of life with everything to live for, they love doing dangerous things. But when they get ancient and too old to do anything, they are scared of pegging out. It's stupid, but it is true.

As I had to work until 12 o'clock on the Saturday morning, by the time I was ready to practise at West Park, everyone else had finished, so I had the track to myself. But I had only done about two or three laps before I was waved in. It was a tricky circuit and as I had not even been inside the Park before I hardly knew my way round. Freddie Frith who came from Grimsby and was a favourite on the East Midlands short circuits, was riding at West Park for his first time. He had been practising all morning on an old Norton, and from 12.30 he had been going round on his TT Norton. But he certainly knew his way round.

The races were organised by Hull Motor Club. There was a good entry that included some good riders. Harry Frow from New Holland, a very good grass track rider, was there with his beautifully prepared 350cc Royal Enfield. Pat Shillings from Howden, who always did well in the TT races was also there with his Norton. Also there was Les Harris, a Velocette rider who lived in Hull, and I believe had fourth place in the Spanish Grand Prix. Also from Hull, were Sammy Worthington and Ray Thompson, and Harold Hartley from

Woodmancy on his Rudge, whom I believe had got a first in the Manx Grand Prix.

The track had a long straight with a right-hand corner at the end, followed by a right-hand corner back onto the straight. I decided to follow them round for a while until I knew the track better and then I would get down to it and start overtaking. Not bad tactics for a sixteen-year-old who had never even seen a road race before. Of course I thought my bike was very fast, but I had never been on a real racing bike. I had practised running my bike off and counting the paces I needed to run before dropping the clutch, as there is no sense in continuing to run when you could be riding. My engine fired straight away and I had made quite a good start, with perhaps four or five riders in front of me at the first corner. I held my position along the tricky sections of the circuit and right until we were back on the straight. I wasted no time in changing gears and getting on full song down the straight. But those in front were pulling away from me and someone passed me halfway down the straight and another rider overtook me before the corner. The rest of the laps had a similar pattern and so by the end of the race, I was a long way behind Freddie Frith, the winner, but there was also a good distance between the last man and me.

I enjoyed my first road race meeting very much. I did not think my riding was so bad, but I had to admit that until that day, I didn't know what a fast bike was. But it was my brakes that let me down more than anything else, because I had to start braking a long time before the riders on the TT bikes. So therefore I knew what wanted doing, but how to do it was the problem. Pug and I continued with grass track racing. We found our road bikes more suitable for the new style of riding than our early low-built grass bikes. As a means of getting more speed for road racing, I ordered some extra strong valve springs, and a couple of valves. I wouldn't have been in a hurry to fit them if it had not been for the exhaust valve getting bent during a grass track race. We took the head off and Ernie straightened the valve by hitting the side, which was not seating, with a hammer until the gap closed up. We had the head back on before the next race and I came third. I have never wasted time on completing valve grinding with metal polish since that day.

I reckon engine development was going too fast for Ernie because he could not see any sense in fitting extra strong valves springs. 'The springs were only to close the valves,' he said. Valve bounce wasn't a disadvantage with Ernie's engines because there was plenty of time for them to settle down before the piston got anywhere near the top of its stroke. He sat on top of a box watching me fit the valves and the springs muttering something about it being just as well to fit bits of tubing as these springs. We went grass track racing the following day. I didn't bother about going round the track before the races as I had ridden there a few times before and my bike was already set up. During the first race my engine began to go off tune, so I went back into the paddock. We found the tappet clearances to be quite large gaps. Ernie began his mutterings again. 'He spends his time and money on his stupid valve springs and does not even adjust the tappets properly.' They set up the tappets and I went in my next race. The engine went well at first, but went off-song again. The tappet clearance was checked, and once again we found large clearances. The poor old pushrods were bending under the strain. New pushrods solved the problem and I was delighted to find the engine performance was better for the new valves and springs.

Pug and I were very busy in our garage at that time and would sometimes work until midnight. We would then put our tools away and have a walk along the beach. Strolling along the seashore in the early hours of the morning is very peaceful and the lovely sea air gets rid of petrol fumes. Sometimes when we finished early in the evening we would have a walk to Roos and drink grapefruit and have a game of darts before strolling back home. Life for us lads was happy and peaceful.

Not for Ernie and the ex-policeman, our landlord. We'd had lots of landlords and Ernie had fallen out with every one of them. But this time was a little different because us lads were involved as one of the landlord's complaints was that the grass was getting ruined and would never again produce good hay. The fact that our ex-bobby was bothered was disconcerting for Ernie. Because hadn't Ernie built the bungalow on the land in hope of having it become his, at the end of the lease.

Bobby had chickens on his half of the field, and not wanting any stray to become our Sunday dinner, he had erected six-foot high wire netting the full length of the boundary. Well it is a well-known fact that wire netting soon begins to sag. But when this began to droop and look sloppy, the silly old fool said, 'Your kids have been swinging on it.' Now this gentleman was very large and there was nothing Ernie liked better than to get tough with big men. He used to say the bigger they are, the harder they will fall. It's a good saying that, I used to like it, until I said it to a chap when I was in the army. He turned out to be some middleweight boxing champion. Theory and practice do sometimes disagree.

Pug and I didn't have much time for girls. But when we did run after them we could never catch them. But with Stan, this was quite the reverse. Girls, lovely nice girls, used to run after him, but they could not catch him. At this particular time when Chicken Joe, our ex-bobby was getting nasty over the wire-netting, Stan had a couple of girls coming to see him over the weekend. As usual Stan did a bunk, leaving us to entertain them. We knew no way of entertaining girls, apart from playing about on our bikes and the girls sitting on our gate while we rode round the track doing stunts. I changed from doing solo stunts to pair's stunts with Pug on his bike. We were coming up towards the hedge with Pug stood on the footrests with arms stretched out sideways. The mudguard was very small, and as we came round the left-hand turn towards the wire netting, I lost my balance. To steady myself I took hold of Pug, and we both dropped off the bike. The bike, thinking it could manage just as well on its own, kept going, but didn't manage to get round in front of the netting. I reckon that was the first time that catch fencing had come into operation at a racetrack. The twist grip, being tightened up for the benefit of doing stunts, remained partly open, and the netting kept the bike upright. The netting was dragged for quite a few yards, before the bike finally fell over onto its side. We had quite a job of untangling and freeing the bike from what had been a wire-netting fence. Pug started his bike and went to the girls; I got my bike and joined them. The girls had mixed feelings about what happened because it appeared to them that falling off and letting the bike fall into the wire netting was a trick that had gone according to plan. This of course was not the case, but if it was not possible to convince the girls that it was not an accident what chance had we of convincing 'Bobby'.

We began to do more solo tricks, setting off one at a time from the gate. This way we were able to do a bit of chatting-up with them and I believe we were making some progress. In fact, I had already decided that we would introduce them to the lovely sand dunes at Sand-le-Mere. My mother was in the habit of hanging some washing across, from the bungalow to the toilet. The toilet being a sentry box affair, with a bucket that had to be emptied by us lads, and at this particular time it was Alan's turn to do it. As we have already found out, Alan was not a lover of such activities as this and had neglected his duty for a few days.

The washing had been collected, but for some reason the washing line had been left trailing on the ground with the ends still firmly fixed. We were riding over the clothesline and no harm was done. At least not until Pug rocked his bike from side to side as he started a stunt. The clothesline was picked up by a footrest and the sentry box was lifted clean off the seat and bucket. The only thing, which could have improved this trick, was if it had been done while Ernie was sat on the seat. But even without Ernie's bare rear end, it was not a pretty sight and after all, our audience was rather posh. This, as with the other disaster, did not look like an accident. Our girls feeling quite sure that they had seen enough of performing lunatics promptly cleared off, never to return.

It didn't take long to fix the 'sentry box', but the fence was a problem. But it didn't look too bad by the time the landlord arrived to feed his poultry. At least it was chicken proof, and we had done our best. But our best was not good enough and we were called some nasty names. Ernie hearing what was being said came up to us and got himself all worked up into an awful temper. There was only one entrance to the field from the road and this was through our gate. The landlord had said, that he would make an entrance to the field from the road into his half of the field. But as the roadside hedge was a large Hawthorn hedge he had failed to keep his promise. Rather than go to the trouble of making a way in through the hedge, he had taken the easy way out and made a gate in his wire-netting fence. Therefore, to reach his land he came through our gate and had to walk across in front of the bungalow. Ernie told him that this must stop and gave him so many days in which to get his own gate.

I was working in my garage a few days later. It was a lovely day, the birds were singing in the hedges and everything was so peaceful. Someone walked into the garage and I had a lovely surprise. There amongst the old engines and things was the most charming lady. She asked me to forgive her for calling when I was so busy, but I had already done that. She had come to visit friends in the village and she'd had trouble with her motorcar. It had developed a misfire just after leaving home so she had called at a garage. They had taken the magneto into the garage to put it right. This they had done, but had made too good a job of the timing when they had refitted it. This caused the car to run hot and sluggish. The car was an Austin Seven and it was a simple job sliding the magneto away from the vernier coupling and refitting it so as to give the correct ignition timing. The lovely lass was soon on her way, but I did not go back to the garage immediately. Instead after closing the gate, I stood with my elbows resting on the top bar of the gate looking down the road towards the village. I thought it was too beautiful a day to be rushing back to work. I could hear the docile beat from the Ariel's exhaust as the road foreman approached. The three men also heard it. As he came into sight, the one who was working continued with his job. One of the others removed his cap and scratched his head while his mate took from his pocket, a large white-spotted, red handkerchief and wiped his nose. The foreman seeing that his faithful gang were all doing something, did not bother to stop. As he passed me he had a great big grin on his face. He was evidently remembering my love letter. He chugged by at his usual ten miles per hour and took ages to get out of sight.

I looked across the road and up the lane where our landlord lived. I was thinking about the young lady and hoping that something else would go wrong with the Austin Seven, so that I could see her again. I glanced up the lane again and saw that someone was coming. But it wasn't a lovely girl; it was our landlord, carrying his two buckets. He was a very large man, and the buckets were very small. I wondered why he did not have decent-sized buckets like everyone else. It would not matter about them being half full; at least he would not look so ridiculous. I could visualise him on the beach with his trousers rolled up and his big flat feet up to the corns in seawater, and his stupid little buckets. The landlord had almost reached the gate when Ernie appeared carrying a garden spade. 'You touch that gate if you dare and your fingers will come off,' warned Ernie. No one knew Ernie better than I did. I stepped back as I did not want to be splashed with blood.

Our ex-bobby put his buckets down and glared at Ernie. 'I am not frightened of you,' he said.

'Well then, open the gate,' said Ernie.

The sneck was on the inside, and therefore he would have to put his hand through between a couple of gate bars to reach it. He was stupid enough to try it, and the spade was swung with such force that its edge stuck into the gateposts only half an inch below the staple. It was a near miss and I hoped he would not be stupid enough to try it again.

But Ernie was taunting him. 'Come on, have another go you old bugger,' and our bobby was getting into such a rage that his face was as red as fire. I was thinking his lovely big moustache would suddenly burst into flames. He made another attempt to open the gate and all of a sudden the spade was swung with all Ernie's strength behind it. Ernie kept the pressure up and his opponent was getting worked up and so reluctant to give up, while I was only wishing he would pick up his buckets and find another way onto his land. He tried once again, but it was not a very good try, but he could feel the wind as the spade dug into the gatepost. There were three great big grooves all within one inch of the sneck and staple. *Surely he will go now*, and to my relief, he picked up his buckets and went.

Ernie, knowing now that at the termination of the five-year lease there could be no further agreements, set about doing the plans for another bungalow. This was a similar style to the first one, but it would be built in sections. Then when the time came for moving again, it could be dismantled and be rebuilt on our next piece of land.

Prefabricated houses and bungalows are not uncommon these days, but I would like to know if Ernie's was the first one in England. Ernie had been doing battle with landlords for as far as I can remember. Very often he was right, and when it came to a court case he would always win. During the time when he lived in a council house in Withernsea, the council was doing a fiddle with the rents. Ernie refused to pay this extra money so the council took him to court. Ernie only needed half an hour to sort them out, and the council had to give the other tenants all the money back that they had collected illegally. So he was not bothered about our present landlord. But there was something that he had on his mind, but that only had to do with motorbikes.

He told us to check over the Royal Enfield and give it a tune-up, and then he wanted the chassis that had the boards fixed to them, taken off the bike and replaced with the Bradbury sidecar. We knew what this was all about. His brother, Uncle Arthur, had just purchased a new Norton and sports sidecar and Ernie had to give him a race. Of course there would be no mention of a race, there never was. They would just go for a little ride and it would just happen and they would find themselves flat on the petrol tanks and the throttles wide open. The women wouldn't mind being left to themselves, as they would find plenty to talk about. Ette and Auntie Ruth were sisters; two brothers had married two sisters. It's a good idea because you do not get many relatives that way.

The Royal Enfield's V Twin engine sounded to be in good fettle when we had completed our adjustments, so we thought it a good idea to see how quickly we could get round 'our road circuit'. We ran it off, as it looked more spectacular that way. Pug was the pilot and I was the ballast balancing on the boards, trying to keep my weight over the sidecar wheel. We had just got the engine nicely spinning in top gear, when the sidecar hit an extra large bump, throwing me onto the rear mudguard. This was no place for the ballast to be at that particular moment and Pug was unable to prevent the bike from going off the road. He was struggling to prevent us going into the deep ditch, but we hit one of those drain ruts, which the roadmen make to drain the water off the roads, and the old Enfield went completely out of control and got itself well and truly jammed in the ditch. Pug's right boot had the sole almost torn off. But apart from that there didn't seem to be much damage done.

I hadn't the slightest idea how we were going to get old Enfield out of the ditch. We could leave it there, as it looked quite comfortable, its width being a tight fit. Pug was sat on the bank looking at his wounded boot. I looked at him and said, 'Pug, I think Daddy is going to be a wee bit cross.' Pug's reply was, 'Sod 'im. What about my bloody boot.'

Two farm men, who were ploughing in a nearby field, came running towards us. They said they had thought that we would both be dead. As we were not dead (I do not think they would have bothered if we had been) they made a few genius remarks like, 'Ba gum, tha's gotten er in a quier fix there' and 'Ous tha reckoning on heaving oud lass out?' They had me guessing there, as I hadn't the faintest idea. But they knew and one of them said, 'Can tha gan to farm und bring a nice lang rope?' I said 'Yes,' but I had collected enough bruises to make walking very painful, so he went himself, while the other man went back to the field for two horses, complete with traces and swingletrees. When they had both returned, they tied one end of the rope to the vehicle and the other end to the swingletree, making good use of the full length of rope. As the horses pulled they kept very near to the ditch so that the angle of force was such as to bring the bike out very gradually and without further damage. We were very pleased to see the Enfield back onto the road and very pleased to see ploughing was a measure of the highest respectability and we were enormously grateful to our friends.

The worst damage to the bike was a bent footrest caused by it digging into the bank. This was the reason for the laughing boot. But the sidecar wheel was very bent, as was the mudguard. But that did not bother us as we were fitting the Bradbury sidecar. We soon had the job completed after getting back home. The following morning Ette and Ernie left to do their visiting, and Pug and I went into the garage to get on with customers' jobs. Afterwards, when we were walking back to the bungalow, we noticed the gate was wide open and we wondered who had been, as there was no one in the bungalow at the time. The children were at school. Then we noticed half the gatepost was missing. It had been sawn off as if someone had run out of firewood. A few days later we had a visitor, a policeman from Withernsea. Ernie was served with a summons to appear before the magistrate at Withernsea police court to defend a charge of assault and battery and damage to property. Then the policeman asked for me. I was in the garage and he came to see me and gave me a summons for assault.

I had never been to a police court before and so I had no idea what to expect. The charges were enough to make anyone feel like a criminal. But it turned out to be so funny. We arrived in good time, but there was already a good gathering of 'nosy parkers' there. If they had gone for a good laugh, then they were not disappointed. The chuckles began when a large man was having difficulty getting through the door because he was carrying a large parcel wrapped in brown paper. Sticking out from each end of the parcel could be seen part of a heavy gatepost as is used for a five-bar gate. He managed to get inside and let the door bang behind him. He went to a seat, and lowered the parcel to the ground and sat down. He was ready and thankful for a sit down. He wiped the sweat from his face, neck and forehead with a large white handkerchief. He looked apprehensive and very uncomfortable.

I was first to be called. I rose from the seat and walked across the courtroom. Everyone was looking at me; I was only 5 feet tall. Everyone laughed when I was charged with assault and battering this oversized chunk of an ex-bobby. Even the old magistrate's stern 'kisser' was showing a faint smile. I wasn't called up to give any defence. A verdict of no charge to answer and case dismissed was given almost immediately.

Ernie was next to be called. He was hoping for something more dramatic and was getting up plenty of steam. After all, he had plenty of court martials as an army officer and was prepared to demonstrate his skill. But this was a comedy show and no one was interested in anything that would spoil it. So Ernie did not get much of a say in the matter as his nibs, the magistrate was quite capable of running the show. 'Where did Nicholson hit you? Have you any wounds?' asked his nibs. 'Oh, he never touched me, he wasn't half quick enough for that,' boasted our opponent with a smug look as he expanded his big chest. That ended the first act. The next act in the comedy was to do with damaging property. 'Who cut the gatepost down?' asked his nibs. 'I did,' said our landlord in such a tone one would have thought that great skill had been called for in felling this harmless post. Then said his nibs, 'It is you yourself who is guilty of the damage.' Case dismissed.

Our landlord had to pay the costs, and he also had to replace the gatepost. Therefore, life was peaceful after that. He got on with feeding his chickens, and Ernie got on with building the new bungalow, and we never had any more trouble. After we had stopped trembling and our nerves had settled down after our ordeal with the court case, we began to look to the future. 'The future is not ours to see,' say the know-alls. But our future as far as the lease was concerned couldn't be any clearer. Ernie definitely had to make another bungalow, but luckily there was no panic as the lease had two or three more years to go. Ernie's load of wood was not due from Scandinavia until the backend of the year, as boats do not run aground in summer.

The road to the sea and Hilston road up to the sharp left-hand corner and the cliffs, form a triangle. The cliffs come in sharply towards the road, about two hundred yards before you get to the corner.

This makes a bay and this is where boats come to shelter during the storms that you often have along the coast. When a boat gets too near to the shore, it runs aground and may tip over onto its side, so some of the load of lovely planks has to go overboard. But getting the soaking wet heavy wood up the cliffs and across a field and loaded and unloaded and carried to where Ernie wanted, was almost enough to kill us slaves. There is quite a narrow piece of land here from the road to the cliff tops. Ernie had quite a lot of joinery work to do on a farm. Some of the land on the cliff top belonged to this farm. Ernie used his own ladder, which he took every morning and brought it home when he had finished his day's work in the afternoon.

There was a piece of wood on one side of the ladder as if it was holding a weak place like a split in the wood. The fact that Ernie was taking the ladder home everyday puzzled the farmer, as there was plenty of room at the farm where Ernie could keep it. No one would want to climb a ladder in that condition so it wouldn't have got stolen.

Ernie finished the job and he also became the owner of this strip of land. He never told me how the land became his. But Ernie did tell me that the farmer couldn't understand why he was so particular about his ladder when it had a strip of wood tied to it. Then Ernie chuckled a bit and said, 'He didn't know it was a fresh piece of wood every day.' So Ernie was getting a supply of wood each day even if it was only a trickle. If his payment for his work was the piece of land, and the wood that he had pinched, he didn't do too badly.

One day, when Ernie was going to see Uncle Arthur, a rider on a Douglas passed him. So it was head down and tummy on tank, but the Douglas left Ernie and disappeared. The next plan was getting a Douglas and Pug and I were performing in sidecar races. Ernie was also interested in speedway and he had seen George Grant riding at Hull speedway on his Douglas.

George was a good rider, but Ernie who had never been on a speedway bike, decided that George would be glad of a few tips. Ernie's brilliant idea was to not shut off for a corner and power slide round it, but to keep the bike flat out all through the race. George thought it was a good idea and won his first heat and did well in his other heats. He was very happy with this and was already expecting to become world champion. George was eagerly waiting for the next meeting. But, oh dear, the bike didn't want any more of Ernie's advice and tipped George off. When you hit those boards from a speedway bike on full song, you don't need any sleeping tablets. George had a nice sleep that lasted until Tuesday.

Ernie, who was under the false impression that he had qualified to be a speedway manager, arranged for Pug and I to ride at Sheffield Stadium. We loaded the bikes onto the Citroen and made sure that the grub old Ette packed for us, was safely in the car on the back seat and then set off for Sheffield. We got all the way there before we found out the meeting had been cancelled. We didn't hang around as Ernie said that we would set off for home. We would go for a few miles then pull up to the side of the road and have our picnic. I was already starving. I was sat in front and Ernie was driving, and Pug was in the back seat, and was very quiet. We thought he could be ill or dying of malnutrition. It became lighting-up time, but the lamps refused to be friendly and remained without a glimmer. I thanked God because I wasn't far from starving to death, but now I knew I would live because old Ette was good at packing lots of currant cakes and sandwiches. I should have known that Pug should have been at the front and me on the back seat. He had scoffed the lot. We slept in the car until daylight and then we went home feeling very hungry and not very much in love with Pug.

After we had finished a large pile of grub, we took the bikes off the car and pushed them into the garage. Pug and I were glad the bikes had come home shining and clean and not covered in mucky cinders. I didn't tell Ernie I was glad the meeting had been cancelled. There was a grass track meeting the following weekend and it was nice to know the bikes were ready.

It was a lovely day for the grass track meeting and the sunshine had brought the crowds out. I always rode to please the people who had come to watch and I liked to hear them cheering us. I felt good, and when you feel good, you ride well. I had two or three laps and the bike was going very well, so I went into the pits and relaxed until the racing started. Pug and I were in different heats and different semi-finals. Pug crashed out of his semi-final and bent his bike quite a lot. I was waiting for the final when I saw Ernie coming towards me. I said, 'Bloody hell, I know what he is going to say.'

One bit of Ernie's wisdom was, 'If you crash you have to get on a bike as soon as possible. If you don't your nerves will be smashed into millions of bits.' It's a load of bull, but we were young enough and stupid enough to do what Ernie told us to do. As usual, it was Pug who crashed and was told to use my bike in my race. 'Let Pug ride in this next race,' he said. So Pug took my bike and I didn't bother to look at the race. I didn't want to see my bike get bent. I did ride in the final and came second.

At one meeting there were a lot of riders and therefore a lot of heats. Only two riders of each heat went into the semi-final. I was in second place during the last lap and in front of us was a slow rider who we had already passed once. The rider, who was in front, passed the slow rider as he went over the finishing line. Then the slow rider went over the line as I passed him, but I was going twice as fast as he was. When it came to the semi-final, they had put the slow rider in it instead of me. So I was done out of the two most important races of the meeting and the prize money. I didn't say anything about it, but the fans had a lot to say about it.

Ernie had a War pension and he had to go to Hull, monthly to collect it. The next time he went, he had a look round a few garages for a racing Douglas. He wasn't successful this time, but he saw a Dunalt. It had a 500cc two-stroke engine, but it wasn't the engine that interested Ernie. Someone, who had similar ideas to Ernie, designed the frame. He liked the young mechanic so they had a good talk about motorbikes. The lad said he would deliver it, so Ernie wanted to pay him for it. But the lad refused to take any money.

When the lad brought the bike, there was nobody at home apart from Ette. She asked him how much it was and he said, 'Just give me something for delivering it.' Ette gave him three shillings and sixpence. The next thing we heard about him was he was at court for selling motorbikes and not putting any money in the till. That frame soon came in handy.

Someone organised grass track racing at Withernsea. It was held in a field on the Roos road where there is a large caravan park now. It was on a Thursday evening, two days before road racing at West Park. I had my EN Special bike ready for the road races and it was in tip-top condition and going well. I didn't want to ride it at the grass track, but there were lots of people looking forward to me riding so I had no option.

Pug had not entered, but he was there with a Panther motorbike. It had a 600cc sloping engine and was very fast. There were a lot of people there, but it seemed a poor show regarding riders, as there didn't seem to be any riders like Harry Frow from New Holland. Pug and I were in the pits talking and admiring the Panther. Pug said, 'It will beat your bike.' All the riders came in leaving an empty track. I said to Pug, 'Come on and let's give them some real racing for their money.' So we went onto the track and made a flying start; and everyone cheered except the officials who stared with their mouths open. We rode as hard as we could and kept on passing each other. It was time we came off so that the others could have a ride, but Pug was in front and I didn't want to finish like that. I tried to go round the outside, but I was going just a bit too fast and went wide onto some rough ground. My lovely motorbike flew high into the air and made a very awkward landing. The back forks and wheel were badly bent.

We took my engine out and also the Dunalt engine. We placed the AJS engine into the Dunalt and it looked good. All four, engine plates had to be replaced. I made patterns for the engine plates and dashed off to a blacksmith to have the plates made. I went in the afternoon and the good man had made them, but instead of clamping them together, he had made them separately and the holes did not line up. I then made another set of engine plates, all extra work and the time was going far too quickly. But when you are working on a motorbike you have to get everything perfect. But when I got older I thought that if I had filed the holes out, it wouldn't have made any difference.

We finished the bike at about 10 o'clock on the Saturday morning. It looked good and I was tempted to have a little ride, but there was not much time to be messing around. I managed to get to West Park all right and went into the pits. I didn't have Ernie and I didn't have Pug and that was good. The pits were on the left, halfway down the long straight. I walked to the entrance of the pits after I had put the bike where it should go. I just wanted to see how they went and soon realised they went very fast. Harold Hartley went by on his Rudge, Harry Frow on his well-tuned Enfield, and Les Harris on his Velocette, and Freddie Frith on his Norton. They all sounded so good, in fact it was the sweetest music I had ever heard. I haven't the writing skill to tell you how I felt as I stood watching them go by. It was my second time at West Park, but the excitement and the thrill was still there. I loved road racing and as I stood there I wondered how long it would be before I was racing them round the Isle of Man.

I got three laps in before we were waved in. I was pleased with the bike, it handled very well. It was the Le Mans type of start so I expected to get a good start, which I did. I passed three or four riders before the first corner and I knew I was going faster than I did in my practice laps. There were some good bends and a couple of corners before you reached the top end of the straight. I don't think anyone gained on me there, but the real racing bikes pulled away on the straight, but only a little, so I finished in a good position. I was looking forward to coming again, but I wished I had a bike that could compete with the real racing bikes.

Our next meeting was a grass track meeting and Pug was with me, but not Ernie. George Grant was riding his speedway Douglas. Everything went well for us and we were in the last race. To make it more interesting, George suggested that the one who came last would have to pay the bill at the café on the way home. We were lucky that the three of us were on the starting line. Pug and I were good at getting a good start, but so was George, being a good speedway rider. As I expected, we all got away together. Pug was on the inside and that is what he was good at. I was on the outside and George was between us. George stayed as near to Pug as possible and I was almost leaning on George. With George being between us and a bit cramped, he couldn't get away from us and that is how the race went on until the last lap. Halfway round, George dropped back; his back tyre had come off one side of the rim. So George didn't get any prize money for that race and he had to pay the bill in the café. As far as I know George never raced again.

Chapter 16

THE DOUGLAS

Ernie didn't mention anything else about getting a Douglas motorbike. So it was a surprise when one arrived. It went very well and so we were pleased with it. We had a ride round our grass track (on our land) and it was easy to ride. We had a grass track meeting coming up so naturally Ernie wanted us to take the Douglas. As we were used to our bikes, Ernie didn't get his wish. Afterwards I felt very mean about it. I even wanted to kiss him after he had shaved, but he didn't have a shave for a few days and by that time I had changed my mind.

Ernie was still keen to have us go sidecar racing. We had a good sidecar, a single seat sports type on a light chassis. I feel sure it was a Watsonian. When we had the bike and sidecar stuck together, it looked well and went good. But the sidecar wheel bearing sounded as if it had rheumatism. I bet that's what it was because it had been hanging around for quite a long time. 'I'll have to make another bearing,' said Ernie as if he had a manufacturing business, which he hadn't. I was only a country Joskin, so naturally I wondered how Ernie could make a ball bearing with just a vice and a file. If it was going to be a phosphor bronze bush, it was still not going to be easy without a lathe. Motorists of Ernie's age were like that. They were brought up in a period when a motorcar was a horse trap with a steam or petrol engine chugging away on a back axle.

With an enormous lot of skill and patience, his chunk of metal had become a bearing. We gave it the best grease we had and fitted it with great care. Ernie gave it a spin; it was perfect, true, smooth and quiet.

'Take it for a run,' the big boss said. 'To run it in you must go very steady,' he advised. Pug was already sat on the bike, while I was trying to squeeze myself into the posh seat. *You are asking a lot,* I was thinking. For Pug to be good, meant that you were going to give him some money or he was very poorly. But at this time Pug was good and with a bit of self-denial and lots of restraint, he drove as if he was at a funeral. We went along the straight length of road from Tunstall to Roos with the speedo hardly moving and in a state of shock.

We reached the Burton Pidsea road and I was wishing Pug would turn round and drive back home. The bearing would be perfect by the time we got home. Suddenly there was a roar of a motorbike passing us and the rider turning round gave us a rude sign.

All Pug's restraint and good intentions cracked. After a couple of miles we were in front of the solo rider. Pug began to slow down so that we could go home, but the sidecar wheel had other ideas. It was enjoying its run out in the country and cleared off down the road on its own. It was a pity we didn't have some eggs; we could have cooked them on the bearing and had a picnic. Pug remained seated, waving his arms about and laughing his hat off while I became a retriever of runaway wheels.

We turned our vehicle round or rather we dragged it round, until its headlamp was facing homewards. I sat in the sidecar holding its damaged wheel as if it was a steering wheel and Pug climbed back on the bike. The problem was how to get a sidecar airborne with only one third of the undercarriage. It was no problem to Pug, he turned the front wheel towards the sidecar and gave the bike plenty of throttle and we were all level. We went home without any trouble, but there was plenty of trouble when Ernie saw us. After this little episode, there was never a word spoken about sidecar racing. It's strange how some people soon get discouraged.

Chapter 17

OUR WORKING LIFE

Pug was getting on for his fifteenth birthday. He was still working at the farm where the mule was. He was just thirteen when he started to work there. It was what you call safe employment, as no one else would work there. The old farmer had moved out of the farmhouse to make way for his son and family. He went to live in a cottage at Roos. His wealth came from buying and selling cattle and pigs. We went every Saturday night to collect Pug's wage, which was ten shillings. Whether the journey would bear fruit or not depended on how well the old chap had performed with his buying and selling skills. The buying and selling was lousy most weeks.

As I have said, my first job after leaving Grant's was at Kirkwood's in Roos. They were a good family and were very good to me and I was living at home, which was great. But Ernie wasn't satisfied with the seventeen shillings and sixpence I gave out of my £1 weekly wage. I left home for the second time and I never lived at home again.

I went to work at Reginald Hall's farm at Halsham and lived in. God was certainly no friend of mine when he let me go there. Some idiot was fitting up a large stationary engine to drive a milling machine. I was stood at one side of it when someone started it with the throttle on a high speed. There wasn't a guard and the belt flew off and hit me in the privates.

When I reached home, Ernie came and linked his arm in mine and helped me to walk into the house (the coastguard house) and up the stairs. I was in agony and groaning. Ernie was imitating my groans and making fun of me. When I dropped my trousers he gasped because he got a shock when he saw the size of my left testicle.

Ernie made a truss and Alan had the job of bathing my injured marble six times a day. I had to go to the doctor and his surgery was at the far side of Roos. Some people may not believe this, but it's perfectly true. I walked or rather limped all the way from home to the surgery. I don't know what the truss was made of, but during that journey I thought it must be a bit of old sailcloth that Ernie had picked up on the sands. That part is still tender and I am always scared of knocking it.

Two of my friends who were my age, one of which was my cousin, were badly hurt in the same place as I was hurt. They were very unlucky because they died. For years, whenever I heard the word cancer, a nerve seemed to run down to that injury. I don't think the word compensation had been invented at that time because I didn't get anything for this injury or the damage the bull had done at Grant's. Ernie may have collected some on my behalf because I had to be fed when I was ill, but I do not know anything about it. I went to work for a young farmer called Wilf Johnson. His farm was at Hilston on the side of our, 'private road racing circuit'. Wilf was from Easington and his wife lived at Kilnsea.

Wilf's parents had a small farm on the left of Humberside road from Easington. During the First World War, there were gunners in a camp near Johnson's farm. So Mr Piggy Johnson got his wealth from keeping pigs. They got all the swill from the camp, so this was a big help for feeding them.

When I lived at Easington, Wilf's mother and father were very good to me. They treated me as if I was their son, except they didn't buy me a farm. One of Wilf's sisters went to work for a farmer. She lived in, and the farmer was very good to her, he made her pregnant. Hilda, (Wilf's sister) purchased, or was given, some of the field. She had a wooden bungalow and some chicken houses and became a poultry farmer.

I used to go to see her and help her a little. Hilda died of a tumour during the war. Her daughter, who was called Ruth, married a local lad and went to live in Australia.

I went to work at the next farm after I left the Johnson's farm; this was Church Farm in Hilston. They also were nice people and so at that time my life was a happy one. Mrs Sally Clark was the boss. She had two sons, one looked after the stock while the other worked the land.

Two or three people, when they knew I was going to the Clark's, talked to me about Sally Clark as if she was a fierce dragon. I think perhaps because she was a woman running a farm some people may have tried to take advantage of her.

One day I took a chance of having my bottom smacked. Mrs Clark had gone out and I was having a bit of grass track practice in the paddock. The maid came into the paddock to feed the chickens; she was having a bit of fun, shouting and doing rude signs to me. I chased her across the paddock and into the yard. She ran to the back door and stood there still full of cheek because she thought I couldn't chase her anymore on my motorbike.

It was a very large kitchen like the one at West Park. The red-tiled floor was always spotless, so it was very naughty of me to chase her into the house. She ran round the big table and I went after her with my rear tyre spinning on the tiled floor. At the end of this daft chasing, we were shocked at the state of the floor. The girl was in a panic and almost crying because she couldn't believe it possible to put the damage right before Mrs Clark returned. Thankfully, with lots of luck and hard work we managed to get the floor spotless once again and enough time to get my bike out of the way.

I must have been good at farm work because I always had some farmer offering me a few extra pennies. I went back to Halsham to another farm; it was quite a big farm, and about 350 acres I think.

There was a large farmhouse and two ordinary houses. The foreman had one of them and the cowman, the other. There were two lads and myself living in. We lived in the foreman's house. His wife was a very good cook and a good housekeeper, so as they say, 'It was a good grub spot and a clean bed'. The foreman was a nice chap and very good with horses and a good stacker.

Our neighbours, the bullocky and his wife were quite different people, but if you were a person who liked athletics, then they were all right for you. Every now and again the chap would run round the garden chasing his wife with a bloody big carving knife. I used to talk to his wife; sometimes I couldn't get away from her. I didn't think she was good for anything, except for running of course.

My youngest sister, Dorothy was about three-years-old. I was ploughing in a roadside field when I saw someone shouting and running towards me. Dorothy had been climbing on a stool, she slipped and one big toe slid down one of the stool legs. A splinter stuck into her toe behind the nail, she wouldn't let anyone at home take her to the doctor to get it out, and she only wanted me to take her. The doctor told me to sit her on a chair. He knelt down in front of her and roughly pulled down her little straw hat over her face and pulled out the splinter. He had no kind words for her, no sympathy he just said, 'That's it, take her home.'

Mr Scott was a farmer at Roos; he also had a small farm at Halsham. He was the next farmer to offer me a few more pennies. Mr and Mrs Scott were the nicest couple you could wish to meet. They were getting on a bit regarding their age, but they only had one child – he was a boy still going to school. Mr Barr who lived in a very small white cottage with his wife, and four children was our foreman. Then there was a lad about nineteen-years-old who worked with the animals.

This lad's mother had a fish shop about eighty yards away. She opened twice a week on Saturday and Wednesday evening, and that was too much for my liking. The lad lived in at the farm. We shared a bedroom and there was a double bed in it and we had to share that as well. Mind you, that was in the days before queers were invented. Every time the fish shop was open he would fill his belly, which gave him fits. Every Sunday and Thursday morning at about 2 o'clock I would wake up thinking I was on a small raft in the middle of the Atlantic in the company of an extra large starfish doing its vigorous morning exercises.

I used to massage his body and legs until I was exhausted. I never knew if this was the best thing to do. But if I had got a doctor I don't think he would have done any better. All the doctors I knew in those days were more or less useless. They looked smart in their black hard hats, pin-striped suits, and patent leather shoes driving their Austin Sevens or a smart horse and trap.

Mr Scott was like most farmers; he could stand about for hours while his men rushed about to get the work done. He always had the same stance when he stood talking, legs apart and hands down in his pockets to his elbows. It didn't take much to make him laugh. His whole body would shake with excitement and his arms like connecting rods would go up and down in his pockets. His privates had a hell of a time; I think his trousers were tailored for extra ball room. I used to be looking at the ground near his boots because I was sure one day his 'willie' would drop off and bounce up and hit someone in the mouth. The victim could be an old maid who had never had such an experience and the shock of it all would cause the girl to dismount from her bicycle too suddenly. Fortunately that bit never happened. It did fall off, but the dog grabbed it and ran like hell. About two or three months later, he asked me what size bra he needed, A, C, or A, D.

You are not forced to believe the last bit, if you don't want to, but the following is definitely true. The farmers were a mean lot and it didn't matter what you did extra, they never crossed your palm with silver. It was sowing time and the land and the weather was just right, but oh dear, Mr Barr was poorly. If he hadn't been sick he would have taken his pair of horses and yoked them to his harrows and I would have taken my pair of horses and yoked them to my harrows but I took the four horses and yoked them to the two sets of harrows, this way I did two men's work. A very pleased boss came into the field and stood and laughed and laughed until his well-polished things were even dazzling the glow-worms.

I used to go to Mr Scott's small farm at Halsham and help out there a bit now and again, to give them a bit of help. The boss of the neighbouring farm was Mr Leckonby; he was the next victim to put up with me. In my opinion he was the best farmer for miles around. He didn't have rich parents, or an uncle to buy him a farm. He had worked at Sunk Island as a farm foreman for a lot of years and worked hard to be able to buy a farm of his own. Anyone who worked at Sunk Island was well respected by other farm people. It was warped land that was hard to plough so they had to have three horses to pull a plough. I thought it should have been the horses that got the praise, as it was they who pulled the plough.

Mrs Leckonby was a very nice person; I liked her very much. They had a daughter who was still at school. She was a lovely girl just like her mother, but they had this real tall lanky son. He was the worst horseman I had ever seen on a farm. His dad should have broken him in along with a young horse.

Mr Leckonby was well built and very strong. I think if he had gone in for weightlifting he would have done very well. He was in the Halsham cricket team. I often wonder how many balls he lost when he was batting.

It was a small farm and I was the only lad living in. The back door was locked bang on 10 o'clock. He knew that I often went racing on a Saturday afternoon. I worked hard for my pennies, but there were no thanks. There were times when I worked on my bike until late on a Friday night and the door would still be locked. If I had a lot to do on my bike I would be working on it Thursday and Friday nights. Therefore, I would do a hard day's work on the Thursday, have my tea and then ride an old pushbike to Tunstall and work on my bike. I would ride back to Halsham and sleep in the cowshed. This was repeated on the Friday. I would be working from early morning until 12 o'clock on the Saturday morning. Then I would have my dinner and go to Tunstall for my motorbike and get to the track usually when the practice had finished. The help I got from the people I had slaved for, amounted to nil. Once, when I was having my dinner prior to going to ride at West Park, Mr Scott was saying, 'Have a good look at him, you won't see him anymore; he is going to kill himself.' He hoped it would make me pack up racing. When we were going to Easington School, Ernie and Ette were bothered about my brother Stan's education because he was a clever scholar and was wasting his time. They arranged for him to go to Brunswick Avenue School and live at Grandma Nick's. The school welcomed him and he was in the football team before he got there. When he left school he went to work at a furniture-maker's in Hull. He was serving an apprenticeship to learn French polishing. Serving an apprenticeship was a big racket and it took six or seven years on very low pay. I reckon it would have taken Stan one week to learn the trade. So actually a lad's time for five or six years was spent making tea, going errands and sweeping up. So you cannot blame Stan for joining The Royal Air Force as soon as he was eighteen. I don't think Ernie minded this move such a lot. Ernie had a lot to remind him of the horrors of war and tried to encourage me to stay on in farming, hoping that I would not have to be in the next war. He would say that they had not finished the war and us lads would have to go and finish it.

Sometimes we would go into Withernsea to take in the flashing lights and the excitement and the thrills of the town's entertainment on a Saturday evening. In other words, we could have our pick from three cinemas. There used to be Tom Mix and Buck Jones. There was a serial with Ralf and Betty and Ralf was Tarzan and he wasn't arf good. He could climb trees better than monkeys. I think that was when I started having nightmares. Going to pictures wasn't my only pleasure when I went to Withernsea on a Saturday evening. I was getting to know a girl called Wendy who worked in a sweet shop. When we came out of the cinema, I would disappear from my brothers and go to the sweetshop to see Wendy. One evening, when Stan was with us he became a bit fed up of waiting for me. He came looking for me and saw me in the shop. As he rushed through the door his eyes were only on me, and didn't notice Wendy until after he said a few naughty words. As we came out of the shop I thought, *that's the end of my romance.*

Wendy was a very nice girl and well educated. Her father was killed in the war. She had a caring mother who did her best for Wendy and her two brothers. They were very musical and the two lads played the violin and Wendy played the piano. I know I was a bit daft, but I had the sense to realise that if Wendy did want to marry me she definitely wouldn't want such a bad-tempered man for a brother-in-law. Although I thought Wendy's heart would be broken, I kept well away from the sweetshop.

About two or three weeks later, Stan announced he was bringing his girlfriend home. This put us into a bit of a spin. Ette heated up some water in a big pan and we took our shirts off. While Ette was washing the bits that show with a V-neck pullover, we went to the shops shirtless to get posh grub for our guest.

Stan was posher than we were, so we knew that his girlfriend would be posh and beautiful. The tablecloth could have done with a wash, but the amount you can get even in a big pan, is very limited. Anyway, by the time we got the table set there wasn't such a lot of tablecloth showing. At last the happy couple arrived, Stan and Wendy. They married and enjoyed a happy and very busy life together.

Pug and I were still making good use of our road track. I benefited quite a lot by practising. I suppose I could handle my bike better and ride into corners faster and quicker with clutch and gears. I was feeling confident for my next ride at West Park. The camshaft engines had more power and speed than my AJS, but I thought I could ride as good as anyone. Therefore, the riders on faster bikes didn't have such a lot of advantage on a difficult circuit like West Park. I think my bike couldn't have been better prepared and was performing well.

Pug came with me to West Park, but not to race; I think he was too young to ride there. The road that goes down to Hull Fair was called Walton Street; West Park was on your right as you went down Walton Street. The main entrance was through large iron gates off Anlaby Road. As far as I can remember, near the gates was a memorial or a statue of some kind and a large iron fence surrounding it. To get to the pits you had to go to an entrance down Walton Street where a short road brought you somewhere near the end of the long straight. For safety reasons you couldn't turn right to get to the pits, you had to go round the track. Of course, Pug asked if he could ride the bike to the pits. I said, 'Yes'. If I had kept my mouth closed after saying he could take it, he would have found his way round at a reasonable canter. But I explained the road in detail and told him where he could open it out. Unfortunately, Pug got a bit mixed up and opened it out just before a sharp corner. I couldn't see Pug as he was going round the backside of the track, but I could hear the engine, and it sounded great. Then suddenly a flash of red motorbike came into view and climbed a tree. By the time we got to the pits the riders were coming out to line-up. I joined them, but it was a waste of time.

I went to both of the meetings the following year. At the first one my carb wasn't set up properly. I had been working on the bike the night before; I think I changed the carb. The people of Tunstall were wonderful towards us so one rule we had was to never start up a racing bike engine after dark, when some people and children were in bed.

As usual, I had to work until dinnertime on the Saturday morning. Some riders had been practising since about 7 o'clock, but I had just missed the practice, and I didn't have much time to see to the carburettor. All the way round the track people were shouting at me to give it some air or to give it some choke. I felt like an idiot because the engine was getting a rich mixture and the air lever was fully open.

At the next meeting, my bike was going well until halfway through the race when I had trouble and stopped. The commentator said, 'Sonny boy and his fire engine have stopped at the café and he is having a cup of tea. But don't worry he will be coming round in a few minutes.' He had always called me 'sonny boy' and my lovely red bike the 'fire engine'. The commentator was young Thompson. He had a brother, but I have forgotten their Christian names. Their father was the boss of Thompson Motors on Anlaby Road. They moved two or three years ago, but were still in Hull. One of the lads was a pilot during the war. I think it was our commentator, but I am not sure. He saw a German submarine surfacing. He ordered the captain to surrender and that is what he did.

God was good to Ernie regarding wood for his new bungalow. His piece of land near the bay where the wood was washed up ashore made the job a bit better.

It is strange to look back on those days and it seems almost unbelievable. How things have changed! No ships have come aground since those days. I guess improved navigation and the size of ships have made shipping safe. A lot of time has gone by since Withernsea and Spurn lighthouses put their lights out for the last time.

I remember the horses galloping past our cottage to go to launch a lifeboat at Easington. There were The Rocket crews at all the villages on the coast. They fired a rocket with a line attached, across the bows of a ship, which was in danger of being capsized. Then a thicker line was attached to the first line and this was winched to the ship, and the breeches buoy carried the sailors one at a time to the cliff top.

All this has gone except the memory of very brave men some of who lost their lives saving sailor's lives. Thank God we have to go and buy our own wood.

Chapter 18

PUG'S FLOP AS A FRUIT SALESMAN

When I became eighteen years of age I wanted to join the Royal Air Force, but there was a snag. The minimum height was five foot four inches. I was only five foot two inches. I thanked Uncle Bill's bull for that. When we were at Easington School, Stan was only half an inch taller than I was. He grew to five foot eleven inches, but I didn't grow anymore after that bullfight. Stan kept on telling me not to join the army as they were thinking of bringing the minimum height for the Royal Air Force to five foot two. Ernie suggested that I try to get a job at Blackburn Airworks at Brough. Lots and lots of years later I did go there and wished that I had gone when Ernie suggested it, when I was seventeen. It was springtime again and Ernie had enough wood to finish the bungalow and was making good progress with its construction. Pug and I were a long way off becoming rich. We had a lot of motorbike and car spares, but there was a slump and we had difficulty in selling and when we did sell something, it was very cheap. Nearly new magneto dynamos were two shillings and sixpence and a nearly new tyre wouldn't be anymore than two shillings.

Ernie had an uncle who was in the fruit trade and seemed to be very rich. He suggested we should get into the fruit trade, so that was what we did.

Pug didn't have any money, but I had a bit and I was earning more than Pug. So of course I was the boss. Ernie had a break from the bungalow job to help us. The Enfield and sidecar chassis was the basis of a three-wheeler fruit wagon.

I can't remember the details of its construction; from the rear it looked like a van; at the serving side there was a half door, which was hinged at the bottom. It opened inwards to make a counter. I don't think Pug had a door for getting into it. I think he just cocked his right leg over the petrol tank and onto the floor.

He went to market with some of my wages and bought a load of fruit. He was a good salesman because by midday his fruit was gone. Therefore, he went to the market for another load. That was except for one little detail. He ended up with less money then when he started. We thought he would soon get the hang of it and make a profit, but he never did.

The only thing to do was for me to go round with him and to seek out the mystery. A woman wanted a pound of apples that would be four apples. Pug just plonked five apples on the scales. The scales went down with a thud and Pug gave the apples to the customer who looked very pleased. When I told Pug he should have taken one off the scales to see if they stayed at the bottom he told me, 'You can't do that, it looks mean.'

Pug's efforts never improved very much, but he was taking fruit round for quite a long time, but I never made any money. Eventually Ernie got fed up of Pug and kicked him out. For the next couple of weeks or so Pug lived on a diet of fruit on the cliff top. I do not know what Pug's next move was.

It was 1935 and I was nineteen-years-old. I was still hoping the Royal Air Force would take in dwarfs like me, but knowing that it may never happen. My thoughts began to drift to the army again. I was still a country joskin and was still hoping for a better lifestyle. Surely the old soldier would not still be hanging round the recruiting office threatening young would-be-soldiers. If he were he would be past his fighting days anyway.

Chapter 19

MOTORBIKES, RACING AND RIDERS

Looking back on those racing days makes me glad that we had a dad who was a motorcycle enthusiast who helped us a tremendous amount. Pug started off with a Rudge Multi when he was seven-years-old. He was a wonderful rider for his age. I didn't get a bike suitable for racing until I was fifteen-years-old. That was the bike that Ernie made out of his 1914 Humber. As soon as my bike was ready, we went grass track racing.

I think that considering how we started and never having any money, I don't think we did so badly. We were very grateful when Harold Miles helped us; me with my AJS engine and Pug with the Black Prince Calthorp. Harold only had a small workshop at that time. Then he managed to get a really good shop on Anlaby Road, and he finished up with Miles Sport, which is a very well known business. I think he was semi-retired when he died of a heart attack playing golf.

I liked racing in the grass track events, but my ambition was road racing and my wish was to win races in the TT races. I am glad I was able to ride against Freddie Frith. He began with grass track and scrambling, which I think is a good thing. He went to the Isle of Man in 1930 and came third in the Manx Grand Prix on a KTT Velocette. He rode in the 1935 Junior Grand Prix and came first and broke the lap record. In 1936

Walter Rusk who was in the Norton team, had received injuries and was not well enough to ride. Freddie replaced him; Norton had made a good move because he won the junior by five and a half minutes. He broke the lap record three times and set up a new lap record of 81.94 mph.

In the senior race he came third behind his teammate, Jimmie Guthrie and Velocette rider Stanley Woods.

In 1937 Freddie won the senior, making the fastest lap. He had beaten Stanley Woods and in the junior he finished second to Jimmie Guthrie. The stupid war came in 1939; in 1947 he was practising on a Moto Guzzi and had a bad accident. In 1948 he went back to Velocettes and rode a mark V11KTT. His teammate was Kenneth Bills. Leading from start to finish, he set the fastest lap at 82.45 mph.

In the TT races of 1949 he was riding against Bill Doran in the junior. He won it and made the fastest lap (sorry I don't know the speed). In 1949 the old championships were replaced by the new series of World Championship races. Freddie Frith won all the rounds in the junior. They were in Switzerland, Holland, Belgium and Northern Ireland. He also won the TT.

Les Graham topped the 500cc class. Eric Oliver won the sidecar series. Reg Armstrong was the runner-up in the junior races with fifteen points, behind Freddie. Reg was riding an AJS. Freddie Frith retired from racing at the end of 1949 to set up a motorcycle business in his hometown of Grimsby. He was the first motorcycle racer to be awarded the order of the British Empire. Geoff Duke was the second.

Stanley Woods was born in Dublin in 1905. His first TT ride was on a Cotton, when he was seventeen-years-old. His engine caught fire while he was refuelling, but in spite of that mishap he finished the race in fifth place. He won ten TT races between 1923–1939. He joined the Norton team in 1926 and stayed with them until 1933. During the time he was with Norton he won the Senior TT in 1926, 1932 and 1933 and also the junior in 1933.

In 1934, Woods rode a lightweight Moto Guzzi and came fourth. In 1935 he rode a lightweight to victory in the TT at a race average of 71.56 mph and broke the last lap record at 74.19 mph. It was a single cylinder sprung frame. This was the first bike to win a TT with spring suspension. It was also the first time a foreign bike had won the TT since 1911 when Godfrey rode to victory on a 500cc Indian. He also rode a two cylinder Moto Guzzi in the senior race and came first and made a record lap 86.53 mph.

Stanley Woods went to Velocettes in 1936 and was second in the senior and made the fastest lap of 86.98 mph. In the 1937 TT senior, he was second and also second in the 1938 behind Norton rider Harold Daniell. He won the junior race with team rider Ted Mellor in second position. Woods' average for the race was 84.08 with a fastest lap of 85.30 mph. The war came in 1939 and so it was the end of TT racing until after the war. In that year there were swarms of bikes, including three super charged BMWs in the second race. Woods rode a Moto Guzzi in the lightweight race. He retired with mechanical problems after making the fastest lap. He rode a Velocette to fourth position in the senior race. He also rode a Velocette in the junior, coming first with Harold Daniell (Norton) in second position besides winning ten TT races. When the Ulster Grand Prix was the fastest road race in the world, he won it seven times.

Jimmie Guthrie was one of the great riders of the thirties. He was a very loveable person and a brilliant rider. He began riding the Nortons in 1930 and teamed up with Stanley Woods until Woods left Norton to go to Velocettes in 1933. Freddie Frith joined the Norton team in 1936 to ride as teammate to Guthrie, when they had exciting battles with Stanley Woods.

Jimmie Guthrie crashed on the last lap at the Sachsenring circuit when he was leading the 1937 German Grand Prix and was killed.

I must mention Harry Frow who lived in New Holland Lincolnshire. He never became well known, but I thought he was a brilliant rider, from my view in races at West Park, which I could see just now and again. Freddie Frith and Harry Frow were mostly side by side, making an exciting race. I never knew who crossed the line first.

Motorcycle racing was a sport where when you were in the pits, the best riders and the newcomers were all treated alike. Pug and I learnt to ride trailing our left leg. Consequently Ernie made our bikes to suit the riding. But the riding style changed, so ignoring Ernie's warning that we would break our legs, we changed our riding style. Harry Frow must have been watching us because he came to us in our pit and told us that our bikes were too low. We told Ernie, but he could not understand how a bike could be too low, and talked about force of gravity and things. Nevertheless we rode with the height as Harry had told us and it was a big improvement.

Chapter 20

JOINING THE ARMY

I told Ernie that I had decided to join the army. I think that for years he had been dreading this. He told me that the only thing he could do was to go with me to the recruiting office to make sure the crafty beggars there didn't put me in the Infantry.

On the 29 of November 1935, I became a soldier in the Royal Corps of Signals. On the way home, Ernie sat against an ex-navy man. I remember hearing them talking about me. The navy man said, 'He should have joined the Royal Navy.' Ernie said, 'There would be lots of aeroplanes attacking ships.' The navy man said that from the great height they would be looking down on a ship it would look very small and the bomb from the plane would miss it. Ernie said, 'In the next war the aeroplanes will dive down to bomb the ships.' Ernie knew what he was talking about.

There was a letter waiting for me from Stan saying, 'You can come into the Air Force now.' I had waited two years for that letter. I wanted to be a fighter pilot: it must have been fate. How long would I have lasted against highly trained German pilots?

I was soon on the train travelling to Catterick camp. I think the part of the journey from Hull to Goole must have been the worst journey in the world.

Before I had even begun my training I had to go back home for an aunt's funeral. She was one of my mother's sisters. I was given a pass for a few days compassionate leave, and now that I was a soldier I had to look like one in a soldier uniform. I was in a hurry to catch the bus that went to Darlington. As I was running for the bus, I saw in the distance some new recruits. One of them was wearing racing leather breeches and racing boots. He looked like Pug, but I knew it couldn't be him. I caught my bus and also my train at Darlington and was enjoying the train journey until I got to Goole, and then it was the horrible line to Hull. During the journey home I never thought anymore about the lad in the racing gear.

Eventually I arrived home and the first person I saw was Ernie. 'Have you seen Pug?' shouted Ernie.

'No,' I called, 'I have only just come home.'

'I mean at your place. He went this morning. He's in the Signals,' explained Ernie.

I said, 'Oh, bloody hell!'

I went into the bungalow with Ernie; Ette had got the kettle on and was preparing some food. In the meantime Ernie was looking at his son's uniform. 'What the bloody hell have you got on?' said Ernie looking at my riding breeches and, putties and spurs. 'I thought you were going to ride a motorbike not a horse,' he said. I tried to explain to Ernie that the spurs were to help you stop if your bike started to go downhill. 'I thought they were for getting your bloody sausages out of the fire when they were cooked,' chirped Ernie.

The funeral went down all right. There was plenty of food and gossip and everyone had a good time. You could sense what the old dears were thinking, *it looks as if she'll go before me, I'm not buying another black hat and veil, and so she needn't think I am.* Soon after all the excitement of the funeral, it was time to go back to Catterick. I wasn't looking forward to the horrible train journey to Goole. I was sat in a compartment from Hull to Brough all on my own. Then at Brough, five girls joined me. They were good-looking and sexy and the young soldier enjoyed every little bit of it. It was the best journey I had ever had.

When I arrived at the barracks, Pug was waiting for me. He looked very sad, and pale and frightened. I said, 'What's wrong Pug?'

'There is an outbreak of meningitis in our barrack room and they are dying like flies,' explained Pug. He didn't look right in his uniform. The breeches and speedway boots suited him better and I thought he should have stayed with his mule.

I was impatient to get training; the king and country wanted me. The storeman had given me some nice things. There was a small thin piece of brass with a slot in it and a duster, a tin of Brasso and a brush. There was a tin of boot polish and some brushes. Someone thought I was going to be busy.

At last we went onto the drill square, and what a thrill that was. The instructor was a nice man with a pleasant sweet voice. If he were two miles away, maybe you wouldn't hear him. If he were two feet away you would hear him, even if you were stone deaf. When you spoke to him you spoke under your breath, but he would know what you were thinking because he had been trained.

My first impression was, *Why did I come all this way to be among a lot of lunatics when there was a good lunatic asylum at Willerby.*

At first our instructor had to teach us to turn round. Well we could do this, but not the army way. You sort of twist your body round on your right foot. If you haven't put your knee out of joint you carry on with the next movement. That is you lift your left foot real high, but be careful your knee doesn't hit your chin or your tongue becomes shorter by half an inch. The next movement must be done properly because if you do it right you will soon become an officer. You must bash your foot down as hard as you can. If you get your knee stuck in the tarmac don't worry because you will soon become a drill instructor.

During this demonstration I was thinking, *You silly man. If there was a big German after you and he had a sharp knife tied to the spout of his gun you wouldn't pratt about like that.*

One of the most important things you must learn to do when you are preparing for a war is to salute. So our drill instructor was very particular about this demonstration. When you bring your right arm up make sure it is stiff. The chap next to you may get his hat knocked off. You will be congratulated if you do it right. The chap next to you will be on a charge for not wearing his hat on parade, but that is his problem. You have to hold your arm up for three minutes. If you happen to have a watch on your right wrist you will not be able to time this bit of salute, and may be stood there when the rest have gone for dinner. But when they come back you have to bring your arm straight down smartly.

Having learnt to salute to the right you are well trained if the German tank is on the right. But the awkward bugger might pass you on the left. So it is essential to learn to salute to the left, because if you give him a right salute and he is passing on the left he will blow your stupid head off and that could hurt a bit.

When you are a soldier you are trained to think of the surprise element. That German tank crew may have stopped to eat their dinner and we would be going past them. So we had to learn to salute on the move. Therefore, we had to march up and down the parade ground like a bunch of idiots. We also had to learn to salute to the front, standing still. But we also had to learn to salute on the move. I was a bit bothered about this because you were going to trample the poor bugger into the ground anyway. We weren't taught to salute from the back and this puzzled me for a bit and then it came to me. If the enemy is running like hell to catch you and you are also running like hell to get away from him, it is difficult to salute. When he catches you there will be plenty of time to salute him. After a week of intense saluting, we were ready for the next important part of learning to be a fighting soldier. This was drills with arms. This means taking rifles onto the parade ground. You didn't put your rifle on your shoulder like a council worker puts his shovel on his shoulder. It had to be done like soldiers do it. You always get the command, 'Ground Arms'. This means you put the rifle on the ground. I was very ignorant at first and I wondered why you did it. It was to do with coming under fire. The army braces had no stretch, so when you put your rifle to the ground a button went twang and clouted the poor chap who was behind you. Then when you bent down to pick up your rifle the other button went twang. We also had to learn to salute when you had a rifle. I will explain it briefly. If you are walking and you are meeting an officer you... Oh sod this! I am going on leave.

If you were a very good soldier you could be judged the best soldier in the squad. The prize for this great honour was a whip. I wondered what Ernie would have said if I went home with a whip to go with my spurs so I decided I had better not be such a good soldier. There were three Geordies in my squad. One of them was very smart and was good at doing all these idiotic drill movements. The other two Geordies cleaned and polished his equipment. They were determined to take the whip to Geordie land.

Pug was in the mess room and these three Geordies were there; they were talking about me. Pug didn't like what they were saying, so he went to them. The big one got up and started fighting with Pug. Someone told me it was a fierce fight and it lasted for about an hour, Pug never mentioned it to me.

One of the corporals had a car. He asked me if I would tune it up for him. I gave it a top overhaul and worked on the carburettor and the ignition. I took it out for a test run and it went well so I was pleased about it. But when I got back to the barracks there was a big policeman hanging about, he was on a police bike. He followed me into the garage courtyard. He wanted to see my driving licence, but he was unlucky because I had never had one. My motorbikes went all right without one.

I had to go to court, and I had to get a licence and I was fined ten shillings. This was one of the best things that happened to me, because I would have been given an Army licence. At the end of the war, those people who got a military licence could not get a driving job. So that policeman did me a good turn.

We did three months of this training that converted sloppy civvies to smart soldiers. At the 'pass out' we did the drill in front of the colonel. He was holding the valuable prize and I guess the Geordies had their eyes glued to it.

The drill instructor walked smartly to the old boy, gave him a super salute and shook the ground when his boot hit it. They talked for a few minutes and then the instructor pointed to me. The colonel began walking towards me and I could see a smile on his face, at least the part of his face that was visible, as he looked like a walrus in uniform. He shook my hand and kept hold of it while he was saying very kind things to me. I think he fancied me and then he handed me the colonel's whip.

We left the parade ground and went to get our wages, holiday pay, and pass. There were two corporals paying out and they were collecting for Dr Barnados Homes. I wondered if there was anything fishy about those two collecting for the homes because I did not trust them. I could see a hat on one of the tables for the lads to put their money into, but there wasn't an official box. I decided to sort them out when I returned from leave. I went to the barracks to get washed and changed to get on my way home for a long, longed for holiday. I put the whip on a couple of brackets below my locker. I was ready for going and was going to pick up my prize. The Geordies had already gone and also the whip so I reckon it had gone to Geordie land after all.

When I arrived home, Ernie was pleased to see me because he had just a little job waiting for me to do. He had bought a field at Waxholme; there wasn't a lease this time. My little job was to be the removal van. I borrowed a horse and a four wheeled flat cart and spent my whole two weeks' leave taking everything from Tunstall to Waxholme.

Back at Catterick I had another flitting job to do. I had to move to the training unit. The training officer said there was a course for despatch riders just starting and one that had completed the first half. Then he said, 'I don't think you will want to sit listening to someone teaching you the theory of motorcycles for three months, do you?' I didn't, so he put me in the squad that was halfway through the course. First I had to sort out the two corporals so I went to see the sergeant major. He definitely didn't want me to go through with it and did his best to make me change my mind. But I was not going to do that.

The corporals talked about the recruits wanting to get off as soon as possible because they had buses to catch. It was only common sense to put a hat on the table so that they could throw money into it as they walked past it. If they stopped to put money in a slot some of the lads wouldn't get away. So it was better for them to transfer the money from the hat into the box after the lads had left. It all sounded sensible and above board and the officer who was the judge thought it was a good idea, and the corporals hadn't done anything wrong.

The second day went similar to the first day and the corporals thought they were scoring all the points. I just let them think they were doing well. It made them happy and most of all it gave them confidence and that is all I wanted. They had already stated that there was only one box.

On the third day I asked the officer if I could have them brought in one at a time. So one of them was brought in. I said, 'I admit that there was a box belonging to Dr Barnados Homes. But you had put the box right at the back of your table so we couldn't reach it, so we were forced to put the money in the hat. I don't believe you put all the money in the box. What you didn't put in the box you shared between the two of you. Therefore I accuse you of stealing money that belonged to Dr Barnados Homes.' The corporal told us the exact position of the box on his table. He went out and the other one came in. I repeated what I said to the first one and he gave the exact position of the box on his table. I then asked for the other one to be brought back.

I said to him, 'You have given me the exact position of where the box was on your table. I told the other one the same.' Then I said, 'These recruits don't get much money, but they were very generous because they were helping a good cause and you two stole the money that they gave.'

The officer said his piece and the two corporals were marched out. I never saw them again and have no idea what happened to them.

In my last squad they were all different types, but in my new squad they were all motorcyclists learning to be despatch riders. About half of them had done racing and were good riders. We began by riding on the moors. You couldn't have a better racing ground. The bikes were 500cc side valve Nortons; they were very good at climbing the steep gradients. I was enjoying myself and this was the beginning of many happy months of riding with good friends.

Pug had been on leave and was transferred to the training unit. He was in the squad that I would have been in if I hadn't jumped the first half of the training session.

The garage where we kept our bikes only had a small door. Pushing a heavy bike through the door was an awkward thing to do, but us learners didn't have any option. But a sergeant rode through it every morning and afternoon. Pug happened to be stood near the door and his hand accidentally came into collision with this clever man's rear mudguard causing him to get tangled up in the doorway. From then on the sergeant pushed his bike through as we had to.

One day a worried looking Pug came to me and asked about some tyres. They were spares for the orange wagon. But with Pug's 'gentle' riding and the heavy weight on the tyres they were soon worn out and also the spare set. Pug, forgetting he had worn out the spares, had sold them to the sergeant major for his small car. When I told Pug the tyres had been gobbled up on a scrap heap he told me that the sergeant major kept asking him about them. The sergeant major had paid him, but Pug had spent the money.

Not long after this and when Pug was fed up with the army, he and a lad called Carpenter, did a bunk. Three months later it was winter and Pug had nowhere to go so he decided to go home.

He had reached Burton Pidsea and the time was 2 o'clock in the morning. Someone had been stealing chickens the previous night and so the police were there hoping the thief would come again. Of course, when they saw Pug they grabbed him and took him to the Withernsea police station. Two army police went to get him and took him back to Catterick where he did some detention.

Chapter 21

DESPATCH RIDER TRAINING

During the time when Pug was having a rough and lonely time I was getting on with my training. The moor was one large trial course that was new to me because there was nothing like it for many miles from Withernsea. One young lad who I became friendly with was very good at getting over boulders. I lost touch with him after I left the training unit so I don't know if he became a trials rider or not. Another lad was 'Spud' Thompson. I think they called him 'Spud' because he was a real farmer type. I kept in touch with Spud for a long time.

After about a month of riding on the moors, we went on different roads to do map reading. Somewhere in the village there would be a message against a gatepost or under a large stone. I enjoyed these trips very much as there was lovely scenery and beautiful villages.

From Catterick camp we went to Bedale and then to Leyburn on the A8684. Leyburn is a biggish village with good shops and I believe it had a cross in the square. This may have come from Wensley, but I'm not sure.

Just after leaving Bedale there was a lovely village called Crakehall. There was a good pub there that faced the lovely green. There were lots of ducks in the pond and on the bank. It was downhill from Leyburn to Wensley and my Norton used to be on full revs.

Wensleydale is the largest of the Yorkshire Dales and in my opinion, the most beautiful. For more than 200 years until 1563 Wensley was the main marketplace for the dales. Then Wensleydale was struck by the plague. The people fled to the high ground round Leyburn and not many returned to Wensley after the plague. Leyburn then became the largest market of the dales. The Holy Trinity Church of Wensley was built in 1245. It looks like a Saxon church. In the nave are wall paintings that date back to 1330. We continued on the A8684 and came to Wensleydale. The River Ure flows through Wensleydale to make the land the most fertile of all Yorkshire valleys. The river flows or rather gushes, down the western slopes of Lund's fill that is fifteen miles west of Aysgarth. There are three waterfalls known as Aysgarth Force within a distance of 1 mile. You can get a lovely view of the upper force from a fourteenth century bridge spanning the Ure.

We came to Bainbridge. We were getting near the end of our journey, as Bainbridge was only four miles from Hawes. We stopped for a while when we got within two miles of Hawes and turned round. There was an old bridge at Bainbridge. It was always worthwhile stopping to look at the view along the Bainbridge River.

Map reading became unimportant after two or three weeks and the run to Hawes became a race. Of course map reading was to train us DRs (Despatch Riders) for the war. Only Ernie knew which war the British government was thinking of. Germany was getting ready for a war with Russia. Anyway, I didn't think much about map reading and finding messages under big stones. What if Churchill sent a very important message like: 'To the soldiers in Tobruk, fight to the last man,' and the DR had to decide which stone it was under.

When we decided on this there could be a big fat German sitting on the stone. He would have to go and say, 'Please Mr German soldier, can I go and get my message?' But it may not be as easy as that. They may not be able to speak one another's language. This would be serious because Churchill would have wasted his time and the last man, not knowing about the message, would have cleared off home.

When the run out to Hawes became a race, it wasn't good for my Norton. We set off at intervals, about one minute between each lad I think. I always set off last and reached our destination first. After two weeks of this treatment the big end was about to watch worms through the bottom end of the crankcase. This isn't good for an engine so two vehicle examiners came to have a look.

I was near the office window, but I hadn't looked in, not until a mate said, 'Nick come and have a look through the window.' On a large piece of white paper was my carburettor in little bits, and the examiners and the two sergeants and the two corporals were scrutinising every part to see why a side valve Norton could knock its big end out in two weeks. They were so busy that they didn't see us. We heard one examiner say; 'This bloke spends too much time going at 30 mph.' This was a joke I think.

For years this country had been making the best motorcycles in the world. But the DRs had ancient belt-drive Triumphs and Douglas bikes. We had the first batch of the Nortons. Germany was making light and very fast tanks for their panzer divisions. We had Churchill tanks – heavy, dead slow and clumsy. They carried a gun that looked ridiculous on the tank and looked as if you could carry it on a motorbike and sidecar. The same eggheads decided on a bike that was heavy and dead slow.

I was near the end of my training and I was thinking about what I had done since I came to Catterick. I considered the first three weeks as a waste of time. If an officer wasn't satisfied with me giving him a salute without going into acrobatics, then it was hard luck for him.

I didn't need the army to teach me to ride and maintain a motorbike and read a map. So the army hadn't taught me anything, but I had the idea I could teach them quite a lot. The sergeant major was still upset over the tyres he didn't get but had paid for. He said he couldn't give Pug a good character, but he could give me one. This was good because my ambition was to get into the Motorcycle Display Team.

The main object of the display team was to get new recruits. Therefore, the members of the team must be good soldiers with a good character. Before 1937 the display team consisted of horses and bikes. But for the 1937 team they would have bikes.

There would be more bikes. But the horsemen of 1936 would be trained to ride them. I thought this was bad news and that there would not be any vacancies. In that case I would be very upset because to get into the team was my greatest ambition.

I wasn't doing anything in particular and I wondered what the army had in store for me, when I was told that Spud Thompson and myself were in the display team. Most of the lads of the team had been in the team for three or four years. They were very good riders, because this was the world's best team.

We had all winter for training until 12 May. The horsemen were excellent riders on horses so it wasn't long before they were good trick riders on the bikes. We had 250cc Triumphs and 500cc Triumphs for sidecar stunts and a 600cc bike, which carried twenty-four men. We were very lucky to have a boss who was a real gentleman. He was a brilliant horse rider and could do most of the stunts on the bikes. His name was Lt Henry Crawford.

Engagements 1937

12 May	Brighouse Coronation Celebration
13 May	Wembley Speedway
17 May	Malling Horse Show Kent
19 May	4th Divisional Signals Sports Canterbury
29 May	Cambridgeshire and Isle of Ely Agricultural Show, Histon
30 May	Cambridge University OTC at Cambridge
3/4 June	Suffolk Agricultural Show at Beccles
8/10 June	Three Counties Agricultural Show, Hereford
11/12 June	Leicestershire Agricultural Show, Leicestershire
14/15 June	Blackpool Coronation Celebrations
16/17 June	Royal Norfolk Agricultural Show at Fakenham
19 June	S Durham & N Yorkshire Agricultural Show at Darlington
26 June	White City Greyhound Stadium (Final–Greyhound Derby)
27 June	Civil Service Motoring Ass. Rally at Castle Donnington
1 –10 July	Northern Command Tattoo at Leeds
14/15 July	Great Yorkshire Show at York
17 July	Selby Hospital Carnival at Selby
21 July	Tunbridge Wells & SE Counties Agricultural Show
22 July	Bedfordshire Agricultural Show at Ampthill
24 July	Scunthorpe Hospital Carnival
28 July	Wick Gala, Caithness
30 July	Stranraer & Rhine of Galloway Agricultural Show

2 August	Durham County Agricultural Show at Chester-Le-Street
3 August	Lutterworth Agricultural Show at Lutterworth
5 August	Tring Show at Tring, Herts.
7 August	Perthshire Agricultural Show at Perth
12 August	1st Cadet Bn DII Tattoo at South Shields
18/19 August	Cleethorpes Carnival at Cleethorpes
21 August	Shilden Show at Shilden, Co. Durham
25/26 August	Royal Jersey Agricultural Show at Jersey, CI
1 September	Hastings Hospital Carnival at Hastings
13–15 Sept.	Scarborough Townswomen's Association
18 September	Masham Show at Masham
24 September	Middlesborough YMCA. Fete, Middlesborough
25 September	Belle Vue Speedway at Middlesborough

Personnel

Officer-in-charge of display team: Lieutenant HN Crawford, R Signals

Secretary: Corporal ES Taylor

Corpl E Turner. NCO I/C	Signalman J Vitale
L/Cpl HR Pescod.	S Moore
J Tomkins	R Boddington
F Keighley	J Paterson
Signalman: T.Hewitt	E Taylor
J Oglanby	GW Rowley
E Pearce	ES Nicholson
C Bridges	CA Thomson
DR McGee	R Richardson
J Farley	CA Friend
R Faraday	R Wintrip
A Gowland	W Chapman

The Motorcycles

Our team consists of:

Sixteen 1936 250cc Triumphs

Six 1937 250cc Triumph 'Tiger' 70

One combination with 1936–500cc Triumph

One combination with 1937–500cc Triumph 'Tiger' 90

One 1934–500cc Triumph with bars fitted.

One 600cc side valve Triumph

Two Skewbald ponies are also included in the display.

Programme

Part 1

1   Entry jump
2   Some individual trick riding
3   A little comedy, introducing Patch and Tintack, the Skewbald ponies
4   Mass demonstration of backwards riding
5   Riding on the rear rests and standing on the saddle
6   The parallel bars
7   Ten men on a 2½ hp motorcycle
8   Jumping through the human circle
9   The combination entertains
10 A method of avoiding an oncoming motorcycle
11 Pair work
12 Climbing a ladder fixed to a motorcycle
13 The 'fan'
14 The fire jump
15 Patch and Tintack again
16 A fire ride
17 The figure ride

Part 2

When I was told I had been selected for the display team, I couldn't get to the quarters quick enough to meet the lads. I had the pick of four lockers and I moved into my new home at record time.

I was very glad when Spud Thompson joined us. We had been friends for three months and we didn't want to be separated. When you are posted from a friend you are lucky if you see them again.

The officer commanding the display team was Lieutenant HN Crawford. I'm sure it would not be possible to find anyone better and friendlier. He was a perfect gentleman and a great sportsman. We called him Henry.

One day, after I had been with the team three or four weeks, I was talking to Henry about different things when he suddenly said, 'Nick, do you know you had such a terrible character when you came to us and what I can't understand is you are not a bit like they said.' I was so surprised at this bad news that I didn't know what to say at first. Then I just told him that I had done my best and couldn't help what they said about me.

A long, long time after this conversation, I was talking to Pug. He began to chuckle a bit. I said, 'What is wrong with you?'

He looked at me and was very amused and then he said, 'When you left training what sort of a character did they give you?' When I told him he laughed again and said, 'Mine was excellent.'

I said, 'Why didn't you stay with your mule, you were just like each other.'

Henry was a good rugby player. I went to see him play two or three times. At that time I was put down for a football trial. Perhaps Henry had something to do with it because we did talk about sport. For some reason the match was cancelled and I never did get a game. So much for those posters I saw in Hull.

'Spud' went home and came back with his motorbike and I went for mine. That made five lads with their own motorbikes. It was good to be on our own bikes to go where we wanted and stay where we wished and for as long as we liked.

We decided to have a ride to Withernsea. Our journey took us to York. We could have gone speeding down the A1 but preferred Thirsk and the A19 because the first stopping place was the Minster. We went through Bootham Bar because this is the North West Gateway and we looked in amazement at the magnificent York Minster and we stared and took in the size of the beautiful stained glass windows. It took 250 years to build and you'd think it was amazing it was ever built at all.

We stopped at the Castle Museum and we spent quite a long time in the streets gazing at the Victorian and Edwardian shops. We had to get on. Our next stop was Clifford's Tower. The weather was good so we went up the mound and were glad that we did because from there you could get a lovely view of York.

We got onto the A1079 for Market Weighton. Just through Market Weighton there was a long steep hill. When you were coming down the hill into Market Weighton there was a long strip of sand. The brakes on most vehicles were very poor and on some vehicles only rear brakes were fitted. So a lot of vehicles went to play on the sand.

When we reached the end of the long climb we stopped to enjoy the lovely view that stretched for many miles, about fifty I reckon. Before Beverley was Bishop Burton. This was and is still a very lovely village.

Bishop Burton, like Market Weighton, had a steep hill leading into the village from Beverley. But they didn't have a strip of sand; instead they had a duck pond. The road carried on straight for the middle of the pond until the last second when it turned right following the curve of the bank. Many motorists unable to make the turn finished up in the pond.

Beverley is a very old town and has a beautiful minster, but the time was going too quickly so we did not stop and carried on to Aldborough and along the coast road to Withernsea. It was nice to be back home, but it was a short stay as we were a long way from Catterick.

When Guy Fawkes and friends were planning to bomb the Houses of Parliament they used the church at Welwick that is about three miles from Withernsea. Dick Turpin was hanged at York; he spent his last night in the condemned cell in Castle Museum.

We had a lovely ride back to Catterick after an enjoyable day out. We were hungry, but that was put right when we had devoured the currant cakes that Ette had baked for us.

As well as riding motorbikes I liked to go for walks. The Signals barracks were on the edge of the moors. The country roads were narrow and rough, but I liked walking along them to see the farms and cottages. The people were glad to see me and were interesting to listen to.

There was quite a good dance hall in the centre of the camp that was very popular. I used to take a girl who served in our NAAFI. She was a very nice person and I liked her a bit, but I have forgotten her name, but I can still see her on the dance floor in her long red dress.

I have always liked Scottish music and dancing, especially when it is a famous military band doing the playing. There were Scottish soldiers in barracks not far from the Signals barracks. They would come onto the parade ground in full ceremonial dress. It was good to see them dancing and listening to the music. It was all free, so I went two or three times.

Chapter 22

PRACTISING DISPLAY RIDES AT CATTERICK CAMP

At first, the Signals Display Team was a combined motorcycle and horse display, but this ended at the end of 1936. Henry had taken command in 1934. He was a lover of horses and a fine rider. It would have been awful if he had lost the horse riders who he liked very much. That wasn't the case. The horsemen remained in the team and learnt to become brilliant trick riders on motorbikes.

The two skewbald ponies called Patch and Tintack, remained in the team. They were used to jumping through fire and having motorbikes jump over them. There were five members of the team who had been with the team for two or three years riding motorbikes. They were Vitale, Moore, Boddington, Patterson, Taylor and Pescod. The new lads admired them for their skills and had to put in a lot of effort and training to become like them.

When Stan joined the Royal Air Force, Ernie persuaded him to make out an allotment to Ette. He did the same with me, Pug and Alan. So consequently we didn't have much to spend, while Ette must have been the richest woman in Withernsea.

A few weeks after going to Catterick, I went to the camp tailor to get him to make me a suit. He made a good job of it and it fitted me. I don't think I had ever had anything fit me before. I was paying three shillings and sixpence every week. I don't think I knew how many weeks I had to pay. I thought the tailor would surely tell me when I had taken him the last payment. I seemed to have been paying a long time and I think if I hadn't left Catterick, I would have still been paying him.

I was glad I had the suit when I saw the old display lads dressed up. They knew all about fine clothes. They put up with my suit, but told me I must get a good shirt. I did and it certainly broke the bank – it cost me six shillings.

When I was going to war I was told I could pack a suitcase and it would go to South Africa and I would get it back after the war. So my lovely suit went to South Africa. It was a good idea, but the people who thought it up had no idea how long the war would last. I was surprised when I received my suitcase, as I didn't think I would see it again. Inside it was just a lot of powdery dust.

Our training went well and there wasn't even one accident. We had a big press day and lots of photographs were taken. I was doing solo and pair tricks. Now and again, a press photographer would get ready to take a photo of me riding solo or doing pairs, but for some daft reason I would get too near him, frightening the poor chap and making him jump out of the way.

Spud said I rode too dangerously and after that I had Patterson for a pair's partner. Patterson was all right and we did some good stunts. Nowadays, the Royal Signals Display Teams have large transport vehicles, but we didn't have any of that. We rode our bikes to the shows except Henry who was more comfortable driving his Triumph Gloria. If there were two shows dated near each other and a long way apart, then it was necessary to go by train. If we didn't, we would miss our sleep.

Brighouse coronation celebrations were a wonderful contrast to being in barracks. There was plenty to see and good entertainment and plenty of beer tents where the team could quench their thirsty throats. I did not drink beer, but I could have been seen with a cold drink or Ovaltine.

Spud may have had an extra pint because he had something on his mind. He came to me and told me his girlfriend was pregnant and her dad wanted to know what he was going to do about it. I told him to tell the girl's dad that it was he who had to do something about it. He had to go to the bank and get some money out for his daughter's wedding.

Spud's wife was a lovely lass. They had two bonny girls. Sadly she wasn't very old when she died. I had lost touch with Spud. I went to an agricultural show at Hawes. I asked the farmers if they knew Spud Thompson, but I didn't have any luck.

Sometimes if I'm watching footballers on television coming through the entrance at Wembley in pairs, I see the display team coming in pairs. But when the motorbike riders got to the pitch each pair parted, one rider going one way round and another rider going the other way. This was the start of the opening figure ride.

It was a wonderful experience to be riding at Wembley. The world's solo figure skating champion was practising at Wembley. I went to see her on the ice and studied her movements. Each movement flowed gracefully into the next one.

I also saw the Cossacks doing stunts on their horses. They were real experts and each stunt flowed into the next as with the skater. I learnt to do the same on my motorbike and improved my stunt riding.

Spud and I went on the Speedway track, riding backwards. The bikes had enough power for broadsiding so it was quite a thrill for us and I think it would have been the first Speedway race to be ridden backwards. I thought it would be good to have real races backwards because you could watch the opposition struggling behind you.

I had been looking forward to getting into the display team. My ambition was to win the TT races, but I needed a lot of money to get a good bike. If I rode for Wembley I would get enough money. Therefore, at the first opportunity, I went to the offices to see Alec Jackson who was the Speedway team's manager. He had a very well-furnished office. Alec was sat in a big posh chair behind his desk. He had a big smile and I thought he looked very pleased to see me. He said, 'Sit down.' I sunk down into the lovely big posh chair. It's a wonder I didn't go to sleep. 'How much will it cost to get you out of the army?' he asked. He had seen me riding and must have been happy about it. I thought it must be a pity if Wembley speedway couldn't rake up enough money to get me out of the army. It would have cost £60. But if I had been in the Infantry it would have cost £30. So not wanting to disappoint him I said, '£30.' He seemed happy with that.

He had already arranged a trial with another lad so he asked me if I could be there at the same time. We would not be leaving London for a few days so that was fixed.

It was unusual for the team to have an extra engagement and it only happened twice during that display period so I was very unlucky when an extra engagement was made on the same day as my trial. We were travelling by train and it was a mad rush to get the bikes and the various props onto the train. There was a telephone near the station so I rang Stan. He was stationed at Uxbridge. I told him to get in touch with Alec Jackson to explain what had happened and to ask him to write to me to arrange another date. I never heard from Alec Jackson and I couldn't understand why, until I saw Stan. He hadn't got in touch with him. I think he had a conference with Ette and had decided that speedway was too dangerous.

Chapter 23

DISPLAYS AND INTERESTING TOWNS

I remember Canterbury very well. We stayed in the barrack rooms and we could relax for a while, but not for long, as besides doing the shows we wanted to see as much as possible of the city. I spent about two hours in the Cathedral. I was amazed at the beauty of it and the structure. It was impossible to even try to imagine how these people could have built it so long ago. There are narrow streets with the first floor hanging over to almost touch the one across the road. Lots of the larger buildings are timber and panel construction. I realised there was more to being on tours than just riding motorbikes.

I was looking forward to the Cambridgeshire and Isle of Ely Agricultural Show at Histon. I wasn't disappointed, but as we did three shows and only had one day to do it all, there wasn't time to look around. But I enjoyed all that riding. I remember the Suffolk Agricultural Show at Beccles because it was a lovely show; a very nice place and the display went really well.

I looked forward to going to the Three Counties Agricultural Show at Hereford as I knew it would be a large and interesting show. But when I arrived at the ground I could hardly believe what I was seeing. I had never seen anything like it, and I felt a mixture of pride and excitement at the thought of performing in front of all those people. We were there for two days so we had time to have a look round parts of the show and see the animals and new farm machinery. The main area was just right and large enough to suit our figure rides and jumps. Everything went really well and we enjoyed our riding. Therefore, the people watching us were excited and thrilled with our display.

There were some fine cows that gave lots of milk. The farmers did not know what to do with it all. We were given buckets of milk, but we couldn't drink all of it so we ended up like the farmers, having so much that we didn't know what to do with it.

We all enjoyed being at Blackpool for the Coronation celebrations. Our display went very well and there was lots of entertainment also. One good thing about being on shows was you were among a lot of happy people enjoying themselves. Also, those people looked upon a Signals Display member as if he was a few degrees higher than a film star. Among other things I enjoyed the good companionship between all my mates, as they were all good motorcyclists.

You have to be a good motorcyclist to get into the team. But you also had to be a good soldier, smart and clean and have a good personality. I think that the beginning of a good trick rider comes from the drill instructor. Every movement had to be quick and accurate and if you were doing a series of three or four tricks, each one had to flow smoothly from one part to the next.

Sometimes an easy stunt was performed and received a loud applause. That may have been followed by a very difficult stunt that hardly got any applause. That didn't seem fair to riders who understood the stunts. But you have to bear in mind that the spectators didn't understand the difficulties of each stunt. So my advice to trick riders is, 'Don't do tricks that you find too difficult. Practice and improve with easy tricks and soon you will find that the difficult tricks will come easy.' When I joined the team it was the back-end of the year and so the training was done during the winter, so therefore we were sometimes doing our tricks and figure rides through snow and ice.

Of course, there was no snow and ice when we went on tour, but we had difficulties because some arenas were small and some were large, some bumpy and some smooth, some were flat and some hilly. If you were going uphill one way and downhill when you had turned round at the end, you found it very difficult to set your throttle. If the arena was small it was difficult for everyone and especially for riders doing jumps. If we had a good-sized smooth arena everyone was happy and we put on a very good show.

I have said that all the team members were very good riders. But a good rider must have good machinery. Therefore, it is time to mention Edward Turner the famous British motorcycle designer. He designed the Red Hunter and the Ariel Square Four and I believe he had something to do with BSAs when their beautiful racing bikes were doing well in the Grand Prix races.

We must be grateful to him for designing our 250cc Triumph bikes that were so easy to ride and powerful, for only 250cc. Also thanks to the Triumph Company for letting us have them. We all enjoyed riding at White City Greyhound Stadium in front of 95,000 people. We couldn't go onto the Greyhound track, so you can imagine the sight of motorbikes leaping out of the entrance to clear the track and then fanning out for the figure ride.

Solo riders going through a series of tricks followed the figure ride. I do not remember the order of the tricks, but here are the tricks that I remember: The bike and sidecar towing a ramp. The solo rider judged the distance the bike and sidecar had travelled; this depended on the size of the arena. When he set off he had to go as fast as possible because he had to jump over the moving bike and sidecar. A motorbike jumped over Patch and Tin Tack. For the human arch, six men come to the centre of the arena on a small cart pulled by Patch and Tintack. The arch was made up of two men at each side and two across the top. A motorbike jumped through the arch. This was a good trick if you wanted your buttons taken off your overalls. The swallow performed with one rider lying face downwards and arms stretched out looking like a flying bird, steering with one hand, one foot on the saddle. We did the Jimmy. It is very difficult and when performed in a small arena, it looked good. We also did the double Jimmy. The ladder trick was always appreciated.

The rider took a bottle of beer in one pocket and a drinking glass in the other and poured himself a drink and drank it on top of the ladder. Pulling a bike and ladder over to an upright position was very difficult and needed a lot of strength. Tricks with the motorbike and sidecar always went down well with any crowd. Not many people knew how difficult it was to drive a motorbike and sidecar.

The pyramid made up of twenty men looked very spectacular. Gymnastics looked very good on parallel bars. It consisted of the driver and the two bars above with the two gymnasts. There was the comic act performed by Signalman Friend, the clown. He made a very good job of it and had the spectators having a good laugh.

We had twenty-four of the lads having a ride on the 600cc Triumph and also sixteen or eighteen on a 250cc. We did the tableau, but I cannot remember how many were in it. One of the lads walked to the middle of the arena. This trick was to show them what to do if a motorbike was coming towards them – jump high enough so that the motorbike and rider go under you. It amazed me how the chap could jump so high from a position of standing still.

During the time we were in London, there was another famous Signals Motorcycle Display at the Royal Command Performance at the Olympia. This was the city of London Territorial Display Team. Captain Firth and CSM Angell trained them. That year 1937, was their first full year of shows. We would have been doing the Olympia engagement, but I was pleased it was decided that they should do it.

We went to their show and gave them some help to get ready. Not being regular soldiers, they had been to work and had to dash to the Olympia to get ready in their display riding gear. There were the bikes to get ready and the props, so our help was appreciated.

They were a good bunch of lads and we got on fine with them. We didn't get to know Captain Firth very well, as he was busy elsewhere. I reckon Henry would have been looking after him. CSM Angell was a fine chap and we got on very well with him. He made a name for himself during the war and he became a major.

One of the lads was called Graham Walker; he became the editor of the magazine *Motorcycling*. The lads used their own bikes, but just before the Royal Tournament they received a batch of Rudge bikes, thanks to Graham.

Not long after the war, I received a letter from Henry to tell me that Major Angell had died. Three of the riders were killed during the war. Graham Walker became famous as a Rudge works rider. He had a son called Murray who followed in his father's footsteps and became a motorcycle racer. One day at a hill climb, the commentator hadn't turned up. So Murray took his place and did it so well they kept him on. Since then Murray has become known all over the world as a commentator and has done Formula One for many years.

We left London and went to Castle Donnington for the Civil Service Motoring Association Rally. From there we went to Northern Command Tattoo at Leeds. When we arrived at Roundhay Park in Leeds, we had a rest from travelling. I think we all enjoyed being there as it was a good arena, lovely people and big crowds to see us. There were quite a lot of army personnel in several different units. This did not make it like Catterick by any means. It added to the pleasure. The lads next to us were well organised with their field kitchen and were good enough to feed us. The cooks dished up some good meals and we enjoyed their company.

We did three shows each day. But the team had time to go and lubricate their tonsils with beer. Sometimes when we were about to start a show, there would be someone who needed a little help. Two lads would hold his bike while someone sat on it. Then all that was needed was for someone to kick his bike off and give it the correct direction and help him to get moving.

I enjoyed the 'figure rides' when they were in this state. They went very fast, but we never had an accident.

Our bikes and the ponies were very valuable so there was always someone left in the camp to watch them. I did this duty on the first evening. All the women went to the ponies to give them a pat and a stroke. Three girls were talking to them so I thought they might get more sense out of me so I went to them. Talking led me to taking one of them home after the lads began coming back.

Her name was Mary Taylor. She had told me she would see me the following day, but I was surprised to see her in the middle of the morning. She had told her parents about me and they had suggested that I go and have lunch with them. I thought she must have done a lot of persuading, but I realised this wasn't the case because they were such lovely people. I was invited to lunch everyday. There was only her mother and father and a young brother.

After having the pleasure of being in Leeds for one week, we had to move. But we stayed in Yorkshire for the next two weeks.

The Great Yorkshire Show at York certainly was a good show. You ride at your best at shows like this and the display team gets excellent marks. As we were there for two days we could get bedded in and enjoy the time between shows and the one evening we were there.

Selby Hospital Carnival Show was a change from the last two shows we had done and to me it was like being at home.

The lads talked about Tunbridge Wells at Catterick. We were now going there and I wondered if it was as good as they say. If they meant the pubs then I would be in for a disappointment. But I wasn't; it was a good show and they were wonderful people.

We travelled through The Garden of England (Kent) and enjoyed the lovely views of the country. We arrived at the eighteenth century spa town of Tunbridge Wells, the day before the show. It is a lovely place and has a lovely seventeenth century church. The people were very sociable there and I wouldn't have minded going to live there. It was a big show and very interesting. I enjoyed looking at the Shire and Clydesdale Horses dolled up with brasses and trimmings.

The display was excellent and the 'figure rides' were very fast, but safe and accurate. I really enjoyed the riding and was sorry when the time came to go. But there were other places to visit.

We had a lovely trip to Ampthill across the country. It is a lovely little town that lies south of Bedford. Once again we were performing before large crowds in a large agricultural show. The display went very well and fast without any trouble or accidents.

We had finished our riding and Don McGee and I decided to have a look round the show. There were two girls stroking the ponies. Seeing us they called out to us to talk about the ponies. But actually they were more interested in us and accompanied us on our walk. They were nice-looking girls and it was not long before we became interested in them. Their names were Betty Laurance and June Peacock, and they lived in a village on the outskirts of Ampthill called Husband Crawley. We had an extra show near to the Ampthill show. It was in the grounds of Woburn Abbey. The Abbey had become a country mansion and it was the home of The Duke of Bedford whose family had been the owners for many hundreds of years. The girls had said they would see us there. They didn't let us down and turned up on their bicycles and we enjoyed having the Duke's estate to roam in. We only had a short time with the girls because there was work to be done. We had to travel north for the carnival at Scunthorpe.

After Scunthorpe we had to go much further north. There was a show at Wick that was as far north as you could get in Scotland, and a show at Stranraer, which is on the west coast. To make things easy, half the team went to Wick and the other half that I was in went to Stranraer.

Stranraer was like Withernsea except for being the wrong way round and looking across the Atlantic Ocean instead of the North Sea. There was this lovely Scotch girl looking lonely. It wasn't difficult to pick up a girl when you were part of the display team. When they looked at me they were not looking at a funny dwarf, but a tall handsome man, who was a dashing and daring stunt rider.

We walked to where the boats came in and we talked. I enjoyed talking to her and listening to her lovely Scotch voice. We walked to the water's edge on the sand. It was a lovely fine night and the sea was calm. The gentle rippling and lapping of the tiny waves were making me homesick. She said, 'I'm not going home yet, I'm staying here until 3 o'clock.' This puzzled my feeble brain because I could tell she was a decent girl and she didn't have a bucket and spade or a ball to play with. She looked across the calm water and pointed a finger at a little lump of it and said, 'My dad is out there fishing and he is not coming home until 3 o'clock.'

We sat there on the sands and talked until eventually we could see a fishing boat coming to shore. I felt sad when I said goodbye and gave her a kiss. Like other girls who became our companions while on shows, when you said goodbye, it was forever, and you never saw them again. But now and again they turn up in your memory to give you a little sadness.

Chapter 24

THE WALL OF DEATH

We left Scotland and did a couple of shows before going to Tring in Herts. We were near Ampthill, but too far away to be able to see Betty and Joan. We had a long journey for the show at Perth. So I had a lot of time to do some thinking. I could have been riding for Wembley Speedway, but that didn't bother me such a lot. I was very conscientious over my stunt riding and I kept myself fit and healthy. I wanted to do a Jimmy with no hands on the handlebars, and the swallow backwards. Both these tricks would take a lot of concentration and perfect balance.

Before I became a member of the Signals team, there was an American who was being billed at Wembley and other big stadiums, as the World Champion. We were expecting to go to America and I was hoping to challenge him. As the Signals team were the best in the world I thought it was time we had an individual world champion. Unfortunately the engagements were cancelled due to the threat of war.

From Perth we travelled south to the 1st Cadet Div, Tattoo at Southshields. This was the type of show that I liked the best. I admired the cadets; they were very smart and well trained. Then there was military music that I always enjoyed.

At the time when we were training at Catterick, Spud Thompson said he was 'glad' to have me as a friend as 'I didn't go to pubs to drink beer and wouldn't be able to afford to'. But when we started on shows, Spud went with the rest of the team. I didn't mind so much because I often had a girl for company. I had a very nice girl for a companion at the Cadet's Tattoo. It is essential to have someone to talk to at shows like that. I was very lucky because all the girls who I met at shows were decent and intelligent.

When we went to Cleethorpes I was near home. If I had a boat it would not have taken me long to get home. But I didn't wish to go home. We were happy to be at Cleethorpes. To make it seem more like a holiday we were staying on a campsite, a lovely change from hotels.

I became friendly with the 'wall of death' riders, two men and a girl. Their 'wall of death' was on the promenade. Planks of wood are used in the construction of a 'wall of death' and built in sections for easy dismantling to transport to different fairgrounds. Shaped like a cylinder, the wall is vertical apart from five or six feet from the floor. This bottom part is at forty degrees from the vertical wall and acts as a ramp. There is a safety rail around the inside, 12 inches from the top. There is a stage fixed to the outside of the wall. This is where the riders are between the shows to persuade people to come inside. There will be two or three motorbikes, and one will have its rear wheel on two rollers and a rider will do stunts on it with the wheel spinning. He has to have a good sense of balance. Also, to do stunts on the wall needs a lot of skill. Steps lead to a balcony, which circles a wall. From there the spectators look over the top of the wall and down to see the riders. I had a ride on one, but I didn't attempt any stunts. I thought the wall looked larger than it really is, and the air pressure due to turbulence puts pressure on your head and neck. You have to sit up straight to counteract this pressure.

The worst thing about falling off is the bike bashing into you. One day a lady was leaning over the top of the wall, her handbag hanging from the straps and the bag a bit below the safety rail. One of the lads' front wheels hit the bag and the bike went into a big wobble and the lad fell off. When he hit the deck he dared not look up because he expected the bike to fall on him. But it didn't fall because a footrest had got hooked under the safety rail. They lowered the bike down with a rope. The bike wasn't damaged, but the lad had broken ribs.

The Indian bikes were slow and old-fashioned, but they made a big noise that added to the thrills and excitement.

Our display went very well and so we were well cheered and applauded. As usual we spent a lot of time signing autographs on programmes and sometimes on scraps of paper. Our two days at this lovely seaside town were nearly over.

During the second evening, two or three of us from the team spent it with some of the lads and lasses who were on holiday. We were sitting in a circle. A girl who was very sociable came and sat down beside me and we got on very well.

The next morning I had to leave the camp early to go to the railway station to help with loading the props and luggage onto the train. As soon as I had left, this girl came to wish me farewell, but of course it was too late. I was told she was very upset and couldn't stop crying. If that girl reads my book at least she will know that I haven't forgotten her.

Next we went to Durham for the Shilden Show. We had some time for practising and I was getting on well with my new trick, the Swallow, backwards. This trick consisted of setting off in the normal riding position. Setting the twist grip (which had a built in ratchet to keep the throttle constant). Then standing on the footrests moving the left foot to the rear footrest, and bringing the right leg over to the left side of the bike and putting my right foot on the forward left footrest.

In this position the rider is stood on the side of the bike and needs good balance and concentration. To complete the trick the left leg comes over to the right side of the bike and the foot on the forward foot-rest. The rider is then stood on the bike facing backwards. Next you lie on the bike with arms outstretched, nose over the back mudguard and feet against the headlamp.

I don't think anyone has done this trick since I did it. I wasn't allowed to do it in a show. It was too dangerous as the rider hardly had any control over the bike.

If I had been educated and learnt posh words I would be able to describe The Royal Signals Team in a manner suited to the brilliant performance of everyone. We were at Jersey for their agricultural show. To a lot of people and myself this was 'The Greatest Show on Earth'!

The combined display with bikes and horses was to end at the end of the 1936 displays, but it was decided that it would end at the Jersey show. This was because the Jersey people were horse lovers and they had a world-famous horse jumping team. I think another reason was that Jersey Agricultural Show was most likely the best.

The most difficult trick was the moving bar. There were two motorbike riders with pillion passengers holding the bar. They moved off from one end of the arena and at the same time Henry and horse left the other end. They met in the centre of the arena. The jump had to be very long and high enough to cover the bar, and the timing had to be perfectly accurate. Henry's jumps were perfect every time he performed, giving a demonstration of his brilliant horse riding.

I must give credit to the bike riders. It needed a lot of skill to drive in a straight line, the exact distance apart and go at the correct speed to reach the centre of the arena at the same time as horse and rider.

The horse riders and the horses were excellent in the figure rides and various jumps, considering it had been about a year since the last combined team.

Another trick that proved the excellent horse training involved four men, two horses and a motorbike. The two motorcyclists set off, followed by the horses and riders. Each rider had the end of a pole. The pillion rider grabbed the pole to transfer himself from the bike to the moving pole.

Patch and Tintack were favourites with the young spectators. They were well trained and they performed with lots of courage with jumping motorbikes.

As we were at Jersey for one week, it was like a good holiday in spite of having three shows per day. I remember the excellent dance hall near the beach. I thought it very romantic.

Our next show was at Hastings. On 1 September, sadly we had reached the last month of the tour. I loved Hastings, but I never went back to visit its lovely town. We went from Hastings to Yorkshire for The Townsmen's Association Show at Scarborough. We lodged in the barracks. I think that was to get us familiar with army life before we went back to Catterick. It isn't far to Scarborough from Withernsea on a motorbike. But my youngest brother Alan turned up on a rickety old pushbike. After we had finished our show for that day and Alan was preparing for the long journey home, someone came in with a mattress and someone else had bedding. So Alan had a comfortable night's sleep and a good breakfast before tackling the long ride home.

The show field was on the cliff top and it sloped upwards and parallel to the cliff. When you began your trick riding you adjusted your speed. It was difficult to judge the slope and so if you had too many revs you were heading for the cliff top and fighting to keep control.

Spud Thompson was doing the ladder trick. By the time he had reached the top end of the field and was turning to look out to sea, he was at the top of the ladder. He was going at a frightening speed. It was a long way from the top of the ladder to the twist grip. Spud hung on like a leech and only just escaped going for a paddle. It took him quite a good way going along the cliffs before he gained control.

We stayed in Yorkshire for the show at Masham, and from there we went to Middlesborough. The last show was at Belle Vue Speedway on 25 September. There were two Yorkshire lads riding for Belle Vue Speedway Team; they were Eric and Oliver Langton. I did not know them personally at that time, but I got to know them very well after the war, especially Oliver.

At that time, small four-wheeled cars raced on the cinders as well as bikes. I was looking at the cars in the pits when I saw a very large jet-black mechanic working on a rear brake of the car that the World Champion drove. His hands were very large and working so delicately on the brake. I thought, *this driver knows how to choose his mechanics*. If I had been in need of an operation on my brain I would have asked for that mechanic.

From Manchester we travelled to Catterick camp. The good time was over and we were back in barracks. It had been the best time in my life and I looked forward to repeating it in 1938. But after a short time my hopes were shattered to smithereens. I was posted to Aldershot.

When I said, 'goodbye' to the lads, it really was goodbye, because I never saw any of them again. I heard of Signalman J Vitale and Signalman E Naylor, getting killed in the war. Sometime after the war, in a letter Henry wrote, he gave me the bad news that Signalman R Boddington had died. He had been in the display team for three or four years. He was a brilliant trick rider and a smashing lad and good friend.

When I was leaving Catterick, they gave me a one-way rail ticket to Aldershot. They were a bit thick and didn't think I would want a ride back to Yorkshire.

Aldershot was what I expected it to be a lot of idiots playing soldier. I think they were preparing for a war. They had old-fashioned ideas, ancient equipment and outdated manuals. They looked good on parade from a distance. It didn't take me long to find out that they never called the role on big parades. I slipped up badly when I went to Catterick and I was asked about my religion. I told them I was C of E. Consequently my name was down for the big church parade. One of the lads told me to go to the office straightaway and tell them they had made a mistake. Therefore, my religion changed from C of E to Wesleyan. I don't know if this will make any difference when I go to heaven because surely they will want you in different groups for organising flights etc.

The priority job was getting myself some wheels. I went to see Claud Rye at his motorcycle shop in Fulham Road. We talked a bit about motorbike racing and speedway because he was an ex-world champion. I told him I wanted a little bike for going home on and a good bike for the Isle of Man. He couldn't help me with the latter wish, but he had a 250cc Ariel. It looked to be in good condition and it needed to be as it was costing me £5. It wasn't a bit difficult to get the weekend off, as I was getting in their way. It was good to get away from the military eggheads and heading for Ampthill and then to Withernsea. There was lots of lovely country between Aldershot and Ampthill and the Ariel was buzzing along merrily. I saw Betty and we went to see Joan Peacock and Joan's mother. Then we went to see their friend Kate White. Although it was getting on for back-end, the weather was fine.

After a good meal at Kate's, I set off for Withernsea and arrived there, after a very pleasurable and trouble-free ride. The ride back to Aldershot was also without trouble.

I went to see Claud Rye again, and as soon as I entered his shop he said, 'I have just the right bike for you.' He certainly had; a Manx Norton in beautiful condition. The price was £15; of course I would have to pay weekly. He made out a form for me to send to Ernie for him to sign to guarantee the payments. After waiting a few days the letter arrived with the form. That meant that I would be going to Ampthill and Withernsea on my Manx Norton and I would have a good bike for racing. Actually it didn't mean that at all, because when I looked at the form there was no signature from Ernie.

From then on I thought Ernie was mean and I didn't like him one bit. Then after quite a long time it came to me that Ernie would not have anything to do with West Park because the road was lined with trees. So I couldn't blame him for not wanting me to ride in the Manx or TTs.

The Ariel was going all right, but I couldn't tell that the driving clutch plates were nearing the end of their life. One day when I was halfway between Aldershot and Withernsea, I was just ambling along because of the Ariel being only a 250cc, when a girl came up alongside of me in a small sports car. She wanted to have a race so I couldn't refuse. The car and the bike had the same maximum speed. There were a few bends to make it more interesting. She was a good driver and we were enjoying this bit of daftness when my transmission disappeared. The driving extensions on the clutch plates that looked like the top of a castle wall had worn away. The only drive I had was a little friction that disappeared when I tried to exceed walking pace.

I didn't have any money with me, not even for a drink in a café. It became dark and I was still slowly moving along with the engine just ticking over. But all the time I was getting nearer to Withernsea. It became light and I reached the new concrete road at Rawcliff to Goole. When I was through Hull I was nearly home, but my petrol tank was almost empty. It was just 12 o'clock, midday when I reached home, pegging out for a drink and a big meal.

Soon after the meal and a rest, the bike and I were ready for the return journey. Ernie knew his stuff about these things and he said, 'Set off in the morning and go to RAF Scampton (I think that is right) and ask Stan to ring up and tell them that you are having trouble with your bike and will be late arriving.' Stan was a big noise, a warrant officer in fact. They had to take notice of him.

When I arrived at the barracks I was told the commanding officer wanted to see me. I didn't like that, not even a little bit. The beds in the army cells are not a bit comfortable and at that time I needed a good bed and plenty of sleep.

The old gentleman shook my hand and said, 'Well done Nicholson.' Not knowing much about these things I thought, *is that what they do when you are going to be shot at dawn*. He called me a fine chappie with lots of initiative and that I was a splendid soldier. I was trying to visualise what the OBE looked like when he said, 'Dismiss.' (That is army language for 'P' off).

It soon became winter; in fact, the winter of 1937 was the worst winter for many years. During the worst night of that winter, the little Ariel skated all the way from Withernsea to Aldershot. I was due in barracks at 7.30 and was there for 7.15. I was ready for bed, but I had to get ready for work. The work was riding a motorbike. It's a blooming wicked world.

One horrible and misty night when I had been home, I was lost on the outskirts of London. I was looking for a building or factory or anything I could recognise, when I saw Wembley Stadium. So I knew where I was, but I didn't have a clue about how to get to Aldershot. It was 5 o'clock then and 7.45 when I reached the Signal's barracks.

I went to see Betty as often as I could. Things had become romantic and we were going to have three children. I was looking forward to the arrival of spring to enjoy the lovely countryside where Betty and Joan lived. This demonstrates the agony and the misery one goes through when you want to do your bit for king and country. I was put on a draft to go to India. The boat would be sailing from Southampton on the 8 March. The length of service was five years. You get less than that for manslaughter.

I went home on leave and I was lucky that darling brother Pug was also on leave. He was going to Hong Kong and that was supposed to be a lot better than India, so Pug took the pleasure in taking the 'mickey' out of me.

I left home a day or two early so that I could spend some time with Betty. I told her not to write to me because I would be away for five years. She promised she would not write. What a stupid conversation for two young people to have when in love.

Pug had a collision with a dog and broke his arm. This caused him to miss the boat to Hong Kong.

When I arrived at Southampton and on the quay I was just looking at this boat and wondering if the Romans used it for shipping stolen cattle to Italy. Suddenly I heard someone shouting out to me. I looked up to see Pug hanging over the rail of this luxury troop carrier. Why must you get all the bad luck in one piece?

Chapter 25

BOAT AND TRAIN JOURNEY TO
RAWALPINDI

It was a lovely trip to India especially going through the Bay of Biscay. Even the bloody ship was seasick. When you are going on a ship, it is essential to have a nice book to read. The army eggheads know this; they are not daft. We all got a beautiful book to keep. It contained about two million diseases that you would most likely catch in India. The weather was very cold, but when you were reading your lovely present it made you sweat with fright. After three weeks of this lovely and interesting boat voyage, we reached Calcutta and we had to disembark with sad hearts. We lined up on the quay and were counted to see if anyone had fallen overboard. What they meant was they wanted to know how many had committed suicide. I don't know why they wanted to know this because no one would want to go back to the Bay of Biscay to look for them.

Next we had a very long journey through gorgeous India. The carriages were lovely and comfortable. Some readers will have seen the ones in the Royal Train at York. They were not quite like that.

We were pegging out with hunger. An Indian entered the carriage with a big bunch of bananas. We scoffed the lot. Some official waited until the last banana had gone to Pug's greedy-guts and announced an urgent warning: Do not eat any of the bananas on this train because they contain cholera. You need a hell of a lot of Nurse Harvey's to shift that. None of us got cholera I am glad to say.

A train was going by in the opposite direction with Indian passengers. The carriages were packed and people were clinging to the sides and some were riding on top. We stopped at a station and there were swarms of hungry children begging for food. This was part of the British Empire and it was a disgrace to Britain. I was there to serve the king and country, but I would have liked to have served the king to the lions.

After a long horrible journey of two or three days, we reached Royal Signal's Barracks at Rawalpindi. Most of us were stationed at the head quarters of the 1st Division Signals. Pug's journey hadn't finished as he was being stationed at Peshawar, which was near the Afghanistan border.

The barracks were very old; you had to go up about a dozen steps. There was a veranda all the way along the front. All this overlooked the dreaded drill square, and behind the drill square were the barracks of the Indian troops.

The people in England used to say that soldiers serving in India would go mad due to the hot sun. When we entered the barrack rooms the old soldiers, who were putting on a show, greeted us. They pretended to be insane and they were good actors, so much so that we thought, *that is how we will become!*

Our stomachs were ready for some packing and we couldn't get to the cookhouse quick enough. The mess was one or two hundred yards from the barracks. The walk loosened up our legs and our bottoms because the wooden seats became uncomfortable long before the end of the journey.

When we returned to the barracks we went to the stores for bedding. It wasn't long before we were lying on our beds, as our bodies were ready for relaxing for a few hours. As I lay on my bed I looked up at the punkah. They consisted of a wooden structure reaching from one end of the room to the other.

Spaced equally were pieces of sailcloth. The wooden structure was connected to a motor by a crude connecting link that made it swing backwards and forwards. This caused the pieces of sailcloth to swing from side to side causing the air to move slightly. This load of rubbish was our cooling system.

I thought about the chap who persuaded me not to join up when I was fourteen-years-old. He was a good man and a wise man. I wondered if he had lived in these disgusting barracks.

An officer came round with the mail and gave me three letters from Betty. She had written one each week. They were very loveable letters, such a contrast to everything I had seen since I left England. I had a problem as she did agree not to write. I still thought it was stupid for a young girl to wait for someone for five years. I didn't know how I would be in five year's time. For a guess I would say absolutely bonkers.

While this problem was troubling my mind a strange thing happened... no, it wasn't strange it was horrible. Two lads came into contact with each other; they were both from the same village. One of them, a part of our group, had just arrived. The other one was going home on the next sailing after five years in India. After they had been talking for a while, the lad who was due home spoke about his girlfriend and that he couldn't get home quick enough as he was getting married.

The other lad void of tact and sympathy remarked, 'Oh! She is married. She married so and so.' That lad was as near as shooting himself than anyone had ever been.

This incident stayed in my mind. After a great deal of thought I decided to tell Betty off and make it an awful letter so that she would forget about me. As I was walking to the letterbox I was thinking I ought to tear it up into little pieces. I arrived at the letterbox with the letter in my hand and pushed it into the box. As soon as I dropped it I would have done anything to be able to retrieve it and tear it up. I never heard from my lovely girlfriend again. This illustrates the wickedness of the British government in sending young lads to a dirty and cruel country for what would normally have been the best five years of their lives.

The milkman didn't have a van for delivering dairy products. His vehicle was like an ice cream cart with a serving hatch. After making a delivery to the cookhouse he went to his pitch outside the mess room. We bought butter, cream, milk, etc, to add to our rations. India was a rogue's paradise.

There were more troops arriving from England. One of these was a young lad who served as a boy soldier. His name was Chippy Wood. He was a despatch rider and when we were at Catterick, I took him out to improve his riding and he became very good on a bike.

The two West brothers arrived and Andy from Catterick. They were linesmen and very good at their trade. For some unknown reason the West brothers seemed to be in trouble quite a lot. I think the fault was with some stupid NCO. After promotion at any cost, they were the kind of people I hated.

There were three despatch riders who I became friendly with. They were Joe Lindsley from London, Frank Browne from St John's Wood, Surrey and his cousin Bill Browne from Manchester. They were all keen motorcyclists. Our bikes were ancient Douglas and Triumph belt drive. The Nortons with 500cc side valves soon arrived. These bikes were not suitable for the rough dusty roads. Our dress was a sun hat, short-sleeved shirt, shorts, socks and boots. Hitting the deck would result in abrasions to arms and legs. I am not exaggerating when I say stupid idiots ran the army.

During the winter months the places we went to were in just a medium radius. But during the summer months all the wives and children and a few of the men went to a hill station called Upper Toper. This was very high up in the hills about forty-five miles from Rawalpindi. This was a regular run for the DRs.

We were timed on the runs because when we left a Signals office they notified the next Signals office and noted the time of leaving. Then our arrival would be noted and so on. On every run my times were the quickest. There was one road that was dug into a high and wide hill. When I was doing that run there would be hundreds of Indians sitting on the hillside to cheer me on.

The lads were complaining about the food ration. It led to a meeting with the sergeant major. After a few suggestions were put forward, I made one. It was, if the people responsible for distributing the food cut out their fiddles so that we got our full rations, we would be satisfied. The sergeant threatened me with a long stay in prison. The army prisons were horrible places so I thought that keeping my mouth shut would be a good idea. India was a rogue's paradise that could not be altered.

I strayed to the back of the barracks a few days after the meeting. I don't know why, perhaps I was just having a walk around. There was a big lad giving a small lad a good hiding. The big lad looked at me and said, 'What do you think you're looking at?' I didn't say anything. Then he said, 'If you don't clear off you will get the same.' Well for one thing I didn't like bullies nor did I like to be spoken to like that. I told him that I was not afraid of big people because the bigger they are, the harder they fall.

The big lad released his grip on the little guy who then ran away (like I should have done). As soon as I had hit the deck my brain told me there must be something wrong with my bit of theory.

Someone said to me later, 'You don't mind who you take on.' He told me the lad was a middle-weight champion, and the little lad was a mischievous little devil and was only getting what he deserved. I decided it was time I stopped living dangerously.

Frank Browne and I became very good friends. For an evening out we went to Rawalpindi to the cinema. After the cinema we dined in a café. My usual meal was a mixed grill and every item was two annas, about three pence. I would get heart, liver, sausage, beef and potato or rice. That would cost me ten annas. I think a drink would cost me two annas. The weather was always fine in the evening and it was a nice walk into Rawalpindi. We would have a steady walk back and talk about various subjects like my farm work and racing. Frank was married and had a son so he would talk about his home, family, and his job. His job was insurance and he would go round to his customers in the St John's Wood district to collect insurance payments. It was good to switch your mind from Pakistan to home.

Up on the walls of the barrack rooms there were some snakes that the soldiers killed in Topee Park. I asked how they killed them and I was told when a snake was hanging from the branch wanting to inject their venom into you, it was easy. All you had to do was to be quicker than the snake and bash its head with a heavy stick. I thought I could do that if the stick was at least 15ft long.

At holiday time, some soldiers went to Kashmir to buy silk undies to send to Britain. But some went shooting tigers. I was beginning to get an inferiority complex. There were such a lot of brave men in this room. The photos were very impressive. I liked their stance. Every crack shot would have his left boot on the ground, the other boot on the tiger's ribcage, and holding the gun perfectly plumb level in his right hand. I wondered if they had to learn this on the drill parade ground before they could go on the trip.

I asked someone to give me some details about these heroes. 'Brave my eye,' he said. 'I'll tell you what they do. They go in a tiger-proof vehicle to a stream, climb up a tree and shoot the poor tiger while it's having a drink.' Typical British sportsmen.

About twelve miles from Rawalpindi, is a statue of General Nicholson. I don't think he was any relative of mine, but someone had told some of the Indians who worked in the barracks that he was.

The general must have been good to the natives because I was treated with a lot of respect. Just a few of the soldiers treated the Indian workers badly. As an example, the tea man came and sat on the veranda. We were often ready for a cup of tea so we appreciated his presence. When someone did not pay him he told me and I made sure the poor chap got his money.

Chapter 26

SORTING OUT BENOIST AND THE
RED CAPS

I had some friends among the Indians (or Pakistan people). One of my friends was a boxer so I had plenty of training sessions. Another good friend was a language teacher. He taught me to speak Urdu as taught in schools and he also taught me to speak to the children who lived in small villages, miles from anywhere, who didn't know what a school was.

I had a friend who was a sergeant and lived in the married quarters with his wife and two young daughters. He was a very good friend, and I was often invited to go to his house for my tea and sit and talk in the evening. People who have never lived in barracks have no idea about how much soldiers miss home life.

Unfortunately this luxury ended very suddenly. My friend's wife was a lovely person and I thought my pal was very lucky. He was on guard duty one evening. It was quite late and I was walking back to the barracks. I saw a soldier climbing out of the sergeant's bedroom windows and scrambling down the drainpipe. I was shocked, but I learnt that this was only one of many 'buckshee' love affairs.

There were a lot of decent people and this includes a staff sergeant, his wife and teenage daughter. He was Scotch and in the Indian Army. The wife was English and the daughter was a very nice young lady who was very good on roller skates. She was my friend for the whole of my time in India.

I often went into Topee Park, but I never saw any snakes hanging from trees wagging their fangs at me. But one day I did see a snake and it was massive. It had been crossing the road and a car had bashed the snake's head. When I carried it into the room the lads looked stunned. My story of bashing its head made me a hero.

I thought about those recruiting posters on the advertising boards in Hull that lured little country joskins to want to join the army. This little joskin was in the football, hockey, and boxing teams. If he had become an officer he would have been horse riding, playing polo and tennis and boozing and eating the best of food in the officer's mess and at fine parties.

When I was writing about Easington, I told you about being on high cliffs at Dimlington. An elderly man who was with us said, 'I can remember two fields out there.' Although the cliffs were high it did not mean that the cliffs wouldn't be washed away. The sea washes away the bottom half of the cliffs, leaving the top overhanging. Hot weather makes cracks, and the rain and the high tides fill the cracks and large pieces of earth fall into the sea.

In later years a gas rig was taken out to sea off Dimlington and a gas complex was built on the cliff top.

At Withernsea they built a pumping station in the middle of Withernsea. The sewage was pumped to the end of the south promenade. From there it went along the top of the cliff for so far and then turned off for Holmpton Road.

Then a miracle happened, the engineers of great skill and learning became aware of the fact that the cliffs get washed away. With an enormous amount of money, sea defences were made to stop the sea.

I mention this because a similar situation was happening in India. The Japanese had conquered half of China and had bypassed Singapore and were heading for Malaysia, Thailand, Indonesia and India.

The Germans were conquering Europe and the Italians were reinforcing their armies in Abyssinia and Eritrea to take over Egypt.

What were we doing in India, absolutely nothing? In the same way as the engineers thought the cliffs would defend their installations, the government and army thought the navy and the shore guns would be able to defend Singapore. How stupid and inefficient those people were.

We had a very good football team and also a good hockey team. One soldier used to be the athletics champion of his county. He was good at football and hockey. His position was outside right. That was also my position. Fortunately he preferred tennis, and I played in both football and hockey teams.

We reached the finals in the football tournament and I was very upset when the team was picked because I had been dropped from it so that the county champ could play. The same thing happened with the hockey final. He received two medals, which I earned. The army could do rotten tricks.

The boxing team were training for a big boxing tournament. I was a lightweight and I would come up against the lightweight champion of India. So this was one bout that we would lose. We had another lightweight in the team, but I think he was going to go up a weight. He was a boxer called Jimmy Gentleman. Jimmy would be a good match for the champion so they decided to let Jimmy fight him and I would go down to Bantamweight. I had to cut down on the delicious army food to get my weight down. After all this palaver the boxing tournament was cancelled.

I had a friend who was a big tough lad. That's the kind of friend you want when you are little. He was in trouble and had to face charges. The officer handling it was a bit of an idiot, which wasn't unusual amongst British officers. He made some remark that my friend didn't like, so my friend got hold of the table and put it on his lap. 'Ha,' said the officer with much glee, 'that's the chappie for that vacancy.' He was talking about the vacancy that had just come up for a sergeant in the Red Caps. So my friend became the boss of the Red Caps, which made him a more valuable friend to me.

Soon after this, one of my friend's lunatics stopped me for speeding. I revved up and let the clutch in: he had never moved as quickly in all his life. About a week later the lunatic came to me in the street and wanted a fight. But since I last saw him I had broken my wrist skating and I had a big plaster on it.

When I was back on my bike the Red Caps were waiting for me and reported me to my unit for speeding on three occasions. I told my friend about it and he said, he would 'deal' with them. I bet he did. I reckon he would have got them in the boxing ring to knock some sense into their stupid heads. I never had any more trouble with the Red Caps.

The worst sneak was a French lad called Benoist. He could sing and he had an officer friend and they went to rich people's houses and Froggy sang to them. I was teaching myself automobile engineering, as my ambition was to become a designer and work for Vauxhalls at Luton. Therefore, I had taken my books to India. Froggy asked me to teach him as he did not know much about it and he would teach me French. I didn't want to learn French, but nevertheless I began to teach him automobile engineering. What I didn't know at the time was a mechanic's course was coming up. This was a normal step up for despatch riders. I reckon his officer friend would have told him about it. Later I was told about the course and I was picked to go on it and also Pug.

The snivelling Froggy talked about this to his snivelling officer friend. They decided that as Froggy was a lot younger than I was, it was more beneficial to king and country to let him go on a course especially as he was well up on automobile engineering. That was a load of bull.

Pug knew nothing about this and helped sniveller with his practical work and so he passed the course.

One day someone told me that Second Lieutenant Benoist was coming back home and they told me the time 'Sir' would arrive so that I could meet him and congratulate him on his promotion. I was only too glad to oblige.

Sir arrived in a horse-drawn gig or tonga. He was pleased to see me and was the first to speak. He said, 'Nicholson take my cases to the officers' mess.' I explained in detail what I thought he was and how much I hated him and where I would like him to go. I used my full vocabulary of swear words and repeated each one about ten times over.

His trembling hands picked up his suitcases and they were shaking so much I thought the catches would open by themselves and tip out his silk dressing gown and silk knickers. I have no idea what happened to him because I never saw him again. If he had shot himself, he would have done at least one good thing in his life.

Getting rid of Benoist was one good thing, but putting up with his friends in high places was something different. Benoist and his officer had been in the wrong so they couldn't do anything about that bit of the story. There was no justice in the British Army. That is how officers in the First World War could send thousands of innocent soldiers to their death at dawn.

Another soldier and I became ill with dysentery so were taken to the military hospital in Rawalpindi. After a week or so we were almost better, but very hungry. We thought it was a good idea to escape and get some food. The ward was fairly high up, but someone had fitted a drainpipe near my window, especially for lads to escape, I thought. So we scrambled down it. We went to a restaurant. We were careful about choosing the food because we didn't want to make ourselves ill again. We decided on toast thinking it would be all right. But in fact it was the worst thing we could have. We staggered back to the hospital in a lot of pain. We had been thinking we would be able to scramble back up the drainpipe and slyly get back into bed. We couldn't have stood on a brick without falling off. So two very poorly soldiers had to go through the main entrance and admit that they had been very naughty and very silly. The doctor gave us a good telling-off, but he was decent enough to keep it from the army people. Not long after I had returned to duty I was sent to Upper Toper and stayed until the families moved back to Rawalpindi.

One day I was resting on my bed as I had covered a lot of miles over rough roads. Some of the lads were talking about different runs and the subject came to a very dangerous road where you climbed so high that you finished up among snow. The time you started a run and the time you reached the next signal office was actually noted and written down.

The lads discussed these timing figures, as everyone knew their own performance. They wondered how much faster the run could be completed and someone suggested a time for this. Most of them said it couldn't be done, but one lad said ' he thought Nick could do it'. The time they were talking about wasn't much faster than I had already done.

My bike was always well tuned as you could expect an out-of-date side valve to be. So I just had to wait to go on that run. When the time came I felt like breaking records and I did the climb in good time.

Coming down was quite different from going up. Your speed depended on how well you could control a heavy motorbike down the side of a mountain. The road was cut into the side of the mountain so there were landslides and boulders to contend with. I had reached a section where there was a sharp left turn and about one hundred yards of straight road. Then there was a ridge in the mountainside that made a right turn and went into a left curve. From the straight section and a very long way down there was a hospital just waiting for idiots on motorbikes.

I needed to be in the middle of the road after I had gone round the left turn, but I was going just a bit too fast and I finished up right on the edge with the bike wobbling badly. The front wheel hit a small boulder that caused me to turn the twist grip slightly and increase my speed. This pulled the bike out of the wobble, but the right turn was rushing towards me. By a miracle I got round it. It was a most horrible experience. I dared not stop to rest because of the road being so high. I just rode the bike very slowly, but I was very scared and relieved when I got to the end of the road.

I did not do that run again, because I had to take charge of the transport that we had for taking the families back to Rawalpindi. This was not a despatch rider's job, but I didn't mind doing it.

The first job was sorting the office out; it was a mess. There weren't any accident forms so that was a priority job hoping I could get some before someone had an accident. But although I rang several times to army units I was unable to get any. The absence of any forms would be someone's neglect.

One of my drivers had an accident and I was in trouble. The officer was one of the ignorant types. Anyway I carried on with the job and everything went well without any accident forms, and everyone was transported back to their homes in Rawalpindi without any trouble.

I was glad to be on my motorbike again, but I was soon in more trouble. There was a unit of soldiers posted to Afghanistan, which was a regular procedure because they only went for six months. The despatch rider was a lad who couldn't care less about his bike and it was in an awful mess. He had to have a bike that was in good condition so they gave him mine and I had to have his.

Before I had a chance to do anything with his wreck I was put on special despatch rider duty. This consisted of going to the unit headquarters dressed in your Sunday best of tunic, horse-riding breeches and your stupid spurs. You had to stand by for these special messages. The messages would most likely read like this: 1st Div Signals officer's mess to 'A' Signals officers' mess. Message begins, 'We are having a party at the officer's mess. There are six lovely striptease artists coming and we have lots of food and drinks. Over to you, Over.'

I set off to deliver some of this rubbish when the bike had a heart attack or something like that and the poor gentlemen didn't get their messages.

I was called extremely inefficient and was dropped down to lower pay. This was hard on me because old Ette was getting a good chunk out of my pay.

Chapter 27

THE POOR PEOPLE

In winter the climate on the plains is similar to England in summer. Therefore, we were comfortable in Rawalpindi. But the summer was very hot. When we were riding down the slopes from Upper Toper it was like riding into a large oven. When you got off the bike the sweat poured down your face making you long for an English breeze.

One very hot Saturday we were listening to the ancient punkahs in the barrack room groaning like an old gate. The flaps we relied on for a bit of breeze were hardly moving. We had a soldier who was an expert on such things, or at least that's what he said. He climbed up to the motor armed with spanners and screwdrivers, muttering, 'I'll speed 'em up.' After all he was an expert.

The punkahs ground to a halt and there was nothing the poor bloke could do to get them moving again. Someone had to get the 'punkah-wallah', the man who would serve the purpose. He was a very nice man. He said he was sorry, but he didn't work on Saturdays and Sundays.

When the punkahs were going, the flaps hardly moved and their old joints groaned saying, 'Yer can't take it, yer can't take it.' But we would have given anything, even the sergeant major, to get the groaners in action again.

I was still playing football and hockey and still not getting any medals. I liked to go skating and wished I could skate as good as my friend. Perhaps my body and legs were too short for me to become a good skater.

I liked walking to Toppe Park. No one was interested enough to walk with me. I felt sure that snakes on the barrack room walls had been bought at the cantonment. That meant I was the only one to 'kill' a snake.

We used to get poor people from the places having famine. I always felt sorry for them and gave them something if I could. One young woman, who I thought would be a teenager and her little brother, followed me into the park. She said she would send her little brother away for a while if I gave her two annas, five pence. I would have given her the money with pleasure, but I didn't even have one anna with me. She seemed to be a very decent person. Someone would take advantage of her. I watched them walk slowly down the road and I wondered how long it would be before they got a drink and something to eat. I thought about the royalty who were friends with the Agar Khan. Would they be thinking of these poor people while they were at their expensive parties?

While I have been on despatch rider duties I have seen women stop at the side of the road to give birth. Later on my way back I have seen the same woman trudging along the road carrying her newborn baby. She would most likely be twenty miles or so from any village. This was part of the British Empire and I did not feel proud to be British.

There was an Indian village on the way to the Signals unit. I would stop close to it, and within a few minutes I would be surrounded by dozens of children. We would have a good chinwag and then I would be on my way. They were just like the children at home except they were a different colour.

Frank Browne went to school in Rawalpindi to learn to speak the language and so learnt to speak posh. Sometimes when I spoke he would laugh at me because it sounded funny to him.

One day we were just strolling along and an officer was coming towards us. As he was walking past us we gave him a real sergeant major type of salute.

There was the dhobi's (washerman) donkey at the roadside and it lifted its head and looked at us. I spoke to it in its language and I'm sure it smiled at me. I said, 'Let's give donk a good salute Frank.' So we gave it a smasher. We glanced back and bloody hell the young officer was looking at us. We tried to think of a good excuse for saluting the donkey. We thought of plenty, but none suitable to tell the CO.

After a while Frank Browne said, 'That donkey wasn't smiling at you, it was laughing at the way you spoke its language.' I'd had enough of this so I said, 'Come on Browne we're going for a ride.'

We got our bikes out and put our armbands on to let people know we were on duty and cleared off into the wilds. We pulled up at the village and my little friends came running to us. Frank spoke to them and they didn't know what he was on about and Frank hadn't a clue what they were talking about. After I had a natter we went back to the camp and put the bikes away. We took our armbands off to let the people know that we had come off duty.

One lad spent a lot of time reading an army instruction manual. We couldn't understand this because the lad was normal. Someone thought he might have a dirty book disguised as a manual. That was a good bit of detective work because that is exactly what it was, *Lady Chatterley's Lover*, in fact.

That lad wasn't a sex maniac and neither were the lads who couldn't wait to read the only sensible textbook we had. Sex is a very important part of life and it was cruel to send young lads of eighteen to nineteen years of age to India for five years. So sex was a problem or rather sexual diseases were.

When I was fourteen-years-old I remember the stinking rich people who had luxury parties. They had lots of good rich food and no hard work. If they were not sex maniacs they certainly acted as if they were.

At that time a lady Member of Parliament suggested that soldiers coming from India should wear armbands as most of them had VD and this would warn the respectable British ladies. As far as I know she couldn't care a damn about the soldiers and I don't think she suggested any ideas to benefit the lads.

There were brothels where the soldiers could go. Frank Browne and I were out walking one day and we were passing the end of a street where there were brothels. We decided to go and have a look.

There were six girls and they had a cubicle each for them to do their work. They were all looking very pleased. As we passed the first girl the smile went and it was the same with the second girl, third, fourth, and fifth. When we were passing the last girl she gave us a mouthful of choice English swear words and said, 'What's wrong haven't you got a ****?'

These girls looked clean to us and may have been all right. The VD came from rough quarters. Soldiers who were drunk became victims of bad men who took them to their filthy headquarters and within a week of worry they would find out they had got the disease, which couldn't be cured in those days.

There was a hospital where these people were taken to be treated. Someone had a brilliant idea of taking us to see these unfortunate lads. There would be no exceptions, everyone must go. I was glad my brains were better than those of the higher-ups.

When they came back they were telling me about how awful it was to see these people and especially when they saw someone who had been a friend. It must have been awful for these patients to feel that they were on exhibition to be stared at.

The lads had good intentions, but a couple of weeks later two of my friends had got drunk and woke up in a brothel in a bad area. They were extremely worried about it as they were sure they would have the disease. I told them they had been taken there to be robbed of their money and not because the women fancied them. I'm glad to say they had not caught anything. Some people had the right idea of having military brothels where a medical officer would examine the girls. Unfortunately the church would not let them do this. The church had a lot of hypocrites.

Many months later when I was wounded in Italy I was taken to an Italian parson's house. He wanted to get into bed with me. I told him what I thought of him and a short time later he said, 'Who are you to say it is wrong? When student parsons go to college they pair up and sleep together.' If I'd had my revolver with me there would have been one less filthy pervert in the world.

I am not including army padres. I can't speak more highly of them. When we were in action there was no one with more courage than them. They were very kind and understanding and a wonderful help when we were in difficulty.

If I'd had some cash when I was in India I would have liked to have gone somewhere for a holiday. I only saw the places I went to on duty. There was Kashmir, world famous for silk. Agra, the town of the Taj Mahal, and Amrista, where the Sikh temple stands.

With a little bit of luck they would have given me my holidays in the middle of the monsoons. When the rains are about to start you are almost in darkness and then the sky is lit up by terrific thunderstorms. Then the rain comes down and it pours and pours for a month. It was much worse than a British holiday season.

Murray Hills is the name of a hill station, which has just dropped from my brain. It is a place where soldiers' families went during summer months. I have only mentioned Upper Toper when perhaps I should have mentioned Murray Hills.

I think the only place where you could go and forget that you were in India was the YMCA. I admired and was very grateful to the ladies who came to mother us in a way. They served us with cups of tea and cakes and entertained us in a way. One of them played the piano and we sang hymns mostly. You couldn't have had a bigger contrast with the barrack room. But you had to watch that you didn't get too religious. One lad became really bonkers and I wonder if Jesus helped him in the war.

I had a crash and a terrible tragedy followed it. I went on a DR run; there and back was about seventy-five miles. I was about halfway to my destination when the crash happened at a corner. An old man was crossing the road and I swerved and missed him, but I hit the deck.

When we went on these runs we were lonely. You passed a village now and again and saw the natives with their sheep and goats and a donkey now and again carrying a large load. You also saw bullock carts going very slowly with the drivers asleep. All these things were dangerous hazards to the despatch rider as well as having a heavy bike and no suspension except the out-of-date front forks. The tyres were too narrow and the roads were narrow and uneven and covered with thick dust. When you crashed you were on your own. There was no one to help you, as some of them would rather knife you. The army couldn't afford to give you a Red Cross box containing bandages, acraflavine for abrasions or painkillers.

I had suffered extreme abrasions because we had no protective clothing. So I had to ride to a hospital, which was not far from the signals office that I was going to. After being bandaged and rested I got up to carry on with my duty of taking messages to the signals office and getting messages for taking to Rawalpindi. A despatch rider must deliver his messages as soon as possible. It says so in the book. But the medics had other ideas and told me I wasn't going anywhere. But I did go somewhere; I rode back to Rawalpindi.

After a run, in fact as soon as you had finished your duty, you had to write in your mileage record book, the number of miles of the outward journey and the distance coming back and give the mileage of the completed journey. I managed to complete this bit of important nonsense and collapsed in a heap on the floor. I did not know anything else until I came round in hospital.

I was in hospital for a couple of weeks and then returned to barracks. I was shocked when I was told I had been put on a charge. I faced a pig-headed officer. The charge was that I hadn't made out my mileage correctly. Pig-headed said, 'How is it that the distance there was further than the distance coming back?' I was at a disadvantage because I hadn't seen this mileage book since I collapsed. Pig-headed said, 'If you haven't got the ability to write down your mileage correctly you are not fit for DR duty.' So I was grounded. On these small charges there was nothing like justice or someone to help you defend yourself. You could be perfectly innocent and there was nothing you could do about it. This officer could have been Benoist's friend. I was off DR duty for quite a long time so I didn't get to see the mileage record book. When I did get back to duty I did see the record book.

The pig-headed officer was right. I had made the outward journey two miles longer than the return journey. That was because I had been to the hospital.

Unfortunately a guy named Chippy Wood died. The stupid officer and a corporal who should have had their heads examined, or blown off, were partly responsible. There was one run that we considered more dangerous than any and should not have been done by a lone rider. I got to the DR garage as quick as I could to find the doors locked. I ran to the guardroom and asked for a key to the garage. They said, 'There isn't one.' I found the corporal and told him I wanted to get a bike to go after Chippy and I was told I couldn't have a bike because I was grounded. Therefore, I told him to get on a bike and go after him. There was no way I could get a bike. All I could do was play hell up. One and a half hours later after Chippy was due back, some of the DRs went to look for him. They found his body by the roadside.

I wanted to tell Chippy's parents the truth about what happened, but I thought it would only add to their suffering. Chippy had only been in India for a short time, but I knew him when I was at Catterick camp. He was a boy soldier training to be a despatch rider. We were very good friends and I helped him with his training. His motorcycle riding became very good. Because of being called 'Chippy' I cannot remember his Christian name.

When the war came I was expected to kill German soldiers whom I didn't know. Just for starters, why didn't they let me shoot a few people I did know? I was unlucky to have another accident at the end of August 1939. I rode to a hospital, put my bike in the porch and went into the ward to be admitted with extensive abrasions on the left forearm and the left thigh.

The following day after I had my treatment of being painted with acroflavine and sprayed with tannic acid, the lad in the next bed said, 'I'll bet you will never ride a bike again.' I told him that I would be riding very soon, in fact after dinner, because I was going to entertain him in the hospital grounds with some trick riding. Soon after that I realised it was stupid. I didn't feel like trick riding, and I didn't want to damage myself anymore. As well as that I would be in real trouble. But I had made a promise.

After dinner I went to the porch to get my bike. But it wasn't there; it had been taken to Rawalpindi. I never even dreamed that there would be a time when I was pleased to have a motorbike taken away from me.

The hospital was BMH Gharial. I had been riding from Upper Toper to Rawalpindi. I was discharged on 20 May.

Things were quite different to what they were after my last fall. I wondered if the officer and corporal had been in trouble. The following is a short statement of the circumstances of the case:

> Whilst preceding from Upper Toper to Gharial the sidestand of the motorcycle dropped lifting the back wheel off the ground while rounding a corner.

Report by Commanding Officer

Q: Was the individual in the performance of military duty?

A: Yes

Q: Was it due to his negligence?

A: No

Q: Was anyone else to blame?

A: No

Q: Court of enquiry (I) has any been. (II) Will any be held?

A: (I) No (II) No

I was in hospital till 3 September, when the Prime Minister broadcast to the nation, 'We are at war with Germany.'

When I left hospital the signals were digging trenches. I don't know if they were to protect us from the Japanese, Germans or Italians.

The Germans were taking over countries in Europe, but no one seemed bothered. Then they attacked Poland whom we had pledged to support. So therefore we had to declare war on Germany. But we couldn't help Poland. Luckily there were a lot of Polish airmen and soldiers who had escaped from their country and were a good help to us.

Chapter 28

AFGHANISTAN

I was told that the reason for being in India was to prevent tribesmen from Afghanistan making raids on India and Pakistan for plundering. If that was true then my time in India was wasted because I never saw any tribesmen. Troops used to go on the North West Frontier as they called it, for a spell of six months. The gods must have been very good to me because I was never picked to go. Therefore, I am not qualified to write about it.

I heard a lot of tales about the Frontier and about the natives. They were fierce fighters and if they caught a British soldier they did awful things to him. There were the Gurkhas on the North West Frontier and spread about were army forts. If the Gurkhas were holding a fort and the fort was being attacked, the Gurkhas would pretend to be asleep and then the tribesmen would enter the fort and the Gurkhas would fight them with their big knives.

All this stuff mystified me and I could not understand how the troops could guard the boundary from forts scattered about enemy territory. I wondered if it was just a load of bull.

The DRs had regular runs and therefore you knew exactly where you were going and the dangers along that route. But when you were a special despatch rider your job was to take special and urgent messages, sometimes to places that were new to you. When you left the garage you wouldn't see any of the lads until you returned from your duty. In the Signal's offices there were only the radio and telephone operators. So when you got a special and urgent message for a place where you had never been to, there was no one who could give you a bit of advice about the dangers or the type of natives along the way.

Therefore, the day when I was on special DR and the office lad had handed me special messages for Peshawar, and a place in Afghanistan, a fort called Fort Lockhart, which was miles into enemy territory, I just thought, *bloody hell that looks dangerous*. I think the trip there and back was a little over 600 miles and included the Khyber Pass.

I had no trouble getting to Peshawar and my timing was good considering I had an outdated Norton. The next part of the journey was difficult as it was mountain roads all the way and became dark before I reached the Signal office. This I think was on the way to Kabul.

I handed in the messages that were for that Signal office. The operator told me I couldn't go any further. The road was closed after sundown and would not be open until sunrise.

I had important operational orders for Fort Lockhart and it was my duty to get them delivered as soon as possible. Also, I didn't take orders from the office staff. I told him I was on my way and that he must tell Peshawar that I was on my way to Fort Lockhart. He said that he would not tell them because it would cause trouble. I said, 'It will cause a lot more trouble if you don't tell them.' Before I left he promised that he would do as I said and get through to Peshawar.

The road was treacherous and the going very slow. I could not use my lights because of being in enemy territory. The tribesmen would fix rifles onto trees on the hillsides pointing to some object at the side of the road, like a boulder that was a lighter colour than the side of the mountain through which the road was cut. The trigger was pulled when the man they wanted to shoot blocked out the boulder. Therefore, putting my lights on would be like committing suicide.

Suddenly it appeared that both the tyres were punctured; it was quite a frightening thought. When I checked the tyres they were all right, but were sunk in 3 inches of sand and dust. Suddenly I saw a dark object approaching; it was a man and I was soon past him. At that time I had covered nearly 300 miles. I was very tired, very hungry and thirsty and didn't know where the hell I was or how much further I had to go.

I had to come to a sudden stop because I could see through the darkness a massive wall of barbed wire. Soldiers came to open the big gates and it took them ages because they were covered with barbed wire. I rode through the gates and the soldiers struggled to get them back into position.

The relief was enormous, after being through miles and miles of dangerous riding and constant concentration and the thought of falling into the hands of fierce tribesmen and dying an agonising death.

I went into the Signal office and asked the operator to bypass the frontier post and get Peshawar straight away because it had been on my mind that the operator had ignored my instructions to get through to Peshawar. My fears were correct and after quite a long time the operator had a grim tale to tell.

As Peshawar had not heard about me it was obvious to them that I was on the road from Peshawar to the Frontier post. Pug and three of his mates got into a small vehicle, perhaps a Land Rover and went to look for me. They had almost reached the Frontier post. There was a sharp right hand corner, which had a fence in the hope that the fence would be able to stop a vehicle or anything else from going over the side. The fence had been broken and there was evidence that something had gone over the side. It was very dark and the bottom of the drop was a long way down. They got the vehicle across the road and jacked up the back end and switched on the headlights, but they still couldn't see the end of the drop.

So three lads lifted up the back of the vehicle while the other looked over the side. But he couldn't see a smashed Norton and me. This manoeuvre almost came to a disastrous end because as there was no braking on the front wheels they nearly lost their vehicle over the side.

They were sure that I would be down at the bottom. They were also sure that I would be past mending when I was brought up. So four very downhearted and very sad lads drove back to Peshawar to tell the awful news.

Pug and mates would have reached base when I was about two miles from the fort, because they had only just reported their adventures when the operator received the messages from Fort Lockhart.

When I was leaving the next morning there were soldiers and armoured cars lining the road almost to Peshawar.

I don't think I need say that I was pleased when I arrived back at Rawalpindi after covering 600 miles of rough and dangerous roads. I don't think anyone at Rawalpindi knew anything about the journey. I didn't get told off and neither did I get a medal.

But now I think of it I may get a medal. I haven't sent for my war medals yet. I still have the card for sending in to claim my medals and lately I have been thinking about sending it. Yes, I will claim the North West Frontier medal I certainly earned it.

Chapter 29

THE WAR

Pug went with the 4th & 5th Indian Divisions to Egypt to sort out the Italians. They certainly did sort them out. But they had difficulty organising the POWs, 200,000 of them.

I was posted to Quetta along with a large number of Signals' men from Rawalpindi. I believe it was the 10th Army that was being formed to go to Singapore.

We went to Bombay and embarked, but there was a problem. There was a danger of the Iraqi oil wells being taken by the Germans. We were with the 3rd Field Artillery Battery. The rest of the army set sail for Singapore, but were held back for two weeks. We then sailed to Iraq and landed at Basra in April 1941.

The Iraqis seemed to be friendly and the men disembarked. Then we began to take off the guns and the Iraqis strongly objected. This caused a problem because Iraq was a neutral country so really we were not allowed to take the guns into the country. We took the guns off and that meant war. But the Iraqis were not ready. They wanted time to bring their guns up and place them into a semi-circle to hem us in. So for six weeks we had Iraqi field guns pointing at us. Of course, as we were British it was against our religion and principles to shoot first. What do we say when we are on guard? 'Halt who goes there friend or foe?' If it is a friend he will say so. But if he is a foe he shoots you. That is a British way of playing fair with the enemy. When they were ready they told us so by firing all their guns at us. I don't think they did much damage. I think they had too much elevation on the gun spouts and killed all the fish in the harbour.

We had 25-pounder guns that were probably the best field guns in the war and the gunners were probably the best as well. After a little shooting the Iraqi guns were scrap and the Iraqis had gone to Jesus.

There weren't any casualties in the Signals. The first casualty was caused by an accident. A DR came in from doing a run. He put his revolver on the table and one of the lads picked it up and it went off, shooting a lad in the left shoulder.

For a time I was attached to the air force at Shyber doing DR duties between the air force and the army. As well as riding during the daytime, I also had to ride at night. I had been a DR for five years and the army had taught me absolutely nothing. I had to find my own way in the desert in the dark. I hadn't been taught anything about finding my direction by the stars. I didn't even have a cheap compass or a cheap pair of binoculars.

At first I found it very difficult to ride in a straight line on the desert. When you walk on a beach try and walk in a straight line with your eyes closed and you will end up walking in a curved line. This happened to me one dark night. I left base to ride to quite a big camp of tents. I reached some tents and there was a soldier outside his tent. I asked him if it was the camp I was looking for. It wasn't so he pointed in the right direction and told me to ride straight and I would get there.

Later I came to a camp that I thought must be the one I wanted. I saw a man outside his tent and I asked him if I was in the right camp and he said, 'Haven't I seen you here before?' I had completed a circle and I was talking to the same man.

The danger was that there were Iraqis in the area. On the run from Shyber to Basra I went in a straight line until I reached a railway line and turned right and went parallel with the line for a few miles. If I had gone left at the line I would have finished up with the Iraqis and I preferred not to do that.

The first time I did this run in the dark I hadn't reached the lines and I was sure that I had gone far enough. If I had veered off to the left I would have been very near to the Iraqis. I stopped my bike and listened for any sign of them. All was quiet. I left the bike and walked round it in as bigger circle as possible without losing sight of my bike. By this method I found the railway line.

The bikes were BSA 250cc with overhead valves. They were easy to ride and manageable if you got into a bomb hole. But they were not sand proof. They may have been tested on a beach and found satisfactory. But the Iraqi desert had very fine sand-like dust. It wasn't long before the plug was oiling up. We had six bikes. We took out the pistons and drilled extra holes in the scraper ring grooves. We hadn't a vice so I held the first piston in my hands. The lad with the hand drill was very clumsy instead of turning the drill and using light pressure he pressed down hard and the drill went right through the bone just below my index finger nail. It was very painful.

Drilling the extra holes wasn't a cure. We also had difficulty with the gear change mechanism, but we did cure that.

The REME called all the bikes in and did a modification on the oil pump. They soldered up the inlet feed hole and drilled a smaller hole to prevent excessive oil going into the engine.

As soon as we got the bikes back I took out the oil pumps to see what the REME had done. I didn't agree with what they had done because the feed down to this hole was only gravity and air atmosphere pressure, which was almost nil. What the REME did with the inlet feed hole I did to the hole at the pressure side of the pump. That was a success and our bikes kept going. All the other 250cc BSAs in Iraq seized up.

Fresh troops were coming into Iraq and were advancing towards Baghdad at a good pace. One day I was miles from anywhere when I saw a wooden cross. I felt very sad to see that one cross which was some poor lad's grave in the middle of the desert. I got off my bike and I walked to the grave to read the writing. It read:

CORPORAL ALAN NICHOLSON
ROYAL ARMY SERVICE CORPS

When I received the last letter from Alan he had been promoted to corporal. He was in the Royal Army Service Corps.

He hadn't been my brother, but I often thought about that grave. Alan was transferred to the REME and soon became a staff sergeant. The REME had a large workshop in Cairo and Alan was there for a time. He built a tank recovery vehicle. That was something the eggheads didn't think about. He put together a little car. I think it was basically an Austin Seven.

Stan was in Cairo at the same time as Alan and they used to drive around in the little car, which had an open top. The commanding officer used to borrow it now and again. Alan didn't mind about that because when Alan got it back there was always a tankful of petrol.

One day when they were sat in the car, two Red Caps came towards them. Because they were sat low in the car their ranks were obscured.

The Red Caps became very clever like they do. Stan and Alan remained down on the seats and never said a word. Therefore, the two idiots took advantage and became very cheeky. Then the two motorists stood up and the Red Caps nearly fell down with shock. Stan was in charge of postings and there were three vacancies at a very bad station. The two Red Caps being in the RAF had the honour of having two of the vacancies. They had to decide on the third place and that didn't take long. Our Kath had a horrible husband so he was picked.

I was going on a DR run when something unusual happened. I wasn't going fast and I didn't realise I was being followed. An Iraqi DR came alongside and crossed my front wheel. I swerved out of his way and picked up speed. I waited for him to come again and the same thing happened. I went a bit faster as I wanted him to hit the deck hard. But he didn't come so I glanced round to see him speeding towards his friends.

I wasn't keen on our Signals officer neither his buddy, the sergeant. But I got on very well with the gunners' officers. The guns were towed by a special vehicle, which carried the gunners and ammunition. When the enemy were on the move, our guns could be towed to an advantageous place like behind a ridge. When the enemy came into range they got shot up and before they had a chance to return the firing, our guns would have been hitched up and taken to another vantage point.

When I was doing my DR runs, I was always on the lookout for moving vehicles in the distance. Most times you could only see the dust and sand from the wheels, but that was enough to let me know that someone was on the move.

One day I had an inkling that the enemy were behind a ridge. I rode slowly towards the ridge hoping that someone would fire at me, but not really expecting anyone to do so and give their position away. Suddenly I saw puffs of sand like small fountains in front of me. I wasted no time and spun the bike around and went to the gunners with this useful information.

About a week later I was up to my dangerous activities again. But this time I had my left wrist hit, as I was turning round to go back to base. I went to the gunners first and then went for treatment of my wound.

I carried on like a good soldier although my hand was painful. I received a message, which had to be delivered to an officers' mess ten or fifteen miles away. I didn't know what the message was, but I didn't think it was important. I was very annoyed when I found out that it was to ask the officers of that mess to go to the officers' mess from where the message had originated.

They had managed to get a good supply of booze and wanted to have a party. As soon as I got to base I went into hospital. My medical report says I was admitted to hospital

24/10/41 left hand wounded. In hospital for sixteen days. Transferred to 6B Con Depot from hospital.

I was soon back on DR duty, which turned out to be lucky for Bill Browne. He was about to go on a run as I was coming in. I shouted, 'Hang on a minute Bill and I will come with you.' I once heard that in the First World War more DRs were killed coming into the camp than the numbers killed by the Germans on their runs. I never forgot this and learnt to take care when coming in off a run.

On our way back Bill was just in front of me and we were taking things easy, as we were not so busy at that time. We were about to pass an Indian camp and I kept my eyes on the sentry. As Bill was about to go by him he called out to the guard and they were out in a flash and four rifles were pointing at Bill's back.

I rode straight at the guard shouting in Urdu, 'We are friends you silly beggars.' If I hadn't gone with him, his own side would have shot him and that would have been terrible.

Bill just kept on going not knowing that anything had happened. He was shocked when I told him how near he was to going to Jesus. But he had learnt a good lesson.

Just after our 'little' war had started, we had a spotter aeroplane. It was a *Lysander* biplane. I used to envy the pilot; I thought it was great just hovering about up there. But one day the poor guy was shot down. I'm glad our lads got to him before the Iraqis did and he was all right, but the plane was not.

When I was attached to the RAF for a short time they had *Wellington* bombers. They were very busy. One of the pilots promised me a ride with them on a bombing trip. I didn't really expect to have that experience because of them being so busy. It didn't happen, but I wasn't so bothered.

We had a squadron of Swordfish aeroplanes (I think that's right) belonging to an aircraft carrier, which was in the Persian Gulf. I liked to see them landing in formation. After they had landed they went round the aeroplanes to count the bullet holes.

We were a lot stronger than we were when the war began and we were fighting near Baghdad. There was Pug, Stan and Alan not far away, but I didn't know at the time, or I would have found them. That would have been a special despatch rider run.

I sneaked into the outskirts of Baghdad before it was safe to do so. I saw a lovely girl and I wasn't dreaming and she wasn't a mirage. She looked very interesting to me. I stopped to talk to her and she told me she was a Greek girl and had come to Baghdad just before the Iraqi war started. Her name was Helena Georgeadise. It wasn't safe to hang about so she showed me her flat and told me to take some dirty washing with me the next time I went so that she could wash it for me.

I set off to get back to base. When I was about halfway across the bridge over the Tigris River I saw an Iraqi wagon. It speeded up and was making for the bridge. I saw no escape and muttered to Jesus to get my wings ready. I can't remember that bit, but it may be true.

What would be in the minds of the Iraqis was to get me while I was on the bridge and help me to go for a swim. I didn't want to go for a swim. My brain was working. If I left the bridge a few seconds before they reached it they would have kept a straight course and would have run over me. That was no better than going for a swim. I had to judge my speed so that I would be near the end of the bridge as they turned onto the bridge. It worked perfectly, but the width between one handle bar and the bridge side and the other handle and the front tyre of the truck was as much as the skin of my false teeth.

We began to get visits by *Messerschmitts*. The pilots were having a great time, but a squadron of *Spitfires* arrived from England. They waited for the Germans and gave them a beating.

I think it was 'Nitor' of the motorcycle who said, 'For the desert you needed small and light high-powered bikes.' Our BSAs were going very well and the little 250cc engines had a lot of power. But sometimes we needed more power. I think a 300cc engine would have been just right.

The British Army instruction manuals seemed to be based on the First World War. The DR was looked upon as someone who went from one Signal office to another that was about quarter of a mile away.

We travelled long distances and amongst the enemy because they were not in slit trenches, but all over the place. So you can say that our bikes weren't as good as they should have been.

Our 'little' war was going well and we were past Baghdad and on the way to Mosul. Now it was almost safe to go into Baghdad to meet Helena. She had a lovely flat. I used to have a bath and put on clean clothes. That was a luxury that the others couldn't enjoy.

We reached Mosul, which is near the Turkish border. I was riding from Mosul to Baghdad a distance of about 200 miles on one trip. I saw five or six Iraqi horsemen. One rider fell off his horse and the others beckoned to me to go to them. I knew that Arab horsemen don't fall off their horses.

When they saw that I wasn't going to stop, the injured man leapt from the ground straight onto the horse's back. Before his bottom touched the horse's back they were galloping after me. I was not on full throttle as I was keeping out of their reach. Then I saw six horsemen galloping to cut me off, and I snapped the throttle fully open and I only just had enough speed to get away from them.

On one trip when I was going from Baghdad to Mosul I became ill. I had a long way to go, perhaps about 100 miles. I became worse and was almost passing out. I kept going and thinking if those horsemen came now I would be kneeling on the ground and kissing their mucky feet. I managed to reach the hospital and stayed for nine days. I had sandfly fever. It was horrible.

About ten miles from Mosul I saw a clump of palm trees. I thought that it was an oasis so I went to have a look. It was the loveliest garden you could ever wish to see. I sat in the comfortable shade of the palm trees for quite a long time just thinking. I felt as if I could remain there until the end of this stupid war.

It belonged to someone and I wondered what kind of a person he was and what he looked like. Because we wanted their oil this person had to leave his garden and get away from the advancing armies. I thought he would be very pleased if he knew that his fruit was being used. So I called it my garden and began to take luscious fruits for my mates.

I called at my garden a few times and my friends looked forward to the lovely eats. But then I lost my garden because we were moving to a place near Baghdad. Also, many troops were moving to Basra.

One evening, our officer came to me and said, 'Would you have a look in Baghdad for my torch; I lost it last night.' He mentioned two or three places where he had been. I didn't believe he had lost his torch; the forty thieves of Baghdad would have snapped it up before he had put it down. I said, 'Yes' to his request and went into Baghdad, but not to look for the torch. I went to see Helena. Of course, I didn't go on my bike. I reckon I would have been walking back. We were camped on the River Tigris so I went across in a small boat.

It was about 2.30 when I was leaving Baghdad. I jumped into a little boat feeling sorry for the boatman because I was thinking he would have to swim for his boat in the morning. Something moved in the bottom of the boat. It was the man who had brought me. The bottom of the boat was his bed.

I wasn't expecting any activity in the camp, but there was plenty. The officer came and asked about his torch. I told him I had looked in the places that he had mentioned, but it wasn't there. I was walking away from him to go and get my beauty sleep when he said, 'Where do you think you are going?'

I replied, 'To my bed for some sleep.'

Then he said, 'No you are not, we are invading Iran at 4 o'clock.' I wondered what Iran had done to him.

It was so important that we set off dead at 4 o'clock as if the Iranians would be vexed with us if we were late. Bill Browne and Joe Lindsey had to dash off as fast as they could go because they were on an important mission. There were two forts to knock out. The first would see us coming and would ring the next fort to tell them to get ready for us.

But they wouldn't be able to tell them because these two brave Despatch Riders had to ride round to the back of the first fort and without any permission from British Telecom, cut the telephone wires. I thought it was a rotten thing to do. The fort offered no protection for the poor Iranians. They were shelled from the 25-pounders and then armoured cars went along the trenches firing machine guns. By this time there would only be a few Iranians left. Next the Indian troops had to go and finish them off. They jumped about four feet into the air yelling their war song, which was enough to frighten the British troops to death. It was sickening and I thought it was just murder.

Our objective was Tehran, the capital of Iran. We didn't have much opposition on the way and eventually we arrived at an Iranian stronghold, which was a little mountain swarming with the Iranian army. The reason why we had to leave Iraq dead at 4 o'clock in the morning was because the main army were leaving Basra dead on time, so we all would be at this stronghold at the same time.

We have military tacticians who are very clever and they work things out in detail so that it is impossible for anything to go wrong. Sometimes you get a slight slip up, like the main army not being there.

An advantage of the North West Frontier is that it was a good training ground. So when you go to a real war you have that advantage and you carry out what you have been trained to do in such a way that you do not baffle the enemy.

On the North West Frontier there are gullies and it's only common sense that you sneak along them. On the North West Frontier there are tribesmen and it is only common sense that a few of them will box you in. That is the best way to run a war.

In Iran the leaders of the main army found the biggest and best gully you have ever seen. So they sneaked along it and got bottled up.

The Iranian army on the hill never said a word to us, not even welcome to Tehran. We had to do something so we went back a hundred years to when we had good generals. I had to find a route where you could take the guns along the lower part of the hill where they could be seen. Also I had to find a route for bringing them back where they couldn't be seen. With this bit of military strategy the enemy would think we had hundreds of guns.

The Iranians laughed so much that their bellies bounced up and down to make the mountain vibrate. I thought, *what a brilliant idea, this is going to cause a volcano and the entire enemy would be blown to smithereens.*

By nightfall I was very tired. I had been on duty constantly for three days and nights. So I prepared my boudoir for some sleep. I got a visitor; it was a Signals corporal. He had a piece of paper in his hand. He said, 'Take this to the signal office.' I told him what to do with it and a few other things and he put me on about a dozen charges. He was lucky he didn't carry out his threat; the Corporal would have been in trouble because I only took messages from Signal Officers. I had a real good sleep. I wasn't disturbed by gunfire. I think they were waiting for the ref to blow the whistle.

I went to talk to three RA officers. A young officer who was on the verge of calling for his mummy said, 'We should make a charge, if we don't they will come down and kill us.' I told him not to bother because they would kill us if we made a charge and they would kill us if we didn't so I'd rather stay here. I don't think I was much help to him.

I was thinking how boring it was when they suddenly surrendered. The reason for this was because the Russians had also invaded Iran and had reached the army on the big hill, at the other side from us. We couldn't believe it and the RA officer seemed to go into a panic and was worse than women at the January sales.

The DRs took charge of the convoys, but we didn't have a look in. RA officers were leading the convoy and they went as fast as they could as if the Russians were going to chase them.

When Frank and I were taking the convoy towards Tehran we noticed swampy ground and we had some difficulty avoiding them. The convoy was going straight for the swamps and as they were going so fast the leading wagons got well and truly stuck.

The signals had a very large wagon with a very large winch and it was the only wagon that could pull them out.

After we had got the wagons out of the swamps, Frank and I took charge of the convoy and we had no more trouble. We were going to a place near Baghdad so Frank took over on his own while I went to see Helena. I didn't want to go to the place where we were making camp because there would be straggles of people who had left the convoy because of mishaps and breakdowns. I would be looking for them as soon as I had seen Helena.

She was very pleased to see me. I had a quick bath and put on clean clothes. While I was doing that she had a nice meal ready. As soon as I had eaten I left because I wanted to get the stray wagons to camp without too much delay. That was the last time I saw my Greek girlfriend.

We spent only a short time near Baghdad. We had someone else to sort out; Rommel, who was a German.

We moved to Basra for a short time to get organised. I went to the air force base where I had been helping, to get the lads some drinks. They deserved it because they had travelled a lot of miles. As I was returning to camp I saw clouds of sand a long way in the distance. I guessed it would have been five or six vehicles. I wanted to get rid of my load of drinks and then bring them in.

A gunner officer came dashing to me saying how pleased he was to see me. One of the gunners had a terrible disease and needed an ambulance or he would be dead within three hours. The other DRs had been out searching the desert, but hadn't found an ambulance.

It took me nearly half an hour of valuable time before I saw the cloud of dust. But as soon as I saw it the throttle was flat out until I reached it, four wagons and an ambulance. I had saved the gunner's life so once again for the third time the RA Officers asked the Signals officer to recommend me for a decoration. But he never did. I was doing my duty, but I did a lot more than that and I think I deserved some reward. The time came when we had to stop playing Lawrence of Arabia and leave the Iraqi desert, my Greek girlfriend and my garden and go to a real war.

Chapter 30

NORTH AFRICA

We reached Egypt and travelled east to Tobruk and changed direction to go to El Adam. There was an airfield at El Adam and a defensive box. This was an outer defence of Tobruk and was eighteen miles from Tobruk and about seven miles from the main defensive line from Tobruk.

We had joined the Eighth Army that was commanded by LT General Neil Ritchie.

We held the main defence line, which was called the Gazala line. Gazala is forty-five miles east from Tobruk along the coastal road. The defensive line extended in a south-east direction from Gazala to Bir Haxheim to Tobruk. It was also forty-five miles long approximately. Along the defensive line was a German stronghold called the Cauldron. The size of the Cauldron was approximately sixteen miles long and four miles wide.

In 1941, the Germans forced the allied armies through Egypt almost to Alexandria and Cairo. But due to shortage of supplies (thanks to the Royal Navy) the Germans were pushed back to Libya and beyond the Gazala line.

For the first few months of 1942 the Germans were building up their supplies and preparing for a massive assault on Tobruk. Rommel spent a lot of time on reconnaissance trips until he knew the area like the back of his hand.

Tobruk's importance was due to the deep water in the harbour for large ships bringing war supplies. But in spite of this, the main defences of Tobruk had been neglected. The British relied too much on fortified boxes. There were five or six of them. I think they would be about three miles square.

The British relied upon boxes when they were fighting the Zulus who only had spears to fight with. Now we are relying on boxes against fast moving Panzer divisions. Auchinleck had said that if it was going to be too costly to defend Tobruk we would leave it and this is why the defences of Tobruk had been neglected.

Auchinleck was at Middle East Command at Cairo. This was another disadvantage. Rommel was in charge and could work out his tactics and change them, as he liked. Ritchie was a good general, but he had only just recently taken command of the Eighth Army and Auchinleck was his boss.

When we reached El Adam it was the first time we had seen *Stuka* Dive Bombers. One lad had been left behind at our last stop and walked to El Adam. He must have been a very good soldier to be able to find his way. Sadly, as he came into the box a *Stuka* bomb blew him up. We realised how unlucky you could be. Just outside was a wagon just like the DR wagon with the big winch. Bill Browne and I scrambled through the wire fence armed with mechanic's tools to get spares. It was a long job and most of the work was under the wagon. But we still ducked when a shell passed by and we laughed at each other. Because when a shell has missed you it doesn't come back, so why duck.

We had a good idea that we may have to get away quickly so we decided on what route to take. We decided to go south-east and keep away from the coastal road for a long time.

A South African division was defending Tobruk and a free French brigade held Bir Hachheim. Rommel's Italian division attacked the brigade in the Cauldron while the Panzers attacked Bir Hacheim.

The enemy drove out of the Cauldron and attacked Knightsbridge. We suffered heavy losses, some 6,000 casualties and 150 tanks. Pug was in this battle and became a prisoner of war. He didn't like being in this situation. There was a wagon near him so he jumped into it and drove across a minefield and came into El Adam. He said the wagon was full of food and it had been nerve racking because he was worried that all the food could be blown sky high. He didn't stay long before he cleared off.

We hadn't any air cover whereas the enemy had hundreds of *Stukas* and *Junkers JU 88*. They were sending waves of bombers to Bir Hacheim and then attacked with tanks and the Free French brigade was overrun. An Indian Motor Brigade was next to go. This box was due south to El Adam. The Panzers turned to attack Bir Buid and also us. Our Henry, at that time Lieu Col Crawford, was commanding officer 7th Armoured Division Signals and defending Bir Buid. It was a fierce battle and the division was scattered losing many casualties. They joined up with another brigade or division (I've forgotten which) and had chance to reorganise, but lost a lot of men. Hundreds of them and many senior officers became prisoners.

Stukas and *Junkers* bombed El Adam almost continuously while a fierce battle was going on between the 3rd Artillery and the German artillery. It was the 16 June; I think I had a few minutes to spare to remember the 16 June 1937 when I was at Ampthill and with Betty Laurence for the first time.

On the following day the enemy overran the El Adam airfield and on the 18th, Tobruk was surrounded. There was heavy gunfire aimed at Tobruk and several hundred *Stukas* and *Junkers JU88* were bombing the defensive lines from El Adam air base.

Six months earlier Auchinleck had decided that we would not fight to defend Torbruk; consequently the defences of Torbruk had been neglected. Richie was ready to retreat, but Auchinleck said, 'No.'

We were holding out at El Adam box against very fierce gun battles. Our guns were in a gully, but the German guns were spot on. They were bombarding us with long-range guns and although our gunners were supercharging the guns as much as they dared, we couldn't find the range.

The enemy kept trying to break through our defences, but they faced everything we had including heavy ack-ack and boofers.

On that day I had been on DR work since dawn to about 5 o'clock. I then went to the main office and they were managing. But the linesmen were having difficulty in keeping communications going because as soon as they put a line down, it would get shelled. Therefore, I went to help them. The linesmen were the two West twins and a lad called Andy and another lad whose name I cannot remember.

I suggested bridging lines in a way that the Signal had alternative routes. That worked well so I left them to find myself another job.

I watched the gunners loading and firing their guns as fast as they could. Each crewmember had a number. Number one had the most dangerous job. He stood up on top of the gully to direct the firing. His life lasted a few minutes and another number one went on the gully. Some of the Signals lads went onto the guns because gunners were getting scarce.

A gunner who liked motorbikes became a friend of us DRs. One of the gunners became wounded on top of the gully. Our friend went to him and picked him up and was carrying him back into the gully. A shell exploded and there was nothing left of them.

The German gunners were so accurate only a few shells landed on the outside of the gully. Therefore, the wounded had been taken and laid on a flat piece of ground about fifty yards from the guns.

I went to the wounded; as they were all lying down I thought they would be a little safer with sand bags around them. So I began to carry sandbags to the wounded and placed them in position; I had nearly finished my task, I just needed one more sandbag to protect a lad's feet. The shells began to stray a bit and were dropping close to the wounded. So as I was putting the last sandbag in position I was on my tummy and a shell dropped too near; my hands received shrapnel wounds and I became partly deaf. I couldn't do anymore for the wounded so I went back to the gully that had altered shape and as it was dark, apart from the flashes, I fell into it breaking my right wrist.

I lay where I fell for quite a while as I was exhausted. I had hardly stopped since dawn. It was the 28 June and it came to me that at that time in 1937 I was sat on the beach in Scotland with the nice Scottish girl waiting for her dad coming in from fishing.

It was very quiet and I nearly fell asleep. People were moving about in a big hurry. We were evacuating El Adam.

I got on the DR wagon, as they were about to move. Then the signals officer looked at me and said, 'Someone ought to collect the gas masks.' I reluctantly got off the wagon to get them and was sure we wouldn't need them. I collected up some and I thought I was going to the wagon, but it had gone.

At one time I said that I would shoot the officer because he was useless. It looked like I was paying for it. He had sent me for his torch and now the gas masks.

I managed to get on the other signal's wagon. The sergeant was in the driver's seat and so I didn't have much faith in going a long way. We didn't because he drove into the Panzer unit's camp. I felt disgusted and disappointed. I had faith in my ability to not become a Prisoner of War. It happened and it was not my fault. It was about 4 o'clock in the morning. I could have made use of a nice comfortable bed.

The Panzer division was soon on the move with us five prisoners. The German lads were just the same as English lads and they spoke English. One of them said to me, 'The British soldier is the best fighter in the world, but they are led by donkeys.' I couldn't agree more. He said, 'British and German soldiers will not be fighting against each other for much longer because Russia is the main enemy and Britain and Germany would be together fighting them.'

We had three or four attacks from British aeroplanes. The wagon driver circled round to get into a good position while the driver's mate fired at the planes and the planes fired at us and dropped bombs. It sounds very dangerous, but it wasn't. No wagons or planes were hit.

I still had my goggles and I was wearing them. We had a despatch rider with us. Every time we stopped I had my eyes on him, I just wanted a little dust storm and I would have been on that bike.

It was evening and we made camp. The despatch rider parked the bike about 30 or 40 yards away. I thought, *thanks Mr German despatch rider, I'm sorry you are going to lose your bike.*

A dust storm started, but some Germans who had come to take us from the Panzer division. blocked our way. I was only seconds too late. We were taken to a point where there were thousands of POWs, and then to Benghazi. I didn't have another chance to wave them bye-bye.

We had become Italian prisoners and we went to a POW camp on the Adriatic side of Italy. We were all very hungry. We were living on stew; I think the meat was camel.

Eventually we got a consignment of Red Cross parcels. They were excellent; whoever planned the contents and packing was a genius. I hope he got a big medal. There were tins of meat and a tin of condensed milk, tea and cigarettes. The condensed milk was for our tea, but I used to think I would just have one spoonful and the rest would be for tea. I had no willpower and I would be left with an empty tin and drinking black tea.

At first the problem was boiling water for making tea. The problem only lasted while some Nicholson brewing machines were manufactured.

My first friend in the camp was John Tatlock. He worked on a London newspaper. He managed to keep his jackknife by fastening it round his neck, on his identity discs line so that it rested between his shoulder blades.

Because there was a lot of tinned food in the parcels I wasn't short of material. The blower consisted of a fan that was driven by a belt or shoelace or a piece of string. There was a handle to turn and gearing was high so that the fan got up enough revs to give a good draft of air. Then there was the firebox. These blowers soon had the water boiling and would burn anything.

Coffee, tea, and English cigarettes brought a good price in town, so these were worth two bread loaves. I didn't want the cigarettes so that became two bread loaves. I wanted my drink of tea. But the Italians also wanted it, so I had to think of something such that both the Italians and I would have my share of tea and I would also get to have two bread loaves in the bargain. Therefore I must give used tea leaves.

The problem was solved. I made a flat tray. I opened my packet of tea very carefully because the packet would be used again. When I made my drink of tea I kept the tealeaves. These were dried very carefully in my tray on the blower. This was a highly skilled job because the tealeaves had to be dried right through so that they crackled, and at the same time they did not smell of burning or smoke.

When this highly skilled job was done satisfactorily the tealeaves were put back in the packet and the packet closed with more skill. The tea was ready for flogging for two loaves.

Next you went to the wire and told a guard that you wanted three loaves for a packet of tea. You never got three loaves, but you always tried. It was a long job, but it was worth it. The guard would go for the bread, and when he returned you threw the tea over for inspection. This took a very long time. The packet was carefully examined. It was shaken and smelt about ten times. At last it passed the test and I received my two loaves. I wasn't really naughty because second-hand tea was plenty good enough for the Italians.

There were about 7,000 prisoners in the camp so it was very heavily guarded and there were a lot of Italian police in the vicinity.

Two lads got Italian uniforms and made rifles out of tin and wood. They walked out of the camp, but they were brought back after three days.

John Tatlock and myself decided not to attempt to escape at that time. But we spent a lot of time working out how we could overpower the guards and make them prisoners when our troops were getting too near camp.

I was transferred to a working camp. I don't know what happened to John as I never saw him again. I went to a village called Abieto Grasso. There were about sixty of us and we were put in a large barn. It was about ten miles from Milan.

We split up into groups of six or seven men and each group went to a different farm to work. There were good farms. Our group was lucky because we had a good farm. The farmer was a fascist sympathiser, but he seemed a decent chap.

There was a family who lived in a cottage at the farm. There was the man and his wife, two daughters and a son. They all worked on the farm. The eldest daughter was sixteen and called Helen and she worked with me. There were other girls working on the farm, but I was closest to this family.

I enjoyed working with them, but I didn't think I would be staying for a long time. The Partisans in Milan were very busy and I thought they might need a new recruit.

First of all Helen did my washing for me. That was a good start. Next I changed my religion becoming a Catholic. All the Italians were Catholics so when I told them what my religion was they were very pleased – Nick is a Catholic, very good man.

I had a ride out once a week to a very large church so that I could carry on with my religion and also get to know the way to Milan.

The barn had a ground floor and a second floor above. There was a skylight, which was always open to let the air in.

This was quite high and the Italians evidently didn't consider it to be an escape route. From the outside it was very high and to make it worse it was built on the edge of a ditch about 8ft deep.

To get down from the roof with a rope would be nothing for a builder. But I didn't like heights. There were no windows in the back of the barn and there was a ditch and a hedge. So the guards never went behind the barn, but walked along the other three sides. The orderly officer paid them a visit at midnight and as soon as he was out of sight, the guard relaxed.

The Italians had known me as a world famous motorcycle stunt rider. So one day they came along with a Moto Guzzi motorbike. I thrilled them with some good trick riding and they enjoyed it. But some military big noise heard about it and there was hell on, and it was the end of my trick riding shows; he must have thought there was a danger of me escaping. It is not nice when people don't trust you.

The weather was glorious and working in the hay field was very pleasant. At first we got rice boiled with a little vegetables. But we told them we didn't have rice like that in England and we told them how to make rice pudding. After that we just had rice pudding for dinner and that was good. But every day our dinner just consisted of rice pudding and after awhile we got fed up of it.

Although we didn't speak Italian at first and our Italian 'friends' didn't speak English, we soon learnt enough of each other's languages to be able to manage conversations. Our teams were very friendly with each other. So we were a happy lot and we all enjoyed the work. The guards were decent men so it was like being at a holiday camp. Only an idiot would want to escape and join the Partisans, but unfortunately I was an idiot and carried on with my plans.

One night there was a thousand bomber raid on Milan. The planes came in from the right, dropped their bombs and departed from our left. The raid took over three hours. This should have put off even an idiot, but it didn't.

The ropes that they used over the loads of hay were not much thicker than clotheslines. As the guards were used to seeing me with my washing rolled up in a towel they took no notice when it was rope.

.

Win and I in 1946

Left: Ette (my mother) with Derrick.
Right: Win's mother.

Ernie (my Dad)

Top: Myself and Frank Browne, with a friend from the gunners.
Bottom: My sisters, Barbara, Audrey, Dorothy and Kath with dog.

The bungalow at Waxholme which Ernie built.

Me on my Velocett on Holmpton Patrington Road.

Hull speedway team, about 1952, at Hedon race track.

Top: David (eldest son).
Middle: Derrick (second son).
Bottom: Peter (youngest son).

Clockwise from back left: Ivy, Win, my Mother, Kath, 'Pug', Derrick with dog and Peter.

Top: Progress at Herberry house. New door and windows.
Barn roof reduced to sloping roof and front wall repaired.
Bottom: Front view of Herberry house on main street,
Hemingbrough.

Top: Work on kitchen finished and larder made into a bathroom
and toilet with new door.
Bottom: View from back road at Hemingbrough.

Top left: View into the garden from a back bedroom window
Top right: Toilet becoming rubble
Bottom: Herberry house, outbuildings.

Top: Henry and Philippa Crawford.
Bottom: Elizabeth.

Win and I.

Chapter 31

THE ITALIAN HOSPITAL

Someone was in contact with the Partisan movement in Milan. So my destination was the Partisan movement in Milan. The contact point was situated at number 10 Farnete Street. This was the home of the Tachini family. Signora Vitoria Tachini was the leader of this group of Partisans. It was arranged that I should meet a man at a place about two miles away. I amazed myself by getting away so easily and I was sure that I was following the directions correctly, which I was because I found the place where my guard would be waiting for me. First snag, he wasn't there. It would be dangerous to hang about because if he had been captured near this spot it would not be long before I was in the bag. So I changed direction for a while and then got back on course. I had done all right so far and I wasn't really worried. I was sure I would be able to find the headquarters on my own.

I had been resting in a barn for about an hour and was thinking about getting on my way. Then I heard noises, people coming towards the barn door. Three Italian policemen entered and I made a dash to get past them, sending one sprawling. Unfortunately he had knocked down one of a number of planks and it hit me on the back of my right leg. I got a bit of a bashing while I was on the floor. People can be very brave when they have guns and you have nothing.

I was slung into the camp with a horrible ache in my tummy and a sick feeling. I didn't get any medical treatment at all and the following day my leg was about twice its normal size.

When I went to bed I went to sleep in spite of the pain. I felt gentle fingers on me, but I wasn't dreaming. It was Helen and two other girls dressing me as gentle and as quick as they could. We crawled out of the camp to a private hedge. We were safe when we were on the other side of the hedge and we passed the sentries. There was a girl waiting for us with a bike. So they got me sat on it and pushed me to Helen's parents' cottage.

Helen's brother sterilised a knife and cut a slit in my leg about two and a quarter inches long and the bad blood oozed out to my relief. They dressed my wounds and made me comfortable.

What to do with me was a big problem because I needed expert medical attention and medication. One of them suggested taking me to a civilian hospital, which was about three miles away.

The next day a horse was yoked to a trap and we went to the hospital. There I was made very welcome. The hospital did their best for me, but after about three weeks the doctor told me he would have to amputate my leg. At that time a new doctor joined the staff. He was a fascist and he soon got to know I was English. He reported me to the authorities and a German officer and an Italian officer came to see my doctor. They told my doctor I must be taken to Germany. The doctor told them I was too ill to be moved and a big argument followed. After a lot of talking they said I could stay for one month. Then I would go into a German hospital and it would be decided there about what would happen to my leg. I think the doctor saved my life because I would not have seen Germany. I would have been shot. I was under guard for twenty-four hours a day and the guards had orders to shoot me if there was any attempt to escape.

I was being looked after while I was in hospital. Therefore, my Partisan friends decided that I should stay there as long as possible. Of course we did not trust the Germans and so preparations for making a dash were made in good time.

I don't think the hospital had much as regards medicine and anti-infection methods. They rammed rolls of bandage into the wound to soak up the infection. I don't think it did any good and it was terribly painful.

I was very upset about the decision to amputate my leg because I was hoping to win a few TT motorbike races. I thought it would be difficult to make rapid gear changing with a wooden leg.

An Italian man and I became good friends because we both had something in common. He was going to have his right arm amputated. He didn't seem unduly upset about it so I put it down to him not wanting to win races in the TT.

After the operation he came to me. It seemed he had not got any relatives to come and see him. As he was speaking to me he put his left hand across to where his other arm should be. It suddenly came to him that he only had one arm and he cried broken-heartedly.

My guards slept across the doorway of the toilets so that I would have to wake them if I needed to go in the night. I never got the same guard twice. This was because they wanted all their men to know what I looked like.

One day I was sitting on a seat in the hospital grounds, my guard was sitting with me. I began to laugh at my thoughts and he asked me why I was laughing. I said, 'You are guarding me while I cannot walk and when I can walk I will be gone and your lot won't find me.' He said, he would 'have to shoot me if I tried to get away'. I asked him what he would shoot me with. He said, 'With my revolver.' His revolver was about four or five inches long. So I said, 'You can't shoot me with that, it isn't a real one.' So he dismantled it to show me it was a real one.

About a week later the Germans made a move to get me and there was sudden and speedy action in the ward. The sentry was sitting on the steps enjoying the sunshine. I had to get into bed and 'die', and I was covered over with a sheet. Two nurses dashed in with a stretcher and I was taken past the sentry and to the mortuary.

We were lucky to get past the sentry because as I was playing at being dead my legs should have been straight. But because of the damage to my right knee it would not go straight, and so the nurse behind was saying, '*Gamba due Ernesto, gamba due.*' Evidently the sentry had not noticed the hill in the middle of the sheet.

There were clothes waiting for me so I was hurriedly dressed and taken through a doorway at the back where a man with a bike was waiting for me. I sat on the crossbar and he pedalled as fast as he could. This was the start of a long and painful journey. Our destination was Vegevino.

Our first part of the journey for about five miles was on country roads and the bumps in the road sent shock waves through my injured leg. My friend told me that we must go onto the main road. He said there were Germans everywhere on the move going southwards to meet the threat of invasion.

We had many more guards to get past who were doing sentry duties on all the bridges. When we had reached the main road I could see that my friend hadn't been exaggerating. I always believed that I would always be able to outwit the enemy. But now I could only rely on friends. I couldn't do anything, but sit on the crossbar of a bicycle, and there was no room for my talents as a despatch rider.

After a few miles on the main road we changed to a more quiet road where there were no Germans. This was relaxing and my friend slowed a little to rest his legs. We saw a man on a cycle coming towards us. He shouted to us telling us to stop. We had been heading for a small town, but our new friend told us it would be impossible for us to go that way because of German guards and checkpoints.

We turned round and went back for about a mile. Our friend said, 'We must wait for two more men who were coming to help us.' We left the road and we sat down to wait. In front of us was a steep hill, which was very high and there were rough steps cut out, which we had to climb.

We did not have long to wait for the two men. One of them had me on his back and set off up the hill in great style. The other man dragged two bikes to the top. My first friend helped to get me to the top and then he wished us good luck and set off for his home at Abieto Grasso. He had risked his life to get me here and all I could do was to hope that he would reach his home safely.

This forced detour took up a lot of time and energy to skirt the small town and the men took it in turns at having me on their crossbars. We saw people in the fields who could see us and may send a message to the enemy and so we were in constant danger. The bumpy lanes and narrow roads were giving me almost unbearable pain and I felt very ill and I thought I would pass out. But I fought against all this as my friends pedalled on and on, so I tried to think more of them and less of myself because of what would happen to them. If we were caught what would happen to them. If we were caught they may be shot on the spot. But their end would most likely be worse than that, and be shot the next day. The Germans would force the people to crowd into the town centre and my friends would be dragged to a spot and filled with enemy bullets. Because this is war and that is how many brave Partisans lives were ended by the cruel enemy whose methods of teaching the people were too horrible to describe.

Eventually we were back on a decent road and were making good progress and expecting to reach Vegivino soon. This was a wonderful feeling to think this awful journey was coming to an end. Then we saw a man coming towards us in a big hurry with a message. There was a checkpoint on a bridge about three miles away and we must keep clear of it.

The detour was a long way round and very hard work and we were all exhausted so we stopped to have a rest. Just a little food would have been very welcome. We were soon on our journey again and when we reached the road we were on the outskirts of Vigivino.

There was an aerodrome for fighter planes on our left and near it was a shed. We saw a young boy coming towards us on his bike and coming as fast as he could. He shouted 'Stop', and then he told us his message, which was, 'Because of the Germans, Ernesto cannot enter the town today.'

I looked at the shed and I guessed what they were thinking, 'Ernesto must stay in the shed'. They made me comfortable on a bed of straw and left saying, 'Someone will bring food in the morning.' I thought I would be dead by then. But I knew that I had to stay alive for the sake of all the people who were helping me.

The fighter planes were very busy and noisy, but I did get some sleep and it was soon morning. I looked forward to my breakfast although I was sure it wouldn't be bacon and eggs. I waited, but no one came.

It was getting dark and I heard someone coming to the shed. I thought this is the end of Ernesto, but they were two Italians with food for me. It was pasta with meat. I thought it was the best meal I had ever had.

After the meal we were able to complete the journey although the place was full of Germans and fascist Italians. The men took me to a house in a street. There was nothing special about the house, but I thought the people of the house were very special. They had an eighteen-year-old daughter, and she was a very lovely girl. Her parents told her that her job was looking after me.

I had a comfortable settee to sleep on; it stood across the front window. The German soldiers who walked up and down the street turned at my window and the cheeky beggars sat on the window ledge to talk a while and have a rest. They were too near for my liking.

I did not look smart at all in the clothes, which I had from the hospital, but they soon became redundant. A man came to see me, he asked me a few questions about my clothes, like what colour did I want and what size shoes and did I want black or brown.

He went away and came back three or four hours later. I was amazed he brought me everything I asked for. The following day three of our aeroplanes paid us a visit; they were *Mosquitos*. They blew up a large building without causing any damage to anything else. It was a German clothing store. Evidently they had been waiting for me to get my new rig out.

My new doctor's surgery was quite a long way from my new home. Also, on the same street halfway down was the Italian Headquarters and at the bottom of the street was the German Army Headquarters. The journey to the surgery and back wasn't doing my leg any good so they needed someone nearer to look after me.

We were returning from the surgery one day when a young lad accidentally ran into us, hitting my leg. I almost gave the lad a mouthful of naughty English words. For my safety I was moved to a house belonging to an ex-school teacher. She was a lovely woman and it was a posh home, but we were opposite the Italian Army Headquarters.

Then, one day, I was being taken for treatment when a boy came dashing along to say German soldiers were at the surgery.

The doctor and the town's chief engineer had been taken down to the courtyard at the bottom of the street. The Germans shot the engineer and told the doctor to examine him and certify him dead. The soldiers at the surgery looked for some evidence to warrant the shooting of the doctor. This could not be found so they allowed him to go back to his practice. But he had to have two German soldiers with him.

I was left without a doctor, but not for long. Almost straight away a man who was a leader of the Partisans in Milan came to the house. He was a Doctor Annessa, a very clever doctor. He took me to his surgery in Milan and he and his partner wasted no time. They put my entire leg in plaster and then cut a hole in the plaster to expose the wound for dressing etc. What a relief from the horrible pain and having the plaster cast to support my leg.

Before we began our journey to Milan, Dr Annessa told me that all traffic going into Milan was being stopped and searched for escaped POWs. We were travelling in a wagon. I was the driver's mate and was riding at the back because I had given up my seat to the doctor.

We were stopped as expected and a policeman talked to the driver and then to the doctor and then came round to the back of the wagon. I was wearing a cap with the tippy pulled down to my elbows to darken my blue eyes. He gave me a good looking over and asked if there were any escaped prisoners in the lorry. There were some big boxes in the wagon and he was looking at them. I gave him a good look over and then I said, 'You can look in the boxes if you like, but I am not going to help you.' He gave me a funny look and cleared off.

The two doctors soon left me because they had other patients to see. The Annessa family had moved to the country so I was on my own. I looked through the window that faced onto the street and had to laugh at what I saw. Across the street was the police headquarters and on guard were two of my friends who guarded me at the hospital.

There is nothing more comical than Italian soldiers and police so I had a laugh every time they changed guard. It reminded me of the time when we travelled on a train to a POW camp in luggage carriages. A guard was sat in one corner and the other one sat in another corner and us lads were sat facing them. They had their bottle of wine on the floor against themselves. We hadn't had a drink and were very thirsty.

After a few hours both the guards fell asleep. We thought this was very naughty of them so we drank their wine. It was Vino Bianca and very good, too good in fact, for Italians. Eventually they woke up. One of them reached for his bottle, removed the cork and put the bottle to his lips. No wine came out and he couldn't understand it. He shook the bottle, but no wine appeared. He shook it vigorously and still no wine. He closed one eye and put the other to the bottleneck and peered into the bottle. By this time the other guard had reached for his bottle and there was the same performance. Then it suddenly dawned on them that the English swine had drunk their wine. A Zulu dance followed with lots of yelling and waving of popguns.

Not long after the doctors had gone, I had a visitor, a nurse from the hospital with good hospital food. When evening came I had another visitor. She was the daughter of the caretaker. She worked quite a few miles away and she had come specially to keep me company. I can't think what her name was, which is very bad of me because she came every evening to see me.

A nurse came every mealtime and so I was doing better than most people by having hospital food. The nurses were lovely girls, very decent and polite. But one day a different type of girl came. She told me she would come back in the evening. I didn't know how to reply to this because I didn't want her to come and I certainly didn't want to fall out with the nurses. I just had to hope for the best.

The nurse turned up looking very sexy. My girlfriend arrived about fifteen minutes later. Both girls were surprised and just stared at each other for a few seconds then they began to talk to each other. This went on all evening and it was getting late and neither wanted to go and leave the other with me. At last they both went out together. I didn't see that nurse again.

Milan had already had a raid of a thousand bombers and they had two more of those while I was at Dr Annessa's surgery. It was the time of the invasion of Sicily, and the Partisans were very busy blowing up the ammo trains etc. I thought it was time I went to my original destination, the partisan headquarters. I had been at Dr Annessa's surgery for about three months waited on by lovely girls and living off the fat of the land. So I left and became part of Signora Taschini's army of Partisans.

There was Signora Taschini, her sister and Signora Taschini's daughter and myself living at the house. So I was still living a life of luxury. They were lovely people, real ladies. Their politeness and cheerfulness was a big contrast to the dangerous life we were living. Sometimes we sang songs in the evening. I'm the world's worst singer, but they said I was good at singing; out of politeness I think.

One regular visitor, who was on duty when she came, was on very dangerous missions. She'd had two or three narrow escapes from the Germans. I remember Dr Annessa asking her to go off-duty for a while, but she didn't. I often think about her and wonder what had happened to her.

My bodyguard was a big strong man, but that wouldn't have helped against German soldiers. My first job was to go to a place, which was at the other side of Milan. There were Germans on guard on the bridge (we had a horse and cart) he patted his side and said, 'We are all right I've got my friend here.' It was one of those 404 revolvers. He had more faith in his friend than I had, as I wouldn't like to depend on it. My dad had one during his war. He said, 'He would not have been able to hit an elephant 20 yards away.'

After a time my bodyguard was missing. People did go missing; you had no idea what had happened to them. They could have been shot.

One day when I had messages that had to go a long way, a man with a pushbike came. He was towing a two-wheel carriage for me to sit in. I was disguised as an old man, which suited me because I had to use a walking stick. There was a young officer walking on the footpath going the same way. He was staring at me all the time we were passing him. I heard someone running a few minutes after he had passed. My heart began to clatter a bit because I was expecting it to be the young officer and he had recognised me. I was very relieved when I saw it was another man. You need two good legs for running away from Germans. So I had no chance.

Large numbers of German soldiers were passing by on their way to the fighting in the south of Italy. So the Germans were using more troops against us, to counteract our activities so we needed a lot more weapons.

One day we heard Germans coming in armoured cars. They pulled up outside the house and the soldiers were dashing towards us. But they dashed past us and went to the house behind ours. It was awful to see the Germans pushing and dragging them out of the house and into the wagons and taking them away. We had an idea what would happen to them and we knew that it could have been us.

There were messages for Switzerland, which were urgent and important because we needed guns and hand grenades etc. I had gone to bed and needed some sleep, but I didn't get much. The daughter came, entered the bedroom and sat on my bed. I was going to Switzerland in a removal van and I would be in a roll of bedding. I hoped they would stand it the right way up or my eyes would have dropped out.

I had to go to several places in Switzerland. I had to learn the names of the places and addresses, and learn the messages and not make any mistakes like giving a message to the wrong house. This took hours because my brain had to take in all the details. I was told there would only be the driver and me. If we got stopped we had to shoot as many Germans as we could before we got shot. I didn't like that, it didn't sound very healthy to me.

During this time the Partisans were blowing up an ammunition train just outside the main station. A lot of Germans were killed, and the German commander put restrictions on all traffic going out of Milan.

One of our top men was captured and this was very serious. Victoria said he wouldn't give away any secrets, but he would be getting horribly tortured and we couldn't take any chances.

There were loose panels in the walls. These were being removed to hide secret documents. Victoria felt that I was in too much danger and had to be evacuated from the headquarters.

I was taken to the house belonging to the parson who I have already mentioned. The following day, Dr Annessa came to see me. I mentioned that the dirty beggar was a sex maniac.

They had me moved as soon as possible. I went to the home of a top fascist. His daughter worked at the German army camp. You can't get anything to sound more dangerous than that. Some of the top fascists were coming over to us and they were very useful.

I didn't go into his house. I had to live in a shed about 80 yards away from the house. There was another Englishman already occupying the shed, but he had only just gone there. I didn't get time to know him. Evidently someone had been helping him and he had been taken to this shed unknown to his helper. This man was disgusted about an Englishman being put in a shed and wasted no time in getting the lad away.

When the daughter came home from work she brought food and drink for me. Her little brother was with her and they both sat down to keep me company. The young lad had a drawing book and some pencils and he started drawing. Then the girl began to draw. She was drawing girls with big boobs.

When they were going the young lad went out first and she stayed back to say that when she came the next day with my food she would come without her brother.

When I woke up the following morning I heard noises outside, so I looked through the window. German linesmen were fitting new telephone wires to the posts just outside my home. I was getting a bit tired of seeing Germans.

They used the back of my home for a 'pee' house and I had to wait until dark before my food arrived. A man brought my food so the young senorita was unlucky. The Germans were there for another two days so I didn't see the girl because on the following day I was taken to Milan, to number 23 Ponte Valero. It was the home of Giustini Orlando.

As could be expected, my leg was getting much worse. A Partisan member came and told me that arrangements were being made for me to go to Switzerland for hospital treatment. I was told to walk as much as I could round the house because I was going to have to walk over the Alps.

In the meantime I had to settle down where I was. The toilet was outside in the yard. During the second evening while I was sat on the toilet, a girl began to sing. She had a lovely voice. I mentioned this to Giustini, and he asked me if I would like to see her. Of course I did, so he went next door and came back with this lovely young lady. After that she spent more time with me than at her own house. Giustini was pushing us together and he went out one day and came back with an engagement ring. This was very embarrassing, as I had no intention of marrying anyone abroad. Only a Yorkshire lass would be good enough for me.

An ambulance came for me. It was the only transport that was not searched.

Chapter 32

GOING TO SWITZERLAND

I was taken to the base of the Alps; I had to wait until darkness fell before beginning the journey. I went into a small church to wait. Every time someone came in to pray I had to kneel down and pray.

It was a beautiful little church and so peaceful. I felt safe and it was a wonderful feeling after being too near to bombs, shells and bullets.

Looking back to June 1942 at El Adam was like a bad dream. I thought about the gunners and how they fought against the German artillery with longer-range guns than ours. I thought about those wounded young soldiers, some of them dying and so far away from home. I wondered what had happened to them.

My mind went back to when I got onto the despatch riders' wagon with a broken wrist and blood dripping from my hands and went for the bloody gas masks. I stood there looking at where the wagon had stood and dropped the gas masks onto the sand. They would soon be covered by a sandstorm.

I remembered a real gentleman; he may have been a professor. He certainly looked like one with his black pointed beard. He had formed a class of pupils and began teaching them. The buildings were being fumigated so we couldn't go to them. Most of us went to the wire for a wee. There was a trip wire about 6ft from the fence. We were not allowed to go past the trip wire.

The professor went for a wee and stepped over the trip wire and began to wee. One of the guards must have been a lunatic because he shot him dead. There was a decent Italian officer at the camp who went up to the guard and slapped his face so hard it sent him sprawling on the ground. I hope he got more than that later.

One of our friends intended living through the prison life and kept himself clean and healthy. He went for a strip wash every evening. There was no heating in the building. He caught pneumonia and died.

I remember the professional rugby player. He was a big powerful man. The rations were not enough to keep him alive. Two days before he died he was trying to shake his blanket, but he didn't have enough strength. He was just like a skeleton.

I thought of Helen and her family and friends and wondered if anyone was punished for helping me and I thought about the two nurses who had taken me to the mortuary. Were they suffering because they helped me to get away?

I thought about my friends in the Partisans and wondered how John Tatlock had got on because I was told that what we had planned turned out successfully.

I also thought about the big chunk of ground called the Alps; which stood between Switzerland and me. Was this really the end of my bit for king and country in this stupid cruel war? It was nearly dark and I had to leave this lovely little church.

Chapter 33

SCRAMBLING OVER THE ALPS

Darkness fell and a guide came with two strong Italian women. At first the going was easy, but it soon became steeper and much more difficult. Then we were really mountaineering and the two women were a wonderful help. We struggled on and on and the climb became very difficult. We reached a small village and were halfway to Switzerland.

Some of the villagers came out to see us. There was a confab between the guard and the two ladies and one or two of the villagers. My guide told me that I would not be able to go any further until the next day because we had to go along a narrow path only 2ft wide. He told me that I would be staying with the vicar. I told him that I wasn't staying with any vicar and that I was determined to get to Switzerland.

They talked for quite a long time and then someone had an idea. They were used to carrying things in large round wicker baskets. So why not carry me in a wicker basket along the narrow path. So that was decided on.

The two women who had been helping me were not going any further and wished me good luck. When I was in Cairo I had three Egyptian notes and I had saved them in case I needed to give them to anyone who helped me. So I gave them to the two women. They were very polite and took them. But I got them back in the post when I was in Switzerland.

The basket was three-quarters full of hay so that I would be comfortable and maybe go to sleep during the journey. I sat in the basket and two men helped to lift the load onto another's back. The path was cut into the side of the mountain so there was no way the man could have a rest before going to the end of the path.

We set off and the basket was swaying from side to side. It was too dark to see over the side so sightseeing was out of the question. The path became steeper and our pace got slower and the basket swayed more. The man was getting out of breath and I had no idea how far he had to go before he could put me down. We kept on going and the pace was much slower and I thought he couldn't go much further. I was sure he would drop with exhaustion. Then the path levelled and became wider. At last he could put me down. He then said, 'Goodbye,' and left. I didn't know what to say. He risked his life for me, but I could not do anything in return.

The second part of the journey wasn't too bad and we were able to make good progress. A group of people came to us; they were similar to gypsies. They talked to the guide and then left. He told me they were robbers. There were a few well-to-do Italian people, mostly business people, who I think crossed the Alps to Switzerland. They carried what valuables they could. These people lightened their load so as to make it easy for them.

We crossed the border and all most straight away I heard dogs and soldiers speaking German. *How do you get away from dogs?* I was thinking. Then as they got nearer I could see Swiss Army uniforms.

They took us to their outpost and we waited for transport. There was an Italian lady who had crossed the Alps as well. She had to leave her possessions behind, but she had brought a case full of silk stockings. For lightness they were the most valuable of her possessions. She thought she would be able to sell them to get some money to live on. I saw her with the sentries and as far as I could see they were not going to let her keep them. The guide had left to go back to Italy to make another journey. But on the next journey the Germans shot him. Our transport arrived; it was a two-horse sleigh. It was a lovely trip and became one large Christmas scene. It was Christmas Eve of 1943. Our destination was Samadan near St Moritz. When we arrived at Samadan, it was like a dream with the streetlights and all the houses lit up. The decorations were a lovely picture and the children were tobogganing down a steep slope on the road.

I went into hospital. There was a lovely Christmas tree and it was beautifully decorated. I was taken to the ward where I was going to be until I was fit to go somewhere else in Switzerland. I didn't know where and I didn't care.

The ward sister came to see me. Her name was Susan Bomann and she spoke perfect English. She had recently returned from England after spending six months in Coventry during the blitz. She had volunteered to go and help in a hospital. I was fed and bathed and put into bed. I was certainly enjoying life here.

The next morning the doctor came to see me and then the treatment for my leg began.

I was introduced to a South African soldier. His name was George Edward Flook, and his home was 231 Windermere Road, Durban, South Africa. We watched Swiss soldiers skiing on the slopes and it was good to see them gliding about. There were fears of the Germans invading Switzerland and the Swiss army were on manoeuvres.

The Swiss army spent most of their time at home. They were responsible for their own area near home so they had all their army kit and equipment with them all the time.

George told me about the escape. He was on a train, which was taking him to Germany. The train stopped at a station and the guards jumped out and walked about a bit. George was in the doorway looking out. For a few seconds no one was looking his way so he slipped under the train and waited for it to pull out of the station. When it did pull out of the station

George saw a man, a station worker. The man spoke to George and he was very friendly and took George to his home.

He asked him, 'Where do you intend escaping to?' George said, 'Yugoslavia.' The man said we would have to get Fritz's opinion. This startled the South African a bit and he wondered who Fritz was. It turned out that Fritz was a friend of their daughter. 'You'll have to meet Fritz,' said the man. George thought that meeting a German was the last thing he wanted to do.

George slept at this house. He didn't get up and was having a lie-in. He heard someone coming up the stairs and then the door opening. George saw this big jackboot entering, which gave him a shock, although he knew he would have to meet him sometime.

Fritz had brought him a radio and some chocolate and asked him what he was in need of. After a few days George and Fritz became good friends. But George still didn't trust him, but only because he was a German.

They were planning George's next move and Fritz had advised George to make for Switzerland because there were more Germans guarding the Yugoslav border. Just to test Fritz, George suggested he came with him.

The German was delighted with the idea and so they had to modify their plans. Fritz had a little business; he and an Italian were flogging German petrol to the Italian civilians. Therefore there was money in the kitty.

Fritz went shopping and bought two suits of clothing. Next he turned up in a German army motorcar, and brought a German uniform for George. They travelled a good distance and stopped to change clothes from uniforms to civilian clobber. From then on it was Shanks' pony to Switzerland.

I said to George, 'Where is Fritz now?' He said, 'I don't know, but wherever he is, he will have big problems.' Fritz had a girlfriend, a Swiss girl, in Switzerland so as soon as he could he wrote her a letter. He asked a nurse to post it, but she forgot to pick it up.

When the doctor came round he asked about the letter and began to ask awkward questions. He realised then that he was a German and sent him back over the border. It was fate, if they hadn't got frostbite they wouldn't have been in hospital, and he would have been with his girlfriend. I was getting looked after very well in hospital and it was good to talk to Sister Susan as she was very good company and she had a lot to tell me about England.

She told me a lot about how England was and how brave the people were during the heavy bombing. I told her about myself and how England was when I was a lad. George Flook didn't stay with us long and I never saw him again.

I had been in the hospital three months and it was time to say thank you very much and goodbye.

Chapter 34

GOING TO ELG

I went to Elg, where I expected to be convalescing for five months. I went to live in an infants' school. I was comfortable and very well looked after and I liked Elg. I soon got a girlfriend and her name was Heidi. She was very nice and respectable. The girls thought that England was a rich place overflowing with cream and honey. Therefore, even I was attractive to them. In fact I could have had twenty wives providing they were all working and bringing money home.

I had news that the Partisans were as strong as ever and still doing a good job of harassing the enemy. I was very pleased to get the following news:

The War Office announces the award of the Victoria Cross to Major (Temporary Lt Col) HRB Foote DSO. Royal Tank Regiment for outstanding gallantry during June 1942 in the Libyan campaign.

The citation describes two actions on 13 June. In the first, though he was wounded, he succeeded by brilliant leadership in defeating the enemy's attempt to encircle two divisions.

In the second, he fought a delaying action that enabled the Guards' brigade to be withdrawn from Knightsbridge. In both he gave an example of outstanding courage.

A battery commander who was in support of LT Col Foote's battalion was awarded the DSO since he reached

Switzerland. LT Col Foote also escaped to Switzerland. Also, to come into Switzerland were members of LT Col Foote's tank brigade. They were Major J Branson DSO, Major J McLean MC Royal Tank Regiment, Capt Burgoyne Johnson RTR.

News 16 June 1944 – Great tank battles in France – Fighting ebbs and flows in all sectors

Heavy fighting continues in France and both sides are being strongly reinforced, the British in the Troain area by parachute and airborne troops. Although the Germans are said to be expecting further landings, Marshall Rommel is considered likely to throw further reserves into what is regarded as a decisive battle.

From Cain to the outskirts of Chaumont great tank battles are in progress. Enemy pressure is strong from Tilly-sur Seulles to Villers Bocage. In the east the storm centre is Troarn, where British patrols are working from house to house. In the Carenten area determined German counter-attacks have been beaten off by American troops.

The Americans have also gained on both sides of Montiboury and are advancing to the west, but positions are constantly changing hands all along the line and the situation is so fluid that it is impossible to make any exact appreciation.

News 23 June 1944 – Allies close in on Cherbourg

Outer defences pierced, 30,000 trapped. American troops have broken into the outer defences of Cherbourg and advanced units were reported yesterday to be only a mile or two from the town, which is being heavily bombed and shelled.

Bitter fighting continues but the Germans are said to be sinking ships and destroying the port, the capture of which now seems certain. Allied engineers are ready to repair it immediately for the landing of heavy artillery.

Rapid progress in Italy

Withdrawing in Italy so quickly that the Allied advance has had difficulty in keeping up with the Germans rearguards. Marshall Kesselring is rushing his forces back to occupy what is believed to be his last line in the Italian peninsular the Livoro-Florence-Remini line.

Already allied troops are within sixty miles of the city of Florence. Towns in Italy have been falling into the hands of the Allies with bewildering rapidity.

21 July – Italy

Having captured this week the important towns of Livirno, Arrezzo and Ancono and established bridgeheads across the Arno, General Alexander's forces are ready for the assault on the Pisa-Rimini line. Both the 5th and 8th Armies are within twenty miles of Florence. Torrential rains are hampering the advance.

France

After the heaviest land, sea and air bombardment of the war, General Montgomery has launched a major offensive into the open plain, south-east of Caen. Heavy fighting continues but the attack has made good progress and Marshall Rommel has had to throw in both his tank reserves and the Luftwaffe. In the west the Americans have captured St Lo.

Due to the rapid advances of our armies and heavy air attacks that caused a lot of confusion it made it possible for thousands of prisoners of war, to come into Switzerland.

Sometime in the near future it would be possible for us to go home. After the war we would have to get work and this could be difficult for a lot of people who had been a POW for three or four years.

Therefore, there were people who were working out a scheme where training for a number of trades could get operational. This had its difficulties because of having to get permission from governments. Also, a lot of the men said they were happy as they were and would wait until they went home. Therefore, all we could do was wait and see what happens.

News 28 July – France

The offensive launched by General Montgomery south of Caen is meeting very stubborn resistance from powerful Germans and is making only slow progress. On the other hand the Americans have succeeded in breaking through the enemy positions west of St Lo and are exploiting their success.

A workshop will soon be opened for American lads for almost any sort of handiwork they like in wood, metal, or clay in the Palace Hotel in Davos. I wonder how long we will have to wait for ours.

There is a building trades' course started at Gossau with about eighty students. The course has been going on for nearly two months and the results so far have been satisfactory.

Flying Bombs – Hawker Tempest is the answer
– What is it like to shoot down a bomb?

Although the flying bomb is faster at low altitudes than most German fighters the *Tempest* can overhaul it without difficulty.

And one accurate burst from its cannon is usually sufficient to blow the bomb in mid-air or send it crashing into the sea or on the ground.

One of the pilots described what it is like to attack one of these flying projectiles:

'As you close up on it,' he said, 'it looks like a large flame with wings sticking out on either side. Because it is so small it is not easy to hit. But the flying bomb is very vulnerable. If your bullets strike home on the jet unit the whole thing catches fire and it goes down with a crash; if you hit the bomb the robot blows up.'

Turned upside down

When we started attacking these things we trod warily, shooting from long range, but as we have got experience of this new form of attack we find that we can close in sometimes to 100 yards. If you are close when the bomb goes up you sometimes fly through the debris and some of our *Tempests* have come back with their paint scorched. The force of the explosion has turned some over on their backs. But the pilot feels no effect except an upward jolt.

Often it is not necessary to hit your target badly. A few bullets sometimes upsets the Gyro (automatic pilot) and then the robot does some queer manoeuvres and crashes. We can catch them without undue difficulty, and making these attacks is helping to make our shooting accurate. It is easy to knock them down and we are very confident of getting a high proportion. During one period we saw seven and got them all.

A new type of flying bomb had a wingspread of about 25ft and about 40ft long. Its speed was estimated at about 600 miles an hour. This was too fast for *Spitfires*. There is a new type of the old model that does 300 miles an hour, 40 miles per hour faster than the old types and very near to the speed of the fastest fighters.

A Russian raid on a flying bomb base has reduced their numbers quite a lot, just to spoil the pilots' fun.

Chapter 35

WALD

My holiday at Elg had come to a sudden end. I had to get off my back and tune up my crutches and get moving. I was required at Wald to take care of the mechanics course. Being an instructor I would be living with a Swiss family.

I enjoyed the journey on a modern Swiss electric railway. The scenery from the train was like a beautiful painting with valleys and mountains and covered with glorious colours of wild flowers. The brown cows with their large cowbells showed up amongst the ground covering, and looked a picture of good health and would give good milk yields for Nestles chocolate. I arrived at Wald too soon as I would have liked to have seen more of Switzerland from that railway carriage.

I went to the home of Mr and Mrs Schoder. Lizy and Tony had a son called Hugo and a daughter called Madi. They were lovely people and I fell in love with them straight away. The house was very large and very beautiful. I liked the Swiss houses that were constructed of good wood. I didn't see the garden because of it being dark. But that was a pleasure I would enjoy the following day.

I couldn't speak German before I went to Switzerland, but I had learnt some Swiss German while I had been in the country and so understood my new friends. The only way I can describe Swiss food is – absolutely excellent.

I was awakened early the following morning and had a welcome cup of tea in bed. I didn't waste any time getting to the window for a view of the garden. I was not disappointed, as it was quite large and well planted with luscious fruit and vegetables. In the distance was the Eiger Mountain.

I was alone that day because Tony had gone to work. The children, Madi eleven years and Hugo nine years, had gone to school. Then Lizy went out. I was enjoying the bit of relaxation when a lady came. She was Lizy's friend called Lena and she came from Ruti. She asked me to go to see her. I was looking forward to that because I would be going on the new railway. It was about two months earlier when they opened the railway from Wald. They celebrated it in carnival mood. Some of the Evades (ex POWs) from Wald were there to join in with the celebrations.

Wald was a lovely little town, absolutely spotless. I liked the verandas in the houses, which stretched right across the front of the house and on some it would completely encircle the house. They were covered with flowers making a wonderful display of every colour.

On the second day of being at Wald, I visited the Evades in their home. It was a large building that had been used for a gymnasium in the past. I didn't know any of them, but that didn't matter because they were all friendly and I would soon know them.

They told me that the British officers were becoming very regimental, as if they were already at Catterick. For instance, it was lights out at 10 o'clock. Their ambitions became spoilt a little when some Australians came.

The lights remained on after 10 o'clock and the orderly officer came in full steam with words like disciplinary action. The Aussies preferred to have the lights on so two of them went quietly to the officer picked him up and slung him through the door. After that no one went through the door and demanded lights out.

I went to have a look at our workshops. We needed a lot of gear and second-hand components. So I went to the Sultza Brothers Engineering Works at Wintherthur, which is on the main line just before Wald. They were extremely friendly and helpful and supplied us with second-hand engines, gearboxes, back axles, a chassis as well as tools, vices etc.

We soon got cracking with our first course and it was a pleasure to teach because everyone was willing to do their best at understanding everything about automobiles. We began lessons at 9 o'clock and finished at 4 o'clock.

At Wald they learnt about engines and welding. Drivers, both army and civilian and for that matter, for any man who in civilian life uses a car, the petrol engine class was particularly interesting. In the lecture rooms the men were learning not only the working of the internal combustion engine, but also about the layout of the electrical system of a car. In the workshop they became familiar with motors by dismantling engines, and by completely wiring an old chassis on the pattern of an ordinary car, they learnt how to trace and remedy simple electrical faults. These men reached the standard of a mechanic of an army vehicle.

I was very grateful to the staff at the Sultza Engineering factory because without their help, instructing would have been difficult. Theory is a good thing if taught with a lot of practical work, without it theory work is useless, and without the help of the Sultza factory, work would not have been possible.

Sultza Bros at that time were one of the largest and most up-to-date marine engineering works in the world. Giant engines, which powered fast, ocean-going ships were turned out at Wintherthur.

A hundred and seventy years ago, Salomon Sultza, a student of theology, abandoned his religious profession and made the journey to Shaffhausen with his life savings. He called on a brass founder and offered him quite a lot of money for the man to teach him his trade.

This was the small beginning to the massive engineering works at Wintherthur where he planned to build his own foundry. But the people at Wintherthur didn't want his factory. He had many arguments with the town council; naturally, as the councils in those days were the same as they are now.

Eventually the council said that 'he could build his factory, but outside the town'. This he did and was soon competing with the coppersmiths, and marketing fire engines, presses and many other articles, which had been monopolised by them. Besides being a brass founder he was an expert turner. In a tiny house, which was still standing and I suppose still is, in the centre of the works at Wintherthur and looking very lonely and dwarfed by the giant factory, he started a small turnery with a good workshop. At the time when I was going to the factory there were 6,000 workers.

Life was very good at Wald, but I missed out a lot on sports like horse riding and dancing. There were talented people amongst the lads. We had a South African world champion boxer and an Australian who was a world champion horse rider. We also had a national ballroom dancer. Therefore, anyone who was interested could get expert tuition. But 'peg leg' as my Swiss friends called me, couldn't do these things.

Nevertheless I was happy doing the instructing. At weekends we did short walks at first and as I walked my leg improved and so I could walk further. The Schoders used to live in a house high up a hill. Going there was their favourite walk and with the exercise and good food, my health soon improved.

I had a double tooth that was playing up. To have it out I had to go to a place about three miles away. The Swiss motorists were not allowed to give us Evades a ride, so I had to walk. Before I reached the place I couldn't make up my mind, which hurt the most, my tooth or my leg.

The dentist was a dental officer from South Africa. His name and address was KR Ware, Shell House, Cape Town. He pulled the tooth out and I sat for a while before making the long journey back to Wald. He told me that he was on a train to Germany. He managed to lift a few floorboards so that he could get through the floor. This he did and he hung on until the train pulled in at the station. Then he dropped down and ran as fast as he could go.

I made friends with a few of the Swiss people who lived in Wald. Two people were Mr O.F. Hattenschwyler and his wife who managed the post office.

Chapter 36

GOING HOME

I had waited six years for the time when I was going home. Now it had come, I didn't want to go home. I would have liked to have stayed in Switzerland. The Schoders didn't want me to leave. Lena cried and the staff of Sultza Bros wanted me to stay and work for them. I could have gone home and then gone back when I had finished with the army. I went home and stayed there. Did I make the right decision? What I do know is that a lot of people in Italy had risked their lives so that I would get home. So for them I did the right thing.

There was fierce fighting going on in France. But the French had advanced from the Swiss border and met up with the British Army units. Here I saw Pug. He had been in the war since it had started. I asked him about home and it wasn't good at all.

Ernie had been working in Leeds as a turner. Ette had stayed in Belle Vue. She had been drawing the allotments from Alan and I and spending it as she withdrew it.

She had been writing to me while I was in Switzerland telling me that Ernie was getting on well with the garage for Alan and I to start a business. It was a load of old bull.

When we left Pug and his friends, we went to a port (I've forgotten the name of it) and we embarked to go to England. When we were going to Gibraltar a German submarine was following us. Three *Corvettes* attacked it with depth charges. The noise and the vibration were terrific. I thought our ship would drop to pieces with the blast. It must have been terrible for the submarine crew. But why be sorry for them after all we had gone through, the Germans wanting to sink us so close to home. The rest of the voyage was quiet so we reached home safely.

Alan was at home, he had married a Welsh ATS girl in Cairo, but she was still out there waiting for her turn to come home.

On my way home for the first time in six years I reached the home of Mrs Ashwell. She was Wendy's mother. Stanley had come home and he and Wendy were living with Wendy's mother. So I called to see them. We talked for a while and then I thought it was time to complete my journey home. Belle Vue was about a mile away. They said, 'No don't go home tonight wait until tomorrow. You can stay here.' I couldn't understand it.

When I went home the following day and saw what home was like, I knew what they meant. I was longing to see the promenade and the sea. I went to look at the shops. A sweet shop was a lovely sight and to be able to go in and ask for a bar of Cadbury's chocolate was like getting a million pounds.

When I went into the shop I hesitated, as making up my mind on which to choose was a problem. I made up my mind and told the girl very politely, which chocolate I wished to purchase. The girl stared at me and said, 'We don't serve soldiers in here.'

There was another sweet shop across the road. When I was halfway across the road a man stepped off the pavement and was coming towards me. I felt a bit afraid and was thinking that I didn't even know his wife. He got hold of my hand and was shaking it with vigour. He was saying things like, 'It's a big honour to shake you by the hand.'

As I stepped into the other sweet shop, the girl gave me a big smile and was very polite as she sold me a bar of Cadbury's chocolate. I was learning that not everyone appreciated what we had done for king and country. I soon found out that there were people who had dodged getting into the services and who now held important position and couldn't care less about us soldiers. These were the next people who we had to fight.

My leave soon came to an end and Catterick camp was my next, 'battleground'. I had a few days to relax and then I had to go to the motorbike garage and workshop. I was told that I would be doing DR duties, but as I had spent time in a POW camp I had to have some riding lessons.

They gave me a bike and a set of tools and so I set myself on doing some maintenance. On these bikes was a very important bolt, which had a slack thread, which soon came loose. I tightened it up as much as I could.

A corporal came to me, and my first impression, was he looked like a bigheaded, clever individual and I hated the sight of him. He explained his task. As it was a long time since I had learnt to ride a motorbike at Catterick he was going to teach me afresh. I could hardly believe his kind consideration for me.

I had a boring day on the moors and the second day was the same. When we went back to the garage on the first day he tried this awkward bolt. He said in a clever voice, 'You will never be able to ride a bike if you don't do your maintenance.' I didn't say anything.

On the third day as soon as we were on the moors he stopped and put his hand up like big chief does when he put his hand up and says 'How'. He looked at me; he had a slimy grin on his kisser and said, 'We are going to do some fast riding today.' I looked at him and gave him a sweet smile.

We were on a well-trodden path where you could reach terrific speeds on these side valve army crates. We set off and after a few minutes, I looked round and the corporal was missing. I had a full tank so I had a steady ride to Withernsea. The funny thing about this is, I never saw corporal anymore and so I never did learn how to do my maintenance and ride a bike properly.

There was a course just starting that I wanted to go on. It was an electrical course, which included compressors, radios, and telephones etc. I put in my application form and was interviewed by the CO. He was a bit sarcastic and said, 'You only want to benefit by it for when you leave the army.' I told him he was correct in what he thought, but I thought it was time I got something back from the army as I had given plenty, so I went on the course.

Pug had come home and was at Catterick. He had made a steam engine and was looking for it. I don't think he found it so I never had a look at it. The lads told me it was very good. Pug and a friend and I were having a stroll and we stopped to look at something. We had stopped at a corner that had a nice curve and I said, 'I would like to go round it on a decent bike.' They agreed and said, 'You should see Geoff, he is coming now.' This lad on the motorbike had style. It was the first time I had seen Geoff Duke.

Geoff Duke was in the 1947 display team. That was the last time I saw him to speak with. I believe our Henry who became a Brigadier, helped to organise this team and borrowed the bikes from the Triumph factory as he did before the war.

A British trial expert, Hugh Viney, was an instructor at Catterick and Geoff Duke was one of his pupils. So naturally Geoff became involved in trials riding and also scrambling.

In 1949 he was winner of the Senior Clubman's and Senior Manx Grand Prix. He became a famous rider of the Manx Norton Team, and changed to Gilera in 1953. He won six World Championships. He was awarded the OBE for services to British Motorcycling.

Percy Tate was another member of the Signals Display Team to do well in the TT races. Alan Shepard was also a team rider, and also an ex-Signals Display Team member.

Alan was a DR at Catterick and was very interested in the display team. The bikes were in the part where the practising was done. No one apart from the team was allowed to go near them. But Alan broke the rules and went to have a good look. He was told to clear off. But later he couldn't resist the temptation to go and finish his inspection. Again he was disturbed and was asked why he was so interested in the bikes. When he told this big noise he was told to get on one and ride round this park three times. That he did and was told to go again and ride round in the opposite direction. The following day he had to report to the CO. He thought he was going to get into serious trouble. But that was not the case. The CO told him he was in the display team.

Alan entered for a TT race with his own bike; I think it was a Triumph. He never stopped practising because he went out to practice with other riders. But he also went out when the road was open to non-riders. His dedication bore fruit and he got a 3rd place.

He became a works rider and at one time rode for the CZ firm. In my opinion he was a brilliant rider, and I would like to tell you more, not only of his riding but a trip across Europe in his van to collect his bike. But I must get on with my own story.

I had a good friend who was lucky enough to have a 250cc Rudge. He looked after it and so it was in beautiful condition. I thought that if I had it I would be able to win the 250cc Manx Grand Prix after the war.

I saw a KTS Velocette advertised in the *Motor Cycle News*. It said, 'In good condition' and it belonged to a motorbike shop called Rennos. I wrote to them and enclosed a deposit, which was 50 per cent of the price.

Next time I saw my friend he asked if I wanted his Rudge because he was getting an Ariel Square Four. I would have rather had his Rudge than the KTS.

The Velo arrived and I was very disappointed with it. It looked a wreck and very scruffy. I wrote to Rennos to complain about the condition and told them to return the deposit and I would return the bike.

They didn't answer my letter so I got working on the bike. When I had smartened it up it looked all right and the engine, gearbox and clutch were good so I was satisfied with it for the price I had paid.

Someone told me where Spud Thompson's house was. It was in the married quarters. So I decided to go and pay them a visit. Spud's wife and two daughters were at home, but Spud was still abroad. That was a big disappointment because I was looking forward to seeing Spud and I'm sure we would have had a lot to talk about.

Mrs Thompson's next-door neighbour was with her. The subject was about motorbikes and pillion riding. Mrs Thompson mentioned that she would love a ride on the pillion again. Straight away the neighbour said, 'I'll look after the children if you want to go on Nick's bike.' I had been looking forward to seeing Alan and his wife, Joan. They were living opposite Fulford Barracks in York, so that is where we went. The lady was a good pillion passenger. She was asleep all the way to York. We stayed with Joan and Alan for about two hours and then came back to Catterick and she slept all the way home.

I was enjoying the electrician's course and making good progress. I had done that course before the war, but at that time the telephones and wireless sets etc were very old, from the First World War. The Signals had to have up-to-date equipment for our war. Our instructors at that time were so out-of-date they were more or less useless.

The post office had kept up-to-date and so post office technicians were very welcome when they joined the Royal Signals and soon got promotion and instructor's jobs.

Ette began to write to me too often to ask me to go and sort out her troubles. This spoilt my studying and I left the course without completing it.

Chapter 37

MARKET WEIGHTON

I was posted to Market Weighton. This was as near to Withernsea as I could get. It was a very small detachment and I was back on DR duty.

I liked being there; it was almost like being on holiday. I just had two different DR runs, one to York and the other to Leeds. I felt at home there and I was glad to have the Velo to visit places, which I knew well. I would have been quite happy to stay there until demob day. But the big fault with being in the army was the moving about.

I was posted to Leeds, but still doing the same job, DR work from Leeds to Northern Command, York. I did not like the people at Leeds. I don't think any of them had been abroad. They had a large garage that had been a normal civilian place before the army took over.

The army vehicles were neglected because the soldiers were still taking in civilian work. There were three motorbikes all in a disgusting state and I was expected to use these for DR work. I had an argument with the sergeant. He said, 'What's wrong with you? Are you frightened of them?'

I said, 'I'll take one, but you get ready with a truck to collect the scrap.' I took it onto a straight piece of road. There was a telephone booth, about in the middle of the straight that was very handy. I intended stepping off when I was near the telephone. But things happened far too soon. The anchor bolt on the brake plate decided to do a bunk, leaving the plate to do a little spin, which locked the brake. It wasn't my day for doing a dainty step-off. I did an awkward flight over the handlebars and hurt my back just a bit. But when I looked at the damage to their precious bike I thought it had been worthwhile.

I went to the telephone and asked for Sergeant 'Fish-face'. I told him his scrap was ready for collecting. By the sounds coming over the phone I thought he must be a little vexed.

Nothing was said until about 10 o'clock the next morning when I was told to report outside the CO's office. 'Fish-face' came up to me and halted, lifting one foot up in the air and cracking it down on the concrete.

Next it was, 'Prisoner, attention, left turn, quick march, left turn, right turn, halt, attention.' I finished up looking at this angry face; it wasn't a bit nice.

Then they started gabbing with loud voices. 'Who are you to criticise our maintenance? I inspect these vehicles personally,' said the CO. They were thinking that their dirty business had come to an end. I knew that it had.

On the following day I rode one of the wrecks to Northern Command for Alan to have a look at. He was in charge of all motorbikes in Northern Command. He wrote a letter for me to give to the CO. I went back to Leeds in a staff car. I still hadn't started my duties because I was waiting for a roadworthy bike.

The CO sent the sergeant to see Alan. He said, 'My CO didn't like your letter.' Alan said, 'Tell your CO I didn't like his maintenance.' He gave the sergeant a good dressing-down for being clever with me.

With my help Alan had put an end to a big racket, but there was still plenty more rackets going on.

I eventually got a bike that was in good order and enjoyed my runs to York. At that time there were thousands of new army trucks on each side of the road. I don't know what happened to them.

I saw Mary Taylor, I've forgotten how, but it was good to see her. It had been a long time since I saw her at the Command performance, when Mary and her two friends came to stroke Patch and Tintac. They were very happy days, but the joy of living seemed to end when the war broke out. We walked into Roundhay Park, and then the memories brought tears to my eyes. She was a very nice girl and still single. Had she waited all these years for me? I don't know. I was wearing my army greatcoat; it looked awful because it was far too big for me. She dropped back and looked me up and down and then said, 'Your coat would look better for an iron.' Much later I thought about this and wondered if she meant she would look after my clothes and me. I can't remember how we parted, I only know we never met again.

My mind was on motorcycle racing, as I still wanted to win the TT races. The fastest speed I could hope for with the Velocette was in the region of 110 miles per hour. I would look a bit daft when the works 350cc bikes were doing in the region of 130 miles per hour.

I thought about Johnny Hoskins. He had been an important man in Speedway for a number of years and was manager of Odsal, until I could afford a competitive road-racing bike.

I had an interview with Mr Hoskins in his office at Odsal. He said, 'You are a bit old, aren't you?' I said, 'Maybe so, but I can still ride.' So I was booked for a trial to ride during the interval on the Saturday evening.

Alan had borrowed the Velo, so I would have to go by bus. On the Friday evening a friend and myself were having a stroll round the shops when we got into conversation with two girls. He told them about my trial and they wanted to come with us and this was arranged and he told them the time we were getting the bus.

I was not happy about this because this trial was important to me and I didn't want to be bothered with girls. So I decided to go on a different bus.

A young lady was getting on the bus as I was getting on it. We sat together and we talked about what we were going to do and I said, 'I am going to Odsal Speedway.' She came with me to the Speedway. I was falling in love with her, and I think she was falling in love with me. When it was time for me to go onto the track, she begged me not to go then, but wait and go another time. Her name was Winifred Bryan.

Things were becoming serious between Win and me. She said, 'I will ask my parents if I can take you home.' When I met her the following evening she was very upset and told me she would not be seeing me again. With a lot of prompting she told me the trouble. Her parents would not see me because I was a soldier. Her father had been a soldier and her two brothers were soldiers, so someone was going to be told what I thought of them.

I went to Win's home during the following day. Her mother opened the door about 4 inches, just to tell me they didn't want to meet me, and then was about to shut the door. But I held the door open and gave her a good telling-off. I must have made a good impression because I was invited for tea a couple of days later.

I took Win to Withernsea for a few days and she fell in love with the place. We were married just a month after we had met and I applied for a council house without any delay.

Win and her parents lived at Thornton near Bradford and we had a lovely wedding in Thornton church and a reception at the Bryan's home.

We set off for our honeymoon on the Velocette. The sky was dull; we were going to Win's relatives who lived in Askern, a few yards from Doncaster. Big black clouds were drifting towards us and then the heavens opened and it was thunder and lightning. I hadn't been on the road before and it was difficult to see in the dark and the rain. We came up to a sharp corner and the rear wheel went into a slide.

We had to go back to Win's home. I rode the bike and Win went in a Samaritan's car because she was injured. That was the end of our honeymoon.

Chapter 38

EARMARKED FOR GERMANY

When you came home from abroad, the ruling was no one could send you abroad again until you had been in England for six months. When we married I had been in England for only just six months. So some lousy individual who evidently didn't like me, put my name on a draft to go to Germany. This was the result of ending a swindling racket in Leeds.

The soldiers on these drafts were transferred to a transit camp just outside Chester. Normally they were kitted out, which took three days and then they left for Germany. Another draft came the following week and so on.

There was a 'B' road at one side of the camp and a ditch; this was the camp boundary. Along the ditch were two or three strands of barbed wire making it impossible to get out. That is what the big noises thought. There were no passes and you were forbidden to leave camp. This was also in the imagination of the big noises. I don't know why they didn't have sentries to shoot us if we tried to escape. I can only describe this place as absolutely disgusting and outdated.

I went to see the medical officer who turned out to be very decent. The verdict was, 'Nicholson is not fit for further service'. This would be a shock for the rogues at Leeds. I had to remain at this disgusting camp and all the rules regarding being confined to camp applied to me for the time I remained there. I had one bit of luck. Another soldier was taken off the draft and he was also a despatch rider who was at Rawalpindi, but in 'A' Corps Signals. I was in 1st Div. Signals. We decided we would not be doing any fatigues, not doing any parades and we would go out of camp whenever we wished, and they could stuff their rules.

I wanted to go and see Win and as I didn't have the Velocette at Chester, I didn't know what the best way of getting there was. During the war and for a lot of years after, hitch-hiking was a cheap way of travelling. So I decided to try it. I don't think I had the knack of giving the right signals because I was still walking two hours after I had left.

After walking so far I was wondering what I should do when a wagon stopped for me and took me to Bradford where I was able to get a bus for home.

I'd only been at Chester two days, but going into the Bryan's home was wonderful. It was such a wonderful feeling going into an ordinary house.

I can't remember how long I stayed there, and as I didn't have a pass, I had nothing to tell me when I should be back, which was a big advantage. I enjoyed my break and I had no desire to risk hitch-hiking to get me back.

I travelled back on a train, which I thought was a good idea. When we reached Chester, the soldiers began jumping off the train, quite a way before the train had stopped and began running in the direction from where we had just come. I thought they had gone mad until a polite voice asked if I had a pass. I said, 'No' and the polite voice said, 'You had better run like hell, there's a hole in the fence just past the end of the station.' No one had a pass and the idiots with red bands round their caps were crowded round the exit gate to check on passes, which nobody had.

When we walked about in the camp we were prepared for people like sergeant majors looking for lads for doing fatigues. They always had a smirk on their faces. Our weapon was just a piece of office paper and it worked like this. When you saw an

NCO coming towards you looking like I have just described, you waited until his mouth started to open, and then you asked him the way to this office that you were looking for, letting him notice that you had something important to take. It worked every time.

Dodging parades was easy because there were no exceptions, which meant everyone was on parade and out of our way. But one day the parade was very special, some very, very big noise was coming to inspect it. My friend was a bit too ambitious. He said, 'As it is special we will inspect it from a great height.' There was a big water tank at the top of some high stilts. I thought, *not from up there, I hope*. He continued, 'We are going to inspect the parade from the top of that water tank.'

I don't like heights so I felt like dashing off to get my button stick, brasso and duster, and get into the parade ground. But it was a smashing view, but all the time we were up there, I dreaded coming down.

Of course, being in the army there were a few rackets. The first week we were there one of the staff was getting married and money was required to get a wedding present. The following week another of the staff was getting married, and the next week and the next until they had all got married. Then the first one to get married had another wedding day as everyone who came in went out after three days and no one knew about these rackets apart from my friend and myself.

Chapter 39

AT LAST I AM A CIVILIAN

I had a holiday and then went to work. I had a job at Motor Distributors on Stanningley Road, Leeds. I was in charge of the motorcycle department. The boss was Mr John Ellis and I was his own personal mechanic. Therefore, I was a very important man and a very busy one, because Mr John had for his own use, thirteen cars. These were classic cars; two were Packards and there was an Armstrong Sidley. Motorcycles were a favourite with Mr John and there were about thirty for his own use and two or three, which were used on his farm.

One favourite bike was a 600cc BMW and Mr John was very upset because it was a bit poorly. They knew it was poorly because of its electrics being out of order. The garage had six auto electricians, but no one could cure the ailing BMW. So when I became the boss of this department, my first job was to sort it out.

There were about half a dozen experts standing around when I started up the engine. Yes it was poorly, so I said, 'I'll take it for a run.' When I had gone as far away from the garage to do the job without eyes watching me, I took out the blocked jet from one of the carburettors and cleaned it, and replaced it and it went as sweet as a nut. Then I took the bike home to show it to Win. I had a cup of tea and returned a fit healthy

BMW to Mr John. He was delighted and satisfied with his new mechanic.

When Mr John had to go to London on business he preferred to go on a motorbike if the weather was suitable. He always had a notebook with him to write down faults on the bike he was riding. Then I would have the little book so I could rectify the faults. The footrests and the handlebars were always at fault. So if the little red book said, 'footrests too far forward', I would make the necessary adjustments.

The next time I had that bike and the little notebook, the footrests would be too far back. So being a good lad I would put them forward again. But then my brain began to work a bit, so no matter what my little book said, I left the bike alone and was complimented for getting it just right.

Mr John's favourite bike and mine was the Montgomery JAP. It was the most beautiful bike I had ever seen, and having a JAP engine the performance was brilliant. It was perfect apart from a fault in the timing chest, like a little man inside tapping with a little hammer. I told Mr John about it two or three times, but he always said, 'The engine is perfect.' Because the fault was so obvious and Mr John so particular, it was a mystery to me why he wouldn't admit it.

I was out one day, riding the Montgomery and the tapping was getting on my nerves. So I took it to the garage and took the timing chest cover off. Mr John came in at that moment and had a fit. 'You'll never get that engine oil tight again,' he shouted. So that is what he was bothered about. There was never a smear of oil on that engine. The tapping was caused by a piece of aluminium bedded into the bottom of two or three teeth of a driving pinion. Being a JAP engine there was never the smallest trace of oil after it had been assembled.

Mr John had a farm at Horsforth. There were two bikes, one with a sidecar, for the benefit of the farm workers to run about on the farm. There were three or four of Mr John's bikes there. There were two cottages on the farm for two workmen. One of these workers drove a wagon and so I didn't see him very often. But one day he came to the farm and saw me sat on straw, eating sandwiches. He told me to go to his house and have my dinner in comfort.

I went to his house and had a nice cup of tea and some pudding or pie and his wife to talk to. This lady and the one next door had fallen out years ago and hadn't spoken since. I thought that was terrible. But I reckon talking to me made up for that.

Win and I moved from her parents to go into a basement flat on Manningham Lane in Bradford. By the way, a basement flat is a posh name for a cellar. We both hated the place, but we were hoping that soon we would have a letter from Withernsea Town Council saying, 'You have got a council house'. Charles Sidney's Velocette shop was across the road, but it only made me feel envious when I saw brand new bikes in the showroom.

Win went into St Luke's hospital to have our first baby. On the 3 November 1946 Win gave birth to a baby boy, and we called him David.

Mr John had a big BMW with a sidecar. When I went into a car park it made the motorists look when I reversed into a space. One day I went out with the boss (Mr John). I was in the sidecar and I found it very scary to be sat low down in a sidecar near to the traffic. At times I wondered if the driver had forgotten that the sidecar was on the right side as the sidecar and I were so near the middle of the road.

I was testing a 3-cylinder Scott and went to the Scott Works a time or two. When you think of Scott bikes you think of a lady's bike, light and smooth running and beautifully designed with its parallel twin cylinders.

Scotts only made seven of the 3-cylinder bikes and that was too many. It was very heavy and I didn't like it one bit. We had two matchless V4s. I didn't like those either. The engines lacked power, which was just as well because there was too much weight on the front wheel. They weren't anything like the Ariel Square Four.

One day Oliver Langton came into my department and asked if we had any cases. I had never before heard tyres called cases, and it was only because he said the sizes that saved me from showing my ignorance. Oliver and Eric Langton had lots of admirers when they rode for Belle Vue Speedway Team. I will write about Oliver later on in my story.

I made a small sports sidecar for the Velocette. So the boss had ideas of making sidecars because they were very scarce and also we had joiners and bodybuilders in the garage. I had to go on sick, but I have forgotten what my trouble was. It may have been the time when my braces twisted and I went sick with a bad back. Anyway I was off sick for quite a while, two or three weeks I think.

When I returned to work they had already made a sidecar. They had made a smashing job of it. I thought it looked like a shed with just one wheel at the corner. The manufacture of sidecars was soon forgotten thank goodness.

I bought a 1,000cc V Twin BSA with a sidecar. We went to Withernsea and I went to the council offices to ask why we had not been allocated a council house. The slimy individual sitting behind the desk said in a clever tone of voice, 'You can't have a council house, you do not belong to Withernsea.'

We were annoyed to think that all this time had gone by waiting for nothing. I had a good job and if I had put in an application for a house near Bradford we would have had one by this time. We had another ride to Withernsea in search of a house and a job.

I saw an empty bungalow on the right hand side of the narrow road going from Patrington to Holmpton, but nearer to Patrington. At the left-hand side of the road and 80 yards back, was a farm. I went to the farmhouse and asked about the bungalow. The youngish looking farmer's wife said, 'You can have it if you come to work on the farm.' I said, 'I will think about it.' I wasn't keen on starting all over again on farm work and so I didn't think I would mention the bungalow to Win.

But when I saw Win I couldn't help but tell her and she was very happy about it.

I advertised the Velocette sidecar and a customer came to buy it. We fitted it onto his bike and he was happy. But about three days later I saw the man coming along with his bike and sidecar. I thought, *I am not taking the sidecar back it belongs to him now.*

When he pulled up he still looked very happy as he told me the reason for his visit. He had left his bike and sidecar in a big motorcycle garage and showrooms in Doncaster. When he returned to the garage the manager wanted to see him. The manager asked him who had made the sidecar and would he come to ask if I would work for them. The manager wanted to give me my own department and be in charge of producing sidecars.

Since I had arranged to go on the farm I was longing to breathe the fresh air from the North Sea, and having trips to Spurn and Paull. You can't have everything. We moved to Eastfield farm on Holmpton Road. But before we moved we went to see Pug, as he was not far from Bradford.

Pug fell in love with an ATS girl called Ivy when we were at Catterick for the first time. They married while they were at Catterick. They were living at Mytholmroyd, a small town south-east of Bradford. Mytholmroyd was an industrial town once famous for its cotton mills. Running parallel with the road was the railway line and a canal, which I think is the Rochdale canal. At one time the canal would have been busy carrying raw cotton to the mills and returning with Yorkshire cotton.

I think you would say the house suited Pug. It was very rough and there were no cooking facilities. There was a range with an oven, but it wouldn't cook anything. But Pug managed to cook a couple of tins of beans in it for our dinner. He went for his welding torch, made a hole in the side of the oven and pushed the torch through the hole and cooked the beans in record time.

The bedroom that we were going to sleep in was at the top of the landing. To provide some privacy for the benefit of the occupants of this bedroom, there was a wall of rough wooden boards. The top of the boards was about 18 inches from the ceiling. But you wouldn't expect a gentleman like Pug to take advantage of that.

I can't remember having anything to eat apart from the tin of beans, but I expect we would have had something. I can't remember what we did in the evening, but I remember going to bed. Just after getting into bed we heard a little laugh from Pug. It was funny to see two heads above the boards that had evidently seen the striptease, which Win and I had provided. Pug and Ivy didn't stay long in Yorkshire. They went to live in Bromley (London) and Pug started a business in the car repair trade amongst a lot of other car repair people like Pug.

Chapter 40

EASTFIELD FARM

We were very pleased with our new home. The bungalow had been well designed. There was an ideal kitchen and nice square rooms making them easy to set out. There was a front and back garden, which had been well worked and planted. Also there was a three-cornered piece of land that wasn't any good to the farmer, so he said, we could have it. A small drain that was a boundary line always had running water. Win had worked for a market gardener before the war. She liked gardening and knew her stuff regarding flowers and plants. So we made good use of this piece of land and saved money by growing plenty of vegetables and we didn't have to carry water for watering.

There wasn't a garage with the bungalow but there was one across the road where I kept my bikes. The road was narrow and had lots of corners and became a good practice road for the Velo and me.

The Tuplins were very decent people as were most of the farming folk, their names were John and Mary. They had a farm at Winestead, which was run by John's mother and brother. It was very pleasant working on the farm and also I was living on the farm and so I didn't have to travel to work and could go home for my midday meal, which was very good.

I liked Mary and she reminded me of Dolly Grant, she was a town lass from Hull, the same as Dolly. She liked sport and in her bedroom was a large photograph of Gordon Richards and another one of Don Bradman.

Eastfield Farm was just small and was worked by John Tuplin and a teenage lad and now the addition of myself.

Speedway had come to an end in Hull, but had begun again on a new track on part of what used to be the Hull Flying Club's aerodrome at Hedon.

Alan used to go to the Speedway and was a mechanic for a rider called Johnson. Alan and Joan were living in Withernsea. Alan rented a building in Roos and turned it into a garage.

The Grants had gone to a farm in Roos. They gave Alan their work, which would have been very valuable to any garage. To start a business you need quite a lot of money in the bank. But as we already know our money was spent and both Alan and I were at a big disadvantage. It is not always possible for farmers to be dishing out money to pay bills. They have to wait for money from selling corn and this comes in large sums, but not very often.

Alan was very hard up for cash and had sent a bill to Uncle Bill. But he had to wait for payment. So Alan decided he would not do another job for the farm until he received some money. It was harvest time and some parts of a combine harvester had broken. It was very urgent, but Alan refused to go out to do the welding job.

Uncle Bill went to the garage to try to persuade Alan to go, but he refused. Joan who bragged about telling people exactly what she thought, and rarely thought the right and sensible things, gave Uncle Bill a good telling-off. Consequently they killed the golden goose that laid the golden eggs.

I was still thinking about road racing and had come across racing cams for the Velo. There was a grass track meeting in Pickering Park in Hull and so I entered. I was still a shareholder of the Hull Motorcycling Club. I bought one share valued at one shilling when I was fifteen-years-old. It wasn't enough to make me a director, but it did get me entry to the ride.

I managed to get a piece of copper pipe to replace the silencer when I went into the pits. But when I reached the vicinity of Pickering Park what I saw was enough to make me want to turn tail and go back home.

I saw special bikes coming in vans and trailers and as I was riding my bike to the track I felt very old and out-of-date. But I kept on going; I had never come in last so I thought it would be a new experience.

I found my pit and settled down to fitting the piece of copper pipe and adjusted the footrests. I looked at the track to give me an idea of the gear ratio that I would need. I saw these lads practising on their special gridirons. I thought, *Bloody hell, a pushbike would have been quick enough.*

I won the heat and then the semi-final and the final. But there was a young lad on a Speedway bike who was a very good rider. His name was Jackie Adams.

When I was at Grants, George had a friend called Dot Adam because his Speedway bike was a DOT who rode for Hull Speedway at the same time as George was with them. He came to the farm two or three times so I came to know him and one day he gave me a pair of speedway gloves. I presumed he must be Jackie's father, but I never knew for sure.

John and Mary Tuplin became very interested in motorbike racing. They came to see me at my next outing, which was a scramble at North Newbald (near Market Weighton).

I had never been to a scrambling and so I didn't know what to do. I went round the track at a slow pace and the crankcase was ploughing through the hilltops. I soon learnt and won my heat, and then the semi-final.

Leading a race from start to finish didn't suit me. I didn't enjoy my riding that way. Jackie Adams began to make the races more interesting and there was a rider from Scarborough who was good. Therefore, we had some good racing and apart from making the spectators happy, we were also happy.

In one grass track race, Jackie was on the inside position and made a good start and I was just behind him. When we came to the corners Jackie's bike slowed up better than mine with having a JAP engine. So as we broadsided round the corners my front tyre caught up and would only be a few inches from the JAP's carburettor until he accelerated round the corner.

I decided to pass Jackie on the last lap at the last but one corner. He was watching for my front tyre, but it wasn't there, I passed him on the outside and won the race.

A lot of races aren't interesting and are soon forgotten, but I think all riders remember one or two races where you have to do some hard and crafty racing. One race I remember but would rather forget. It was a semi-final and only the 1st and 2nd riders of each race went into the semi final. Jackie was in good form and in this race he had the inside position and got a good start. I tried my best to pass him and failed. We were on the last lap. There was a slow rider in front and when we came to the finishing line he was between us. Jackie flashed over the line; the slow rider crawled over the line as I flashed over the line. Jackie was given 1st place, the slow rider was 2nd, and I was given 3rd place, and so I was done out of the final.

I didn't say anything, but the spectators did because they had been robbed out of a thrilling final.

My mother, Ette, at that time was some bloke's housekeeper who lived at Newbald. She came to the scrambling and was there for one particular race. By now I had a fan club, which were Mary Tuplin and my mother.

I got a good start and then I didn't see any other riders anymore. The crowd were shouting for me to slow down so I kept slowing down. There was a length of the track that was straight and flat and the start and finish line was halfway along it. On the last lap but one, I looked back as I came onto the straight piece and there was no one in sight so I took it easy down the straight, but as I went round the corner at the end of the straight still taking it easy, Jackie Adams passed me and I had no chance of passing him on the narrow part of the track.

Ette was very upset about this so I told Jackie that my mother didn't like it and he had to blow his horn in future when he was about to pass me.

John and Mary stopped coming when harvest began.

I began going to the Speedway, but I didn't spend a lot of time watching the riding, most of it was spent in the pits. I felt more at home there. If anyone was having trouble with the bike and needed any help, I gave it. One rider's mechanic was his girlfriend. She was a sweet young lass and her hands were small and dainty. He was awful to her when she was rushing over putting the bike right and he was always impatient and often swearing at her. I felt sorry for her and so I often helped her.

They had a good support from spectators at first and then attendance began to fade a bit and the finances shrunk. They needed an additional rider and they would have been glad to have me, but they couldn't afford to buy me a Speedway bike, and I couldn't afford to buy one.

As Jackie Adams already had a bike he went to help them out. I was well known for my trick riding as well as racing. Therefore, it was a pity I was without a Speedway bike as I'm sure the two of us would have drawn the crowds back.

The crowds didn't come back so I promised the management that for a month during the interval I would do a stunt. So I went to see Charley Burn who was the blacksmith at Roos. I borrowed long iron poles of tubing.

Then I borrowed some planks and scrounged some straw. I set it up before the racing, and during the interval I did the fire jump two or three times. The little stadium was full.

I had done my fire jump weeks too late, because unfortunately the Speedway was closed for good after that meeting. I was told that Jackie Adams went to a first class

Speedway team. I was glad about that, he was a good rider and the right age.

Preparing for the fire jump was a rush job and I should have had a lot more straw, as I didn't have much of a fire. This was made worse because only one side was alight. After I had done the first jump the flames spread to the other side. But the cameraman had gone when I did the second jump, which was a pity because it would have been a better picture. But not to worry, the picture was good enough to go between Don Bradman and Gordon Richards in Mary Tuplin's bedroom.

Life was good. I had given up all hopes of winning the TT races, but I was happy to go grass tracking and scrambling. By now the bungalow was decorated to our liking and we had good furniture to make it a lovely home. Life isn't supposed to be that good, so when it is good you had better be prepared for a shock.

The shock came from John Tuplin who said with no hesitation, 'I'm selling spot so ya betta find somewhere else as soon as possible.'

I hate having to look for a job and especially when you have to find another house as well.

Chapter 41

MOVING TO HOLMPTON

We didn't have far to go. Mr John Herd, a farmer at Holmpton was prepared to take a chance and take me on.

There were two good houses not far from the cliffs. They had been coastguard houses and had become redundant by the coastguard people and were now occupied by people who didn't have anything to do with coastguards. It would have been nice to have one of those.

But one old house was empty and this became our next home. It was quite a good house. There was no frontage, but the narrow garden and hedge ran from the gable end along the roadside. At the end of the garden was a pigsty and near the house was a shed.

Mr and Mrs Ted Lyons lived next door at the side nearest the sea. Ted was the foreman for Mr John Herd.

The Herds owned almost all of Holmpton, having three farms and a fourth on the way to Welwick. They were all very religious people except little John, Mr Herd's son. Mrs Herd was very nice, very quiet and a kind person. I liked her; in fact, I liked the whole family. Three daughters made up the family and the youngest was Hannah. She was about sixteen-years-old, very nice looking and a good singer. I would liked to have taken her home, but being a coward I dared not ask Win for her permission.

I told Mr Herd how much pay I wanted. I was never interested in what the usual pay was. He told me that the amount was 10 shillings more than the laid down wage. I would be working with Al Hunter and if he gave me an extra 10 shillings he would have to give Al the same. So Al received a raise of 10 shillings in his wage packet. I had no conscience and even slept well after causing a poor farmer an extra £1 per week.

I had a week's holiday before starting work at Herds. I went to see Frank Browne at his home in St John's Wood – a nice ride on the Velo. He was an insurance man and went round to his customers to collect their insurance payments. So I kept him company on his rounds. He would have a large box of Rennies and he was constantly eating them. I thought there must be something wrong with his chest or stomach.

Frank wanted a family type sidecar, but there weren't many about at that time so I said, 'I will make you one.'

Back at home and to start work too soon for my liking. I can't help being lazy. Al and I were the dairymen. We milked the cows and when that was done we put it on Al's wagon and he took it to Hull, for those greedy Hull people to drink. Of course, we had lunch first, a drink of tea, cheese sandwich or a piece of pie. When Al cleared off I had cows and sheep to attend to.

When I went grass tracking, Al was my mechanic. He felt very proud when he was in our pit, flashing his mechanic's badge. I'm pleased to say there was never any mechanical fault for him to rectify.

I bought some young pigs to make use of the pigsty. I bought the meal from the boss. He trusted me to go and get it. I was very careful, when I weighed it, not to get too much from the religious gentleman. There may have been a slight error now and again, but not more than a stone.

The little shed became a sidecar manufacturing works. When it left the production line a letter was sent to the customer to inform him of this and he came to the factory in the garden, and it was married to his bike. Frank was delighted with the sidecar and after a few lessons he was in the same class as Eric Oliver or maybe not quite. Anyway, he had no trouble on the journey home.

Madi, Frank's wife, had two friends in the motor trade. One was a skilled mechanic and the other wasn't skilled, but he had loads of money.

They had a garage halfway between London and Brighton. I think it was called Crossroad Garage. The garage became a financial success and they wished to expand by getting another garage. They came across a garage that suited them and were able to buy it. They needed a manager for the Crossroad Garage and Frank and Madi strongly recommended me. At this time, a relative of Madi's gave them a house that suited them, so they were getting ready to move.

The garage men trusted the recommendation given to them and arrangements were being made for me to go down there. This was being done through Frank. I did not have their new address and I could only wait for a letter from Frank, but I never received one. The Rennies wouldn't go out of my mind and I wondered if he was heading for a heart attack. He was educated and his letters were well written and interesting. I missed them very much and I lost a valuable friend.

Win used to pass by on her bike to get the shopping from Patrington. Two elderly workers, who were brothers, would say how well and fit she was and say how she 'cudenharf push them pedals round wi' them strong legs'.

What they didn't seem to notice was that Win was pregnant and the day for the birth wasn't far away. At the birth, I was officer in charge of kettle, which consisted of having plenty of boiling water at the ready. But I failed my duty when Amy Savage came to say, 'Dad needs his car urgently and it refuses to budge.' I thought an Austin Seven doesn't need much sorting out and I may not be missed. But I was, because our Derrick had got himself born before I got back. Flipping kids are always awkward.

I had plenty to do at home. David was growing up and there was baby Derrick to look after. Therefore, I stopped going motorbike racing. I went for walks with my family and usually we walked down Main Street. There was the school on the left and opposite it was a grass field with ponies grazing and then there was the private road to Herd's Church Farm, which carried on through the farm to the back lane. The chapel was on the left and so was the paddock where we played cricket when we rode our bikes from Easington to try to win against Holmpton School lads.

Turning right on the Withernsea–Easington road on your left was a quaint looking cottage where Ken Gell lived with his wife Bertha and son who was the same age as David. Next on the left was a wide grass verge. A narrow road made a semicircle to make access to the post office and the cottages where two families of Gells lived. Next you came to the pub and a road, which led up to John Herd's farm.

To carry on with the walk there was a row of old houses with long gardens. Mr and Mrs Savage and their daughter Amy, lived in the first one with the tired Austin Seven. We turned round the corner onto the back road. If you turned right after going a good distance along the back road you came to our house, but usually we walked straight on to the cliff tops. On the right, when you came close to the cliffs was a road that went through a farm.

We turned right, passed the new coastguard houses and next to the coastguard's rocket house was the Lyon's house and our house. By this time you would have had a good walk and would be ready for the Sunday roast.

I got on very well with young John Herd. He was a terrific worker, but whether or not he gained anything from his efforts I do not know.

Win's parents had taken on a pub and they asked Win to go for a few days. I wasn't invited; I think it was because they didn't expect me to be able to get the time off. But I did get a couple of days off. So I told Win to ask her parents if I could go, and write to me and I would come on the Velo.

I was looking forward to a ride out and waited for the letter. It didn't come so that meant I had to go to work instead. I was so upset about it that I wrote Win a letter and told her off. When she saw my letter she was so pleased and expected it to be a real love letter. This taught me to be more patient and not be in a hurry to tell people off because of self-pity. She hadn't taken me seriously and did not think that I wanted to go, so I was sorry about the letter.

Mr Lyons and the two labourers worked with the horses and there was more pleasure in working with horses than sitting on a cold smelly tractor. This was a time when machinery was replacing the faithful horses. Ted Lyons and the two labourers were coming to the end of their working lives and the changes must have been terrible for them. They loved their horses and the horses were faithful and obedient to them. They had worked together for many years.

Of course, I was for machinery as I thought it would mean a better standard of living and shorter hours. But this only showed my ignorance as I found out when older. It put lots of people out of work and the people who were working didn't have shorter hours, they still had to work hard for fat cats and shareholders and greedy bosses.

One day little John's love of tractors faded a bit. He was going amongst rows of turnips or something similar and he wanted to get a tractor ready for this work on Monday morning.

The chapel preacher was in the house and the whole family were getting themselves ready in their Sunday best. They would be walking through the stackyard on the way to chapel. Little John was waiting for them to clear off so that he could get on with his job. He only had to jack-up the tractor and adjust the track of the wheels to suit the width of the rows. He would have the job ready before God's disciples returned.

God may have been good to the chapel goodies, but he certainly let little John down.

The wheels had been put to where John wanted them and the jack put away. He thought he had better start it, to make sure it was right for Monday morning. But alas, he only got a chuff-chuff instead of a bang-bang.

He thought it could only be the magneto. There was another Fordson tractor nearby and he knew its magneto was all right so he swapped them. It should have gone bang-bang, but it still went chuff-chuff.

His patience was only just ticking over and kicking the tyres as hard as he could didn't make it start. The people of God had entered the stackyard after hearing a lovely sermon and singing their heads off to Jesus. The stackyard was no place for them when a stray lamb was doing an Irish gig and playing football with the tractor tyres and using the most terrible language at a poor defenceless tractor. His mother went up to her frustrated son saying 'Oh come on John, don't upset yourself so much.'

There are two ways to put the magneto on, one way is right and the other is 180 degrees out. They could think what they liked about John's behaviour, but it was God who made the engine stop in that position, which caused the air to be blue on that Sunday afternoon.

We were getting to the beginning of winter weather and so John couldn't keep warm on the tractor and needed shelter to protect him against the cold winds. So I made him a cab and fixed it onto the tractor. When he came back to the farm after knocking off time, he praised the cab and said, 'he had been warm all day'. He told me it was the first tractor cab in Holderness.

David wanted a two-wheeled bike, but we couldn't afford to get him a new one. There was an old lady's bike in the shed so from that I made a little bike. I cut a length out of the rims and joined them up to make small wheels. I shortened the front forks to match, but I had to leave the long steering head as it was. It was certainly a 'sit up and beg' model and David could only just look over the handlebars. It was a pity there wasn't a contest for the funniest bike in the world. I am sure David would have won it.

Christmas 1950 was getting near and Amy Savage asked me to make a pedal car for one of her nephews. I made it from aluminium with beautiful curves. Amy was pleased with it and so was the lad. But I wondered what David thought of it in comparison with his funny bike.

Chapter 42

HENSALL

A lot of changes came about in 1951 and it started with Win's grandma passing away and Win going to the funeral. Win's parents lived at Hensall, a village between Snaith and Castleford and Win went home with them after the funeral.

When she returned home she was very excited about a cottage in Hensall, which she had looked up. She said, 'It is a good place and has a very big garden.' We had waited six years for a council house in Withernsea, or Withernsea district and it seemed we would never get one.

As Win had said it was a good house; I didn't go to see it. I gave my notice in at Herds and prepared to move. While we were loading the removal van the postman came with a letter from the council to say there was a house for us. However, we decided to continue loading the van and moved to Hensall.

The first shock was the house; it was horrible. It was semi-detached with the gable end on the roadside, apart from a narrow footpath. There was a yard stretching from the road to just past the next door's gable end, and beyond this was the big garden knee-deep in wick grass and other weeds.

The ground in the yard was very rough and stood on it was a square brick building. This building was the toilet for the two houses and it had a brick partition. At the front there were two doors and through each of them there was a wooden seat with a hole. These were the toilets backed by the partition. There was no entrance from the toilets to the other parts of the building. This was gained by a large hole, like a window hole for fitting a window in the back of the building. As the toilet was being used you added ash from the fireplace and when the space under the hole was full you had to go with your shovel, scramble through the hole in the wall and shovel out the toilet and sling it to the back. You did this for six months and then someone came to empty the place and then you started again. I thought Win must love her parents an awful lot to come here to be near them. I was soon asking the council for a house.

I went to work at a garage in Selby run by a Mr Waddington. The mechanics were young people, pleasant and good to work with. The lad who did the car spraying was very good at it and was a good mechanic. There was a sixteen-year-old lad who was very good with cars and was the boss' favourite. I soon got settled down and was happy to be working there.

The young motorcyclists of the district soon admired me for my speed on the Velocette. One lad who was the son of the Tune's family who were farmers in the village, had a very good bike and as he thought himself a real speed merchant, he decided to wait for me on a country road and ride behind me to check my speed. This is how he described it to his friends: 'I was waiting for him and when I heard him coming I started my bike and put it in gear, and he was out of sight before I could get going.'

But there was a lad and he was a good rider. He worked at Selby and two or three times I saw him go by Hensall Road where it joined the Selby Road. One day I had just turned onto the Selby Road when he went by.

I followed him and most of the time we were on full throttle. At Brayton Church there were two bends in the road and we were flat out and my fingers were itching to close the throttle a bit, but I had to remain flat out to keep up with him.

We had to stop at the railway crossing. He had a big surprise when he saw me at the side of him.

At work they began to sell Bond Mini cars. They had a lovely aluminium rounded front, which made them look good.

A customer came in and bought one. A week or two later it came in after hitting something and bashing the front in. The young lad started work on it and when it was finished, it looked like new.

It wasn't a wide garage, but it was quite long. The lad was proud of his work and thought he had earned a drive, so when the boss left for lunch the lad got in it, drove it to the forecourt, turned round and went down the garage with a look of, 'ain't I good' and bashed into the wall. It was brilliant because the front was now exactly the same shape as when it had come in. I don't know if the boss had enjoyed his lunch or not, but he didn't look very happy when I saw him looking at the crumpled Bond Mini car.

Another Bond Mini car was sold. The driver couldn't drive, so I had the job of teaching him. I found the brakes to be useless. I wrote a letter to the company telling them that the brakes were useless and told them how to improve them and made some drawings.

They wrote back kindly, and thanked me. They told me that their engineers were already redesigning the brakes in exactly the same way as my letter suggested.

They could have been honest about it as my only intention was to cut down on accidents.

I don't think my pupil was very bothered about passing the driving test. He sold footwear and as long as he could get round the village houses with his wares to flog, he couldn't care less. I don't know who was paying my wages, but that had nothing to do with me, I was only a working man. We used to call at my house now and again for a bit of lunch. Every time he came he would give Win and the two lads boots, shoes, slippers, and whatever else. This teaching was taking a long time and the lads would soon have enough footwear to open a shop.

There was a doctor who lived at Gilberdyke who had a lovely Alvis car. He thought too much of it to put it into a garage, so I looked after it for him. I wanted to make some small adjustments on it. It was a long way from home so we went round the villages, flogging boots and shoes. I can't remember how it ended; perhaps he went to prison.

Peter was born on 14 June 1951. Win wasn't well and the doctor called often. The landlord also came at short and regular intervals with his shovel, sand and cement, to patch up the walls. I think his mixture of sand and cement must have been about 20:1 so the patching up was never-ending.

Likewise the digging in the garden was never-ending, as it had been neglected for years. But after weeks of hard work it was ready for planting.

Win's dad was working at a corn merchants and they had a litter of piglets for sale. There were ten of them and Win's dad, Bill, bought five. He asked me if I wanted the other five. I thought it was a good idea and bought them.

I sowed most of the garden with sugar beet seed and I had a good crop. I made a slicer and fitted it above the trough so the pigs got their sweet chips as I was cutting them.

The method of feeding pigs had changed because people no longer wanted fatty bacon. When pigs were killed, the fat of three parts of the pig were measured and graded into A,B and C. Therefore, money was lost by over-feeding.

My pigs were fed on a small amount of meal and a lot of sugar beet and because they were thin, Bill was always saying I should feed them as they were starving. When they became bacon I got three (A) grades while Bill had lower grades. Therefore, I received a lot more money than he did. Having to admit that his knowledge of feeding pigs was a big disappointment to him, as well as being out of date.

Chapter 43

WORKING AT MR BAKER'S GARAGE

We were expecting a long wait for a council house and so we began to look for another house. We didn't have far to look. There was a farm almost opposite, and like most farmers they preferred a modern bungalow and were having one built at the end of the stackyard near the back road, which gave them a good frontage.

They asked us if we would like to rent the farmhouse. We certainly did and were looking forward to moving out of this place and living in the farmhouse.

We had been living in Hensall about two and a half years when we moved into the farmhouse. It was a typical old farmhouse with large rooms where you could arrange your furniture as you wished and not be too crowded. The house was in good condition, as it had been well looked after and very clean. The decor suited us and so there weren't any big jobs to do.

There was a large frontage with level and hard ground, suitable for parking vehicles and working on them. I could make things with metal or wood and the first thing I thought about was making a little pedal car for Peter.

I bought pedals and wheels from a bike shop in Selby. I was able to get a sheet of aluminium from an engineering shop also in Selby. I used aluminium rivets to hold the joints together.

There were no difficult curves to make, only straight curves, which could be bent round something of the correct circumference. Therefore, Peter didn't have long to wait for his little car.

He was enjoying his rides, but unfortunately there was a little lad who lived across the road who came for a ride. Peter, not being selfish, let him have a ride then Peter got back in his car. Before he had a chance to move, the lad was asking for another ride. But he was impatient and picked up half a brick and hit Peter between the eyes. He was rushed to hospital and he has always had to wear glasses since.

A glazier's shop in Selby had stacks of sliding glass doors. They were 19 inches by 12 inches, just right for bathroom cabinets. They were very good value for the price so I purchased sixteen of them. I made six cabinets and sold them. I had the remaining doors for a number of years until a friend and myself needed a bathroom cabinet.

I went to work at Baker's garage in Kellington, about four miles from Hensall. It was a family business that had been running since the turn of the century. There were Mr Baker senior with his son who was married and had a family of five girls and a very lovely wife.

They were agents for Austin cars. They repaired cars, but their main work was with tractors and farm machinery. They owned threshing machines and steam engines to tow and drive them. Apart from the garage, they had the blacksmith's shop and a machine shop with suitable tools and lathes for making large parts and small parts for the threshing machines, carts, wagons and agricultural machinery.

Mr Baker and his son worked in the garage. They worked mostly on cars and tractors depending on how busy each department was. Then there was the mechanic who had a horse that he rode around the village. He had worked at Baker's for donkey's years and thought he was the foreman; he was a real crawler. There were also two men who did the labour work. Then there was I, the main motor mechanic.

The blacksmith was also the machine operator and turner. He was a big powerful man and as gentle as a lamb. I got on well with him and we became good friends. He had been at Baker's for donkey's years as well, and the men who worked on the threshing machines had worked there for a number of years too. It was a very happy place and I enjoyed working there. One day a lady brought her car in with clutch trouble. She said she had taken it into a garage in Castleford and they had done some work on the clutch, but it still wasn't right. I drove the car into the garage and onto the ramps. Crawler came to me, but not on his horse and said that I mustn't do the clutch because when cars have been bodged up, we turn them away.

I decided to change their rules and dismantled the parts to get at the clutch. Crawler came to ask how I was doing. I told him that I was doing all right and that someone had done some welding, but it needed a bit of grinding down and when that was done the clutch would be as good as new. He went away feeling pleased.

I finished the job and the lady came to drive it home. After about a quarter of an hour she came back with a smile and praised the good work. They called me Ernest, which was my first name. I heard Crawler talking to the boss about the clutch. He said, 'I thought the job would be difficult for Ernest so I explained to him in detail how he should do it.'

Mr Baker's late father had made a car round about the year 1900. It was at the back of a shed as if it was a piece of scrap. It was a pity they hadn't found a place in the garage for it and kept it in good condition. There weren't many cars made at that time and most of the people who did make them, became well known.

Two new cars arrived; they were an Austin A30 and an A40. I prepared them for the customers and delivered them. I hadn't driven a new car until then and I was amazed with everything about them. The engines had a lot of power and the gearboxes were so quiet and it was so easy to change gears.

Such a contrast to the side valve engines and gearboxes without syncromesh, which we often drove.

I thought I would be able to make a car, which would be an improvement on a lot of cars that I had worked on, and I began to think about it. We had plenty of room at the farmhouse. Therefore, it had to be built before we got that council house.

I liked Kellington. There was a row of Swedish houses, and I wouldn't have minded having one. But they were made mostly of wood and I was afraid of having a fire.

There was a new estate nicely set out and I liked the look of the houses. I was hoping that if the council ever got round to letting us have a house it would be there.

Win was nagging me to change my job. I liked being at Bakers. They were very good people to work for and I was happy there. But Win wanted more money and the trouble was, the road from Whitley Bridge to Snaith was having big improvements carried out.

Win's young brother was working on the road as a labourer and was getting a lot more pay than my pay. I eventually told myself that you only go to work for money so why not go where you can get the most. Therefore, I gave Mr Baker a week's notice. I was very miserable during that week and was glad when Saturday came.

Chapter 44

I BECAME A ROADMAN

My first job was in the council yard at Snaith. There was a load of hardcore in the way and I and another man had to move it. After a few shovels full I was ready to take my jacket off. Joe, my mate asked why I was taking my jacket off. 'Because I'm too warm,' I replied. 'Well, slow down then,' advised the old timer. So I had learnt my first lesson for working on the council.

In spite of Joe's advice and having dumpers to do most of the work, manpower was still needed and there was plenty of hard shovelling to be done. Win's brother, Jack, was big and strong and he was a good worker, but he also used his brains.

Jack was married and had four children. He loved his children and during his time off he usually had the kids with him. They would go fishing and Jack was good at snaring rabbits, so rabbit pie would be the following day's dinner.

No matter where we were working, Jack would go missing about an hour or maybe two hours before the foreman was due to come to us. Jack would always have one or two rabbits for him when he arrived.

The dividing line between the road and the verge, or footpath is made with kerbstones. But not this road, it was concrete, a channel was dug and filled with concrete and a man with a levelling float smoothed the concrete.

As the concrete was almost set it was sprayed with sealant, which sealed the moisture in to prevent the concrete from drying too quickly. This prevented cracks and also and made it stronger. I had the job of spraying on the sealant.

In the late afternoon a small gang of men put oil lamps along each side of the road, which gave a red light to warn motorists of work being done on the kerbs. There was no work on Saturdays and Sundays. They gave me the job of looking after the lamps on these two days. The work consisted of going to all the lamps on the Saturday evening and filling them up with paraffin and relighting any that had gone out. This was repeated on the Sunday evening.

I did a little experiment and found that if I made sure all the lamps were filled to the top, they would last from Saturday until Monday morning. Therefore, I didn't have to work on the Sunday evenings. No one ever knew about this so I was still being paid for the Sunday work.

Brough aerodrome became the venue for motorcycle racing with a programme of top British riders who provided the spectators with exciting riding. It would be 1953 when we first went to see them. The bikes were mostly British makes, but it was a time when foreign bikes were able to compete with British bikes in world championships.

The tourist trophy races began in 1907 and up to 1953 the British manufacturers' racing bikes were similar to ordinary touring bikes. The German NSU 250cc bikes had six-speed gearboxes, and our manufacturers didn't think that would be suitable for an ordinary road bike and you couldn't learn anything by having them. Therefore, they were losing interest and the Italian manufacturers of MV Gilera, Moto Guzzi, began to take over.

In 1954 Gilera and MV's fitted five-speed gearboxes on their 500cc bikes and MV's fitted six-speed gearboxes on their 125cc. Moto Guzzi had five-speed gearboxes on all their machines. Therefore, British riders were changing to Italian manufacturers.

There were also small racing cars racing at Brough. This made a change from watching motorbikes and still gave us exciting races to watch. The most popular make of car were the Coopers that used a 500cc Norton engine. They were lightweight and were very quick; this was Formula 3.

At the end of the war, racing cars were very scarce. Hence the 500cc Coopers built by Charles Cooper and his son John in their small factory. The Norton engine was at the rear of the car. They went from the Formula 3 cars to front engine sports cars and Formula 2 cars, also with front engine.

In 1955 their sports racers had rear engines. The Coopers Coventry climax engines were used in fire pumps during the war, and after more engine tuning, was used in their Formula 1 racing cars.

David, Derrick and Peter were developing a love for cars, motorbikes and speed. So I bought them a go-kart. There was a disused aerodrome about two miles away where learner drivers learnt their skills. This was the place where they became very good go-kart drivers.

Win had a nephew called Woods who lived at Upton near Doncaster, who was an expert on go-karts and I think that he was the English Champion at this time. There was a track for go-karts not very far from home so this also became a regular outing. One driver who needed more speed asked me to work on his go-kart, so I gave it a tune-up. He was a good driver so his first race after the tune-up was very exciting. One of the competitors was the wife of the boss of Fletcher's sauce factory in Selby. Also in the race was Tony Wood.

Tony Wood had a good start and was leading and the chap on my tuned kart was in second position and Mrs Fletcher third. Mrs Fletcher had a great battle for second place that gave her a lot of confidence and she thought *I've passed him, now I'm going to pass Wood*. So there was another fierce battle and she passed him on the last lap and she kept her lead to win the race. Unfortunately our go-kart wasn't suitable for racing.

The road job had come to an end. During the last couple of days of my time on the road job, I had a lot of pain and felt poorly. Our doctor's surgery was at Snaith and because I was too ill to ride a motorbike I had to go by bus. But to get to the bus was about a mile to walk and when I left the bus I had to walk to the surgery.

By the time I reached the surgery I was very ill and in agony. If the man I saw had been a good doctor, or just an ordinary doctor, he would have called for an ambulance urgently and I would have been taken to the hospital and would have been operated on. But unfortunately this man who they called a doctor, was just a stupid idiot. He made an appointment with the hospital for the following day. But he didn't arrange any transport for me.

I had to walk from the surgery to the bus stop and wait a long time before the bus arrived. The bus ride was torture and then I had the long walk home. Win and I had to leave home early to catch the bus and the trudge from home to the bus stop began. Win was wishing she had been able to borrow a pram for me to sit in.

Getting to the hospital felt like a 100-mile journey. But when I was in the hospital they didn't waste time and I was rushed to the operating theatre. I had some kind of growth on my bowel. My appendix was healthy, but the surgeon didn't want me to have another operation in the future in the same place. So my appendix was taken out as well as the growth. After only one week they needed my bed for someone else, so I was kicked out. The journey in the ambulance nearly killed me. I was on sick leave for three months. During that time I was thinking about the car that I was going to make. And I did some drawings.

Chapter 45

WORKING FOR THE WAR DEPARTMENT

At Burn, which is between Eggborough Power Station and Selby, there is a wartime aerodrome. The army used this for examining, servicing and distribution of every kind of army vehicle. I went to work there as a vehicle mechanic, on 25 November 1954.

I had been studying with the British Institute of Engineering Technology, and was awarded the Institute's Diploma of Associate Membership on 4 January 1955. Soon after this I was promoted and became tester and inspector of all types of tracked and wheeled vehicles.

There were two ladies in the office; one was young and she lived with her parents who ran the Burn Post Office. The other one was older and lived in Selby. During the war she was with the Dambusters and used to go to their annual dinners. She told me all about the Dambusters and before long I was thinking that I must have been with them also.

Win's parents were still living in Hensall and Bill, her father, was employed with us and was a driver. Also, from Hensall was a friend called John Todd. He had an Ariel motorbike and we used to ride together to work and home again. When I worked in Selby, I bought my petrol from a small garage. When I called, the boss nearly always had a problem with either a back axle or a gearbox or engine etc. So I always have to sort things out for him. Once again I was going past his garage and stopping for petrol and sorting out his problems.

One day I was looking for a Morris truck. It wasn't my job to chase after vehicles, but this one was wanted urgently. I went to have a look in the paint shop. There were two ladies at their work who I knew. I was asking them if this Morris truck had been in their workshop and had gone out again.

The foreman naturally thought I was a driver and started to give me a good telling-off for talking to his girls. I thought if that is how he talks to the drivers it was time he had a good telling-off. I checked everything in his shop and really gave him a dog's life, and warned him that I would be back to make another check, and he would be in real trouble if there wasn't any improvement. I did go back and give him another good telling-off. I didn't like to take advantage, but I thought he deserved it.

There was a lot of thieving and twisting going on. One day the army wanted about three hundred, one-ton two-wheeled trailers. There were several long rows of them. You could drive past them and not see anything wrong, but when I went to examine them most of the inner wheels were missing. It was a mystery to me how they managed to get away with them.

When I examined wagons I did the checking over first and then the road test. One day it was getting near to morning break and I decided to go home for it, so I took a wagon without checking it.

The wagon seemed to lack power and the suspension didn't feel right for an empty wagon. When I arrived home I looked in the back. There were three motorbikes with tools and clothing. No one knew anything about them so I could have unloaded them at home and kept them.

I was thinking it was time to make a start on my home-made car. But a fitter who lived at Selby had an SS100 Jaguar. He and his wife had worked on it for two years and it was like new, but they had sickened of it and wanted to sell it. He wanted £76 for it. I felt sure that I could get that amount for my V Twin 1,000cc BSA. He had promised to wait a couple of days. I sold the motorbike and sidecar straight away and went to collect the Jaguar. Someone had offered him £80 for it and he had taken it. So I was back to making a car.

To get the measurements for my car I had the family sitting on stools arranged like sitting in a car. I don't know how I worked out how much the lads would grow and how quickly.

I decided to make a three-wheeled car; this would be cheap on tax and also there didn't seem to be any factory making a first class three-wheeler. It would have a thousand cc V Twin Engine, as I didn't want to be loitering as I was travelling quite a lot to army depots.

I began studying for the AMIEE (electrical engineers). I didn't have to start at the beginning because my AMIET exam covered the first half. My first book was Higher Maths and as I had already done books I and II, it was just a matter of adding a bit more knowledge to my brain.

A friend who was a maths teacher at school told me to go to him if I needed help. To be helped with difficult problems can save a lot of time so one day I went to him with two or three difficult calculations. But he could not work them out.

I had another friend who I knew would be able to help me. He had a sports car and I maintained it. He worked at Brough and was an expert on jet engines. He had a quick glance as if they were just simple arithmetic. He said, 'Oh this is nothing, you just do this... and that... and... here's the answer.' I felt very stupid, but that didn't matter, I had learnt something.

A lady whose husband was killed in the war was doing her best for her son. I was teaching him maths and basic engineering. I had bought some motorcar building material, and so I was having a very busy time.

The engine, gearbox, and back axle, were from a 1935 James three-wheeler. The engine was air-cooled so I was not bothered about a radiator and all their faults. The chassis and the floor were made of wood, and the body was mostly marine plywood. The windscreen was from a Humber car. I liked it because one part of it opened to allow air to come in. Not for the purpose of keeping you awake because the noise from the engine would do that, as it was almost sat in my lap. There would be no crawling underneath for topping up the gearbox and back axle; this was done through the floor.

Fitting the gearbox was no problem and the dash panel had the benefit of my wood experience and looked good with its small oil amp meter and petrol gauges. The wings were fibreglass, but they were not made in a mould. Time goes too quickly when you mess about with such high-fluted methods. I used ½ inch wire mesh and with a bit of bending and pulling and stretching it soon came into shape. Then the fibreglass was worked into the netting and smoothed off.

My boss called to see how I was getting on with the car. I said, 'It is coming along nicely.' Then he told me I was going to Uttoxeter in three days' time and did I want a rail ticket. I said, 'No, I am going in my car.' He laughed because he thought I was joking.

He could be excused for thinking that because I had quite a lot to do on it including making the doors. So he left me saying, 'If you don't want a rail ticket I won't get you one.'

Work began at 8 o'clock, and I would be travelling on the day before that. This meant I only had two days to get the car ready. When I knocked off on the day before I would be travelling, I had a one-door car. So I had to get up early and make the other door.

I finished the door and fitted it; of course I didn't have door-windows. They make the car stuffy and unhealthy. I was hoping the engine would start. The starting handle went through a hole in the side of the car and connected up with a shaft coming from the timing box. One swing was all that was needed to get the engine singing.

I felt confident about how the car would go so I switched off and went in for some food and drink and prepared myself for a test run to Uttoxeter.

The car was going well and I was as happy as a sand boy. Then there were big black clouds drifting overhead and then the rain poured down. It suddenly came to me why car doors have windows.

There were big puddles on the road in Thorne, and there was a coal wagon. I remember it well because in spite of all the wet, my carburettor burst into flames. The coalmen were real fire fighters. They picked up a coal sack apiece, dipped them into a deep puddle and knocked hell out of my new car.

There didn't seem to be any real damage done and I was soon speeding on my journey. Everything was going fine, but when I reached Nottingham I was very tired and so I stopped in a lay-by and didn't know anything until I woke up in the early hours of the next day. I reached the army barracks at 7.30 a.m.

My job at Uttoxeter lasted for two weeks. I had good digs that had been arranged by the army. There was just the man and his wife. The house was quite a long way from the town. They went to a pub every night and I took them in my Rolls Royce. I don't drink beer so I drank orange juice. But the lady knocked back about half a dozen stouts every night. She was small and fat so if you saw her you would guess that she went to the pub every night to drink fat-building liquids.

On the trip home the weather was good and I was very pleased with my little car. The chassis that was part of the body had lots of strength and was low, about 7 inches from the ground. I could make it broadside round sharp corners at a good speed and there was no danger of it rolling over.

It is very naughty to make a car and just go driving it on the roads, except of course a little road test to Uttoxeter. To be right you have to have an engineer to fill in forms. Then you must have insurance and then a licence. So who best to get for doing the forms? – My friend at the little garage at Haddlesey, Jim Sykes.

I took the forms and his eyes goggled. 'I don't know anything about filling these in, can you do it?' he said. So I filled in the forms and he signed his name. Needless to say it passed easily.

One day when I went home from work, Win and the lads were ready for a quick dash into Lincolnshire. Win had seen a cottage advertised in the newspaper. So off we went, speeding on the straight roads and sliding round corners.

It was a lovely cottage with a garden and orchard. The lads liked it and so did I; it was exactly as described in the paper. But Win came out with her usual saying, 'No thank you, I'll leave it.' We enjoyed the ride out and I was back at work the following day.

There are two types of examiners. Good ones were the conscientious ones who failed every component with the slightest fault or wear. They cost the taxpayer millions of pounds. Then there were the others who would let slight faults go and didn't miss anything, which needed to be changed or repaired. Then there was myself, if a part was serviceable it stayed on the vehicle.

But I was particular as far as safety was concerned, when I rejected two tanks that had special work to perform.

There was going to be very important manoeuvres in Europe and it was essential that a special tank would be taking part. It was so important that they prepared two in case one failed its inspection. They both came to me and I failed both of them. Our boss received a letter from the War Office to say how disappointed they were over not having one of them. But they could not have them without my signature.

We often had a ride to Withernsea. Ernie was living in the bungalow that he built, with his three dogs, and Ette was in a prefab. We always called to see Ernie first and he was delighted to see us.

Next we went to see Ette, and Alan and Joan. Ette had a grandchild called Christopher, a favourite although she would say she had no favourites. He was always saving up for something and was always about £2 short. When we arrived at Ette's it wasn't long before Christopher turned up.

They had both learnt their little speeches off by heart. It would go like this: 'Did you manage to get that, which you were saving up for Christopher?' He would look at me with a sad face and say, 'No Gran, I've been saving for it for a long time, but I haven't got enough money yet.' They would both look at me and Ette would ask how much he wanted. He would tell her, but he really was telling me. Then Ette would make some remark about Uncle Jack will have enough money to spare.

Win would be itching to go. We would have a cup of lukewarm tea. Win hadn't come to look at Ette, so we would set off towards the shops.

First shop would be Ella Ashton's; she sold all sorts of things and Win would be looking for a bargain. Then next we would read adverts at newspaper shops. Suddenly Win would become interested in something and say, 'I want to go and have a look at that.' I would say we don't want one. Win would say, 'you can have a look for nothing.' We would go to have a free look.

Win, during the war, was an inspector at Avro aeroplane factory until a piece of steel went in one of her eyes. So she had to come off inspections, and then Avro began to get aeroplanes back in the sky again.

Whatever we went to look at, it had a thorough inspection from Win. Then she'd suddenly ask, 'What's yer bottom price?' £5 comes the reply. 'Oh, I'll leave it,' says Win.

We would go back to Ette's and it would soon be time to go home, and I would wonder why the heck we bothered to go.

Chapter 46

WIN'S FAMILY

Win's mother was called Hilda and before she married she was a Johnson. Her brother, Charley had a garage in Askern and I was told that he had a bus service. His buses were the first to run from Askern to Doncaster.

Bill, Win's father, had been in the First World War and suffered the effects of being gassed. He had been a miner and I think he gave it up on account of his lungs being damaged. They had four children. Charles was the eldest, and then came Kath, Win, and Jack who was the youngest.

Bill and Hilda went into the ice cream business. Jack, although being very small, thought he should have a share of the profits. No matter where they kept the income from selling ice cream, even in the top cupboard, Jack would always find it and help himself. He kept these skills to the end of his life.

Win's granddad Johnson died sometime before I met Win and no one seemed to mention him. But I do know that Grandma Johnson had a café. She took the ice cream business and also Charley. He went to live with them.

Charley went to war and later when Jack was old enough, he also became a soldier.

Bill and Hilda began baking and whatever Bill did, he always became very good at it. He won trophies for his cakes and they sold pikelets to Marks and Spencer. He began breeding fox terrier dogs and won at a lot of shows. They took on a fish shop at Worksop and were very disappointed when they only had about half a dozen customers on their first night. But they progressed quickly and were able to replace the old range and have the shop fitted with everything new. There was an REME Barracks at Worksop and Alan was there. He used to go to the Bryan's for fish and chips. When I took Win home for the first time Alan was surprised to meet the girl who served him in the fish shop in Worksop.

Grandma Johnson had a café at Askern, well situated in the park at the side of the lake. Win and Kath used to ride their bikes, about eight miles to Askern, every Saturday and Sunday to serve in the café. So everyone helped to keep the business going during the war.

There was a fairly large grass field near the park where horses grazed when they were not pulling the ice cream carts. There were also a lot of pigs, which also belonged to Grandmother. After the war, Charley went back to the business. He had married a Scotch girl called Cath and they lived in the house where the business was. There was a large square yard flanked by the house and a wall at each side with good buildings across the back.

They invested in new machines to step up the production and to turn out choc ices etc. But when Jack came home from the war, he had nothing to come back to.

Charley's horses always looked well and the drivers could feel proud of themselves when the horses were yoked to the flash ice cream carts, with the curved and straight lines, the work of experts. Charley's competition was Masarella. When there was a show there would be Bryan and Masarella's ice cream carts, side by side, racing to get the best pitch at the show.

Charley and Cath had one big problem. They said that they knew the driver's were lining their pockets with some of the takings, but they didn't know how to stop it. I didn't know how to solve their problem and if I did I wouldn't have told them.

Sadly the horses and lovely carts were replaced by motorised ice cream vans. Johnson's garage was about a quarter of a mile from Charley's place so naturally that is where the vans and the car went for maintenance and repairs.

Uncle Charley wasn't pleased about Charley getting everything while Jack had nothing. He told me that when he made out Charley's bills he added some on because of Charley having Jack's share. That would have been okay except that the money he thought was Jack's share never went to Jack, he kept it for himself. I didn't attempt to tell him this as I don't think he would have understood.

Charley began to realise that his Uncle was cheating him, so he began to bring his repairs to me. I didn't like Charley any more than I did the other Charley. So I charged a good price for my work until I became too busy and he had to go somewhere else.

One day Win was walking along with her mother. Someone had dropped a shilling and Win picked it up. But Win's mother said that it was her shilling because she saw it first and it was only because she was old that Win beat her to it. Win also had a handicap because she was about five months pregnant. They agreed to change it and have sixpence each, and they were both happy.

These two women were not mean; it was just their nature and how they had been brought up. When we went shopping we also shopped for Win's mother. When we reached Bryan's house we would have a cup of tea and a bun or something. After this, Win would fish out from her purse the two shopping receipts. The rest of the evening was spent working out the amount of money she wanted from her mother. This had to be exact to a halfpenny.

When Grandma Johnson died, Win's parents and Win got nothing. In other words, Charley got the lot.

Win was hoping for a daughter. She was a very good daughter to her parents and I was hoping she had her wish, as she certainly deserved to have a daughter who would grow up to be as she had been.

It was a weekend and the weather was good and there was motorbike racing at Brough and we were getting ready to go. David had a friend who lived just down the road and he went to see him. Why we let him go to see his friend when we were going out, I will never know.

I was ready, but Win was still upstairs. Ladies like to look good when they are going out even if they are going to motorbike racing. But she was an extra long time so I went upstairs wondering if there was anything wrong. She was on the bed in agony having a miscarriage. David's friend's mother had come to our house in a temper over something that had happened between her boy and David. She had played up hell with Win and upset her so much that she began to have the baby.

She was rushed to Wakefield hospital and I stayed at home to see to the lads. When things were in order at home I went to the hospital. I was walking down the centre of the ward looking for Win. There was a lady looking at me and she looked extremely poorly, but she gave me a lovely brave smile. I almost walked past her before I realised it was Win. I felt really bad about it, but there wasn't much I could do about it.

The doctor told me that they couldn't save both of them and according to the law in such cases they had to save the baby. Therefore, they had to just let Win die. Sometime later, the baby was unlucky and died. It was a boy. Win pulled through, but she was very ill and stayed in hospital for six months.

Working on Burn aerodrome was not such a good job in winter as the cold winds and the snow blew across with nothing to stop it. The tanks would become covered with snow and ice and it was impossible to be warm no matter what you were wearing. Inspecting and testing wagons and tanks, armoured cars, gun carriages, troop carriers and tank transporters and trailers and even bicycles, went on day after day.

Christmas and New Year would come and go and then it was spring again and gradually the vehicles became warm and the pleasure of working at the aerodrome came back to us.

Derrick's dog, Peggy, had a litter and one of them was extra small. Always, when Bill came to our house he would have something to say about this small pup. He said that he would take it home otherwise it would die.

Derrick didn't want to part with his pup, but his granddad kept on about it until Derrick gave it to him. This had been a crafty trick on Derrick because the smaller they are the better they are for showing.

The little bitch won at Crufts and other big shows, and then she had a litter and in this litter there was a small pup. It won at Crufts and became a champion.

An American Griffin breeder offered Bill a large sum of money; so large, that Bill forgot about what he had said about what they did to the ears. The dog went to America and became an American champion.

Bill became rich from Derrick's little bitch. But not only that, he became admired by the kennel club supporters and looked upon as being some special gentleman by the lady dog owners and he lapped it up and couldn't get enough of it.

But what about Derrick? He was content with Peggy and that was as well, because that was all he got.

Egypt wanted some tanks and as British governments are always hard up for cash we had to sell them some. But there were complications naturally. The Government was not allowed to flog tanks to Egypt. But they were allowed to sell agricultural machinery.

Someone in the War Office said that if a tank were rid of its gun barrel, it wouldn't be a tank. The paint on the tanks was grey so without the barrel there wasn't much difference between a charioteer and a Ferguson tractor. That is if you work in an office.

So the deal was done and all these tanks were lined up and the welders began their long task of removing the gun barrels. Of course they were class four tanks. But someone had driven a nearly new class one tank amongst them. The welders didn't notice this and so it lost its barrel with all the other tanks. I wonder if Nasser had a friend amongst the drivers.

Chapter 47

BUY ONE AND GET TWO FREE

Somewhere north of Filey were approximately one hundred enormous engines left over from the war. They were American engines. They knew that inside the cylinders there was a coating of rust. But not all of them were rusty.

My job was to remove all the cylinder heads, which would be quite a lot of work for one man. The cylinder heads of the rusty ones had to be left off. But those with no rust had to have their cylinder heads reassembled. I was expected to have the job done in three weeks.

I noticed that if the spark plugs were clear of rust the inside of the cylinders would be clear. Also, if there was rust on the spark plugs there would be rust on the inside of the cylinders.

Therefore, I first removed all the spark plugs of an engine and checked them for rust. If every spark plug was clean I refitted them and that was that, engine finished. This was all I had to do on 40 per cent of the engines saving myself a lot of work.

Of course I trusted my theory, which may not be 100 per cent correct. But that wasn't my problem, as I didn't expect an armed guard to come from America to take me back with them to do my job properly.

I was lodging in a large house and they had enough accommodation for Win and the lads. So I came home for them and we had a good holiday as they stayed for two weeks. I had finished my job at the end of the second week. So I had a free week with them.

Back at Burn they were getting ready for a large sale of all army vehicles and equipment. One farmer came to me asking for just a little favour. He had been looking at a three-ton Bedford truck and he liked it and it would be very useful on his farm. But it was a class one vehicle, but if I brought it down to a class four he would be able to buy it. There would be something for me he said. A bag of spuds, I reckon.

When the sale was in progress, I was busy with examining wagons, but I had a look. As Win would say, 'You can have a look for nowt.' There were three motorbikes. They were in lovely condition and being sold, while in the workshop there were motorbikes, which were in poor condition and were being prepared for being returned to the army. I thought about the bag of spuds I might have had.

While I was looking, the auctioneer had come to three bikes and a young man had bought one of them. At least that is what he thought he had done. As he was pushing his purchase away the auctioneer's clerk told him not to forget the other two bikes, which he had just bought. That wasn't bad shopping, buy one get two free. I wondered if they were the three bikes that I had taken home. I had a day out at an army depot in Beverley. There weren't any tanks, just lorries and Landrovers, so I had an easy day.

Chapter 48

SUEZ CRISIS, 1956

President Nasser of Egypt nationalised the Suez Canal Company in order to finance construction of the Aswan Dam. Eden denied Nasser's right to nationalise. This caused a lot of argument with Britain and France against the Arabs.

This gave us a lot of work. We had recently received tank transporters from the army. These had to be inspected and road tested and then go into the workshops. There was a lot of work to do on some of them, which meant the army were short of tank transporters. Luckily Pickfords were able to help out.

There was an order for 300 Landrovers. Some very keen examiner had noticed that incorrect brake fluid had been used. This gave the workshop a big load of extra work draining off the brake fluid and replacing it with the correct type. When this was completed the brakes had to be bled to remove all the air in the system.

Two main types of brakes were Girling and Bendex. If you used Girling fluid in Bendex brakes the sealing rubbers would be ruined and vice versa. It was a sales gimmick; the only difference between Girling brake fluid and Bendex was that Girling fluid was red because they added a red dye. When the fitters finished each of the Landrovers, a driver would bring it to the examiners to road test. If there was any air left in the brake system this would be shown by the brake pedal having a spongy feeling and going down further than usual. In this case the vehicle would be driven to the reject park to wait until it could be taken back to the workshop for re-bleeding and once again tested by the examiner.

To keep up with the work we had to work overtime. We didn't mind this. The weather was good and there was a good moon, lighting up the hares as they zigzagged in front of us.

Eventually the Landrover order was completed and they went on their way to Egypt. But there was still plenty of examining to do on lots more vehicles.

Together with the French government, who thought Nasser was the main supporter of Algerian rebels, Eden planned the invasion of Egypt and occupation of the Suez Canal, to coincide with the Israeli attack on Egypt. America disapproved of British action, which was condemned by the United Nations; the Labour Party objected strenuously. Britain was forced to withdraw. The affair was embarrassing and a blunder for the British government, causing loss of diplomatic prestige and resulted in the resignation of Eden in 1957.

Chapter 49

MOVING TO KELLINGTON

At last we had been allocated a council house and we were moving to Kellington; it was 1957. Not too bad – we only asked for a council house in October 1945.

It had been a long wait, but we were happy to be in a nice house at last. It was a well-designed house with nice rooms set out in a sensible order. So good that I think the design was the work of a lady designer who was a good housekeeper.

We had two gardens, one at the front and one at the back. There were twelve garages over a spacious square area giving room for manoeuvring and also working on the car in the open. There was a vacant garage, which belonged to our house.

The residents were mostly miners and retired miners. They were very sociable and easy to get on with. Mr Robinson who was a miner and his wife and two or three teenage daughters, lived next door to us. They were very good neighbours and our lads played with their girls. David was eleven-years-old.

The distance from Kellington to Burn was about the same as the distance from Hensall to Burn.

We had struggled through another winter and those large chunks of steel called tanks were warming up and the tedious job of inspecting all the brackets and containers and tracks didn't seem to be so tedious now that we could keep warm.

I was still going through Haddlesey and still getting petrol from the little garage and still helping my friend Jim Sykes with his problems with cars. The garage was built on low ground, a lot lower than the road. During the winters, his garage would be flooded. I do not know why he stayed there. He must have been close to retiring age and was probably hanging on for that. Or he may have been like most people who have a small business, just wanting to hand it over to his son.

When the son had left school he went to work on Burn aerodrome with the army vehicles. I think that would have been upsetting for his dad. But you can't blame the lad for that as I reckon he would have been much better off.

My little car had another test. Not a load of theory stuff like it got at the little garage. It was a real practical test. A man, who I gave a lift home to and who lived at Haddlesey, came to me with a problem. Not his own problem, it was a lady who needed to get home from work that day in quick time. She was his next-door neighbour and he had asked if I would take her home. She normally travelled home on the buses and always had a long wait before the bus arrived at Burn entrance from Selby. As I was a glutton for punishment I said, 'Yes'.

When she came to my little car it's a wonder the little car didn't have a heart attack. She was enormous and I couldn't see how we were going to get her into the car, and what would happen to my little precious if we did get her inside.

There were plenty of cranes about and I could have removed the top of the car and lifted her in. The man who lived next door to her was a regular occupant of the front passenger seat, so I couldn't leave him behind.

He had to occupy the off-side rear seat. He was normal size, but still he had to do some acrobatics and crawling to get there. This was a special car built to size for the Nicholson family. The headroom had to be worked out by the algebraic process. First I had to estimate the working life of the car in years (not weeks), say four years. Then get an accurate measurement of David's height and calculate how tall he would be in four years. Call that 'x' which would be the minimum height. Minimum height plus thickness of hat plus 4 inches in case his head was itching and he wanted to scratch it. Ignoring thickness of paint these calculations gave the exact height of the distance between floor and top. The top sloped towards the back, but you don't expect kids to be wriggling all over the place during the journey, and we still hadn't got jumbo loaded yet. But my friend was sitting comfortably, his top button on his jacket was pressing into his chin, but that wasn't my problem, I hadn't made his jacket.

Jumbo got her bottom onto the seat, but there was no way I could get her legs in. She dismounted as they say in the army and we had another try. She put her right leg in first and squeezed her body into the car that made some rolls of fat go to her neck, which was better than making the door aperture too wide. Most of her was now in the car, but the awkward beggar wanted to take both of her legs home. Three workmen had watched our struggling and came to our rescue and with lots of pushing and pulling we got her sitting comfortably.

The journey to Haddlesey was good and I was pleased how well the wooden chassis and the large front forks stood up to the weight. Getting Jumbo out of the car was much easier than getting her into it.

During the journey the next day, I asked my passenger why she was so fat. 'Because she eats too much,' was his reply. I was satisfied with his answer and didn't ask him any more questions about her.

There were bad rumours about. Some people were saying the army was leaving Burn. I tried not to take any notice, as they were only rumours. But rumours have a bad habit of jumping around in your mind so you worry. They say there is no smoke without fire.

Win had become poorly, when she lost the baby. I couldn't carry on with the AMIEE course. I gave it up. For one thing, I was very busy with work and also at the homefront and doing odd jobs on cars and motorbikes, helping people out.

No one seemed to know much about Japanese motorbikes. I was keen to learn, as I was interested in them. Germans and Italians had already given the British factories a rough and lean time. I didn't think it would be long before we found out about the Japanese.

I bought an Ariel twin with a large sidecar. It had telescopic front forks and plunger type rear suspension. I was longing to ride a motorbike and sidecar for a change from my three-wheeled car. It was summer 1958 and Win and I and the lads thought it was a good idea to have a ride to Withernsea to see Ernie, Ette, Joan and Alan, and Ette's grandkids. They had no doubt been saving up to buy something for the last couple of years and only needed £2, which I, Uncle Jack, could afford to give them.

After this I would have to take Win on a bargain-hunting spree as usual. It was the beginning of the week, but I thought I should have a ride on the Ariel to make sure it was all right for our 'long journey'. I knew the engine was all right because the man who had sold it to me said it was. He had stripped it right down and carefully assembled it while making sure all the components were in good order. That was enough for any one to take the bike out and test it.

Gradually there was a slight knocking sound from the bottom of the engine that became worse quickly. The engine had to be completely stripped. I found the nuts, which hold together the bearings and found that the big ends and the connecting rods had come loose. Jobs like these are easy in motorcycle workshops, but not so easy when done in a council garage on a council estate.

When I had finished the work and was taking the motorbike and sidecar on another test, my ears and brain were on full alert. At that time a new roundabout had just been made at Ferrybridge. The roundabout was a typical piece of highway expert's genius. The first time a bus went onto it, the bus fell on its side. There was quite a lot of traffic about so my brain had to sort out idiots in tin boxes on wheels as well as be on full alert for nasty noises. I was on the roundabout amongst these boxes, concentrating like mad when there was this most dreadful noise that made me look down at the engine. I had just passed a workman holding one of those big chisels that work by compressed air and the rotter decided to pull the trigger as I was passing him. What a relief to know all was well. So we enjoyed our ride out to Withernsea and back and without any trouble.

The following week I had to visit Uttoxeter again. I went in my three-wheeler car. It was running well and by this time I had some windows in the doors and it was painted blue. I went to the same lodgings and the couple were pleased to see me, but maybe only because they would be having a ride to the pub.

I was there for two weeks inspecting and road testing lots of Bedford three-ton trucks. They had been inspected and road tested before they left the factory by Bedford's examiners and so they only had slight faults. It was a waste of time. But the army rules must be obeyed.

Not long after I had returned to Burn I was told officially that the army were moving from Burn. I would be transferred to a depot in Derby.

Win and I and David, Derrick and Peter went to see a house in Derby. It was just what we wanted. The front of the house faced a large park, which pleased us. The house wasn't large, but it was tall, three stories. The top floor looked as though it had been a bedsitter. We could keep it like that and have someone living there and paying us rent.

My pay with the War Department was good and with the help of the rent from whoever took the bedsitter we would be able to buy the house with a mortgage. I liked the idea of living in Derby.

I was a very happy man as I drove us home. But when we were at home Win wanted to talk about our new adventure.

But during the conversation she said suddenly, 'I don't want to go.' I gave my notice in reluctantly and left on 3 October 1958.

Most of the workers were given notice and a lot of them would get paid redundancy money. But I could not get that because I wasn't redundant.

Three days after finishing at Burn I went to work for the National Coal Board. Two miners were pleased about it because they had a lift to work and back in my little three-wheeler car. Win would be pleased also because she would be getting her ton of coal each month.

My job was being a fitter on mining machinery. The pay for fitting was quite good, but I never got it. I was a bit ignorant about mining and the ways of the National Coal Board. I was expecting to work on machines above ground. But I was told that I would also have to work on them at the coalface. Therefore, I had to be trained for underground working at Bentley training centre.

When I arrived at the training centre I had to go to the stores. I remember being given a helmet and a lamp, which fitted on the front of the helmet, but I cannot remember anything else. But I remember very plainly going up a lot of steps with a lot of miners in cages. I would have rather been going over the Alps in a wicker basket.

We went into the cage and it was so full there wouldn't have been room for a little mouse. I wondered how many broken strands there would have been in the cable. We didn't just go down, the cage just dropped and then it began to come up again and the cage door opened and we got out, but not at the top we had actually reached the bottom. We had pulled up so quickly that you got the sensation that you were going back up again.

It was horrible being down there in the dark. The sun was shining up at the top and I wondered if I would ever see the sun again. One young lad who also just started that day had to go to the coalface with a bucket of whitewash and a big brush. Where I stood there were two openings in the cages so that the tubs could be pulled through. The tubs were joined together by a longish heavy chain. The chains were taken off the tubs, and thrown on the ground at the coalface side off the cages. The tubs would be taken up to ground level and emptied. Two tubs would then come down. As the cage door opened the tubs would come out of the cage. It was downhill from the cages to the coalface, so away they went. But they have to have the link chains with them. My job was to throw these two chains into the tubs as they were passing me. It was hard work and the most horrible job I have ever done. I think we were down in the pit for eight hours. But when knocking off time came round, it seemed like two or three days.

I saw the young lad who had gone down near the coalface. His job was to put the whitewash onto a piece of coal of each tub as it passed him. It was very dark and the poor beggar was by himself. He didn't have a watch so he didn't know the time.

The tubs stopped so he thought it was the mid-morning break. He was hungry, so he ate half of his sandwiches. The tubs started coming again and he thought it had been a short break. After what seemed to be a very long time the tubs stopped again. So he was sure it was dinnertime and he ate the rest of his food.

The tubs set off again and he was very tired and just hoping the tubs would soon stop so that he could go home. It was a very long wait and at last they stopped. But no one came to take him to the lifts. The tubs started up again and so he had to keep dabbing the whitewash on.

There had been two or three breakdowns and when he thought it was time to go home it was only midday.

Three months passed and I was still on training and on a low pay and still on the same job, slinging those heavy chains into the tubs as they went past me. There was no sign of me going on to fitting.

One day I found out how superstitious the miners were. We had set off on our way to work. For some reason I thought I shouldn't be going to work. I mentioned this to my two friends. That got them worried and they wanted me to turn round so that all three of us could go back home.

I kept on going and one of them was getting agitated and worried. When we reached work this one went back home on the bus. But the other miner and I went into work.

I have mentioned that I worked near the lifts at the coalface side. The other side of the lifts was out of bounds for trainees. I hadn't any chains so I told the deputy who was in charge of the trainees. He said, 'There's plenty at the other side of the lifts so go and get some.' I hesitated because I did not know whether to disobey him or not. He shouted, 'Get on, we need them in a hurry.' So I went to the other side. Two or three tubs that had broken away came speeding down the slope. It was very narrow and I stood with my back against the coal wall. As they passed me all my buttons where ripped off my overalls.

When I saw the deputy, he began to tell me off. I told him that he had sent me there. If I had been killed this ignorant man would have lied and Win wouldn't have got any compensation. I never went back to the pit.

Chapter 50

NEWSOMES

There was a small oil refinery and lubrication factory belonging to Newsomes. I went to see the foreman. He said that he was sorry, but he only had a labourer's job at present, but he may have something else later. I asked how much did he pay labourers. It was more than what skilled fitters got in garages. So I didn't hesitate about becoming a grease monkey.

I had my own building and my own grease barrels and some clogs to wear. I had a ram that was nothing to do with sheep. It was a long cylinder about 9 inches in diameter and about 10 feet long. Inside the cylinder was a piston that moved backwards and forwards drawing grease in at the back end and pushing it out at the front. Before switching on, it was advisable to remember to have a barrel in position because grease is funny stuff to shovel up.

When a barrel was full you switched the machine out of gear pulled the barrel out of the way and replaced it with an empty one. I couldn't understand why the pay should be more than a fitter's job. But I wasn't going to argue about a little thing like that.

When there were enough full barrels to make an order I had to stencil the name of the oil firm whose order it was, on every barrel and also the kind of grease, like soft, high resistance, medium, wheel bearing grease etc.

I think Shell was the number one customer and Mobil came next. The worst part about doing an order for Shell was putting the Shell badge onto the barrel lid. This was done with an expensive stencil made of very fine silk. It was so easy for a thread or two to break making the stencil useless and it was a cap in hand occasion going to the office for another stencil, which was very expensive and Shell didn't have much money.

One day, two Shell male representatives were looking round the works. They came to my department and it pleased me when they spoke to me in a very pleasant manner because I was just a labourer. We became very friendly and just at the point when I thought they were going to give me a barrel of grease for my pushbike, one of them said, 'We are from Shell.' I already knew that. Then the other one said, 'We make the best oil in the world.' So just for devilment I said, 'Oh, didn't know you were from Castrol.' That was certainly the end of that friendship. I didn't care about that because if they had given me a barrel of grease it would have had to live in the kitchen, which was a bit on the small side for things like barrels of grease although it would have been handy for the chip pan.

I was promoted and I got my own pan, not a pan that you cook your dinner in, but a big pan for making hand cleaner and lots of other oil substances. My first job was making a textile lubricant. The other men on the pans were a bit amused that this stuff should be my first. Because it was so difficult to make, they said, that if I could make it then I could make anything.

I had the temperature right and I was careful to put all the ingredients into the pan in the correct quantity and the exact weight. The ingredients had different colours, but the end product is white and it doesn't stain textile material. My pan of bubbling stuff was turning white and everything looked good to me. When I had finished it was good, in fact, it was perfect.

I continued with other successes with oil-based substances and was thinking I must be an expert on a pan. Another order came in for the textile lubricant so having wisdom; they gave it to me. With all the confidence of an expert I set about making it. I did everything the same as I did the first time. It began to turn white and that was good. But when I finished I did not have a textile lubricant. I had a pan of lovely rubber.

One thing which amused me was, say you were making grease. You were brought hundreds of one-pound tins ready for filling with their labels round them. All the tins were alike; mostly they were all made at the same factory. But each firm had its own label telling you that they were sole manufacturers of this grease, or that this was the best grease you could get, or that they had their own secret ingredients and all that rubbish, and it was all made in this one pan.

They made brake fluid. It was all made in the same pan. But for one make they mixed a red dye, and for the other make, they left it as it was.

Since I had started working at Newsomes, my friend John Todd, the one who lived at Hensall and went to work at Burn and rode the Ariel motorbike, had gone into a small motorbike workshop starting up on his own. I had been giving him a bit of help working on the few Japanese bikes that came in.

John rang me one morning at about 2 o'clock to say a good customer had broken down with gearbox trouble and he needed his bike for going to work at 7 o'clock. I stripped the gearbox and repaired it and the man had his bike at 7 o'clock. I don't think many garages could beat that for good service.

There were two young men who I knew who were taking over a garage about a mile from John's garage. They were making extensions to the place and would be opening soon to sell second-hand cars, and they asked me if I would work on any motorbikes that came in as part-exchange for cars. I told them I would do providing I had time to spare.

Chapter 51

CASTLE MOTORS

I heard that Castle Motors wanted a motorcycle fitter. Mr Thompson and young Mr Thompson, were the bosses. This was just what I wanted. They had the agency for Honda, Yamaha, and Suzuki. So I went to have a look as soon as possible.

Young Thompson interviewed me. I had seen him racing at Brough, but he also rode at the TT races. I told him what wage I wanted. That seemed to give him a bit of a shock and after a few minutes he said, 'I can't give you that, it is more than my foreman gets.' My reply to that was, 'I know more than your foreman.' So I got the job and got more pay than his foreman Geoff.

The start of my first day began with this young foreman striding towards me with his hand outstretched saying, 'I'm Geoff.' I thought, *I don't care who you are as long as I get more pay than you do.*

When the Honda 50cc bikes came they arrived in crates with three bikes in each crate. They were taken and stored in a building about half a mile away from the garage. We wanted some bringing to the garage. So Geoff and an apprentice and I picked up a few tools and we walked to the building. We opened a crate and took out three Hondas. They were not completely assembled for packing reasons.

Geoff had been a few times and he had become very quick at it so before ours were half assembled, our foreman had petrol in the tank and was on his way to the garage. The young lad said, 'He always does that just to show you up.' I had already decided on the type of man he was. I said, 'When we come back for another three we will hide one of his small parts and when we are ready to go we will help him find it.'

We walked to the building again and began to fit the components and Geoff was like a sand boy and he was soon in front of us and this was pleasing his little mind, until he needed the hidden part and he began searching.

I hate having to look for things. You drop something and you expect it to go straight down to the floor. But it never does and your brain gets all twisted up and you finish looking at the roof as if it has gone that way for a change.

Geoff had reached that stage and we may have felt sorry for him if we had liked him just one little bit, which we didn't. We finished our bikes and then went to help our foreman. We kept asking whether he had looked here and looked there. He said, 'I've looked everywhere and I cant find a bloody thing.' He was getting very cross so the lad decided to find it for him.

We rode together back to the garage. I think Geoff had learnt a lesson. The next time we needed some little Hondas for the garage, the young lad and I could keep up with Geoff and so we always rode together. I found Geoff good to work with after he had dropped his foreman attitude and he never bothered me.

During my first day Mr Thompson came to me to have a chat. He wanted to tell me about his lad's racing and I let him, not letting on that I had seen him and not saying anything about motorbike racing. He told me how well he looked after his lad's racing bike and how good he was when it came to fitting tyres. He said, 'If we are not busy tomorrow I will show you how to fit a tyre.' I thanked him and looked forward to the lessons. I think in the meantime he had learnt a bit about my racing and me. I didn't get the lessons and he never mentioned about tyres or his lad's racing anymore. Young Thompson did win one race in the Isle-of-Man. It was a scooter race and I think he was riding an Italian Lambretta.

There was a consignment of 500cc motorbikes arriving from Japan. The crates from the last ones were littering up the place where we stored them. We needed a fence at home so I took off the sidecar body and brought the crates home on the sidecar chassis. I had served an apprenticeship about moving wood on sidecar chassis. But this time the wood wasn't at the bottom of high cliffs.

My transport to work was always one of my motorbikes and never the car. Young Mrs Thompson often asked me to take her home during working time in her husband's car. That was one thing I didn't want to get involved in although her intentions could have been quite innocent. I used to tell her I couldn't drive a car. I don't think she believed me so she kept on giving reasons for wanting to go home, but I left that for her husband to do.

I settled down at Castle Motors. It was a comfortable garage with plenty of light. I didn't like dark scruffy places. I got on well with everyone and the main thing was I was working on Japanese bikes.

One day a Yamaha came in. It was an insurance job having had an accident. The insurance representative was having a big argument in the office with young Thompson. It was only a small thing to argue about. Brazed onto the steering head downtube, are two pieces of metal one at each side. Their purpose is a stop for the steering so that it doesn't become too much in lock. One of them was missing due to the accident.

The insurance man's argument was, it did not warrant a new frame because another piece could be brazed onto the downtube, and it would be the same as it was before the accident.

Thompson stuck out for the customer's rights and he wanted nothing less than a new frame. I thought the insurance man was right and I admired him for keeping insurance costs down.

On the other hand I admired Thompson for fighting for his customer's rights. At the end, after about two hours of fierce argument, the insurance man had to give in and went on his way. The end of the story is two pieces of metal were brazed onto the steering head. The work took about fifteen minutes.

Although this had nothing to do with me I didn't like it. Mr Thompson senior, was a likeable man and he often came over for a chat. But I had gone right off his son after the insurance job and I had no more interest in Castle Motors.

A motorbike came in one day, which was a scramble bike, or motocrosser. I had no idea why it came in. I think Castle Motors had bought it; perhaps young Thompson was going to have a go at scrambling.

There was some wasteland behind the garage so at midday the bike was taken there and all the staff followed expecting to see a one-man display. Young Thompson began his ride and that was all we got. No wheelies, no broadsiding, no sitting on the handlebars, just a ride round wasteland. Everyone was disappointed, so I gave them a show of riding backward and broadsiding and a few of the White Helmets' Tricks. I had shown Thompson up a bit and I felt he had been paid back for the insurance trick.

Chapter 52

MACLAUCHLAN'S GARAGE

At Knottingley on the Main Street, was Maclauchlan's garage. I stopped to have a look and came into conversation with Mr Maclauchlan. This led me to giving in my notice at Thompson's and working at Maclauchlan's. Besides having the garage, Maclauchlan had heavy machinery for laying down roads. But the highway part of his business would have nothing to do with me. He was a rally driver, and also his brother-in-law. They both drove Sunbeams and tuning them was the most important part of my work there.

We did not have a foreman, but a works manager. My first impression of him was he was a big head and I didn't think he was any good at his job. They didn't have anything to do with motorbikes so I could just concentrate on cars. This was easier than flitting from one place to another.

I was soon wondering how big head had become a works manager because he didn't have much work knowledge about cars. One day I came across a stupid nut, which none of my spanners would fit. I've always hated adjustable spanners, but I had to use mine on the awkward nut. He came and stood over me for a few minutes. That was another thing I hated. Then he said, 'You will never be an engineer while you are using one of them.' To which I replied, 'You will never be an engineer whether you use one of these or not.'

Our love for one another never got any better. One day, two mechanics were trying to solve a problem on a car engine. We had a small Crypton tuner, but I don't think any of them knew how to use it. They had already fitted a new coil and distributor. They had spent a lot of time working on it, which meant the customer would get a big bill.

The works manager took these two mechanics off the job and put them onto another car. I heard him say, 'This job is more urgent than the one you are doing.' I felt like asking him why he hadn't put himself onto the urgent job.

The two mechanics began working on their fresh job. It was not long before big head took me off my job to go on the one the mechanics had left.

I began by taking off the new parts and taking them back to the stores and putting the old parts back. I don't think big head saw me doing this, as he didn't come to me straight away. I reckon the store man told him. He was very polite when he said, 'We do not do that here, when a new part goes onto a car, it stays on.' I told him politely, 'Not this time.'

It was an intermittent fault caused by a broken low-tension wire. The trouble could have been caused by a fault in the distributor, but you wouldn't expect it to be the coil. The coil has two different coils, one is high tension and the other is low tension. It converts low-tension voltage from the battery to a high voltage, which jumps across the spark plug points that ignites the petrol and air mixture. This is your driving force on the pistons.

Coils rarely give trouble, but when they do it is when the coil heats up and causes a short circuit. That is how I knew the coil on that car was not causing the fault.

I think it is likely that a Crypton sales person had visited Mr Maclauchlan because a large Crypton tuner had arrived. It didn't do much more than a small Crypton tuner. But everything about it was big and would impress the customers.

To get the customers into the garage we had one full day of free Crypton tuning. An expert from the Crypton factory came to use one of the machines. Lots of cars came and they formed two rows so I had a row and the expert had the other. My first car was a good example of DIY tuning; the carburettor was well out of adjustment. I began to adjust the mixture control and I heard someone say, 'It's better already and he hasn't even put it onto the machine.'

Because I was concentrating on what I was doing I didn't take much notice of what was going on in the next row. But now and again I heard a car leaving the expert, sounding terrible.

Someone, most likely the works manager, put the boss's car in to be tuned (not the Sunbeam) and it went to the expert. When the boss came back from his lunch he was like a raving lunatic. He shouted and swore at me saying, 'Why have you let that idiot mess up my car?' I told him that I didn't know the expert had touched his car, but I would soon tune it up again.

I had bodywork to do on a car. I had removed all the rust and treated the bad places with rust killer and primed them. The next job was to fill in the deep rust spots with what they called cellulose stopper, which was special putty. This job was done with care, or else you would have a lot of work sanding down the hardened putty to the shape of the bodywork. But before I could apply the putty I had to leave the bodywork job to work on the Sunbeams, as they were going into action at a rally at the weekend.

After I had finished the rally cars I happened to notice that someone had put the stopper on this car body. It was someone who didn't know anything about the job.

The culprit was the works manager and by that time I had had enough of him, and I played up hell with him. I don't know who finished the job, but I just became an ex-member of Maclauchlan's garage.

I was passing the showroom a few days later. There were two lovely silver cups on show that Mr Maclauchlan and his brother-in-law had won. Mr Maclauchlan came out of the showroom looking very happy and I congratulated him on his successful drive.

We were talking for a while and he was proudly telling me about the rally. Then I said, 'I wonder if you will do as well next time as I won't be tuning the cars for you.' I told him what I thought of his works manager and he went mad. He tried to persuade me to go back, but I had to disappoint him.

I knew where I could get a lot more money and that is what you go to work for.

Chapter 53

BP AND POLLARD BEARINGS

Before leaving Maclauchlan's, I had applied for a job at BP (British Petroleum) and I had an interview. I was just one of about 120 other applicants. Five were picked to go on a final interview. I was one of the five. Before I left after the interview, I was told that I had most of the qualifications and was sure to be picked for the job when I went, which would be on the 5 February 1966.

There was a vacancy for a turner at Pollard Bearings, an engineering factory in Knottingley. They made nuts as well as bearings and supplied 40 per cent of Ford Motor Company's intake of nuts. I applied and was successful and arranged to start work on the 1 February. My brain let me down badly because if I had said 7 February I could have gone for the interview at BP and then decided which job to take.

My second mistake was I wrote to BP telling them that I wouldn't be on the interview because I had another job to go to. It is all right having decency and doing what is right sometimes, but definitely not when dealing with engineering firms.

I learnt this when I went to work and was told that the turning job had been given to an inspector because it had been promised to him before they had advertised the vacancy. I had two choices, either go home or be an inspector. I decided to be an inspector until I found something else.

The factory was in a large and very old building on the banks of the Aire canal. In days gone by it would have been a storage place or perhaps a mill. The factory floor was well worn and uneven by many years of cast iron wheels rumbling over it with heavy loads off the cargo boats.

Inside the factory you breathed a little carbon dioxide mixed with a large percentage of hot oil fumes from the cutters of the noisy machines. Outside the factory in the yard were lots of racks filled with long bars of steel and men placing them onto barrows. These were made of heavy angle iron and consisted of a square at the top and bottom and were joined together by four corner members. They had four very small wheels. The world's strongest man could maybe push one without much difficulty, but for the ordinary man they were killers. They were the most horrible contractions I had ever seen and made me realise for the first time that there wasn't a glut of engineers in this factory.

The large piles of scrap impressed me and I thought well at least that is one thing they are experts at making.

Inside were the stores with large amounts of chucks, drills and tool steel. There were two separate departments; in one was a row of single spindle machines that made the nut blanks. The nuts were cut from the hexagon bars of mild steel, high tensile steel and aluminium. The hole was drilled and part of the hexagon turned down to form a turret as the blanks were for self-locking nuts. The tool had chamfered the front of the nut when the previous blank was parted because as the tool parted the blank two chamfers were cut. I worked on this department.

The other department made the saw cuts in the turret part of the nuts, tapped the threads and pressed the turret end to distort the threads at the saw cuts to make the nuts self-locking. There were about 300 machines and about 125 women operated them.

All the machine operators were on piecework. They worked as quickly as possible to make extra money. It was a typical engineering works for that period where workers' wages were very low and so they did piecework by making themselves slaves to get a little extra money. They were making the fat cats a heck of a lot fatter.

In the women's department the women worked very hard and their fingers moved very quickly as they operated their machines. But they were let down on some of the machines, because of these machines making scrap.

There was a woman in charge of these workers. Also there was a man known as the works manager. He spent most of his time walking from one end of the department to the other. All day long he walked up and down, never even glancing at the machines or operators. He would have been on a high salary and earned nothing.

This works manager had a brother-in-law who was in the same department as I. He was working on a modification to improve the machines in the women's department, which were turning out the most scrap. He was a decent chap and I got on very well with him. His modification worked well for a short time only. The nut blanks had to enter the machine magazines the correct way round, every one that didn't became a piece of scrap. The modification had two ramps, which tipped the blanks onto the hexagon end. When it did this the blanks became nuts, but when they didn't it was scrap.

I do not know whose idea it was, but they should have scrapped it and thought of something different. I didn't interfere while the chap was playing about with it. He was getting a living out of this work and I didn't have to pay his wages.

I carried on with the inspections job. Each part of the nut blanks measurements had to be within five thousandth of an inch. If they were not, they were scrap. Well that's what the bosses thought. I wasn't related to the bosses or Henry Ford and so if I thought they were good enough they passed.

The machines were out-of-date, but I was just an inspector and they had nothing to do with me. But I did say how they could be improved and the bosses were interested, but not a lot. I didn't know that a new machine was coming.

The new machine arrived and this would take the place of about half the old ones. It was a six-spindle machine, which meant it took six of the hexagon rods at once and as it was much quicker than the old ones, it would most likely do as much as nine times the output.

They soon had the new machine working and it was going well. But so it should be, there was about £25,000 of machinery there. The fat cats were not satisfied evidently and I was asked if I could improve it. I said, 'Yes' and that ended my career as an inspector.

The new machine had a big fault the same as the old machines. Simple non-technical faults will carry on forever because the people who make machines do not have much common sense. They make and fit chutes, which at the top end fits below the cutters and at the bottom end it goes through the side of the machine taking the swarf with the nut blanks (in this case). Operating a riddle to separate the nuts from the swarf takes two men on each shift and there are three shifts, i.e. 48-hour's work per day.

If the machine that was making the swarf automatically separated the swarf from the nut blanks, then there would be no need for the riddle and the 48-hour's work could be spent on some other jobs. This was achieved by simply fitting two Nicholson chutes.

My chutes fitted under the cutters and onto the side of the machine as the others fit. But the difference was they didn't go straight from the cutters carrying oil and swarf into the container until it spilt all over the floor.

The chute came from the cutters almost at a right angle for 3 or 4 inches and then curved to almost a right angle where it came through the side of the machine. It was straight after the curve to the container.

A strip of metal was taken from the side of the chute at the bottom, to around the bend at the top. This left a gap just a little smaller than the size of the blanks. Therefore, the blanks couldn't be washed through the gap into the base of the machine. But that is what happened to the swarf and oil.

The part of the side remaining was a strip of metal that vibrated with the vibrations of the machine. This was sufficient to keep the blanks moving until they dropped into the container, dry with no swarf.

I also did smaller improvements to the machine. This pleased the fat cats very much as they were able to buy shares and get even fatter. But they wanted more.

Would I take over the machines in the women's department and could I improve on the scrap situation? I told them that the scrap situation didn't need improving, they were making enough. It seems I had misunderstood them. They meant they wanted me to cut down on the scrap. I said, 'I hope so. It couldn't be any worse.'

I cut out the scrap in half a day. This was an engineering factory. I don't know where the engineers had gone. Most of the scrap was caused by the machines, which cut slots in the nuts. These were the machines that brother-in-law had been trying to improve for six months.

The machines were a poor attempt at engineering, but they were not the cause of the scrap, but they were good at breaking down. It was the feed to them that caused the destroying of the blanks.

The feeders were made during the war for bullet cartridges. They had dome-shaped bottoms with the opening at the top. You filled the bottom with nuts. There was a ramp on the inside and vibration caused the nuts in the centre to create pressure, which forced the nuts to go up the ramp. When they reached the top they had to go through this gadget with the little ramps created by brother-in-law. These let blanks, which were the wrong way up, go into the magazine. The small circular saws that made the slots didn't care a damn where they cut the slots, so lots of the nuts had the slots in the hexagon and were scrap.

So I had to solve Pollard Bearings long-standing problems, which had converted ordinary, poor scrap dealers into millionaires. I had no relatives among these millionaire scrap dealers so I did my duty to my millionaire bosses.

I cut a hole in the ramp near to the top and large enough for nuts to fall through, so that when I switched on, all the nuts fell through the hole. So that bit was all right, but the machine wanted some of them.

The nuts that went up the ramp the right way had the turret facing the wall of the feeder and it was these, which I did not want to fall down. So to hold them onto the ramp I cut 2½ inches from a strip of bright steel, which was ½ inch wide and ⅛ of an inch thick. I drilled two holes and slotted them for screws and drilled and threaded holes in the wall of the feeder. The piece of metal was adjusted so that it held onto the nut turret as it passed by the hole in the ramp.

Therefore, the nuts going the wrong way round were pushed off the ramp and fell down to the bottom and had another turn at climbing the ramp, but those the right way round were held by the strip of bright steel, until they had passed the cut out.

There were about ten of these machines and in half a day's work I had solved the problem and it was impossible to make even one piece of scrap.

One of the big noises came round just looking at things. He stood looking into one of these bowl feeders for half an hour or more waiting to see if a nut went the wrong way. After a while he cleared off without saying a word. Not even thank you.

The nuts went from the slotting machines to the machines that made the threads, and then to the presses, which distorted the thread at the slots. The distorted threads gripped onto the bolt threads to lock the two together. Some nuts went on to be cadmium plated.

I liked the man who was in charge of the plating shop. I think he would be about 55-years-old. His son had been to university to become an engineer and had returned to Pollard Bearings.

His son came to my department as charge engineer, so he was above me. The slotting machines that I described as being badly designed had very long chains that did not run smoothly and vibrated. Cams controlled the circular saws.

These cams were not suitable for their job and one day I was trying to explain to the works manager how they should be and doing little sketches to try to make him understand. Without me knowing, he took the sketches to this young engineer.

For a few days the engineer was not speaking to me so I went to his office to ask him who was rattling his cage. He said, 'Those sketches you gave to the works manager were not right.' I gave him a bit of a telling-off and pointed out that the sketches of cams were just to explain a point and were not supposed to be the same as diagram drawings in the office. Then he said, 'I know ten times more about cams than you do.' I thought this was a very childish thing to say, so I sorted him out.

After a while he said, 'You have a funny way of going on. You design something and then you make it. You should go to the drawing office for them to do it.'

My reply was, 'I'm not giving you idiots the chance to gain from my ideas.'

There is always a lot of jealousy amongst engineers and I knew I wouldn't be at Pollard Bearings long enough to get a gold watch.

There were only three of us working on these machines, but by keeping them well maintained we were able to keep them going and that kept the girls happy.

The eldest of my staff was nineteen-years-old and he lived in Knottingley. He was very skilled, pleasant, and an excellent worker. He had salmon sandwiches for his lunch every day. I liked salmon, but I wouldn't want it every day. Now and again he ate my sandwiches and I ate his to give us a bit of variety.

The other lad was seventeen-years-old. He was always happy and was always an excellent worker. By talking to me he developed the motorbike-racing bug and it became so bad there was no cure. He became the passenger in sidecar racing and paired up with a well-known rider.

I liked working with the girls. To me they were all lovely and pleasant and they got on with their work. In the other department I was friendly with a lad called Clive Dickinson. He played rugby for Castleford. His girlfriend worked on slotting machines, she was a lovely girl.

By this time we were having good weather and so we sat on the canal banks to have our sandwiches. There were some boats, but it was mostly the 'tubs'; a barge would pull about ten or more loaded with coal.

The works manager, who walked up and down all day, was sweet on one of the girls. She worked on one of the tapping machines, and one day an oil leak covered her lap. I grabbed some cleaning rags and dashed to her and wiped her skirt and when her skirt was rid of most of the oil I pulled her skirt up and cleaned her legs. I noticed her knickers had escaped the oil slick, which was good because up and down Charlie was staring with very jealous eyes.

When the girls went to toilet they never went on their own, there would always be a bunch of five or six. I wondered if they were afraid I would follow if they were on their own. But I think it was the girl with the cleanest hands who did the knicker pulling down for all.

One of the women lived near me so she had the honour of riding to work in the Nicholson three-wheeler. One of the workers told me to be careful because her husband was an all-in wrestler. This person didn't know that the husband was my friend. But it was good of him to warn me. Her departure from being a passenger came suddenly.

One morning one of the girls wanted to go to the bank at lunchtime. She said that it was very important and she hoped I would take her. Of course I said, 'Yes'. So at lunchtime we walked out together and cleared off to the bank in the little car. We then went straight back to work in time to have lunch.

My girls didn't want to know me and at finishing time my passenger had gone home on the bus. I was told that the girl I had gone out with had a bad name for being a rum lass and taking her had given me a bad name.

In spite of this, a lady in the stores asked me to give her driving lessons. She was having difficulty getting to work on time so she had bought herself a car. So I arranged to go to her house and take her out.

There was a disused aerodrome about seven miles away so I was taking her there. On the way to the aerodrome I told her to learn as much as she could by watching my driving as she would be driving the car back home. She laughed at that thinking that I was kidding her. But she did drive it home and she was learning quickly.

It is strange that after I had been out with her teaching her to drive, a friend who was a driving instructor came to see me. He had heard of something new, which interested him a lot. It was dual controls in a car, which was a good thing for driving instructors. I made the dual controls and fitted them, so his car became one of the few round there with dual controls. The following day he was out with a young lady learner. Suddenly a car came out of a side road and he applied the brakes while the poor girl was sat motionless with wide eyes staring through the windscreen. He came to tell me all about it and how lucky it was to have fitted a lifesaver just in time.

I had never seen dual controls so this was all my own work and design and it had stood the test. Perhaps I should have patented it. I made a few parts, but they didn't get put together. I had a busy life, now I think about the things I should have done, but you can only do so much. Sometimes you think you have done the wrong thing, but that may lead to something good and that is life.

A wagon driver came from Fords for nuts and bearings. He was talking to someone who suggested he should come to my department and have a look at the machines. He was staggered when he looked at the feeders on the slotting machines because he said that it was just what Ford needed and he begged me not to let Pollard Bearings have them.

He suggested I should do some patenting, as I could become a millionaire. It is only when it is too late do you realise the value of people's suggestions and you wonder how hurt they must have been when their kindness and consideration for you is not grasped and put to good use.

Everything was going well at work, the machines having the benefit of our loving care, were running merrily and all the girls were very happy as they were getting good bonuses. Then one morning a fitter turned up to work with us, as we needed help. He seemed to be a slimy crawler and we were not pleased with his presence. It was obvious he had come to take over from me after he had received sufficient free lessons.

After a few days, when I went home there was a very interesting advertisement, which Win had read in the newspaper. It was about a country cottage for sale. It read:

> FOR SALE, A COUNTRY COTTAGE, CALLED HERBERRY HOUSE AT HEMINGBROUGH, FIVE MILES FROM HOWDEN FIVE MILES FROM SELBY, WITH VACANT POSSESSION.

It was detached, built of brick with a tiled roof. There was a small entrance, living room with Yorkist range, lounge with modern tiled fireplace, cupboard under stairs, kitchen with sink (cold water only), and two bedrooms.

Outside was a barn, coalhouse and earth closet. There was also a large garden to the rear and side with vehicular access.

It was offered for sale by auction on the premises on 30 June 1966 at 6.30 pm.

Frank Hill & Son was auctioning it. Frank Hill was an auctioneer at Easington and his son Charley was in Pug's class at Easington School.

About a week later Clive Dickinson's girlfriend came to me looking very upset. She asked me to take all our gadgets off the machines. I couldn't understand this and so I said, 'Why, they make the work so easy?' She replied, 'Yes, I know and because they are so easy to work they have stopped our bonuses.'

We sprang into work and we certainly did work until every item we had made for the machines had been removed and buried under loads of swarf.

The following day the youngest lad saw our new fitter take one of our gadgets from under his bench and began to copy it. It was a spare that I had made. The lad hung around until he had the opportunity to grab it and bury it in the swarf.

The management were too slow to sack me as I had given my notice in after the girl had told me about the dirty trick with the bonuses.

All the work I had done at Pollard Bearings had cost them nothing and I had saved them hundreds of thousands of pounds.

Chapter 54

HEMINGBROUGH AND FERRYBRIDGE POWER STATION

I decided to build a power station. It's not everyone who builds a power station. So my next trip out was to Ferrybridge Power Station where they had made a start on the power station. It was evening and I only went to have a look round. There was no one about except one man and he was looking up at a crane, which was on top of the steel structure. This was the 200ft level, which to me was very high because I do not like high places.

He asked me if I was looking for work. I told him I was and so the conversation turned to what I could do as regards engineering. He was a manager and he was very interested in the crane up there 200ft above us and hardly stopped looking up at it while we talked.

I told the manager that I was willing to work for his firm. He seemed to become more relaxed and looked at me for a change, and not bothering so much over the crane. Then he said, 'We want to get that crane down so that will be your first job.'

My mind was only thinking of the crane and I had no sense of fear, only a sense of responsibility as I wondered about how I was going to make a start. I decided that the jib would have to be removed first and lowered down to the ground.

There was an office near us so I didn't want to make a fool of myself by asking him where his office was. I went to this office next morning and got signed on. Unfortunately, or most likely fortunately, it wasn't his office and I had signed on with a different firm. I had become one of Yarrow's men. Yarrow was a shipbuilding firm and was manufacturing and installing the ducting for the combustion air and flue gases.

One thing that was sticking out like a sore thumb was this driving instructor's job. I would have to go to see the cottage and if I was lucky enough to get it I was going to have loads of work.

The woman was almost ready for the test, but she wanted to take it in her own car, which wasn't in a fit condition. The brakes and steering required working on. So I decided to go to her house the following day to make a start on it. I rang to tell her to leave the keys where I could find them.

I was glad the weather was fine the next morning as the job would have to be done on the road and that is something I hate to do.

I gathered up jacks, axle stands and loads of tools and went on my way. I decided to dismantle everything that needed to be repaired. Everything went well, which was very rare with old cars. I was just making a list of what parts I wanted, when her husband arrived home.

He was very friendly and was kind enough to assure me that if there were any spanners I needed I could use his as he had a toolbox full of tools. He had been on a job and there was a maintenance fitter working not far away. He had kept an eye on this fitter and as soon as he had to go somewhere he swiped his tools and hid them. At knocking off time he had retrieved his prize and taken it home.

He was very proud of his clever achievement. So I said, 'You had better go and get your tools and put your wife's car together.'

I had a bit of difficulty getting my axle stands and jacks from under the car and then I left and never saw him or his wife again. It was the end of another payless job, but I was pleased it happened suddenly.

We went to Hemingbrough to look at Herberry House. As I expected, there were a few small jobs to do. The roof tiles needed replacing with new ones. The windows and the front door needed doing. The barn wall was bulging out about 10 inches, and also the gable end of the barn.

The earth closet was a long way from the back door, but the pigsty was near to it. I suppose it is easy to get used to pig muck so they had a good point there. The back door was very narrow and I had to bend my head to get into the kitchen. The outbuildings required smartening up.

There were no bedroom windows at the back of the house. A lean-to at the back was a food larder and left of this was the kitchen with a very small old-fashioned window.

Inside the kitchen was an old-fashioned square sink and wooden draining board. Under the sink was an old bucket with an old piece of cloth, which I thought was a pair of the old dear's knickers. The cloth would have been for the floor if it had the crutch piece, but without the crutch piece it would have been the dishcloth. There was only one tap; a cold wash on a frosty morning gets rid of pimples.

The kitchen was small and the stairs were steep because there wasn't enough room to be anything else unless they went through the front door and obstructed pram traffic, which the police would not like. There was a very old oak beam from the front wall to the kitchen wall that was 12-inch square. This divided the kitchen from the stairs.

We went up the stairs not rushing, as we wanted to have a look at them because they were brilliant. They began with a large slab of stone for the first step. It was a bit high, but you can't expect everything to be perfect. The rest of the stairs were just right and made out of good orange boxes.

The bedroom doors were painted green, as they should be to suit the style. They were the same as the shed doors with

343

the T-hinges and snecks to match. How the ceiling stayed up is a mystery to me.

When we were coming down the stairs, Win made some remark about them. She must have thought the old dear had flannel ears, but she hadn't and her voice came over loud and clear. 'There's nowt rang wi' stairs, they've done us.' The cottage had been very small with no upstairs many years ago. This was changed and the bedrooms were built. The bricks that were used were large and handmade. So this alteration was made at least a hundred and twenty-five years ago. The original bricks below were small hand made and hundreds of years old. The garden was about three quarters of an acre.

There would be lots and lots of work to do, but I liked it and hoped it would become ours.

Sometimes we do stupid things and regret it for years. Selling my pride and joy, my ever faithful Velocette was one of these stupid acts of madness. For some reason I bought a 175cc ohc Honda. It was a lovely bike easy to ride and very fast for such a small bike.

On my first day of work at the power station I went in the Nicholson three-wheeler. Three of us were walking together to our work on the site. My companions were lads and they talked about motorbikes. I said, 'They are noisy dirty and dangerous.' They were not surprised at this, as I was 51-years-old and it was a typical remark for an old man to say. They talked together for the rest of the day, not saying much to the silly old man.

I went on my Honda the next day. I did a bit of fast cornering and a few stunts. That made them talk to me when we went back to work after our lunch. In fact I was so fed up of bike talk I was glad when it was home time.

I was at work on the 30th, and that evening was the auction sale so I rushed off home as quickly as I could go. We had our tea and I was ready to rush off to Hemingbrough. Win was washing up like women do, everything had to be clean and tidy and I was getting mad as I wanted to get to Herberry House before the auction started. The lads were not ready so I went without them and I felt awful about that.

We were only just in time as the auctioneer stood on his box and began the bidding. There was only one person, a man, bidding against me. The bidding reached £700, it was my turn and I said £735 and that was the last bid and we became the new owners of Herberry House.

The lads turned up on their bikes just after the bidding had stopped. As they came through the full five-barred gate I said, 'Get off my grass.' They were delighted and kept saying, 'Is it ours?' as if they could hardly believe that we had actually got it.

The deeds made very interesting reading and they went back to the year 1765. They stated that we could graze our cattle, sheep, goats and horses on the common land. That was good to know and there were no worries about our stock going hungry. Peggy the dog was the only stock we had and she wasn't so keen on living on grass.

The old people had a house to go to and had moved two days after the sale; therefore I had no excuse to sit about reading comics.

Yarrows had a good workshop for me and another fitter. We were kept busy with no foreman or works manager to interfere. My workmate was a good chap to work with and so we had a happy shop. Sometimes I passed the crane on top of the girders waiting for someone to get it down. After about two weeks the work began. But next time I looked the jib had fallen through the girders and come to rest across the girders about 30ft below the top. I didn't envy these people and I had no intentions of pinching their job.

When I was in the pits at West Park a young man came to talk to me and to have a good look at my bike. He told me I was very brave and daring. I enjoyed the compliments and it made me feel good. About a week later I was in Hull and there was a long ladder that reached to the windows of the third floor. At the top of the ladder, cleaning the windows was this young man who said, I was brave. It flattened my pride quite a lot because I wasn't brave enough to do his job.

I had the same feeling at the power station. I admired the steel erectors for their skill and their guts. They were just ordinary people who had feelings and fears like everyone else who were brave enough to do what seemed to me, a very dangerous job.

The building of the chimney was completed. It was 700ft high so red warning lamps had to be fitted. 700ft of ladder arrived in short sections and two men to erect them.

I watched them start on this enormous task. They leaned the first piece to the chimney and bolted it, and then the second section and so on until they reached the top.

Some heavy 1-inch brass brackets arrived and a man to fit them. He put one of them under one arm and began his climb up the ladder grasping the ladder spells with his right hand to pull himself up. He reached some fixing studs and I saw him trying to fix the bracket. He looked to be having a problem and then he came down, still carrying the bracket under his arm.

The holes in the bracket were too small for the studs. This must have been quite annoying, but he didn't show it. I felt very annoyed because it was someone's stupid neglect. I was also against him having to carry the brackets when a block and tackle could have done it and he would have had two hands to make his climb much safer.

He took the bracket into the fitter's shop and my workmate drilled the holes out. The man then took the bracket and fitted it and when he came down with another bracket my workmate had gone on another job, but I was there to do the drilling.

When you drill any material you must clamp it down. With brass you need extra care because it is the worst for jamming the drill. So I took extra care clamping it to make sure the bracket didn't spin. This man who was climbing one-handed and carrying a heavy bracket up a 700ft chimney said to me, 'Thank goodness for that. Your mate didn't clamp them down and almost frightened me to death.'

The main building of the power station houses four large turbines and four large boilers and so the size is massive. I was on the 40ft level one day when it was only a shell with no floors. I was doing a job halfway along one side. There was a girder going across the middle, it was 10 inches wide. The majority of girders that the steel erectors ran about on were 4 inches wide.

I needed to go across to the other side, but it was a long way and I felt I would be ashamed of myself if I didn't go across the girder. There was a crane overhead and the steel ropes passed the girder about 2ft from it, near the centre. They were motionless so they were not a problem.

I stepped onto the girder and as I walked along it I felt quite safe. I was about 4 yards away from the ropes when the crane was started and the ropes did a merry dance swinging about. I almost lost my balance, but I was able to keep walking. As I passed them they were almost touching me and I was really scared, but when they were behind me I was able to continue and reached the other side.

I thought the chap in the crane must be a mental case. I never walked across it again, crane or no crane.

We remained in the council house until I had completed some big jobs. I began with the bedroom ceilings, which I thought would collapse at any moment. Going by the type of bricks used for making the cottage into two storeys I estimated the year would be around 1866, so the ceilings had been there for a long time. When it came to the demolishing job my idea of them falling down was way out. They were very thick and much stronger than anyone would think, and I had a very hard job knocking them down.

Eventually they were down and a new ceiling of battens and plasterboards was put into position. A friend with a trailer helped to get rid of the rubble and when the rooms were clean we moved all our belongings from the council house and handed in the keys.

I had bought a Reliant van, cheap. It wanted some jobs doing to it so my idea was to use it along with the Ariel and sidecar chassis. Then later I could do what was required on the Reliant and sell it.

When the removal job had come to an end we refitted the sidecar body and I used it to go to work. I was given a regular job, fitting grease pipes. There are hundreds of grease points on the sides of ducting. Most of the grease nipples are accessible from the ground, or a gantry or from the top of the ducting.

So my job was to fit the nipple onto the side of the ducting and connect a copper pipe from it, fix it onto the ducting and connect with the bearing of a huge damper or perhaps a small access door grease supply.

I was given a fitter's mate, that is someone who stands around and passes you a spanner now and again. It is against the union law to give him anything else to do or you may have a shop steward round, which means having to tell him to get stuffed. But we didn't get anything like that and we were good pals and worked with much happiness.

The only spanners I used were two small ones and I carried those in my pocket. But he did hold the ladder with his bottom on the spell, which was conveniently positioned for fitters mates bums.

I had to struggle without him on two days per week. Those days he had the mucky job of sweeping, and shovelling inside the ducting. His wage during the days with me was just below mine. But during the other two days in the ducting his wage was a lot more than mine. So therefore we had the same amount of money.

I missed him very much when I was on my own, but I did have more output. He was well educated and a very good talker and his conversations went like this: 'I went to Red Lion last night and there was this bird sat on her own so I went to her and asked her what she was drinking, and she said, "double whiskey." Go! By gum she was a smasher and she smelt right yer know. She took me to her house, a lovely place and we went upstairs and started to get undressed and do you know, she hadn't any tits. It put me right off.'

When you have someone like that talking to you all day you learn a lot, and since then I have never taken a girl home from a pub without asking for the size of her bra.

My work friend in the fitters shop was very lucky. He had been sent a load of 3½-inch pipes. They were 18 inches too long so he had to cut them to the required size. He had worked like a good lad and had nearly finished them when he noticed one of them was 18 inches too short. He must have cut it twice.

He was so upset I thought I should bring his mother. 'What can I do?' he said with a face enough to turn milk sour. I told him not to panic. 'What can I tell them?' he asked. Just tell them the silly people sent one too short.

His problem was only half solved. 'What can I do with this?' he asked giving the pipe a little kick. I said, 'Just tell them that the one they didn't send is 18 inches too short.' It took him a few minutes to work that one out. I knew what was going to happen to it. Herberry House wanted a rotary clothesline and that piece of pipe was the right length. I put him out of his misery saying I would look after it.

It went below the sidecar body and was tied to the chassis. There was a foot or so stuck out at the front and the back, but it got home without any problems. The rotary clothesline was not a priority job because the old lady had left a length of clothesline. But I got on with it much to Win's pleasure.

I don't think the lounge had been used except for funerals, weddings, and Christmas. So apart from the coal fire smoking enough to choke you it could remain as it was for the present and likewise the living kitchen.

There was a lot to do in the kitchen and also there was the job of converting the larder into a toilet and bathroom with a handbasin. Luckily the larder was large enough for a decent-sized toilet and a wall to divide the toilet from the bathroom. This left enough space for a toilet and washbasin. So I made the toilet and bathroom a priority and then the kitchen would come next.

After measuring and studying and having a sit-down, something came to my mind. I was thinking of days gone by and I asked myself why was I doing this work. The old lady said the stairs had done them, so what was wrong with them. The sentry box, which stood at the end corner of the barn with the daily mirror cut into six inch squares held by a piece of wire, turned at the bottom end to hold onto the valuable paper was all in good condition. So what was wrong with it?

There used to be pigs in the sty not motorbike parts, I was wrecking a large useful larder. I was knocking down large useful shelves that held large bowls of fruit, vegetables and eggs all fresh on that day. I could see people salting a pig and someone turning the handle of a sausage-making machine. Hanging from hooks in the ceiling would be what was left of the last pig, a ham, ribs and some back.

The old-fashioned living kitchen door was open and in my mind I visualised the old man sitting at his breakfast of two eggs and two thick rashers of bacon and the juice running down the sides of his mouth. He wouldn't have been going to work in a power station, not him; he would be in the sunshine turning hay. Candles were good enough for him. How much would the cottage be worth in years to come if I had left it alone?

With some help from Win, David, Derrick, and Peter the old larder soon became a beautiful toilet and bathroom. The old sink unit was pensioned off and a new sink unit took its place. I went to Porters in Selby for wood to make the kitchen cupboards and worktops. I was happy to make those and it reminded me of being in my father's workshop in Cottingham when I should have been at school. You only have one life, but even so there are happenings, which take you away from what you wish to do and that, which you are best at.

The front room (or lounge) chimney was on the gable end facing Bulmer's house. I went through the Bulmer's gate with my drill and extension and drilled holes through the bottom of the chimney below the fire grate. The extra air going through the holes was enough to stop the smoke coming into the room.

There was a terrible tragedy at work near the top of a cooling tower. One worker needed a hammer, but as he hadn't one with him he walked so far round on the scaffolding to another workman and borrowed his. Later the man who had loaned his hammer needed it, so he went to see if his workmate had finished with it. He had almost finished with it so the man waited for it and as they were talking, he leant back onto the safety boards that are fixed on the scaffolding and it gave way and he fell down. From halfway down, the cooling towers become wider and his body was ripped to ribbons. I heard that the part that gave way was a piece of plywood.

My job became more dangerous as the ducting sections reached higher heights. The worst came while I was on my own. I had to climb about 60 or 70ft on vertical fixed ladders. I had to fix pipes up to 2 or 3ft from the top. I was very scared; I scrambled onto the flat top hoping I would become used to it. I could see vehicles down below that looked like Dinky toys and the longer I stayed up there the more scared I became. The only thing I could do was to scramble back over the edge onto the ladder, do my job of fitting the pipes and get down as soon as possible.

The next day men were erecting the gantries. I felt very annoyed because with those in position my job would have been much safer and not so difficult. Power station work is difficult and they expect everyone who goes for a job to be a steeplejack. The weather was rough and two men were inspecting a cooling tower for cracks like you often get in concrete. They were stood on a moving platform or crate. There is a fence round it so you don't fall off. Nevertheless, I would have hated to be up there with them. Suddenly there was a gust of wind, which blew them and their crate outwards quite a long way and of course much higher. As suddenly as the wind had come, it was gone leaving nothing to hold the crate and it swung back hitting the cooling tower with tremendous force knocking the two occupants down onto the floor of the crate.

I was told that they were not injured. Perhaps they were not, but an awful shock like that could be the beginning of a heart attack or a stroke.

We had a ride to Withernsea to give Win the chance to get a bargain or two. However, it was my turn for a good buy. An old couple on Holmpton Road had an old Austin for sale because the poor old chap had become too old to drive.

It was an Austin 1300cc in very good condition and the old couple hadn't used it much so we were lucky to get such a good car at a reasonable price. Of course we didn't always go to Withernsea.

We used to go to chapel nearly every week. I used to go to chapel on a Sunday with Granddad Grant, but it wasn't like that. Just after the war, a demobbed RAF man set up a business selling almost anything for people like Win to browse through. He had a very large chapel at Cawood and for the sake of Win getting a bargain now and again, it was our Saturday evening ride out and very enjoyable. We also went to the Bryan's, Win's mother and father. Win would always take some shopping and for some reason they could never get the change right. During the mathematical struggle Bill would be in his Sunday best waiting for his pocket money. Eventually the old woman would notice him and give him it. She always took a long time to notice him and when she did she would be thinking, *that's saved the price of a pint.*

Bill was a good chap; he liked to talk to people. He spoke very slowly and quietly as if he didn't want to wake up the kids. He would explain every small detail and if he thought you did not understand, he would start again. He was better than any sleeping pills. Our Peter talks like that. If you ring our Peter, ring him before 10 o'clock or you will miss your breakfast.

We also went to the Bryan's, but this time to Charley Bryan and his wife Cath. We always had a lovely tea there. Cath had worked in a mill in Paisley and she fell in love with the rich Yorkshire soldier. If she had any ideas of taking things easy she shouldn't have been marrying Charles. But Cath was a very good worker for Charlie's ice cream business, and went out with an ice cream cart.

Cath liked company especially a lot of people at parties. Win's relatives had some good parties just after the war. Cath was brilliant on her accordion when she played Scottish music and gave us a few Scottish dance steps.

No matter whether we were visiting them or they visiting us, we had the exciting party games. It would begin like this: 'Everyone get a piece of paper and a pencil, draw a donkey and put the piece of paper on your head and draw the donkey's tail onto the donkey.' It was ever such a lot of fun and David, Derrick, and Peter got so excited they couldn't sleep. I used to feel like getting Granddad Bryan round to talk them to sleep.

Another ride out was to Barnby-Dun near Doncaster to visit Win's sister, Kath who had married John Brown. He had a joinery shop. It belonged to Mr Richard Attey. John went to him when he left school to serve his apprenticeship and stayed with him all the time. When Mr Attey retired, he moved out of the house in the yard where the joiner's shop and Chapel of Rest were and let John move into the house and run the business. John was a councillor and was usually in some pub on council business. That is what they called it. He became the lord mayor.

Kath was a lovely person, but she seemed to suffer from sleeping sickness. Perhaps due to her dad talking to her too much when she was a little girl. She was always doing competitions from newspapers. You spent the first ten minutes tidying up because the chairs were buried under lots of newspapers, magazines and you might find a dictionary and a bit of washing. But with a bit of patience you always came across a chair.

Kath and John had three children; they were Eileen, Ian, and Barbara. One of Barbara's children is called Sandra. She spent a lot of time with Grandma Kath. She was a good worker and a good help to Kath and was a girl I liked very much.

I was going to get some window wood and make windows for the front of our house. But John said, 'Don't do that, we have the wood and tools here so I will make them for you.'

He soon had the windows made and fitted. As regards the front door he told me about some doors at Upton School. He was working there at that time. There was a classroom that was divided into two, by three doors hinged together so as to fold back when a large room was required.

The people of the school decided it would be better for the room to revert back to just being a single room making three doors redundant. So I went and bought one of them. They were well made and were good-looking doors and it was a pity I didn't know about them before I fitted the back door.

We were very happy living at Hemingbrough. We had lots of good friends and Win was in the Women's Institute and had a job at the school as a supervisor. The lads had good motorcycle friends.

At work I had finished fitting the grease pipes and was spending some time in the workshop. The rough weather became rougher and a lot of damage occurred amongst the buildings.

I was looking out from the workshop door at the cooling towers. Two or three towers were facing the wind and two or three more were behind them. The wind was very turbulent and speeded up as it passed between the facing towers to hit those behind with more force.

As I watched the tops of two back towers, they began to turn and the narrow waists twisted until they collapsed and dropped straight down.

There was an awful lot of rubble to get rid of, but they had the gear to do it and the work of rebuilding two water towers began. The remaining towers had to be inspected for cracks. I saw three men climbing to the top of one of them. The leading man, when he scrambled from the ladder to the rim of the tower, stood up and began walking round the top, bending over as he looked for cracks.

The next man went round on his hands and knees. The third man put a leg over and shuffled round astride the top. I thought they were very brave, especially the second and the third because they showed signs of being afraid. I watched them come down and I was thinking they would be glad to be back on the ground. I'm sure I was glad to see them touch down.

Work at Yarrows was about finished. I had to go round all the moving parts like dampers and shafts, access doors etc. and rectify all faults. This took me three days and then moved from Yarrows to Parsons who made the turbines. I was only doing odd jobs in the turbine house, because their contract was almost completed.

One man was laying paving on the turbine house floor. He had a young man as his mate. The mate had very little to do, which was getting on his nerves as the job had been going on for a long time. It was a massive floor and although there was four turbines it left quite a lot of floor to pave.

The layer was going on holiday so I had to do his job. The mate had been watching him doing the floor for weeks so it was obvious he could do the job himself.

I suggested to him that I would be the mate and he would be the boss. He could hardly believe his luck and he began putting the paving down with no faults.

I enjoyed the rest and the lad was doing something that put a look of satisfaction on his face.

He wanted to do me a good turn. Win and I had reached our twenty-fifth wedding anniversary. He came from Batley and Sandie Shaw was on at the Batley Variety Show so he invited us to go for tea and then to the show, sleep at his home and then go home on the Sunday.

When I told Win she was very excited about it and really looked forward to going to see Sandie Shaw's show. But the lad gave me a problem on the Wednesday. He said, 'Of course, you will be sleeping with my wife and I will be sleeping with yours.' I was wondering if all fitters' mates were like this. I didn't say anything to him because I didn't know what to say, and I didn't know what to say to Win.

I made up my mind not to say anything to Win and just hoped for the best. We arrived at his house in good time to have our tea and so as not to have to rush to the show. His young wife was absolutely gorgeous.

They had put a good spread on the table, which we enjoyed very much and then we went to the show in his car. His wife made a remark about his driving. That made him angry and use bad language. By that time I disliked him.

It was a wonderful show. Jack Charlton was sat at the table behind us. I think it would be his wife and his mother and someone else, but I don't know for sure. They were talking and enjoying the show so I didn't like to butt in.

After the show we went back to their house and had a nice supper. We talked a bit and then I said to Win, 'Let's go to bed now.' And that was it.

The fitter was back from his holidays on the Monday morning and his mate became just a fitter's mate once again.

There was nothing left to keep me at Ferrybridge Power Station so I was ready for something else. I handed in my notice and said 'Goodbye,' a week later.

Chapter 55

MAKING THE NEW STAIRS

This was an ideal time to get rid of the horrible stairs. Win and the lads could have lived in the barn for a couple of weeks, but I was very kind and took them to Withernsea for a two weeks' holiday. I was ready for a holiday myself and would have loved to stay in Withernsea with them for the two weeks and we would have visited the old places, Spurn, Hornsea, Bridlington and a few more towns and villages, but I had to get on with my work. There was a large garden to see to as well as working on the house.

The stairs were on the dividing wall between the kitchen and the lounge. This wall required all the old plaster and cement being knocked off. Therefore, I left the stairs standing until I knocked off all the old plaster and cement above them. Then I knocked the stairs down and finished knocking off all the old plaster and cement. I had the rubble and old wood to get out of the way and sweep up. My next job was very important I had to cook myself a dinner, I was missing Win already.

Plasterers are a special breed with large shoulders and long straight arms and they slap it on in great dollops. The little skinny amateur can't do that, but with a lot of concentration the wall looked good.

Next I had to do some careful measuring and take the results to Porters of Goole for them to cut correctly the stair sections from lovely beech wood. They cut it out and the next job was planing it. But they were too busy and I only had a few days left to get them made and fitted, as I would be going for Win and the lads on Sunday. I went early on the Friday morning and waited and waited and it became the middle of the afternoon. But then a man shouted, 'It's your turn next.'

There was plenty of time for them to get it planed before knocking off time. But after they had planed just one piece, the foreman shouted to the men to stop the machines, as they wanted the shop floor cleaned up, as they were not working on the Saturday. I had wasted all that time and now I had to work like mad.

I planed quite a lot before I had my tea so that I could relax after. The side pieces, which went from the floor to the landing, were 10 inches wide and 1½ inches thick and very heavy. Therefore, it was very hard work, but I had finished them by Saturday night.

Sunday morning was like being at Pollard Bearings because five ladies turned up to help with lifting the stairs into position. We were a bit crowded, but we didn't mind that because we needed all the lifting power.

Derrick had not taken Peggy, his griffin dog on holiday. I gave her dinner to her before I began to get ready for our journey, but she wasn't hungry and didn't eat any of it. I'm sure she sensed that we were going to bring back the family and was too excited to eat.

We went in the Reliant van, and I lifted Peggy into the back and also her dinner. I was very tired and looked forward to reaching Withernsea and having a sleep. I went through Hedon and onto the Burstwick road. About two miles along this road you could turn left for Burton Pidsea and the Burstwick road turns right and then straight until you get to Burstwick. There was a road on the left to Halsham before Burstwick so we turned left. About 100 yards further was a sharp turn, which you should go round, but not as I did. I think at this point I fell asleep and hit the side of the road on the right. In those days they used to dig gullies to drain the roads. These were great for turning vehicles over if you wanted to have a good look underneath, which I didn't.

The Reliant was upside down and the engine oil drained out and made a pool slick in the underside of the bonnet, and the top, which was now the bottom, was plastered with Peggy's dinner. But where was Peggy? After a few minutes poor Peggy staggered out of the back as the back doors had conveniently opened themselves. You could say we were in bit of a mess. I had to wait for Alan to come to get the van onto its wheels and tow it to Withernsea. Alan worked on the Reliant and made it ready for our homeward journey, which we completed without anymore loop the loop stunts.

They had enjoyed their holiday. The weather had been good and they all had a suntan to prove it. They had been in a chalet on the park down Holmpton Road. Charley and Cath had a chalet there so Win had company for the two weeks.

They were glad to be home and could not get over the improvement the stairs made. We were all tired and after some food and a chat about Withernsea and my relatives, we went to bed early for a good night's sleep.

Chapter 56

WIN'S FEET

Win had to go to hospital on the Tuesday. When Win was a young schoolgirl, lads' shoes were cheaper and stronger than girls' shoes. Therefore, it was sound economics, thought Mother Bryan, to buy Win lads' shoes, which resulted in years of suffering for Win. She had a very large bunion on one foot, but the one on the other foot was only half the size. She walked pigeon-toed, which apart from the pain, spoilt her looks, which was a pity because she wore clothes to suit her and so always looked smart.

She went to hospital to have her bunions removed. The surgeon said he would make a good job of the big one, but he wouldn't bother much with the one, which wasn't so bad. The one he made a good job of didn't give Win any more trouble. But he made the other one worse and she always had a lot of pain from it.

I found out in later years that a lot of these high-up people in hospitals were what is known as educated idiots with not much common sense.

Win always had a fear that I may run out of work and be bored. So she would be planning something for me to do while she was away from home. Being an old cottage the rooms were small. We had a sideboard with its back to the dividing wall between the living room and the back kitchen. It was the only piece of furniture, which stood near this wall and stuck out like a rock against the cliffs and needed skill to negotiate it without getting a bruised knee or elbow.

My bit of homework was straightforward and I would have lots of time to sit in the village pub. All I had to do was knock the wall down and build another 18 inches back. This would make the kitchen 18 inches smaller, which she would be able to put up with and, the living room would be an extra 18 inches. Of course, the sideboard would still be sticking out, but further back, which would be great until some nuisance offered Win a larger table at a bargain price.

As soon as Win had left for the hospital I promoted myself from deputy leader to boss giving myself greater power and scrapping Win's plans. There were two good-sized recesses caused by the fireplace and chimney, which I could make use of.

I was going to use the Reliant van once again, but I had evil plans for it later. I knew where I could get caravan wood, doors, and worktops, so that was where I was going, to get a load.

I made two units, which consisted of two drawers and two cupboards below. The tops that reached the ceiling consisted of two side panels the width of these being 4 inches less than the depth of the cupboards to give the finish a well-balanced look.

I connected two panels by fitting a top and a piece across the middle. This made a cupboard with sliding doors. The space between the underside of the cupboard and the worktop was left open for small pictures or wall plates or cup hooks, etc.

When the second top was made and fitted and the two cupboards stood in the recesses they looked very good. I emptied the sideboard and made it redundant. So in less than a month the living room and kitchen had new stairs and two new cupboards.

Now I moved from woodwork to metalwork. First I had some 2-inch by ¼ inch angle iron to saw up. I wanted two lengths 2ft long and two lengths of 3ft long to weld in a frame. Then I had to measure up the length of an axle of ¾ inch round mild steel. The axle would fit into the bearings, which were bolted onto the frame. I required two motorcycle rear wheels fitted with small chain sprockets. I used phosphor bronze bushes to take the axle and fitted it into the wheel hubs. I needed two temporary stands at the front. The front is nearer to the axle than the back of the frame.

The next job was to remove from the Reliant van, the engine, radiator, gearbox and clutch, starter motor, and generator (dynamo). I left the propeller shaft and back axle on the Reliant for the present.

I needed the engine mounting brackets to fit on the frame. Then I lifted the engine and all that goes with it, onto the angle iron frame and marked out where to drill holes and lifted the engine onto the frame after drilling. Next I bolted down the engine, gearbox and radiator.

I went back to the Reliant and removed the propeller shaft from the back axle leaving the universal joint on the back axle. I removed the back axle leaving the road springs on the van.

The half-shaft housings were too long and needed cutting down so that the overall length was 2ft 2 inches. The half shafts had to be cut so that they were protruding 2 inches from the half-shaft housing.

Next I placed the axle on the frame, which was now the chassis and bolted the two universal joints together as we were not using the propeller shaft, and clamped the half-shaft housings to the chassis. I used two motorcycle chains for the drive from the back axle to the wheels. I removed the temporary props from the front and fitted some cultivators at the back and I had a better garden tractor than you see at agricultural shows.

David, my son, was always interested in engineering. He started a course at night school. He used to go on his motorbike, but once I took him and went for him later. I arrived at the school twenty minutes too early and so I went up to David's classroom to have a nosy. In my opinion the instructor's knowledge in engineering wasn't worth David's time, so he didn't go anymore. He started at an engineering works in Knottingley, not far from Pollard Bearings. Like them, this firm could turn out first class scrap.

One of the jobs was making presser feet for sewing machines. That is the plate that goes onto the material when you move down the lever. There is a hole, which the needle passes through. It was usual for half of those made to break the needle because the hole wasn't in the correct position.

They put David on this job as soon as he went to work there. Instead of making scrap he began by making a jig, which cut out the scrap. He gave the jig to me as a keepsake. I was very proud of it because it was so well made. Unfortunately it has got lost, but I am still hoping to come across it.

When David had completed three months he said, 'I am going to leave.' I asked him for what reason because he was serving an apprenticeship. He said, 'I can set up all the machines as good as anyone there so I'm not staying there on a very low wage and not learning anything.'

He went to work at Askern in a hardware shop working on washing machines and fridges etc. Then he worked on televisions and built up a very useful knowledge of all electrical machines. He didn't smoke or drink alcoholic drinks, as he was never a vandal or anything like that.

He and a friend were on night shift. After having three or four hour's sleep they went out to look at shops. Two policemen came across the road to them when they were looking in one of the shops.

One of the policemen asked them what they were doing. David said, 'We are just looking in the shops.' The other policeman said, 'You should be working for a living instead of idling your time away.' The lads explained that they were on night shift. The police did their best to try to get them to say something, which they could get against them, but the lads had more sense than to bite their bait.

From then on a police car would wait for David to leave work and follow him home. During this time David was in Selby near the Aire and Calder Canal. There were five children playing on top of the bank and David was afraid they were in danger of falling in, so he didn't go away. Then they began to shout, 'Someone has fallen in.' He ran to them and could just see a little girl in the water. Luckily he was a good swimmer and managed to rescue her. Then he ran with her in his arms to her grandmother's house, which was 100 yards away. She was only two-years-old. Her name was Briony Tatham.

In spite of this, David was still harassed by the police and by a dirty trick they got him. David went round a very slow corner onto a main road. About 50 yards away from the corner, they had the road up. It was impossible for David to break the speed limit in these 50 yards.

The police would feel proud of themselves when David had to go to court. They could have been doing something useful instead of hounding a young innocent motorcyclist.

We grew a lot of fruit and vegetables in our big garden, a lot more than what we needed for ourselves. I had a good idea: the next time we went to Withernsea I would stop at Boothferry Road where those posh houses were and sell some of our garden produce. I went to the back of a row of houses and went knocking on back doors. The occupants didn't seem to be vegetarians and my big wicker basket didn't get any lighter. I reached the last house in the row and went into the yard where three women were busy. I asked very politely if they wanted any vegetables. They told me very impolitely to stick my vegetables. I immediately lost all confidence regarding becoming a salesman. I went from the back of the house to the road and saw that it wasn't just a house; it was a fruit and vegetable shop.

I waited until I was well away from there and tried again and I sold out. One old lady told me to call whenever I was passing. She said, 'If you want to live to be old, have a sleep in the afternoon.' I was so busy making money for my old age, I didn't have time to sleep in the afternoon. I think I had a problem there.

Win was a good gardener; she had once worked for a market gardener and knew the names of all plants and flowers. We would walk along the garden path together and she would be talking about this plant and that flower giving them their names. I would pretend that I understood. Then she would say, 'You don't know, which one I am talking about do you?' My pretence would come to a sudden end.

One day when I came home from work, Win had something to show me in the garden. There was an old hen house in the middle of the garden and the ground around the hen house hadn't been worked, as it would have been a large hen run before we went there. So it was this ground, which she wanted to show me as it had been dug and weeded and nicely raked over. I was feeling very pleased about her good work until I stepped round a corner of the hen house where a rake was waiting for me. My right foot went down on the curved prongs and the shaft gave me a hard hit on the side of my head. What should have been a pleasant evening turned a bit sour. Whenever I see a rake in that position, no matter whose it is, I make it safe.

Mr and Mrs Bulmer and their son lived next door to our left and Mrs Hinchcliff and daughter Peggy lived to our right. Mr Hinchcliff had died two or three years before we went to Herberry House. Two large hedges marked our boundaries. There was a large hedge and a deep ditch across the end of our garden. There was a very large willow tree in the left-hand corner. It supplied me with the supports for runner beans.

An oldish couple had a bungalow built on land across the back road. It stood on its own, which I thought was not good for an oldish couple if they became ill and needed urgent help. The bungalow overlooked our garden; therefore I could look across to see if they were moving about and I would know if they were all right or if they needed help.

Our house was at the end of Main Street where it joined onto Mill Lane. Branching off was Landing Lane. When you were in Landing Lane you got a good view of the Drax Power Station, as it was only a few fields away. But to get there was a 12-mile journey.

Just down Mill Lane there were quite a number of greenhouses. Jimmy Smith lived near them. He had a large garden and people who lived near, bought fruit and vegetables from him. So everyday he went round to his customers with his flat wicker basket with his fresh produce. There was often a bunch of lovely fresh flowers for some lucky lady.

You didn't have to be one of Jimmy's customers to get a big happy smile and a few pleasant words because he was always jolly. His mother's small farm was opposite us. Mr Smith died before we went there. Kathy Smith looked after her mother because she was an invalid.

Joan Drew and her husband Richard and children, two girls and a boy, lived at the beginning of Landing Lane.

Just past Drews' was the Chilvers' farm. Mr and Mrs Chilvers were a lovely couple. Bill was interested in old stationary engines. He also had a steam engine.

To satisfy insurance, all the steam tubes in the boilers of old steam engines had to be replaced with new ones. Bill and his son Gordon were doing this replacement one day when I visited them. It was a very awkward job.

Mrs Chilvers was a wonderful lady. She used to do a lot of baking for people in the village who weren't very well off. She was a good friend of Win's and so we often had her coming round with a freshly baked cake or a fruit pie. We had a lot of friends at Hemingbrough, Mavis and Norman Fields were a couple that I liked very much. They had two children, a boy and a girl. Norman was the manager of a small engineering factory in Selby. They lived at the end of the back lane and were about 60 yards from us.

My job with the turbines was easy and a lot different from my job at Yarrows so I wasn't going home as tired as I used to be. Therefore, I was in good shape for my jobs at home.

The little tractor cut down on work and almost made garden spades, forks, and rakes redundant. When it was pulling cultivating tools it went dead straight so you could just walk at the side of it until it needed turning round. It was easy to turn because of the rear axle differential. I used to grow about 200 spring cabbages. Scuffling between small plants was easy with my tractor because of the low gearing. It went straight and very slow.

The Reliant engine was basically an Austin Seven and it was brilliant for the little tractor. It started easily and never missed a beat and what was important to me because I do not like disturbing neighbours, it was quiet.

We had a large freezer, which just fitted in the pig house and we spent most of our time in summer filling it, putting in enough to last until the following summer. We went to Withernsea often and came through Beverley (not the centre of Beverley) on our way back home. We went by the horse racing course and to Bishop Burton. We used to stop there and go to a large house, which faced the pond where they sold meat in freezer packs. That is where we bought all our meat for the freezer.

We were pulling peas all summer. You could sow early peas in February although we usually waited until March. Later the intermediate peas were sown and then the late ones, or you could sow early ones late in the season. The advantages being you had fresh peas to eat and also there was a longer time to pull them for the freezer.

Sowing peas by hand is slow and back-aching work; therefore a Nicholson drill was designed and produced. Fresh runner beans were one of my favourite vegetables so we always had plenty. By sowing the first crop under cloches and then later sowing outside, gave a longer harvesting time for eating during the summer and a longer time for preparing them for the freezer. This was made much quicker due to the manufacture of the Nicholson bean slicing machine that sliced the beans as quick as you could feed it.

I made large cloches for growing carrots. They used to be harvested before the carrot fly had a chance to ruin them. I also grew carrots out in the open. They would be sown next to the onions because the carrot fly didn't like the smell of onions, and the onion fly didn't like carrots. So both the carrot fly and onion fly would clear off to another garden.

We had all kinds of fruit, red and black currants, raspberries, gooseberries and strawberries.

If you have gooseberries you will go to them one morning and find thousands of fruit buds under the trees. If you are not an expert gardener you will most likely wait until the following spring and cover your gooseberries with netting to keep the birds off. Your crop will be hundreds of small berries. So give the birds some credit because they know what they are doing. They will only take off the right amount of buds and when they are ready, you will have a lovely crop of big juicy berries.

I am very lucky because often when I need something someone else wants to get rid of the same thing. This happened when I needed lots of cloches for strawberries. A man was dismantling an old fashioned greenhouse with small panes of glass. So I bought the glass.

I needed lots of $\frac{3}{16}$ inch galvanised wire, which I purchased at a hardware store. Going by the measurements of a glass plate I made a wooden jig, which was like a letter H. The wire was looped round the bottom, which would hold a piece of glass. Then a sharp bend 1 inch below the top loop would complete the top loop.

My jig was 12 inches wide. I bent the wire round to form the top loop and to go to the bottom and make the bottom loop.

I made another one on the jig. Then I fitted a glass at each side and put a piece of glass on the top. I made enough to cover three rows of strawberries, which were about 100 cloches.

We were growing more than we needed at home so I loaded up with fruit, vegetables, and flowers and went to about thirty houses in Selby. I only needed twelve customers so I picked out the best dozen and called on them once a week.

Since I made the wardrobes out of the caravan doors, Win had been waiting to decorate the bedrooms. So I bought some suitable wood to make the back windows. I knocked out the bricks and made and fitted the windows.

I was glad the rear windows were fitted, as this was the last job for me on the house apart from rebuilding the chimney stack, which was in the barn. I had made up my mind to get a builder to do the roof tiles.

The barn and other out-buildings would be a big job. But I decided to leave them until the work in the garden eased up.

Win's mother was much worse and had to go into hospital in Wakefield. Win's dad was going by bus to visit her, but as he wasn't well the journey was too much for him. After two or three days, Win and I went to the hospital and Win's dad came as well. The poor old dear was very poorly and very unhappy because she was in hospital. She had never been in that situation before, having people to feed her and run after her. She was a quiet person who was never at ease amongst people.

She said, 'Take me home, Bill.' Bill's reply was, 'Yes, all right.' But I knew he didn't mean it and Hilda also knew that he was just putting her off.

She kept on asking to go home and I felt very sorry for her. I said, 'Let her come home Bill. I'm sure Win and Kath (Win's sister) and Cath (Charley's wife) would be able to look after her.' Hilda came home with us.

At that time unfortunately, Kath and Cath, were not in very good health so most of the work fell on Win's shoulders. Hilda didn't mind this because she preferred Win (naturally) as Win had helped at home during hard times and had been a very good daughter to her mother and dad.

Hilda was deteriorating quickly and Win was getting very tired. One day, Hilda said to me, 'Look after our Win for us won't you, Nick.' I told her I would look after her. Then she said, 'I just want to be able to hang on for our David's wedding.'

David was married at Hemingbrough church. During the reception, an honest, good worker, who had never done anyone any harm, went to Jesus. I said goodbye to Hilda.

It is a terrible part of a daughter's life when her mother dies. Win was very sad because they had been so close. But as well as being sad, she was exhausted.

Win was a dinner lady at Hemingbrough School. She had been allowed time off when she was looking after her mother. As they had been so good and considerate to her, she went back to work almost straight away although she wasn't well. Two or three days later she wanted to see me about something. When I reached the school she was at the school gate waiting for me. We talked for a few minutes and then she turned to go back to her job. I watched her walking away; it was a wide path and she was walking on the right hand edge. Suddenly she veered to the left and was walking like a drunken person. To me it looked like she'd had a stroke. She went to see her doctor who was about to retire as he had reached retirement age. He said to her, 'There is nothing wrong, you are too fat.' I thought this was a ridiculous thing to say because she was well built and muscular.

A young doctor came to take the place of the ancient one. Win went and he said, 'There's nothing wrong with you, you are too fat.' So we were rid of a useless old doctor, but had to put up with a useless young doctor.

It was July 1969 and we had been at Herberry House for three years. We were very busy in the garden and in the kitchen, blanching vegetables. I had not begun work on the barn. I must have been born lazy. It was time I made a start.

The new power station at Ferrybridge was almost completed, so they could do without me now. I gave them a week's notice to leave and I would get another job when I was ready.

The chimney stack had been getting on my nerves for three years. It had been plastered every now and again for many years and had become rounded in shape. So that is where I started to knock off the thick coat of plaster. The bricks were not too bad and I only had a few bricks to replace, so that job was soon done.

I wanted a pit for working under cars so this was my next job. I dug it out making it 6ft long. I had to get rid of the soil. The barn floor was just soil so it would have to have a concrete floor put down, but not yet.

The next job was the tiled roof. I dropped the tiles onto the barn floor so the soil floor was covered with broken tiles. The tile battens were levered off next and the roof spares loosened and dropped down. The barn had become topless.

I had the gable end and the front wall to do; I didn't like the look of the gable end. The apex bit was bent over about 9 inches. If a bored bricklayer had come along and pestered me to let him take it down I reckon he could have persuaded me to let him do it.

The job had to be done by someone and there was no one else but I. So it was up the ladder to remove the bricks very carefully. There was only a small door so as I was going to fit a large door into the gable wall for getting a car through, there were a lot of bricks to take down. I was surprised how quickly I did get them down.

I cleaned up next, throwing the bricks all over the floor for a base for the concrete. Then I took the front wall down and cleaned up once again.

Rebuilding the walls had to wait till the floor has been converted to a concrete one. Therefore I broke up the bricks to form a base and cut some wood for shuttling the lining of the pit with concrete. Then I ordered the mix.

By leaving the walls until last, the mixer shoot reached most parts of the floor cutting down on work.

There was a job vacancy for a maintenance fitter at Eggborough Power Station. It lay off the A19, about nine miles from Selby. I felt sure I could get the job so I applied for it and was called for an interview.

There were three men behind a large desk at the interview. One of them had a list of questions and I was wondering if I would be able to answer any of them. It's an awful feeling. He looked at me with a little smile on his face. That is usually a bad sign to start with. 'Good morning Nicholson.' He said in a low polite voice. 'Good morning,' said I. 'I'm not going to insult you by asking you these simple questions,' he said, and that was the end of the interview. I had a few days left to get the walls built and then I started work at Eggborough Power Station. It was September 1969 and there wasn't a roof on the barn yet.

The autumn leaves have begun to fall from the trees and it would soon be winter with frosty mornings and fog to blur your vision on the roads. Roll on spring.

Autumn Leaves

When the autumn leaves fall down
To whirl about the street
In shades of russet, gold, and brown
They gather round our feet.

The oak tree stands in golden splendour
A scarlet cloak from the maple falls
Yellow, orange and purple render
The chestnut gay as winter calls.
Trees stand gaunt against the sky
Resting giants awaiting longer days
Their sleep will last till spring is nigh
Whom on green buds the warm wind plays.

David Nicholson, 1958

Chapter 57

EGGBOROUGH POWER STATION

As I had worked at Ferrybridge Power Station and seen it grow from many acres of components and ducting etc. I knew what the inside of a power station looked like. Nevertheless, I had a lot to learn about the situation of hundreds of valves and many other things to learn.

On arrival at the station I found the car park was very large and it was good to know that someone had realised that more and more motorists would come onto the roads.

From the car park I went to the main office. After the usual procedure I was given keys for lockers. One of the Bakers' girls was in the office and it was lovely to see her and have a little talk about her family and how the garage was going on.

I went to my locker and changed into my working clothes and then went to the workshop. There were about eight squads of fitters and mates, and two foremen with each squad of about eight fitters.

You were not told, which job you were going on. Instead there was the jobs card rack. You took out the card with your name on it and you read your instructions, which were very brief. I had to repair a leaking valve. Most of these valves were in line with the gantries so you had to reach over the safety fence, which made it hard work.

There is a very high pressure of steam, about 600 degrees centigrade, passing through these valves. Usually this is switched off before the fitter goes to the valve.

Eggborough was the type where four power stations are built into one. There were four boilers and four turbines. There was a river at Haddlesey and from there a large pump, which was near Jim Syke's garage where I went for my petrol when I worked at Selby and Burn, fed water into a reservoir near the cooling towers.

To condense the steam in the cooling towers they are filled with wooden structures built like the honeycombs in a hive. The condensed water pours down and goes into the reservoir to be used again to make high-pressure steam for driving the turbines.

The coal plant and ash plant take up most of the space at a power station. The coal came from a large modern mine at Kellingley. The trains were controlled from a control room and so there was no one on them.

There were large bunkers at the coal plant. When the trucks passed over the bunkers, the bottoms were opened automatically and the coal fell into one of the bunkers and then the bottoms were lifted back into position and locked.

The coal went by a conveyor system to the coal stacks. To stack the coal a very large machine called the moxey was used. It was on a turntable carried by a huge chassis. The ball bearings used in the turntable were the size of footballs.

The conveyor system for supplying the coal to the boiler house consisted of wide flexible belts supported by rollers. They entered the boiler house at a height of about 150ft and dropped down into the bunkers on the 40ft level.

From the bunkers the coal was conveyed to the mills, which were on the ground floor. The mills looked like large boilers and stood horizontal. From the mills the coal was blown into the boilers. Therefore, the coal had to be crushed to 'slack' and the mills did this. They were half full of iron balls just a little smaller than a tennis ball. The mills spun on their axis slinging the balls about and crushing the coal.

Up against the inner walls of the boilers and all the way round, were the water tubes. The tubes were of high quality steel and about 4 inches in diameter. The high-pressure steam drove the turbines as it passed through the turbine blades.

Working in a power station was an unhealthy job, due to dust and noise and it was also dangerous. Nevertheless, the people were cheerful. Most of the maintenance fitters had served their time in garages. Then there were the most important people, the fitters' mates. There was none of that nonsense from the trade unions about a fitter's mate just passing the spanners. As soon as the fitter read the job card the mates would be on their way to the stores to draw out what was needed on the job. They were brilliant; a good mate made the job easy and every one of them in our team was good and reliable.

There were more and more new cars coming onto the car park and most of them belonged to fitter's mates and labourers. They would collect brochures from car showrooms and study them. While we sat in the canteen having our lunch the subject for discussion would most likely be about cars. They knew all the cars' names and all the different models. They were far beyond me and so I had to keep quiet. It's doubtful if they could change a wheel if they got a puncture, but that didn't matter. There is an awful lot to learn on a motor vehicle. There are petrol and diesel engines, gearboxes and ordinary clutches and automatic clutches. A differential needs skill when overhauling one. There is also the high and the low voltage circuits. Therefore, in my opinion, a good motor mechanic can tackle any type of engineering job.

I found my workmates to be well skilled, reliable and very helpful to each other. There were two foremen in each group. Ours were called Gordon Wedgwood and Hugh Owen. They were good at their job, very pleasant and always helpful.

David joined us. He began working at Eggborough on 7 November 1969 as an instrument mechanic. Now there were four Nicholsons working there. The other two were a married couple, no relation to David and I. The young man worked on clearing up and drove a forklift truck. A bucket could be fitted to replace the fork. His wife worked in the stores. They were a lovely couple and everyone liked them.

Our Derrick and Peter had their talents. Derrick took after Granddad Bryan and worked at a bakery and was very good at his job. He was also a keen angler and often took first prize, usually a goose for Christmas. Peter was good at art and as a budding artist his drawings and paintings were very good. He was musically minded and could play an organ well. He could entertain and take off Irish and Scottish talk. There was a young group in Selby, I knew one of them and he kept telling me to persuade Peter to join them. I don't know why he didn't.

He left school and became a painter and decorator with Mr Tomlinson who lived on the main road.

It was near Christmas, and time to go to Withernsea with presents. We also took lots of Holly because we had four large Holly trees in the hedge on Bulmer's side.

My eldest sister Kath lived about 100 yards away from my mother. Win liked Kath very much and Kath always looked forward to us going. My other three sisters, Audrey, Barbara, and Dorothy, were all married and lived away from Withernsea so we didn't see them at Christmas. Barbara lived at Marlow with her husband and three children. Her husband was Ken Paterson who was brought up on North Road, Withernsea. He lost both his legs in the war.

Audrey and Dorothy went to my mother's sister's farm during the war. They were called Young. Dorothy came back home to Withernsea, but Audrey stayed in Lincolnshire and married there. They live in Billingborough.

Dorothy married an air force lad from down south of England. But they stayed in Withernsea. Dorothy's husband worked on the buses, but looked out for something better. He went to work at Blackburn Aeroplane Factory at Brough, which is on the North Bank of the Humber. He learnt to be a Capstan lathe operator.

Dorothy and Ron moved to Havant in Hampshire. Ron became successful working on engineering. They all came to Withernsea during the summer months so we usually went to my mother's bungalow to see them.

We missed Win's mother when Charley and Cath came at Christmas and brought Win's dad. He wasn't well and of course he would be thinking of his Hilda. Bill hadn't been well for a long time. There was a comic who used to put on a sad face and say, 'I'm not well'. Bill used to mimic him, saying, 'I'm not well, and I am proper poorly.' I do not know if anyone else noticed it, but I knew he wasn't kidding and was more poorly than what we thought.

We had some good food and drinks and talked for a good while and then Cath played a few Scottish songs on her accordion. Cath didn't tell us to get our pencils and paper. As David was 23-years-old, she may have thought they were too old for playing games like drawing the donkey's tail.

Charley and Cath used to bring the lads good presents. I thought this was one-sided because they didn't have any children. But we tried to make up for it by giving Cath and Charley a good present.

We went back to work and soon it was the new year of 1970 and I was looking forward to spring. It wasn't cold in the power station where the turbines were. But it was very hot near the boilers. You could be working on a valve amongst very hot pipes and then your next job may be at the coal plant out in the cold.

When I was on nights and going to work on a very cold night, I dreaded the thought of having to go to the coal plant to work on conveyor belt rollers. They often wanted changing or wanted new bearings fitted. It was a horrible job when there were icy winds chilling your bones. When you became cold that was how you were for the rest of the night.

My Swiss friends, who I lived with in Wald, had been asking me to go to see them for a long time. Spring was getting closer. Win could get about with the aid of a walking stick, but I was afraid she would become worse. Therefore, we could go as soon as the weather became warmer. So I wrote to Tony and Lizy to say we would soon be seeing them.

During my last week before going to Switzerland, I was on night shift. Always when I had been on nights I would have my breakfast and then do some work with the intention of going to bed after dinner. Then I would decide to go out again to just do a little job. So I would be going to bed for a couple of hours after tea.

This is how it was during the week before going to Switzerland. I was very tired when I left work after the last night. I had almost reached where you turned off the Selby Howden Road to go into Hemingbrough Main Street, when I fell asleep. A car coming towards me was evidently going at a fast speed. The car woke me up as it went by and I saw it through my mirror speeding along. I was on a short stretch of straight road, but there were bends in the road just ahead.

It was a miracle that my car kept going straight. It was an awful feeling for me, but as for the other driver I don't think he noticed anything wrong.

We went by train to Dover and then the ferry and then on train to Wald. We enjoyed every bit of the journey and as Win's longest journey previously had been to go to Pug's in London, it was exciting and interesting for her.

I looked forward to seeing Lizy and Tony and their son Hugo and daughter Madi. I would talk to them fluently in their own language and Win would be so proud and look at me with love and amazement.

Lizy, Hugo, and Madi were at the station waiting for us. I think I had tears of joy when I saw them. But how they had changed and Lizy was looking old. I can't think of words to describe the thrill and wonder of being in Switzerland again, with my kind and wonderful friends.

The house was only a short distance from the station and we were soon there. Win went into the kitchen to help Lizy with the food and drinks. They got on like wild fire. Win spoke in English and Lizy spoke in her language, Swiss German, and they understood each other clearly. I spoke to them in my fluent Swiss German and no one understood me. It's amazing how a language gets lost in thick fog in your brain when you are not using it.

Tony came in and we sat down to a delicious Swiss meal finished off with strawberries and cream. 'Where would you like to go tomorrow?' asked Tony. I said, 'I would like Win to see Wald tomorrow and the next day I would like to go over the hills to that restaurant that has the fish tank in the wall.' There was a 'yes' vote through the chair.

We talked during the evening, had supper and Win and I went to bed early. We both slept soundly, but it wasn't late when we got out of bed and dressed and went to the window to look at the view. It was the same window, which I had sat at many years ago. The Eiger Mountain was still there in the distance; no one had pinched it while I had been away. Someone had heard us and brought a welcome cup of tea. We talked for a while and then breakfast was ready; we could smell the lovely aroma of bacon and eggs frying. Swiss bread is delicious and goes very well with fresh eggs and Swiss bacon.

After breakfast we sat in the garden. Madi came after a while. Lizy, Madi and Win and I went into Wald. It was a beautiful small town of Swiss wooden cottages all with their veranda's decked with colourful flowers. I think they were most likely wild flowers.

We had a nice meal in a restaurant. I took out my wallet to pay the bill, but Madi said, 'No, put your wallet away.' Madi paid the bill and then she told us it would have cost us a lot more as I was a visitor.

Lizy said, 'Lina is coming tomorrow.' During the war, Lizy, Lina and Jaffe Davis and I often walked to the restaurant. It was high up in the hills, a lovely walk, which we enjoyed very much. The pleasure of the walks was just a memory now, as we had grown older.

We were still having good weather and we looked forward to the trip. But our walking was no more than walking to a taxi and into the restaurant at the end of our ride. It was lovely to see Lina, and she hadn't changed. The restaurant still looked the same. The fish tank was still there sitting in a hole in the wall so that it could still be viewed from two rooms. I didn't recognise any of the fishes so I think they had been changed since I left.

It was quiet because it was the middle of the day. When we were younger we preferred the middle of the night, when there was dancing and a Swiss band playing, or an Austrian band. I couldn't help my memory taking me back to the lovely moonlit early morning walks down the slopes to Wald.

We talked about it quite a lot and many pleasant memories came to our minds. Switzerland used to be something very romantic in my imagination when I was a schoolboy, and I was glad that fate had given me a chance to get to know it.

The journey back to Wald was very pleasant, what with the lovely scenery and herds of Swiss cows ringing their large bells hanging from broad coloured ribbon or belts. They looked very healthy and so they should be, living in such beautiful and healthy surroundings.

By the time we were back at the Schoder's house we all had a large appetite, which was soon satisfied by the delicious Swiss food.

When Lina wished us a goodnight she said, 'Come and see me at my house tomorrow. You haven't forgotten the way?' She was right. I hadn't forgotten the way and about the new railway, which they opened while I was living in Wald.

The journey and being at Lina's house, brought back memories of the walks in the long grass and the woods where we collected bucketful's of toadstools, which were delicious when cooked in a large pan.

Some of the woods were free, like the common lands in England. People went to get wood and they would pile it up until they came to take it home.

There were lots of piles of wood spread about. I asked Tony if anyone took wood from another man's pile and put it on their own. Tony said, 'You do not have that in Switzerland.'

I went for a walk with Lizy to a farm. Win stayed behind to have a rest. Lizy bought eggs, butter, bacon, and some potatoes. She left her shopping to pick up on our way back home. The road was on the side of the hill; therefore, when you looked left you could only see the fields by the roadside. There were men and women working. But they all noticed us and spoke or waved. The weather was good and the friendly people also helped to make us feel very happy and important.

When you turned your head to the right you were looking at the most wonderful view. There were fields with cows grazing and hay fields where people were turning the hay so that all the hay would be ready for carting to the farms for winter-feeding.

Mountains stood out in the distance capped with pure white snow. On the sides of the mountains, flashing in the sunlight, were electricity towers (or pylons). I could imagine the difficulties of getting them there and a much more difficult task of erecting them and the linesmen connecting up the heavy wires.

The road turned sharp right and became a very steep hill. A lad came round the corner on his pushbike and rode down the hill as fast as he could go. I have often wondered if he ever became a World Champion Motorcyclist.

We walked slowly back to the farm and were told to come in, which we were glad to do as we were ready for a sit-down. The farm lady found pleasure in showing me round the house. I couldn't blame her for being so proud because it was the most beautiful house I had ever seen with its lovely beams and panels, doors and stairs, all made from Switzerland's own pine.

The furniture was also made of pine and I felt at home in a comfortable chair, drinking coffee with real cream and eating a large slice of fruitcake. I thought, *you don't need a lot of money to keep you happy, only a walk in Switzerland amongst lovely people.* My own regret was that Win hadn't been with us to enjoy the lovely walk.

The following day a friend of the family came in a very large car and took us for a ride over the hills, which was similar to going to the restaurant that had the fish. But it was a much longer ride. It was also brilliant as regards the scenery. Although we were almost at the top of the mountains it was an excellent road.

That night, soon after we had retired to bed, there was a thunderstorm, which became violent and went on and on for hours. I was conscious of being in a Swiss wooden house, but there was no need to worry because it was built to stand up to strong gales.

We went to have a look at the damaged road two or three days later. We went just a few miles and were staggered at what we saw. The road was completely washed away and the water was gushing down where the road had been. We went round Wald again and did some shopping. I had to go to the toilet. I heard voices, two men talking to each other, but I couldn't see anyone. I had never been in a Swiss haunted toilet before. Then I saw under the toilet door, two pairs of man's shoes all pointing the same way. Yes, it is true; the Swiss people are very friendly. The time went far too quickly and sadly we packed our bags to leave beautiful Switzerland and the friendly people.

We had a good send off as they all came to the station. I was glad Lina had come along to say farewell. Madi said that she would come to England and bring her two daughters, the following year. I don't know what happened to her husband if she had one.

I was sorry that Tony and Lizy hadn't been to England, and neither had Lina. I had the awful feeling that I would never see them again. *What can you say to them? How can you thank people enough when they have been so wonderfully kind to you?*

The train set off and they were soon out of sight and it is impossible to put into words how I felt. The weather was good for travelling and my mind began to take in the views and activities of that, which sped by.

We were very tired by the time we were at Herberry House. Susan and David had a good meal ready for us, which we devoured greedily as we were very hungry.

I had been worried about Win's health, but she had taken it all very well and had enjoyed a very good holiday.

I took things easy the following day. Sunday and Monday morning came too soon. I was hoping Saudi Arabia had bought Eggborough Power Station in my absence, but it was still there and I had to clock in and get a job card and spend the day amongst the heat and the dust. What a contrast to last week. Our lads and their best friends were all motorbike crackers and had been wallpapering the barn, but not with cheap wallpaper. There were dozens of pictures of motorcycle riders covering the walls.

To mention just a few there were pictures of Mike Hailwood, Ralph Bryans, Giocomo Agostini, Jim Redman, Phil Read, Stuart Graham, Jarno Saarinen, Bill Ivy, Helmut Fath, Kel Caruthers, Rod Gould, Jack Findley on his G50 Matchless, Max Deubel, Spaniard Angel Nieto on his Spanish built Derbi, Fritz Schiedegger and many more.

I had a lot of work to do in the garden. The crops of spring cabbages were excellent. Now I had to study where the next year's cabbages would be. I wanted to know this before I sowed the peas.

Plants take food out of the soil. But they also put something back. If one knows this then they can cut down on expenses. Peas put lime into the soil and cabbages take it out because they need a lot of lime. Therefore, cabbages are planted after peas, and benefit from the lime.

When Win was about 22-years-old she met someone and fell in love with him. They wanted to marry, naturally, but Win's parents didn't want to be without their loving hardworking daughter and so they talked her out of getting married. Her mother said to Win, 'If you stay single and stay with us until you are 27-years-old, I will give you £700.'

After Win's mother died, Win said to me, 'My dad has looked everywhere for that £700, which my mother promised me and he says he can't find it.' I didn't take this seriously. It may have been there or it may not, but I felt sure that if he had found it Win would have no chance of seeing it. Win was 27-years-old when we married, so I think the promise was broken, they had never been over generous to her.

Win's sister and her husband decided to have Bill at their house rather than have him be on his own. So there was a sale of house and furniture.

A long time before this, Win and her mother went to a furniture sale. In the sale were four old dining chairs, which were first class and beautifully made and in good condition. Win loved good furniture so she bid and they were knocked down to her. Her mother wanted two of them, but Win said, 'No, four are valuable, but just two on their own would not be worth anything.' Hilda kept on nattering and told Win she would get them when she died. So in the end she took the two chairs. Win asked her dad for the two chairs, but he refused and sold them in the sale, so the chairs never made anyone rich. You can be good to your parents during what should be the best part of your life, but your reward is forgotten.

Kath had their dad living with them in Barnby Dun, near Doncaster. The house was in the yard opposite the workshop and the Chapel of Rest. The last time I went to see him, a coffin was being carried from the Chapel of Rest, which was opposite his bedroom window.

He said, 'I will be next.' Then he told me to go and see Jack's eldest lad who was his favourite grandson. I had to tell him to go to see his granddad as he had a £100 for him. Bill died just before the lad arrived.

The money from the sale did not amount to much. It was an old house. It was to be shared between Charley, Kath, and Win. I explained to Charley about the £100 for the lad and Charley didn't seem interested.

Power stations are highly complicated and run from the control room by the engineers. Steam leaks are very dangerous because of the high pressure. You cannot see the stream of steam. You can hear it, but as the echoes bounce around off many of the pipes it is not possible to detect the direction. A piece of rag tied to the end of a long stick will find it.

A very young engineer who was new to the job may have been trying to find a leak and didn't know about the stick method. He went onto a gantry to be closer and was hit by the steam, which knocked him off the gantry and he was killed.

An electrician was surprised to see me at work one day. When I enquired why he was surprised he told me that David was motorbike racing and I should have been there to help him. David hadn't mentioned it because he didn't want his mother to be worried.

The next meeting couldn't come too soon for me. But before it did, I made a trailer to fit the bike for holding it upright. I used a sidecar connection, which bolts onto the frame under the seat. The bottom end was bolted to the trailer floor. Two padded clamps held the wheels. So there was no need for clotheslines and straps.

We had been at work until midday while other riders were practising. So David hadn't had time to go round the track. To reduce the speed down the straight length of the track, a chicane had been marked out. David told me to walk to it and go back with details. This track was on Elvington aerodrome that was used during the war.

My knowledge of cornering was no more than going round on a comparatively slow KTS Velocette, which did not handle like the modern bikes. I thought the corners were too sharp. If I had been able to get back to David my information would have been useless.

But my return journey had not started before the racers set off, and all I saw was bikes flashing by with two flicks and they were gone. I felt very old and certainly past my action date.

David was a very good rider and the bike handled well. But the Ducati engine wasn't built for racing and so he began to look for a Yamaha 250cc engine as we thought one would fit the Ducati frame.

Social Club

As you entered Eggborough Power Station, if you looked left you would see the social club. But to get to it you had to keep straight on to the end of the car park and turn left going between the end of the car park and the power station main building. Then turn left and to the social club.

Before you entered the building you got the idea that money had been no object. When you got inside you were sure it wasn't. It had been well planned and well built and very well carpeted. The well-decorated walls had interesting pictures. There were games rooms for adults and children. Then there was a large room with two bars down the centre to make sure that throats were kept lubricated during gossiping and shop talk.

Then there was the main part where you could eat any time, but which was decorated extra special during parties, and Christmas dinners for the retired. They had plenty of music, but what I enjoyed most was the music when it was a colliery band. The Mills Blackdyke band was just one of many excellent bands.

Small Turbines

Six small turbines were a standby if needed when a main turbine was closed down or being worked on. Changing the filters was a job I didn't like. They were situated at the top of the building, which was 200ft high. The size I reckon would be 4 yards square and made of cloth or nylon or a mixture of both materials.

The used filter had to go down to the ground to be picked up by the labourers. The easy way was to roll it up and drag it to the edge of the building and push it over and it went whizzing down to the ground and made a loud thud. Watching it going down made me feel a bit giddy and afraid that I would lose my balance because there was nothing to get hold of.

Chapter 58

VETERAN AND VINTAGE CARS

A nice change from motorcycling and car racing is a visit to a Veteran and Vintage Car Rally. I always feel a lot of gratitude for the people who have restored them to their original condition. They are such lovely people and so proud of their cars. They always have framed certificates and also the information about the car for you to read.

They will wait patiently while you are reading. Then they will talk about the car to you because they are so pleased you have taken the trouble to see them.

I enjoy going to shows and galas where the cars are an additional attraction as you can take your time and spend more time with each car. But when the weather is good I like to enjoy the ride to the large rallies. There is an annual rally at Bridlington, which is one where I like to go, and another one is Sledmere, which is an interesting journey through interesting villages and lovely views.

You have to do a lot of walking at Sledmere to see all the cars. But it is a luxury to be able to wander over many acres of grassland and enjoy the shade of the trees. When you are tired of cars there are the wonders of the great house to enjoy.

I had friends among the car owners who I only saw at the rallies. There was Mr and Mrs Fattorini senior and their son Michael and his wife from Harrogate. They were lovely people. They were rich and I was very poor, but that didn't make any difference and I received lovely Christmas cards from them. One day, Mr and Mrs Fattorini were leaving, sitting high up on their Armstrong Siddley; they gave me a good wave. I remember it well because that was the last time I saw them. Michael and wife went to Guernsey and somehow we lost touch.

The people who went to see them racing on the cinders at Belle Vue Speedway will remember Oliver and Eric Langton. Oliver had a Rolls Car dated 1904; that was before Royce joined Rolls. Oliver must have been rich because I was told his car was worth £1,000,000, but he was always one of the lads and a real gentleman. When a field was being prepared for a rally, Oliver would be working as hard as anyone, running about with wooden stakes to fix the ropes. He wasn't a young man and his wife would be worried. She used to say to me, 'He doesn't need to do it and I am worried and afraid he will have a heart attack.' The awful day did come when Oliver did have a heart attack and died.

Chapter 59

GOING BACK TO DAVID'S MOTORBIKE RACING

David was looking out for a Yamaha racing engine, and eventually was lucky enough to be able to buy one. It was an old engine so we didn't expect the Ducati to be as quick as the new Yamaha's. It fitted into the Ducati without much trouble, and its name was changed to Yamati.

The Yamati was a lot quicker than the Ducati and so with Ducati handling it, it was a good racing bike and David enjoyed his racing very much. It wasn't fast enough to win races, but his fourth and fifth places against good riders and fast bikes were good achievements. Mechanics are very important people who no one gives credit to so it is time to say, Peter was David's mechanic.

One of the lads who David rode against was sponsored, and the man who sponsored him wanted David to join them. David was not so keen on the rider so he remained on his own, and he was looking for a faster Yamaha engine, which was not so old as the one he was using.

Even when you are an old-timer it is good to be in the pits and mix with the riders. Mick Grant, who was a favourite of all of us, became works rider. The late Pat Shillings' son was a friend of ours. He was a good rider. His mother was always at the races. There was Bill and Alan Jackson who were famous for their Isle-of-Man Tourist Trophy successes. They always brought their large caravan for the family to sit in. Mrs Shillings and myself spent quite a lot of time in their caravan talking about motorbike racing and other things.

Even if you do not see all the races you enjoy meeting people and it creates a wonderful and happy atmosphere. A few of our friends rode in the Isle-of-Man races and I was thinking David would be going with them if he found a better engine.

One rider called Phil Mellor was my favourite. He was brilliant when he rode at Scarborough, but sadly he crashed and was killed, riding in a TT race. I longed to ride in the TTs in days gone by, but the thought of David riding there was different. I would have been worried and scared, as Ernie was when I rode at West Park.

One day David said, 'I've seen your Velocette engine. It was in a modern frame.' A few months after this he was riding from Hemingbrough to York. At a house, the garage door was open and David saw a man inside the garage. Outside the garage were three lovely motorbikes. David stopped and went back to have a closer look at the bikes and to talk to the man.

David was very surprised when the man said, 'Hello I have got your dad's engine, do you want to see it?' David followed him into the house, and there in the centre of his sideboard, stood on a worthy plinth and looking brand new, was my faithful friend, my Velocette engine.

The engine had been put into a decent frame and taken to the Isle-of-Man where it was clocked at 110 miles per hour. I think the engine would have been standard because the racing cams went to Ireland.

David said to me, 'You can have a look at the engine.' But I did not go; I would rather see it on my own sideboard.

David found out about a more up-to-date Yamaha engine and he was keen to have it. He asked if I wanted to go with him to get it and of course I wanted to go with him. The engine was in Wales and the weather was fine. We went in David's car.

When we were going through Buckingham and were near Ampthill, my memory took me back to the Signals Display Team. It was at Ampthill where my friend McGee and I met Betty Laurence, Joan Peacock and Kate White.

I asked David if we had time to visit a friend. He said, 'Yes, we have got plenty of time.' We went to the house of the Peacock family and knocked on the door. I was expecting someone to open the door and say, 'Oh, they left years ago.' But no, I was in luck; Mrs Peacock came to the door. She asked us in and was so pleased to see me. As we talked she put the kettle on and prepared food for us.

Her daughter Joan, who became McGee's girl at the Ampton Show, had married and was living in America. Betty, my sweetheart until I went abroad, had waited for me until the end of the war and then married. She was happy; she had a good husband and two children.

We left to get on with our journey and me with the knowledge that these lovely people who were my friends many years ago, had survived the trauma of that stupid war.

David's new engine looked good in the Ducati. David had made one or two small parts and linkages, but what he did make looked very good and the bike looked beautiful when finished.

We took it to a disused aerodrome for testing. We had a problem. Although we knew the techniques of starting a racing Yamaha we had a little difficulty with starting this one. When it was going it was very quick and lovely to ride.

The man who had sold the engine had told David not to do anything with it because it had been stripped and tuned by an expert. Therefore, we thought the problem with starting was some fault, which may rectify itself, or we may just find it accidentally.

David soon learnt about the workings of a power station and became a foreman. Now and again we saw each other while we were working and would try to talk, but some engineer or other wanting to know how this or that works, would interrupt us. He was an instrument mechanic, but he could not be promoted to engineer because it was against union rules.

He did some good modifications and inventions. Therefore, when the power station was to be brought up-to-date by computerising, David was responsible for the job, which consisted of ordering the equipment and the construction work.

The components were American, naturally, and the American firm were based in London. David spent three days of the week at the power station, and three days in London to sort out the equipment etc. Therefore, he was very busy.

David was racing at Elvington, Carnaby, and Cadwell Park. He was still having the starting problem. He loved his racing and would be very upset if he missed a race because the bike wouldn't start. Because of the extra work at the power station he had no chance to dismantle the engine and had to leave it until the end of the racing season.

Eventually the engine was taken to pieces and the problem was found. A small seal had been badly fitted, which let sufficient air into the crankcase to upset the carburettor for starting only. David was very particular about fitting jobs and so you could say it would have been better if the expert had never seen the engine.

Before the next racing season David had glandular fever and this left him with diabetes. He was very ill and he lost his strength and soon became tired. He rode well in spite of his handicap, but there was always the danger of getting badly hurt in a crash. The beautiful Yamaha was sold and that was the end of David's racing.

Chapter 60

EX-BUILDER

A worker was sent to help me on one job. He asked me how was I getting on with Herberry House so I began to tell him and mentioned the old tiles on the house roof.

He said that he was a builder by trade, and offered to re-tile the roof for £100. This was excellent news so I said, 'all right'. He came to do the job and a load of new tiles followed him.

I did the building on the pig house, which was now the freezer house. When we had both finished it was the last of the building jobs on the house and also the outbuildings. He told me I could get a government grant because he had received one when he re-tiled his house. I applied and was refused, which annoyed me at first. After thinking about what I had done I thought to get a small grant on the last job would have spoilt my pride.

Chapter 61

THE MOXEY

Seven night shifts came round every sixth week. I was on my way to start my first night. It was such a beautiful night, so I wouldn't be going onto the coal plant, I thought. I would be working in the hot dusty boiler house.

My stargazing was way out because my job card said coal plant. The Moxey had come off its turntable. But all I had to do was to lift it back onto its turntable. I had a gang of ten men.

I sent them to the stores to get lots of jacks and ratchet chain pullers. I went to study the job. There had been a massive side thrust, which had displaced the turntable ball bearings and allowed the Moxey to overlap by about 14 inches over the bottom ball race.

The Moxey had moved in the direction away from the coal hill. The first job was to place the ratchets at that side giving some tension to be sure of no more movement.

The heavy ball bearing had almost gone out of sight in the coal. All must be retrieved, cleaned and put onto sheets. We put half of the jacks into position for the first lift and half for the second lift.

We operated the jacks and the monster began to rise slowly and more tension was put onto the ratchets. It was a slow and difficult operation and very hard work. There was side pressure on the jacks, which had done the lifting so the other jacks took over until we could get to clean the coal from the ball bearing tracks and replace the balls.

More tension on the ratchets and the Moxey slid into position back on its chassis. We had more hard work to do taking the heavy equipment back to the stores.

Because of the slow and careful working, no one was injured. We went to the baths and our lockers and went home feeling satisfied with our night's work.

The bunkers on the 40ft level were filled from the bunkers near the top of the boiler house. They were filled by coal from the large coal heaps on the conveyor belts.

The bunker, which I had to go to work on one morning, was on 40ft level. They fed the mills, which crushed the coal and it was fed into a boiler.

It is very dark in the bunkers so I needed my lead lamp. I went to the nearest sockets and plugged in. My cable was three or four feet too short. At the back of the bunker was a small hole as if a bolt had come out. If I disconnected the plug from the lead and pushed the lead through the hole I would have a light.

I stepped into the bunker and fell through. I would have hit the mills below and been killed. But I was saved because there was a plate across the bottom of the doorway, which I managed to grab with my right hand. My arm was almost pulled out of its socket and my arm and hand were very painful.

The reason why I fell through was because the contract men on night shift had removed the bottom of the bunker from underneath. I had stood on a floor of coal dust.

David had made his house look nice, but it remained an old railway house so he was looking for something better. There were new houses in Hemingbrough and with a struggle he sold the railway house and moved into one of the new houses.

Derrick had moved to Cambridge to work for a large food concern. They turned out to be a bad firm and Derrick left them and came back to Hemingbrough. So the family were altogether again.

I was worried about Win's health and made an appointment for her to see the doctor. Fortunately her doctor was on holiday so she saw a different one. At last there was some action; he sent her to Wakefield hospital.

From Hemingbrough to Wakefield is about thirty-two miles, and as I visited her most days, I did not get a lot of time for the jobs at home and was pleased my building was completed. To make matters worse, the hard work and the climbing at the power station was getting too much for me. My legs and my hand were giving me a lot of pain.

I became a regular visitor to the work's medical room. The medical orderly was very good to me and his treatment helped a lot to relieve the pain. The work's medical sister was also a good caring nurse and showed a lot of interest in me. Therefore, I was lucky and grateful to two very kind people.

Changing my job on the Power Station

Parkinson's disease struck one of the foremen. You couldn't wish to meet a finer person. He had been a motor mechanic on cars and wagons and had a good knowledge of diesel engines. They took him off the normal work at the power station to go and work on power station vehicles. There were a number of large diesel-engine driven vehicles on the coal plant so his knowledge was well used. He had too much to do on his own so I was also taken off power station work to help with the vehicles.

We got on well together. There were small engines to look after also, therefore the job was sometimes easy.

Two Tragedies

There were two awful distressing tragedies. A man who was at the social club had a sudden heart attack and a message was sent to the medical room. The orderly picked up the oxygen bottle and breathing apparatus and set off running to the social club, which as I said earlier, was a long way off. I can't understand why there wasn't a vehicle there to take him.

However, his exhausting dash had him there in no time and he saved the man's life. He walked back to the medical room, again carrying the heavy load. He went up to the locker room that was up a high flight of stairs. When the next shift came on, they found him slumped on the floor near his locker. After saving a man's life in such a heroic way, he died alone with no one to do anything for him.

I was working on my own assembling a small stationary engine. There were some contractors not far from me. One of them left the gang and returned later. I heard him say, 'One of the Eggborough men has been killed, and his name is Nicholson.'

To hear such awful news is distressing enough no matter whom the unlucky one is. But when it could be your own son your feelings are beyond description. If it wasn't David then it was someone else's son so I tried to shut it out and wait, but that was impossible and the turmoil in my brain nearly drove me mad.

It was the poor man who worked on the forklift truck whose wife worked in the stores. They had been working on the 40ft level picking up heavy metal objects. They had unbolted a section of floor so as to drop the load through the space and drop it on the floor 40ft down. The truck had nose dived through the space tipping the man over sending him to his death.

Chapter 62

MY LAST JOB AT THE POWER STATION

Going back to job cards. Before you picked up your card and read it, you had no idea where you would be going or what you would be working on. Because there are hundreds of different parts to a power station it can be difficult to remember what spare parts you will need or when you got there, the best procedure for dismantling and reassembling.

Someone thought up a time-saving idea. That idea was to have an instruction card with every job. So someone had to make these cards. They gave me an office and told me to get on with it.

I liked the job. My leg was feeling better because it was getting more rest and being on the job gave me the satisfaction of knowing that I was doing some good.

I had been on that job for about a year when one day there was something I wasn't sure of regarding dismantling a piece of equipment; therefore I went to check up on it.

I saw one of our fitters had just begun to work on one of the mills. He had reached the stage where he must lift off the manhole cover. Normally he would have had his mate with him, but he hadn't come in that day. The mate would have brought in all the gear he needed including lifting tackle for lifting off the manhole cover. He had been looking out for someone passing who would give him a lift, when I turned up.

I should not have been doing any lifting because I had been put on light duty only.

He was a very strong man and had helped me two or three times when I was doing fitter's work so I didn't like to be mean with him. He had a long iron bar that he slotted into the ring on the hatch door. He was holding one end of the bar and wanted me to get hold of the other end so that we could both lift together. But we didn't lift together. He lifted before I was ready and I got most of the weight. That put my back out of action and I couldn't carry on with my job.

Fortunately Win had come home two days before I hurt my back, which spared me the agony of driving to Wakefield. Two good friends of mine came to help me. Joan Drew and a nursing sister who worked at the Selby hospital.

I also had good friends at the power station. They let me go on sick and the nurse came to see me now and again. I was on sick for about three months on full pay, and then they gave me an early retirement. A collection for me made me £80 richer. I was well favoured because usually the collections were around £35.

They trusted David with this large sum of money. Knowing Win, and knowing that I could not have a large sum of money in case I ran away from home, David had written £30 on the envelope so that his mother didn't get too excited. The power station management let me draw my work's pension.

Sometime ago, Win's mother had let her have a beautiful dressing table. Because we hadn't space in the house it had been put in the barn. I put my collection money in the drawer to keep for a couple of months because that was when Madi and her two girls were visiting us.

Before the two months were up, a scrap merchant and his lad came round. They were nosy beggars and they did not miss anything. 'How much do you want for the dressing table?' he asked. 'Ten shillings,' was my reply. I was in a big hurry to go somewhere so I said I would see him soon. 'What time will you be back?' asked he. I fell for this smart trick and without thinking, I told him. He made sure of getting to the barn first. When I arrived home the dressing table and my money had gone.

Because the management had recommended my early retirement the social people gave me a disability allowance. This was very good of them. I only received one payment when they stopped it and said I must be examined by one of their doctors.

Their doctor said, 'You can't tell me there is not something, you can do.' That was the end of my disability allowance.

I went to the employment exchange to sign on. I had Win with me in her wheelchair and waited my turn. I was given a card to take to an engineering firm. The manager was a friend who I had worked with. I asked how he was getting on. He replied, 'Over worked and under paid.' I said, 'Your firm is no good to me then; just write unsuitable here.' I dropped the card into a letterbox and never heard from the job shop anymore.

I had already applied for a job at Hawker Siddley at Brough. My dad suggested I should go there when I was seventeen-years-old. I was a fool for not going, as it was a very good place to work at. In those days it was Blackburn Aircraft Ltd.

I worked in the experimental department. A component would be designed and we collected the drawings and made it. Next it would be tested on an aircraft and if it passed the test it would go into production. It was an interesting job and compared to being at the power station it was free from dirt and dust and the work was easy.

My pay was that of a skilled fitter plus bonus. I liked the way the bonus was worked out. We were given a time to complete making the part. If we completed it in less time, then we were paid a bonus on the time we saved.

During fine days we went outside to eat our lunch. We sat on the grass on the edge of the aerodrome, and five girls kept me entertained with love stories, knitting, husband bashing and lots of other entertaining activities.

If we travelled to work on the trains we were given a ticket for just one way because as long as you arrived at work they couldn't care less about us getting home again.

They didn't give us any petrol payment for going in our cars. Therefore, it was much cheaper to go on the train. But for some of us it wasn't worth it. As for me, Hemingbrough station wasn't in Hemingbrough, it was at Cliffe, two miles away.

Coming home wasn't convenient because it was quite a long walk to the station and a half hour wait for the train when we had reached the station. Therefore, I went by car. Apart from these small snags it was the best job I had ever been to.

There were some wonderful machines not like the crap at Pollard Bearings. Making a wing for an aeroplane was easy. You put a large piece of aluminium on the machine and switched the machine on. The cutting tools, which worked automatically until there was an aeroplane wing, cut out to $\frac{5}{1000}$ of an inch.

I heard that an American firm who made drills were advertising their smallest drill, which they described as being the smallest drill in the world. One of these smallest drills in the world went to Brough. Someone drilled a hole down the centre and sent it back to America.

In spite of the highly complicated machines, I liked to go into the propeller workshop to watch propellers being carved by hand; I envied the skill of those workers.

The year was 1976 and my mind went back to the end of the war. Sadly my mother and father parted, but I'm sure they still thought a lot of each other. My dad stayed at his bungalow (Belle Vue) and my mother went into a prefab bungalow and later she went into a one-bedroom bungalow on Kirkfield. Back then my dad was about 83-years-old and my mother about 82.

When I was working on Herberry House my dad rode his pushbike from Withernsea to Hemingbrough just to see how I was getting on. I had just fitted the stairs. He said, 'It's a good man who can fit stairs like that.' To hear a compliment from someone with my dad's skill for woodwork really made my day.

He decided to live in a caravan still on his land near the bungalow. He said, 'It was warmer than the bungalow.' He had a shed at the end of his caravan for two very big dogs. He loved his dogs and I am sure they loved him. They were very obedient to him.

One evening his caravan caught fire and he just froze and couldn't move his legs or anything not even an inch. Suddenly he remembered that his dogs were fastened in the shed and would be burnt to death. It was like a miracle he dashed out and freed the dogs and managed to get away from the blazing caravan and the shed.

During their late years I think my mother and dad would have lived together if it hadn't been for relatives who lived near my mother. When they saw each other in the main street of Withernsea my dad would ask my mother how much was a cup of tea. My mother told me it made her feel awful as she would have liked to have taken him home, then she said, I dare not because of them.

It was a long way for my dad to walk to the shops in Withernsea. One day he told me about having run out of medicine and it was very important that he didn't miss taking it. He said that on his way back he was only about 80 yards from home and he couldn't walk much further. A car stopped to give him a lift because the driver had seen the state he was in. As he was getting out of the car and thanking the man for his kindness the bottle slipped from his hand as the car set off and smashed on the road. Consequently he became very poorly.

We often had a ride to Withernsea. We used to go via Burton Pidsea and Roos and call at my dad's first. He was always very pleased to see us. He had a good brain, which didn't deteriorate with his age and so we enjoyed talking to him. He would say that so and so factory would be closed in six months, and it would be. He should have dealt in shares.

Win liked to call to see Kath, my eldest sister. It was very difficult to get through the back door with Win in her wheelchair and if we went to the front door we had to negotiate a drain hole in the path.

It was all right when the assault course was conquered and you had reached the sitting room. A nice cup of tea was welcome after a long journey. Kath had a friend called Tom. He was a pattern maker. He liked to come and see Win and I at our house, as he liked the garden. Unfortunately it took Kath a couple of hours to get ready with her soak in the bath and her make-up and hairdo. Tom would be very disappointed when darkness came before they arrived.

After our stay at Kath's we would go to mother's bungalow and get told-off because the dinner she had made for us was dried up. We had to eat and tell her that was how we liked it.

Most times relatives would come to see us. We were very popular because we took loads of vegetables every time we went. Sometimes we would see Pug and Ivy as they went now and again, coming up from London in their big Jaguar car. They often called at Hemingbrough on their way to Withernsea. The Jaguar engine was always short of oil when they called. It must have known that I always had a can of the best oil.

Pug had a small garage. He never put any cash in the bank. It was all in a large metal box, which always came with them. He had some friends, all very select gentlemen. I don't think he used a bank because if he did there would be a danger of his friends robbing that bank where his money was and that would be very embarrassing to all.

Sad news from Switzerland

Madi's holiday was postponed because her dad was ill. Poor Tony had something seriously wrong and only a short time had passed when Lizy wrote and told me he had died. My next letter from Switzerland was from Madi with more sad news. Her mother had died. I missed writing and receiving letters from Lizy. Madi wrote now and again, but it was not the same.

Hawker Siddley

At Hawker Siddley we had prepared for making the wings for the airbus. I believe there were three countries involved, England, France, and Germany. We were held up because of arguments between politicians. We were not able to get on with any other projects and could only hang around waiting for the big men to come to an agreement. The worst thing about this regarding us workers was bonus pay, which had almost finished.

Leaving Hawker Siddley

My friend Norman Fields was willing to take a chance on me and let me go to work at the engineering firm, which he managed in Selby. This had advantages, namely I would have more time at home due to less travelling and my wages would be the same.

So I decided to leave Hawker Siddley, but not happily because I liked being there and everyone liked me. Good jobs where you could make a good bonus were scarce, but I was given one about three weeks before I left. The job was making brackets to fit on the noses of two different aeroplanes. The brackets were large and very strong and made from ¼-inch aluminium. Their purpose was to carry large heavy cameras. I made them in half the time and therefore I received a 100 per cent bonus, which they sent to me a couple of weeks, after I had left them. This was in 1977.

Norman Field's small factory was just to my liking. I liked the building, which was large enough to give plenty of working space and light enough through large windows to make lamps unnecessary. The floor was neat and tidy. Norman had qualities not usually found in managers and so as I expected, it was a happy atmosphere.

They were making conveyers, which were used in drinks factories. Return bottles at the drinks factories went onto the conveyer belt. The bottles were steered by ½-inch thick nylon discs cut out to hold the bottles. The bottle tops were removed by chucks, which lowered down to the bottlenecks. The bottles were conveyed to a cleaning bath and later filled with orange juice or any other drinks and conveyed to the chucks to receive new bottle tops. They were then ready to be sent out and delivered to shops.

The machines were well designed, but I found faults in the production methods, which I improved bringing the output from two machines per week to three machines per week.

About eight months after I began there the little factory was taken over by a large firm. I believe the large firm had an interest in it from the beginning.

Norman then worked at the large firm, still as a manager. It was a long way home to travel after a day's work, as he was no longer a young man. There were a lot of managers at the firm who were not really practical engineers like Norman.

Chapter 63

MADI IN HEMINGBROUGH

In the spring of 1978 Madi and her two daughters at last came to England to enjoy the moors and the dales of North Yorkshire and the plains and seaside resorts of East Yorkshire, which are so much different to her country. We brought them to Withernsea to my relatives, but not to spend too long as I was eager to show them Spurn Point and Paull and the flat land of Sunk Island.

I didn't go out to work anymore after I had left the factory at Selby, but I kept very busy looking after Win, taking her out in her invalid chair and rides in the car to Selby to go shopping. We also visited Win's relatives who lived round Doncaster. Then there were the rides to Withernsea to see my relations and to take Win round the shops and the market.

In between all this there was work in the garden. There were the vegetables to eat, and some to go in the freezer, and the surplus to sell. The summertime passed and the garden work became much less. But Win had become very ill and my nursing job became almost full time.

Win had always been in love with Withernsea, and now she wanted to go back. I had a big problem because I didn't think Win was well enough to be house hunting and then moving to Withernsea, but she had made up her mind.

I had a lot of spare parts for cars and motorbikes that I had to get rid of. I advertised and got some response, but the selling price was rock bottom. For example, I sold five motorbike engines for 5 shillings each.

I wasn't in a hurry to sell my tractor in case the move to Withernsea did not happen. I decided it would be the last to go.

Win rang a dealer to come and look at the many items she had bought mostly from the big chapel at Cawood. She spread them out on the lounge floor and covered all the spare space with them. There were some beautiful items of pottery, vases, and brooches, everything you could think of. There must have been something there that was valuable. But the dealer only gave her £5 for the lot.

The spares of mine that I hadn't sold went to the scrap man. When I built my tractor I used a motorbike oil tank for a petrol tank. The oil tank was a special Rudge racing tank and I intended changing it for a BSA tank. I eventually advertised my tractor and a man came and bought it for £45. I hadn't had time to change the oil tank so he had a real bargain as he had the Rudge racing tank.

We came to Withernsea and had the complicated business of going to estate agents and having a look at the properties. We looked at a few properties, all different, but none to suit us. I had glanced at a photo of 4 Louville Avenue, but I wasn't so interested. So we returned home to try another day.

We advertised Herberry House and a builder who was building houses in Hemingbrough came to see us. He made an offer of £20,000. I had chosen a solicitor in Howden. He came to see me and after having a look in the garden he said, 'I would tell that builder to take a run and jump at himself.'

Win was very poorly and I thought there wasn't much time left for her and moving became urgent. I thought selling to this builder who didn't have to sell his house, would not be complicated. Therefore, I told the builder that he could have it. I regretted this decision later, and realised that I should have taken notice of the solicitor.

We had another ride to Withernsea. This time we went down Louville Avenue and saw lots of bungalows being built. The avenue had been extended down to the promenade. There was a new road branching off called Oak Avenue, and another road at the end of Oak Avenue called Turner Avenue. The price of these new bungalows was £16,000. We decided to have number 4 Louville Avenue. The price was also £16,000.

It was one of four bungalows, which had been built in 1933. There was a large carport and a wooden shed. The front garden was small and had a wall at the side and also a front wall. The garden at the back was also small. Neither of the gardens looked healthy. They hadn't been worked on for years and there was a lot of wick grass, which had taken all the goodness away.

The front of the bungalow comprised of two large windows. The window on the right was in the front bedroom and the other was the lounge window. The windows were the original ones and in very good condition. I didn't like the front door.

The back door was at the side of the bungalow and had a porch, which was half brick with wooden windows. The bricks were good, but not the wooden windows and door. The outside brick wall and the porch were in a straight line. There was a window in the porch that looked into the kitchen, and another under the carport that looked into the kitchen and there was a small window in the toilet.

If you stood with your back to the back door you saw through the porch and onto the road. Enter through the back door and the toilet door was straight opposite. Turn right and walk into the kitchen. There was a sink unit, which would soon be at the council tip. The bathroom was on the left with a bath, following the sink unit. The kitchen was L-shaped and had a fair sized window looking into the back garden.

In the kitchen was a double floor cupboard. On the wall, which was the lounge wall as well as the kitchen wall, there were old electric switches and fuse boxes housed in an old-fashioned cupboard. Across the corner near the sink unit was a hot water cistern in an old fashioned cupboard. All these things would help fill the skips in the council tip.

The lounge was of a good shape and size and also the front bedroom. There was a lovely dressing table, where once stood a fireplace and it was flanked by two double wardrobes with louvre doors.

A passage led to the front entrance hall and the front door with a window at each side of the door. There were plenty of cupboards in the entrance hall and another passage led to the two rear bedrooms. On the back wall were three double wardrobes with top cupboards to the ceiling.

Halfway along the passage was a small bedroom with a large cupboard on one wall. Both these bedrooms had patio doors opening onto the rear garden towards the sun.

The rear garden fencing was a mess and new roof tiles on the bungalow would be an improvement. High up in the toilet was an ugly black flush tank and the toilet seat was also for scrap.

All the guttering was of wood with round cast iron downpipes. The bedroom at the end of the passage was for a double bed, but along one wall were three double wardrobes with cupboards above, reaching to the ceiling. Because of the wardrobes taking up a lot of space the bedroom could not be used for a double bed.

The property belonged to Mrs Johnson who occupied it. She said, 'Will it be long before you can come into the bungalow?'

I said, 'No we haven't any complications.'

'That is good,' she said, 'because I am going to Bridlington, and the lady who owns the house in Bridlington can't wait much longer because the lady in the house which she wants, can't wait any longer.' I began to wish I were a gypsy.

I asked Mrs Johnson about the old electric switches, and she told me they weren't used because all the electrics had been replaced.

I had a big decision to make because it seemed obvious that a new house that didn't want work doing and no complications must be better than an old house with a lot of work needed and a train of nattering people. After a lot of thinking I told Mrs Johnson we would have it.

Chapter 64

THE GREEDY BUILDER

While we were at Withernsea, the builder had looked round. He had found a job that needed doing and he wanted £500 knocked off the price of the house. I hadn't much option and he got the money knocked off.

The greedy man came again and had another £500 knocked off. I should have told him then to take a run and jump at himself. He was buying the place without planning permission, but he had the cheek to say he would not settle up until he had the plans passed. This was a big con and he was really taking advantage of our circumstances.

A council meeting had been held only a few days ago and so we had a month to wait. After waiting the month, the council refused the application, which was for two link houses. Link houses were two houses linked by two garages in the middle. The reason for the refusal was because he planned to build too near the road. It was the road belonging to Back Lane. He submitted plans, which were passed at the next meeting. So we had waited two months.

Straightaway the bulldozers arrived to remove the hedge and fill in the ditch. Then it only took a few minutes to destroy my pride and joy, the lovely big garden.

The builder advertised Herberry House, the barn, the pig house, and the large entrance to the land. There was the lawn at one side of the garden path and garden at the other side. He sold that for £17,000. Therefore, all that was left cost him only £2,000.

We moved to Withernsea on 17 December 1979, the day before my sixty-fourth birthday. We did not forget the holly and so that was the last Christmas that the relatives had excellent Herberry House holly.

The deeds of Herberry House went back nearly three hundred years. They were very interesting to read and the writing was so beautiful if I tried to describe it I would not do it justice. I hesitated before handing them over to the builder, but I did give them hoping he would pass them to the next occupant. But the rotter kept them.

Win settled down and I took her out quite a lot. But I am sure she missed Hemingbrough and being near David, Derrick, and Peter. A number of Withernsea people knew us and would stop to talk to us when I had her out in her wheelchair. She was always very sociable and enjoyed a good laugh with everyone.

Spring arrived and with it came visitors to stay in chalets and caravans. Louville Avenue goes down to the promenade so we were not far from the sea and enjoyed going into Withernsea that way and coming back along the main street.

The visitors were friendly and so the walks were very enjoyable. Win liked garden parties so we never missed any when the weather was good to us. There was the lighthouse garden party, Seacroft, Holmpton, Ottringham, and Rimswell. All the garden parties were enjoyable, but we liked Ottringham the best. Everyone would be so pleased to see us as if we were someone special. The time when I was not taking Win out was spent working on the bungalow. We went to a builder's merchant in Hull. I asked about baths and a man said, 'Come with me I have got just what you want.' We went into a dusty warehouse and below inches of thick dust, were six baths. I wished I hadn't bothered, but when he pulled one out and cleaned off the dust, it sparkled. He said, 'They have been left over from a contract job.' I've forgotten how much the price was, but I remember I was very pleased because he had almost given it away. There was a chrome bar, which was bolted across from one side to the other to help old people like me to get out.

The man benefitted from being good to me as I bought all the plumbing requirements. Taps for the bathroom sink unit, and hot water cistern and stopcocks. There was a lot of copper tubing and joints and bends.

I did all the work on my own. I had a struggle with the bath to get the side right up to the wall. It was only quarter of an inch off; it was because of the copper pipes. I made a sentry box in the loft for the cistern to go inside and the cold-water tank on the top. That was a struggle.

I bought the kitchen cupboards and sink unit and they looked good. I sold the big freezer and bought a nice chest freezer. The old cupboard and the outdated electrical switches and fuse boxes were still on the wall. I didn't check to see if they were still connected because the old woman told me all the electrics were new. She had told me an untruth and I received an electric shock. All the electrics for power had been done, but all the light wiring was old.

Whenever David came to see us he would say, 'What do you want doing?' I had already done the additional power circuits, which were required for the hot-water cistern and the shed. I said, 'The lights want rewiring.' So he did them, completing the electrics.

We had a wedding on the 20 June 1980. Peter and Marian got married. Win had made wonderful progress regarding her health and was able to get to the wedding and she enjoyed every bit of it.

Kath, my eldest sister, had three sons, and the youngest was Paul. He married a nice young woman called Elizabeth. She used to come to see us when we visited my mother. Elizabeth and Paul went through divorce about eighteen months before we moved to Withernsea. Elizabeth was still friendly with Win and often came to see us and cleaned up for us.

Chapter 65

WITHERNSEA, WIN'S BIG STROKE

Win's health was still improving and she began to say, 'When I get better', instead of, 'If I get better'. The air was healthy there and I felt a big improvement in myself and wasn't regretting leaving Herberry House.

The people who bought the new houses were struggling to do their gardens, which is usual in new houses. I regretted getting rid of my tractor as I think I would have been able to hire it out.

Suddenly Win's health became a worry to me and I kept on telling her doctor about it, but nothing seemed to be done about it. One morning after I had dressed Win, I went into the kitchen to do the breakfast.

When I took Win's breakfast, she was in the midst of a very bad stroke. Her doctor told me that if someone is having a stroke there is nothing one can do about it.

Win was taken to Hull Royal Infirmary. She wasn't in there long before the doctors wanted to put her in the psychiatric ward. I told him that she wasn't going to go into that ward and I wanted her to come to Withernsea Hospital (convalescent home).

We argued for quite a long time and then he went out and came back bringing another doctor to help him to persuade me that Withernsea hospital wasn't a proper hospital. But I wasn't having any of it and Win came to Withernsea Hospital.

I never regretted my decision as Win was amongst people she knew and at Withernsea where she wanted to be. I went to see her nearly every day and took her out whenever the weather wasn't too bad. She always tried to do things for herself, as she did not like people running after her. She read books and magazines and kept her brain active and so she was reasonably happy under the circumstances.

There was a sad start to 1981 as my dad was taken into Withernsea Hospital in January. He was very poorly and his voice was very weak. He had something to tell me, but I couldn't make out what it was. A male nurse came into the ward so I said, 'My dad is struggling to tell me something and I can't understand him. Please ask him what it is.'

The nurse could understand him, but he said in a nasty tone of voice, 'I don't want to know about your money.' The nurse walked away and Ernie was very upset. He had been trying to tell me where his money was.

I went home with a feeling that I had let my dad down. I could have done some drawings of the inside of the caravan or inside his bungalow and if I had drawn the spot where his money was he would have let me know. But he passed away before I could visit him again. He was 92-years-old.

Later Elizabeth and I went to Belle Vue to clear the land of Blackberry briers and other weeds. We went for several weeks until the land was clear. We didn't get any thanks from anyone for our hard work.

Chapter 66

THE RAILWAY AND HOTEL

Going back to when the Hull to Withernsea Railway was built, a lot of rich people came from Hull to Withernsea. Of course, they had to have a large hotel to accommodate them, where they could dance and get drunk and do all the other activities like sleeping with other people's wives. So the hotel was built near the station.

After a short time, the rich decided that Scarborough, with its large hotels like The Royal Hotel, were better than Withernsea. Therefore, the Withernsea Hotel lost its trade.

Consumption was a terrible disease in those days. The Rickets family, business people in Hull, had the hotel converted to a convalescent home for people who were sick with consumption. This disease became more or less wiped out in this country and so the convalescent home became a hospital. Most of the senior people still refer to it as the 'Convalescent Home'.

Win was still very poorly when she came home. Looking after her became almost impossible and I was exhausted after three days. On the fourth day Elizabeth came to see how I was getting on. She told me to go to bed and have a good sleep. I slept for four hours and by that time Elizabeth had done the housework and had everything under control.

To make the workload less for me, we had a nurse coming in the morning to wash and dress Win. Another nurse came in the evening to undress, wash, and put Win to bed.

Elizabeth came every day and so everything was under control, except Elizabeth was feeling the strain as she was going to work. I told her I would apply for a home help. Elizabeth said she would rather do the work herself. But I did get a home help and I was glad; it was the right decision.

Before Win became poorly with the stroke we went to Oulton Park and Cadwell Park to see motorbike racing. Some of my enthusiasm for motorbikes also got into Elizabeth so we began to go to races. A neighbour who was a good friend came in to look after Win.

We used to go to Oliver's Mount in Scarborough. The Humber Bridge was now completed, which shortened the distance to Cadwell Park by a lot of miles. Therefore, Cadwell had become our favourite track. Of course we did not go very often, as we had to look after Win and take her out in the car.

I heard of a very good residential home, which took people like Win in to look after them for a two-week's holiday and to give the carer a break. It was near Scotch Corner, a long way to go, but she took the journey very well. It was an excellent place and the carers were very kind and loving towards all the residents. The food was very good and the residents were taken out into the countryside and also to a show. Win had a very good holiday and was looking well and happy when I went to bring her home.

The weather was fine and so I enjoyed the ride out. Win never stopped talking about her holiday and never complained about anything. It must have been very good.

My sister Kath's eldest son, Leslie and his wife Rosemary, left their home in Kirkfield Road to live in Louville Avenue. They had two sons, Christopher and Andrew and a daughter called Penny. Penny liked to come to our bungalow and we were glad of her company. There was something special about her; she was lovely and very polite.

When she was fifteen-years-old a tumour grew in her brain. She soon became very poorly. Her right eye closed completely and she became thin and pale. But her lovely smiles remained; she was a very brave girl.

The summer passed and the winter was soon here and another Christmas. But it was Penny's last Christmas, as her life ended after five weeks, on 2 February 1983.

Kath was very upset and she never got over losing her lovely granddaughter. She was still working nights at the hospital and she still had her large house. But she would be sixty-years-old and would be retiring and going on that extra special holiday, which she had promised herself.

Summer days were here and Win went on another holiday at a residential home. But this time she went to Harrogate. Harrogate is a lovely place; there are some parks and lots of flower gardens. The school children were on holiday and some of them were very good and took disabled people out. Win was very happy because it was a good home and the carers were good and so was the food. But what she liked most was being taken out everyday by the school children. I also felt very grateful to the children for their kindness and consideration.

There was good news from Howden, Marian was expecting. Of course Win was delighted and borrowed a knitting aid from the Withernsea Hospital and began to knit. I noticed she was having difficulties with the knitting aid.

Win stopped knitting and looked at me and said, 'Nick go into your shed and make me a knitting aid.'

For the base I used a piece of wood, 3/3/1 inch. To make a channel for holding a needle I used two blocks of wood, 1¼-inch square and 2 inches long. Two spring-loaded ball catches were fitted into one of the blocks. The blocks were fixed to the base by screws with a ½ inch space between them and the catches facing inwards. I clamped this gadget onto Win's table. She placed the needle between the blocks and the catches held it. The needle could not fall out, but it was easy to take out.

Win was delighted because with just her one good hand she could knit as good and as quickly as she did when she had two good hands. I decided we would go into production, as there were so many people who needed a knitting aid, which was easy to use. Our aim was to help these people and so we did not do it for profit.

Fewsters at Patrington were manufacturers of windows and doors. They also made coffins and carried out funeral work. They were an excellent firm and very helpful.

I ordered a lot of lengths of beech wood from them, and they machine-cut them to the exact breadth and thickness required.

I ordered $\frac{3}{8}$ inch and $\frac{1}{4}$ inch plastic-threaded rods and wing nuts and a box of cupboard door spring-loaded ball catches.

I made jigs so there was no marking out. The shed was too small so Elizabeth and I made it larger. Then we fixed up the benches and arranged the tools. We had two new drills on stands, and a new electric saw. The saw was made to slide in plastic guides at an accurate right angle for the lengths of wood. There was a $\frac{3}{8}$ inch bolt, which was a stop for the lengths of wood and could be adjusted to give the exact length to the small pieces, which were cut off.

The reason why we had to be so particular about the accuracy of setting up the machines was for two reasons. The pieces of wood had to be a good fit in the jigs, and the finished product had to be very accurate because they were designed to be used with twelve different sizes of knitting needles, which could be changed with very little effort.

As I cut off the pieces of wood Elizabeth placed them into a jig and drilled the holes.

Win was presented with the first knitting aid to come from the production line. Lucie was born on 14 May 1984 and by that time Win had made some baby clothes for her granddaughter.

I applied for Win to go for another holiday at the same home in Harrogate. This was granted, but we couldn't get the same dates as the previous year.

Elizabeth and I were busy on the production line in the knitting aid factory, i.e. the garden shed. It was easy to imagine ourselves having a factory as we were getting letters for the managing director, or sales manager, EN Knitting Aids.

We began by supplying Withernsea Hospital with three aids followed by another three going to Hull Royal Infirmary and three to Kingston General Hospital. After that the sales spread fairly quickly.

I advertised in the *Dalesman* thinking I would get sales in Yorkshire, but a woman in Australia who had lost an arm in a farm accident had the *Dalesman* sent to her and she ordered a knitting aid. One also went to a woman in Canada. The letters of gratitude we received from people who were using our knitting aids were rewarding enough, as we were glad to be able to help people.

We also helped children. In about 1961 the drug Thalidomide was produced. It was responsible for many children being born deformed. Soon after we began selling the aids I received a letter from Wales written by a woman whose granddaughter only had one arm.

It was a sad letter. She told me about her granddaughter and how she longed to be able to do some knitting. They learnt knitting in her class at school. But she was sent to the library to get a book to read during the knitting lesson.

The loving grandma had already bought knitting aids that were useless so she wrote 'Unless you are absolutely sure that my granddaughter can use your knitting aid please do not send one, as she has had enough disappointments'.

I sent one straightaway and a few days later I received a very happy letter. It read 'My granddaughter took her knitting aid to school and was able to knit along with the other children. Thank you very much please find enclosed my cheque'.

Kath retired near the end of the year. She had been a nurse at Withernsea Hospital for many years. She was dedicated to her job and I guess a lot of sick people will be missing her. Her youngest son, who had been married to Elizabeth, had married again. Kath had some good news for the New Year: they were expecting a baby.

Kath was waiting for her grandchild to be born and then she would go to Leeds to see the baby. As soon as she saw the baby she would come back home, book this fabulous holiday and have a good time. The good news came; she had a granddaughter. So she went to Leeds and had two or three happy days. When she was packing up to come home she had a heart attack and died. She was sixty-years-old and it was 24 April 1985.

A nursing sister, who came to see to Win, died in a road accident. There were two trees planted in the hospital grounds, one for Sister Susan Grazier, and the other one for Nurse Kathleen May Roberts.

Win went on her holiday to Harrogate. Staying there cost an awful lot of money, but because the schoolchildren were at school, Win never went out. Too many residential homes brought in large profits and the people running them couldn't care less about sick people.

We have some good shops in Withernsea. The Co-op is a very good shop for drapery and William Jackson's is a favourite for groceries.

My mother dealt with them when we were at Tunstall. Mr Brown used to come round to their customers once a week for orders. The orders were delivered in a van; it was an easy way to shop.

We had a Woolworth's, which was popular, and also Dee's – a grocery shop. The market was very good, but it had to be moved further back to make way for Proudfoot's superstore.

There were the remains of the railway ticket office and platform. These were demolished and the ground levelled. There was a scrapyard, which I thought was an eyesore, which went. Station Road was extended and these alterations converted an eyesore to a very smart area, which was in the centre of town.

Proudfoot's superstore was completed and Dee's had gone and Heron's had come to Withernsea. It was a very popular shop.

When I was a schoolboy there was the rink that was very popular. I liked to go roller skating. The rink became the Grand Pavilion with a lovely dance floor and restaurant; it was very popular. I used to dance with my sister Kath.

Win's idea was for me to take her on holiday instead of her going to a residential home. She said that it would not be a holiday for me, as I would be looking after her. But I could go on my own later. We went to Bridlington without booking, but we found a place to stay. It was near the promenade and also near the shops. So that was good, but the boarding house had faults. We found a boarding house, which seemed very good, so we booked for the following year.

Soon after we came home from Bridlington, my mother had a heart attack and went into Withernsea Hospital. I was told that she was a lot better on the second day. I didn't go to see her as I was told she had a lot of visitors. I didn't think that would be good for her. I went on the following day to see her, but the Staff Nurse told me she'd had a serious heart attack during the night and she had died. This was on 4 July 1986. She was aged ninety-three years. Her name before she married was Ethel May Grant. It was a pity she was called Ette when she had lovely Christian names.

Our next-door neighbours at number 2 were called Pedrick. Mrs Pedrick was an invalid and her husband looked after her. Mr Pedrick drove East Yorkshire Buses. They were lovely neighbours.

Mr Pedrick died and his wife went into a residential home. A young man who was a builder took their bungalow and was doing a lot of work on it. I thought he might be doing it up to sell.

It was a busy life looking after Win and taking her out. Elizabeth was working and there was her house and garden to do and the same at this end. We were also making knitting aids and posting them to customers. They just fitted into the small cardboard boxes that we made from the boxes we got from Proudfoot's.

Win and I went to Bridlington again. The landlady was called Dorothy Constable. Her husband went out to work and helped a little in the evenings. They were really good people. It was hard work for me. But the weather was good and I enjoyed it as well as Win.

The young man who was doing up number 2 had moved and a retired couple came in. They are called Wally and Win Howard. They are a smashing couple and so we have the good fortune of having good sociable neighbours next door.

Stanley and Wendy had two children, Trevor and Wendy. Trevor married and went somewhere down south. Then Wendy married and went to live in South Africa. Wendy has been back two or three times to see her parents. Also, Stanley and Wendy have been to South Africa. Wendy senior has become very poorly and I don't think she will be able to make any more trips to South Africa.

Pug and Ivy have left London and are living at Castle Acre, near Kings Lynn in Norfolk. Their rides to Withernsea are shorter by half the distance. But Ivy regrets leaving London and her family. They have had two or three holidays on Golden Sands Chalet Park, which is on Holmpton Road.

Ivy died and she is buried at the little church in Castle Acre. A short time after Ivy died, Pug had a stroke. This was terrible for Pug as it is for lots of other stroke victims because everyone likes to be active. It was also bad for Pug because he was many miles away from relatives. His daughter Jacqueline makes regular trips to see him.

Callipers

Win had to wear a knee-length calliper and one of her shoes had to be drilled to make an anchorage for the calliper. She needed a new calliper. When this had been made, the expert took it to Hull Royal Infirmary, and I took Win to have it fitted.

We were sent to a room; there was no one else waiting outside, so they were not busy. I pushed Win into the room. There were the two experts waiting for us. One man who had made the calliper was in his best suit and the other was the medical man in his white coat.

The medical man was sunk into a large comfortable chair and he had no intentions of getting out of it. The mechanic picked up the calliper and fitted it onto Win's leg. I didn't make a move and so the medical man said, 'That's it, you can go now.' I said, 'No it isn't.' He gave me such a strange look, as he wasn't used to being spoken to like that. I said, 'The calliper is to help her walk, not for when she is riding in her wheelchair.'

I helped Win to stand up and she walked a bit. The calliper was hopeless and so the expert who had made it began to bend it over his knee. I told the two of them not to bother anymore and I would put it right when we got home.

I put the old calliper onto her leg and the new one was never worn. Knee-length callipers were no good to Win because her knee kicked back.

Dr Heaton ordered a full-length calliper. While we were waiting for it, Win's right leg was giving her trouble and she had to go into Withernsea Hospital.

The new calliper was sent to the hospital. It took a nurse a very long time to fit it, which put Win through a lot of pain. When I saw the calliper I thought that there must have been a mistake. It had come to the hospital instead of some horse racing stables. The man who had made it was at the hospital. I thought, *that man is going to get to know me a little better.*

Dr Heaton told me to tell the expert to make another calliper, but to my specifications. I thought this sounds like trouble. The man came to see me to tell me he had been making them for twenty-five years.

No matter what the man thought he still had to obey the doctor's orders and make another calliper. But needless to say it was hopeless. When you are designing a calliper you have to think of basic mechanics. It has to be easy to fit, light in weight, comfortable and able to help the patient to walk and not hinder movements of the leg.

If you place a cane over your knee as if you want to break it in half, there are three pressure points. The knee is one of them, and the other two are your hands. With a calliper, the back of the calf is a pressure point and also the front of the thigh and the shoe is the other one. The pressure points have to be correct because we want the leg to be in a straight line with no kicking back of the knee. Therefore, the calf strap must be solid round the back of the calf with the fastening at the front. The thigh strap must be solid at the front with the fastener at the rear. Don't get these mixed up, like the experts do, their way of putting things the wrong way round may be patented.

To fit the calliper, the patient's foot goes over the calf strap from behind and into the shoe. The two straps are closed and the calliper is fitted.

Win's home-made calliper weighed 1¾ lbs. The other two callipers that went to the council tip weighed 3½ lbs. I have given these details because I hope that any badly made or badly designed callipers will become scrap and be replaced by more useful ones.

It was a fine day so I took Win for a ride in the car. It was a mystery trip because neither of us knew where we would finish up. Eventually we finished up at Bridlington and we parked the car in a car park near the centre of the promenade. We looked at the shops and had a nice lunch and eventually we decided to go home. Win had a tripod type of walker. Win used it when I took her out of the wheelchair to get to the car door. I helped her into the car and then put her wheelchair in the boot. Then I got into the car and drove off leaving the walker behind. I cursed when I got home; I had to get someone to look after Win and go back to Bridlington.

I went to the police station. There was a very large policeman behind the counter in case they had burglars. Someone had taken the tripod; it was a young lady who took the particulars. She took so long over it I thought I would be sleeping in a cell.

The policeman spoke to me, and he was friendly. I could only just see over the counter. I said, 'I used to be in the police force.'

He said, 'Were you?'

I said, 'Yes.'

He said, 'What happened?'

I said, 'I was only in the Police Force for six months.'

So once again he said, 'Why, what happened?'

I said, 'Someone spragged on me, they told them I had lied about my height.'

He looked over the counter and looked me up and down and he did not know what to say. Then he said, 'Well what height did you tell 'em you were?'

My brain had reached a stage when it refused to help with this daft conversation. The policewoman brought the papers for me to sign and I hurried away.

Chapter 67

LARGE BOULDERS TO PROTECT THE PROMENADE

Halfway to Holmpton was a sewage station. It was necessary to have a large pumping station. But where could it go? In the centre of the shopping area of course! They spent weeks digging out the hole for the large pump. But where was the best place to take all these thousands of tons of soil? On the top of the cliffs of course! The road was covered with mud for weeks, but eventually the hole was large enough and in time the rain cleaned the roads. Then a funny thing happened, the council found out where the soil had gone. The council told the contractors to move the soil. I reckon they would have put it back in the hole if the large pump hadn't been put there. I don't know what the contractors said to the council, but it doesn't matter because I don't think it would have been fit to write here. The soil isn't there anymore; it went into the sea along with the cliff. Not to worry it will have extended Spurn's existence for two or three years. This story is as I learnt it and I think it must be true.

The paving slabs on the promenade began to lift with the seawater. That meant that the groins, and the foundations, of the promenade were damaged and could not be repaired. The only solution was to protect the promenade with large boulders. These boulders were brought on boats and how they piled them on so high was a mystery to me. I was also surprised to see the boats coming so near to the shore with such heavy loads.

The boulders were tipped into the water and picked up by a large crane. The long jib swung round and tipped the boulders onto the dry sand. Then they were put in large heaps and some were carried in lorries to be tipped along the bottom of the promenade. It was a long and costly job. Perhaps some day The Hull Motor Club will get to know about the heaps of boulders and organise rock climbing events.

The promenade sea wall was remade and the walkway was relaid. This looks very good and we are proud of our promenade. But the wall is too high so visitors to Withernsea can only look at the wall and not the sea and the beach.

I was pleased to see a lot of seats along the promenade because we get quite a lot of old people among the sand diggers (visitors). They were placed about three feet from the wall and facing it. Therefore, you could sit on a seat and have a good look at the wall.

A lot of people complained, but I thought it was a crafty move on the part of the council. I thought they were going to make holes in the wall and charge people for the loan of periscopes. The seats were turned round and everyone was happy. They couldn't see over the wall, but who wants to look at mountains of boulders.

Drainpipes were sunk into the cliff top at the end of the south promenade. Someone noticed that the cliff top moves as the sea washes the cliff away and so the edge of the cliff came very near to the pipes. This was no problem as the boats brought another £6,000,000 worth of boulders to put along the bottom of the cliffs.

The fact that the cliffs get washed away became common knowledge and the people at Easington Gas Terminal found out about it. This caused a lot of concern and a lot of brainwork. Some people suggested moving the whole gas works further back, not taking into account the expenditure of another mile of 30-inch gas pipe.

They got an idea from us; they would protect it with boulders. Therefore, for a long time the boats brought the oversized pebbles and there was much dashing about of wagons. But at last the gasworks were safe from the sea. The only remaining problem was, the little country from where the boulders came from has become so light there was a danger of it drifting into orbit. I hope they demand the return of the big stones before this can happen.

Chapter 68

WIN DIED DURING MY HEART ATTACK

Two or three years ago, Win bought a little red invalid car. It was a BEC and very well designed and constructed. The following morning she drove onto the promenade and I walked with her. It was too quick for my little legs to keep up with her and so she had to keep stopping to wait for me to catch up. But it was a lot better than having to push her in a wheelchair.

We went as far as the Pier Towers. On the corner of Pier Road and the promenade, was Mr Whippy's ice cream parlour. We sat outside and had tea and cakes. After a good rest we went back home again along the promenade.

During the afternoon, Win went for another ride. I didn't go with her, I thought as we had been out for a long time in the morning she would not go far. But she was gone a long time so I went in our car to look for her. I couldn't drive on the promenade so I went up and down the short roads, which went from Queen Street to the promenade. But I still couldn't find her. I had another look at the café, but this time I went round the back, and there was Win knocking back a big ice cream cornet.

Win spent a lot of time knitting and she made some lovely things. But there were times when she was poorly. She used to get a lot of pain and very bad headaches. One day while I was getting breakfast ready there was a really loud bang on the bedroom door. Win had been getting out of bed without my help and had fallen against the door. I couldn't move the door to get in and Win could not move away from the door.

Mr Shakesby and his wife Caroline lived across the road. He was an ambulance man and a crewman on the lifeboat. I went to get him and it was not long before he was in the room putting her on the bed. I have no idea how he managed it.

Win's health was deteriorating quickly and so we were back to the wheelchair. Pushing the wheelchair was giving me a lot of pain in my right ankle, calf of my leg and my knee as a result of wounds received during the war.

One day she said she felt bitter. It was the first time she had said anything like that. Another day she told me she wanted to be buried in Hemingbrough. If I buried her in Withernsea she would haunt me. I was having pains in my chest and difficulty pushing the wheelchair.

I began to feel very ill. Elizabeth was on night shift. I went to pick her up from work. I wanted to buy two bunches of flowers on my way home. But I did not have my wallet with me so I had to go home for it. When I reached home I began to have a heart attack and so I got in my car and set off to go to the hospital. There was a car park at the hospital, but usually it was full because a lot of selfish people would park there and go shopping. To get to the hospital and then not be able to park would be terrible.

I went into the car park at the Municipal Buildings. My walk was downhill, but that was no help because when I reached the hospital grounds it was a very steep climb up to the hospital.

I went to the casualty waiting room. There was a man in the waiting room and some one with the nurse. I sat and waited and the person with the nurse came out, and the nurse called for the man. I was in a lot of pain so I stood up and was walking beside this man to make sure the nurse knew I was there.

After a long time the man came out and the nurse called me. 'I knew that you were there, I had seen you,' said the nurse. Then she said, 'Anyway what is wrong Nick?' I said, 'I'm having a heart attack.' I think that gave her a shock and sent her into immediate and swift action, and another nurse was soon in top gear.

A friend was looking after Win because she was poorly; her name was Dorne Gilchrist. Alan came to the hospital. For some time he had been saying he wanted me to leave him my shoes. As soon as he came in he mentioned about my shoes. At that time I couldn't care less who got my shoes. He soon realised the seriousness and dashed to get Elizabeth.

They were putting me in the ambulance when Alan came back with Elizabeth. Alan went home, but Elizabeth came in the ambulance. Mr Shakesby was the ambulance man. Elizabeth said he had worked on me for most of the journey and almost lost me a couple of times.

Elizabeth went to see Win to tell her about me having a heart attack. The shock was too much for Win. Perhaps it was two days later when Dorne brought Win to see me. She brought her again on the Thursday. Dorne left us; she may have gone to the waiting room. But when Win was talking to me I couldn't understand a word and I was wishing Dorne would come back, as she would have told me what Win was saying. I became partly deaf at Aladam.

Friday was Elizabeth's birthday so she had brought some extra tasty food and so we ate it, thinking we were having a birthday party.

It was usual for people with heart attacks to leave hospital on the seventh day after admission. Therefore, I would be going home on the Saturday. But the doctor wanted me to stay in until Monday. On Saturday morning Peter came to the hospital. The staff nurse told us to go into a small room, and I began thinking the worst. When we were seated Peter told me that his mother had passed away.

I went home on Monday morning. David was arranging the funeral for Withernsea cemetery. I told him to change that as soon as possible or I would be haunted. During this sad time, Elizabeth was absolutely wonderful. Saturday was 19 November 1994 and Win was 75-years-old.

With a lot of loving care Elizabeth nursed me back to good health. Besides our local rides out to Spurn, Paull and Beverley, and Howden and Hemingbrough we went to Austria. This was a coach trip and we enjoyed every bit of it.

We went to Havant four times, three of them were invitations to weddings. Their weddings were really posh ones with about a hundred guests. We always stayed one week with Dorothy and Ron at their house.

It became our turn to have a wedding. Elizabeth and I were married on 6 March 1998 and we were well supported by the Havant relatives. It rained all day for our wedding, but I am glad to say the photographer (our Peter) was able to present us with a lovely album of his expert work.

Chapter 69

A FACE LIFT FOR WITHERNSEA

When Win and I moved to Withernsea, it was a very drab place and needed a lot to bring it up to a reasonable standard for a seaside resort. We had a good market, which drew a lot of people, but we needed much more than that.

The view from the north-facing windows in the hospital was shocking. There were remains of the railway station, the platform, and wasteland where the railway line stood. The coal yard as it had been when the trains were running, and further back was a large scrapyard.

The council bought the land from the railway company. Taking into consideration the awful mess, I think the railway company should have paid the council.

Work on the Grand Pavilion began, and the result was the leisure centre and sports centre. The sports centre has a 25-metre indoor swimming pool. The leisure centre has a gymnasium, sports hall, solarium, saunas and catering facilities. All this was completed in 1989.

The market was near Queen Street, but it was moved further back to make room for Proudfoot's supermarket. The restaurant and post office face onto Queen Street. This was completed in 1988. The north end and the south end post offices were closed.

The rugby field became unused and soon became a disgrace, which was a pity because visitors pass it as they are coming into the town. We were pleased when Tesco decided to build bungalows further back and a supermarket at the side of the road. The bungalows were built, but not the supermarket and so the eyesore remains.

Withernsea has had a golf course for ages. It is a nine-hole course, but there is talk of it becoming extended to eighteen holes.

We are proud of our lighthouse; it is beautiful and 130ft high. It is a joke because it is built in the middle of the town. Someone who lives down south asked me to send them a postcard of the lighthouse. Actually it wasn't built in the middle of the town. It was built in 1894 when Withernsea was only about six dwellings.

I recommend a visit to the lighthouse. It is an interesting museum and a memorial to Kay Kendall who was a famous actress in the fifties. Another famous lady was Nurse Cavell. The Germans shot her during the First World War. I remember her sister.

Many years ago we had to take our household rubbish to a tip near Preston. But we had the good fortune of getting a tip on Hull Road. In recent years this part has become Beacon Industrial Estate. This is very useful and an improvement to Withernsea. There is a good reliable garage, a boat-building works and a builder's merchant.

The railway line, built by Bannister, was opened in 1864 and closed in 1964. The railway company had built the forty-bedroom hotel, which eventually became the hospital.

There was talk of the hospital being replaced by a new one. This upset a lot of the residents and they began a petition to keep the old building. A new hospital must be better than an old one, which had originally been built as a hotel.

A beautiful new surgery called St Nicholas, was named after the nearby church, and was built in 1996. In my opinion every one of our doctors are excellent and deserve a good surgery.

Work began straight away on dismantling the hospital and the new one opened in 1997.

A new building to house the inshore lifeboat has been built on the south promenade.

The memorial gardens near the municipal buildings were nice to walk through and step out onto the promenade, but the area was shabby. A lot of work has gone into this area with pleasing results. The library has been improved and adjacent is the Council Information Centre. The regeneration office is on the other side of the library.

The car park has been improved and grass turf has been laid between the car park and the promenade.

The Valley Gardens have always been a central pleasure area. At one time there was a lovely bowling green, and many people enjoyed watching them play. It was missed when it was transferred to Lascelles Avenue.

The recent work on the Valley Gardens has transformed it immensely, to a masterpiece in fact. Last July there was a sea festival that was a huge success. Opposite the Valley Gardens, a large amusement arcade has had a facelift with the addition of a bowling alley and restaurant. This is called Game King.

The gasworks land, which is down Park Avenue, has become a childrens' play area, and work is progressing with the Millennium Green Park and wildlife habitat.

The Proudfoot Group have announced that building work on a 7,500 square foot extension to their supermarket will commence soon.

The council will soon renovate a property, which has been an eyesore for years and was a takeaway fish and chip shop and restaurant.

The council have been negotiating to purchase the property for quite a long time and I am glad to say that the deal is almost finalised. It will become a Recourse Centre.

With these improvements the visitors are coming back and on Saturdays and Sundays, the town is full of cars. There are still properties, which need smartening up. But we have come a long way in a short time and we will go on improving.

I would like the road, which passes the market to be extended to where the railway line was. From there it could pass over the old railway track and join the road after bypassing Hollym. We could have one-way traffic from Queen Street to Patrington Road. This would help to eliminate the traffic problems, which will become much worse when Proudfoots have built their new store and perhaps a new petrol station.

Elizabeth and I were very happy. We had the bungalow looking very homely with cavity-wall insulation and lots of insulation in the loft to keep us warm in winter and our fuel bills low. The gardens looked nice and delicious apples grew on the three apple trees.

We had five rabbits, extra work, but they were very loveable. Also, there was Bluey the budgerigar and Charlie the Kakariki (parakeet). They played together all day. Bluey was an expert tightrope walker.

We needed a better car. David bought a new Audi and gave us his BMW so then we could do longer journeys in a shorter time, and with comfort.

Sadly our loving marriage ended due to the interference of a woman who was not related to either of us, on 16 June 2002. Elizabeth has lost such a lot, but has gained nothing and is now living in Cottingham.

Win had done some writing just a short time before she died. I have found this writing in one of her handbags, and the following is some of that writing.

17 October 1993

Soldier's Bride – Married: 16 October 1945

I first met my husband to be at a bus stop. I had been for a holiday to my gran's. I loved to go and see her, as she was on her own, my granddad having passed away when the war was declared in 1939. This was in August 1945. I had to get back home to help my parents. My father was a master baker. He had his own business and made on his hot plate, muffins, crumpets, oatcakes, and scotch pancakes etc.

My gran lived in Askern, near Doncaster and I had to travel to my home in Thornton near Bradford. I had to change buses in Leeds. I had got to Leeds and was waiting for the bus to take me to Thornton when this soldier boy came and stood next to me in this khaki great coat. I couldn't even see his feet as his coat almost buried him. But he had the loveliest bluest eyes I have ever seen.

The bus drew up and I jumped on and went upstairs and sat down, and then the soldier sat next to me. I put my case on my knees and got comfy for the journey home. My new-found friend and I got chatting on the journey. He said, 'I can smell apples.' I just laughed because my case was packed with apples from my gran's, for home, but before I reached home only a few apples were remaining, being consumed by my new friend.

We reached Bradford; time to say cheerio I thought. But instead he invited me to go to a café nearby, so in we went. The café was rather full so we sat at a table where two old ladies were already having a meal. As it was wartime the only food we could have was that good old standby, beans on toast, for two.

I could hear the old ladies saying, 'I'll bet the soldier has just come home on leave.' Needless to say, I just laughed inside and thought they did not guess we had only met about two hours ago and I had never met him in my life before and he was a long way from home. But I found out later that he had been for an interview with the manager at Odsall Stadium for a test ride, prior to becoming a Speedway Rider in the Odsall Team.

I put him off going to do this, as I did not want him to get hurt riding motorcycles. So he gave it up just for me. Having never seen anything like Speedway before I was glad in a sense. But I also had a feeling of guilt, as this was his only hobby. He was a despatch rider in the army and also in the display team of the Royal Signals.

The day he met me he was waiting for a bus because his younger brother had borrowed his motorbike and had not returned it in time for him to go on it to Odsall for his trial.

His motorbike was a KTS and he wishes he still had the bike. I remember when I said we cannot afford a couple of vehicles and sold the bike for a mere £12 in 1955 as by now we were married. August 1945 we met and on 16 October 1945 we married at Thornton Parish Church and we have just had our forty-eighth year anniversary. I do hope we reach the big fifty years.

We have three sons. David is the eldest at 46-years-old, Derrick is 44-years-old, Peter 39-years-old and one more we lost who would have been 36-years-old, if he had been spared.

All the years we have been married my husband always says, 'Maybe next year,' and as he did grass track racing and scrambling etc. I still did not like him to go road racing. But his ambition all these years has been to watch the Isle-of-Man Tourist Trophy races. He is seventy-nine years of age. I am seventy-five-years-old and I would dearly love for him to see the TT races as I always would say, 'Never mind love, maybe next year.'

Thank you, for reading my story.